THE SHIFTING MEANING OF LEGAL CERTAINTY IN COMPARATIVE AND TRANSNATIONAL LAW

The principle of legal certainty is of fundamental importance for law and society: it has been vital in stabilising normative expectations and in providing a framework for social interaction, as well as defining the scope of individual freedom and political power. Even though it has not always been fully realised, legal certainty has also functioned as a normative ideal that has structured legal debates, both at the national and transnational level.

This book presents research from a range of substantive areas regarding the meaning, possibility and desirability of legal certainty in the context of a rapidly changing global society. It aims to address these issues by bringing together scholars from various jurisdictions in order to examine changes in the shifting meaning of legal certainty in a comparative and transnational context. In particular, the book explores some of the tensions that now exist between the conventional expectation of legal certainty and the various challenges associated with regulating highly complex, late modern economies and societies.

The book will be of interest to lawyers concerned with understanding the transformation of core rule of law values in the context of contemporary social change, as well as to political scientists and social theorists.

The Shifting Meaning of Legal Certainty in Comparative and Transnational Law

Edited by
Mark Fenwick, Mathias Siems
and Stefan Wrbka

·HART·
PUBLISHING
OXFORD AND PORTLAND, OREGON
2017

Hart Publishing
An imprint of Bloomsbury Publishing Plc

Hart Publishing Ltd
Kemp House
Chawley Park
Cumnor Hill
Oxford OX2 9PH
UK

Bloomsbury Publishing Plc
50 Bedford Square
London
WC1B 3DP
UK

www.hartpub.co.uk
www.bloomsbury.com

Published in North America (US and Canada) by
Hart Publishing
c/o International Specialized Book Services
920 NE 58th Avenue, Suite 300
Portland, OR 97213-3786
USA

www.isbs.com

First published 2017

British Library Cataloguing-in-Publication Data
A catalogue record for this book is available from the British Library.

ISBN: HB: 978-1-50991-125-7
ePDF: 978-1-50991-126-4
ePub: 978-1-50991-127-1

Library of Congress Cataloging-in-Publication Data

Names: Fenwick, Mark (Law teacher), editor. | Siems, Mathias M., 1974– editor. | Wrbka, Stefan, 1976– editor.

Title: The shifting meaning of legal certainty in comparative and transnational law / edited by Mark Fenwick, Mathias Siems and Stefan Wrbka.

Description: Oxford ; Portland, Oregon : Hart Publishing, an imprint of Bloomsbury Publishing Plc, 2017. | Includes bibliographical references and index.

Identifiers: LCCN 2017020059 (print) | LCCN 2017020417 (ebook) | ISBN 9781509911271 (Epub) | ISBN 9781509911257 (hardback : alk. paper)

Subjects: LCSH: Legal certainty. | Comparative law.

Classification: LCC K262 (ebook) | LCC K262 .S53 2017 (print) | DDC 340.1—dc23

LC record available at https://lccn.loc.gov/2017020059

Typeset by Compuscript Ltd, Shannon
Printed and bound in Great Britain by Lightning Source UK Ltd

Preface

Legal certainty is of fundamental importance for law and society: it has been vital in stabilising normative expectations and in providing a framework for social interaction, as well as defining the scope of individual freedom and political power. Even though it has not always been fully realised, legal certainty has also functioned as a normative ideal that has structured legal debates, both at the national and transnational level.

This book presents research from a range of substantive areas regarding the meaning, possibility and desirability of legal certainty in the context of a rapidly changing global society. It aims to address these issues by bringing together scholars from various jurisdictions in order to examine changes in the shifting meaning of legal certainty in a comparative and transnational context. In particular, the book explores some of the tensions that now exist between the conventional expectation of legal certainty and the various challenges associated with regulating highly complex, late modern economies and societies.

We hope that this book will be of interest both to lawyers interested in understanding the transformation of core rule of law values in the context of contemporary social change, as well as political scientists and social theorists.

This book would not have been possible without the financial support of Kyushu University, which allowed us to host a series of workshops on this issue. Special thanks go also to Hart Publishing, especially to Roberta Bassi, who has accompanied and supported this book project from a very early stage.

Mark Fenwick
Mathias Siems
Stefan Wrbka
Fukuoka, Japan/Durham, UK
31 January 2017

Contents

Part III: Transnational Perspectives

Part IV: Applied Perspectives ('Certainty through Law')

List of Contributors

Mateja DUROVIC, Assistant Professor, Faculty of Law, Hong Kong City University, Hong Kong

Mark FENWICK, Professor, Faculty of Law, Kyushu University, Japan

Monika HINTEREGGER, Professor, Faculty of Law, University of Graz, Austria

Geraint HOWELLS, Professor, Faculty of Law, Hong Kong City University, Hong Kong

Lisa JOST, Research and Teaching Fellow, Department for Legal Studies and International Relations, Danube University Krems, Austria

Jonas KNETSCH, Professor, Faculty of Law and Economics, University of Reunion Island, France

Gabriel M LENTNER, Research and Teaching Fellow, Department for Legal Studies and International Relations, Danube University Krems, Austria

John LINARELLI, Professor, Durham Law School, Durham University, UK

Mikael Rask MADSEN, Professor and Director of iCourts, The Danish National Research Foundation's Center of Excellence for International Courts, Faculty of Law, University of Copenhagen, Denmark

Kunihiro NAKATA, Professor, Faculty of Law, Ryukoku University, Japan

Henrik Palmer OLSEN, Professor, iCourts, The Danish National Research Foundation's Center of Excellence for International Courts, and Vice-Dean of the Faculty of Law, University of Copenhagen

Elina PAUNIO, Legal Secretary to Advocate-General Nils Wahl, Court of Justice of the European Union

Patricia POPELIER, Professor, Faculty of Law, University of Antwerp, Belgium

Thomas RATKA, Professor, Department of Business Law and European Integration, Danube University Krems, Austria

Mathias M SIEMS, Professor, Durham Law School, Durham University, UK

Yo TERAKAWA, Professor, Faculty of Law, Kansai University, Japan

Charlotte VILLIERS, Professor, Faculty of Law, Bristol University, UK

Stefan WRBKA, Associate Professor, Faculty of Law, Kyushu University, Japan

The State of the Art and Shifting Meaning of Legal Certainty

MARK FENWICK, MATHIAS SIEMS AND STEFAN WRBKA

INTRODUCTION

HOW DO WE achieve legal certainty today? This, at first sight, rather simple question leads us to many interconnected further questions. For example, why do we need legal certainty at all: could a strong emphasis on legal certainty not be counterproductive for 'justice' in the individual case? And what exactly do we mean by '*legal*' certainty? Is it a well-crafted, precise piece of legislation? Or do we refer to the way law operates, socio-legally, in practice? And what exactly is legal '*certainty*'? Does it refer to knowledge which citizens should have about details of specific substantive rules? Or rather that there is a system of procedural rules in place which is applied in a certain way? And then what is so special about legal certainty '*today*'? Does it imply that, in a contemporary context, legal certainty is less or more important, for example, due the growing impact of transnational soft law as a flexible means of governance, on the one hand, or due to the need to counter the uncertainties of globalisation, on the other?

This book cannot promise to answer all of these questions comprehensively. However, it can address some of the core themes raised by these multi-layered issues from a comparative and transnational perspective. Of course, we are not the first authors to write about past and present challenges to the meaning of legal certainty. Therefore, this introductory chapter intends to set the scene and outline the 'state of the art', as well as our own contribution to this topic.

The structure of this chapter is as follows: the next section discusses current definitions of legal certainty, starting with some of the case law, but then exploring the literature on this issue in more detail. This is followed by a further analysis of the literature, dealing with the focus and scope of the previous publications. This provides the basis for the two subsequent sections: an analysis of the 'shifting meaning of legal certainty'; and an overview of the contributions of this book. The final section concludes with an outlook to possible future research.

DEFINITIONS OF LEGAL CERTAINTY

The concept of 'legal certainty' has been used in some court decisions. These decisions provide some indication as to the meaning of legal certainty. According to the European Court of Justice (ECJ; now Court of Justice of the European Union, CJEU), 'rules should be clear and precise, so that individuals may be able to ascertain unequivocally what their rights and obligations are and may take steps accordingly.'[1] According to the European Court of Human Rights (ECtHR),

> the law should be accessible to the persons concerned and formulated with sufficient precision to enable them—if need be, with appropriate advice—to foresee, to a degree that is reasonable in the circumstances, the consequences which a given action may entail.[2]

According to the House of Lords (now Supreme Court of the United Kingdom), 'a citizen, before committing himself to any course of action, should be able to know in advance what are the legal consequences that will flow from it.'[3] There have also been judgments accepting the concept of 'legal certainty' in other countries, for example, in France and Germany.[4]

By their very nature, these judgments address legal certainty within the context of specific factual scenarios. By contrast, the academic and policy-oriented literature is not bound by such restrictions, but can attempt more general definitions of legal certainty. The following will therefore focus on these latter definitions. For this purpose, we screened the recent literature published in English, French and German for books and journal articles which have the phrase 'legal certainty' (or their French and German equivalents, see below) in the title; we also included selected further publications.[5] The following two tables provide a list of these publications, together with short summaries on how they define and/or understand the concept of legal certainty.

[1] Case C-110/03 *Belgium v Commission* [2005] ECLI:EU:C:2005:223 para 30 with references to further cases.

[2] *Maestri v Italy* Series A no 39748/98 (2004) ECLI:CE:ECHR:2004:0217JUD003974898 para 30 with references to further cases.

[3] *Black-Clawson International Ltd v Papierwerke Waldhof-Aschaffenburg AG* [1975] AC 591 at 638 (HL) per Lord Diplock.

[4] See Conseil d'Etat, Assemblée, 24 March 2006, Société KPMG and BVerfG (German Federal Constitutional Court) NJW 2013, 2103 para 34 (referring to earlier case law).

[5] A recent book which we could not include any more in the subsequent tables is H Avila, *Certainty in Law* (Cham, Springer 2016) (with tax law certainty as the main substantive concern).

Table 1: Legal certainty in English-language publications (selection)

Author and title	Type	Definition/understanding of legal certainty
V Gessner and AC Budak (eds), *Emerging Legal Certainty: Empirical Studies on the Globalization of Law* (Farnham, Ashgate, 1998)[6]	Collection of papers	'relatively stable action patterns which reduce the uncertainties with respect to the behaviour of other individuals in the process of human interaction'
P Popelier, 'Legal Certainty and Principles of Proper Law Making' (2000) 2 *European Journal of Law Reform* 321[7]	Article (and monograph)	'predictability of the application of the formal law by the judge, the government and the administration, who are in turn bound by the law'
J Braithwaite, 'Rules and Principles: A Theory of Legal Certainty' (2002) 27 *Australian Journal of Legal Philosophy* 47	Article	certainty as 'consistency' and 'reliability'
J Raitio, *The Principle of Legal Certainty in EC Law* (Alphen aan den Rijn, Kluwer, 2003)[8]	Monograph (and article)	'predictability and acceptability in the legal decision-making process'; 'balancing between predictability and acceptability, between formal justice and material fairness, in legal decision-making'
JR Maxeiner, 'Legal Certainty and Legal Methods: A European Alternative to American Legal Indeterminacy?' (2007) 15 *Tulane Journal of International and Comparative Law* 541[9]	Article	law provides definitive answer to a legal question

(continued)

[6] See also V Gessner (ed), *Contractual Certainty in International Trade* (Oxford, Hart Publishing, 2008).

[7] See also P Popelier, *Rechtszekerheid als Beginsel van Behoorlijke Regelgeving* (Antwerp, Intersentia, 1997); P Popelier, 'Five Paradoxes on Legal Certainty and the Lawmaker' (2008) 2 *Legisprudence* 47.

[8] See also J Raitio, 'Legal Certainty, Non-Retroactivity and Periods of Limitation in EU Law' (2008) 2 *Legisprudence* 1 (the statement about the need to balance between predictability and acceptability is from this article, ibid 23); J Raitio, 'Legal Certainty as an Element of Objectivity in Law' in J Husa and M Van Hoecke (eds), *Objectivity in Law and Legal Reasoning* (Oxford, Hart Publishing, 2013) 85.

[9] See also JR Maxeiner, 'Some Realism about Legal Certainty in the Globalization of the Rule of Law' (2008) 31 *Houston Journal of International Law* 27.

Table 1: *(Continued)*

Author and title	Type	Definition/understanding of legal certainty
S Bertea, 'Towards A New Paradigm of Legal Certainty' (2008) 2 *Legisprudence* 25	Article	'legal certainty should be regarded as an intrinsically theory-laden notion, which needs to be discussed in relation to particular theories, and not treated as a largely pre-theoretical idea'; not possible to give it one overarching definition.
O Raban, 'The Fallacy of Legal Certainty: Why Vague Legal Standards May be Better for Capitalism and Liberalism' (2010) 19 *Public Interest Law Journal* 175	Article	'clear legal rules' where 'people' can 'predict consequences of actions' and 'lawyers' can 'predict consequences of applying the law'
K Crawford, 'The Paradoxical Relationship between Econometric Effectiveness and Legal Certainty' (2011) *Comparative Research in Law & Political Economy Research Paper No 5/2011*, available at ssrn.com/abstract=1755153	Working paper	'lawyers and clients are able to predict what the outcome of a particular legal question is likely to be in the light of previous judicial decisions. Also, once the legal rule has been established ... individuals can orientate their behaviour with regard to that rule'
KE Davis 'The Concept of Legal Uncertainty' (November 2011), available at ssrn.com/abstract=1990813	Working paper	legal uncertainty is 'unpredictability' and not simply 'disagreement about the law'. 'Legal uncertainty is nothing more than uncertainty about what legal officials will do'
A Raynouard and AJ Kerhuel, 'Measuring the law: Sécurité juridique as a watermark' (2011) 8 *International Journal of Disclosure and Governance* 360	Article	'the dimension of predictability is at the core of the concept. It is joined by two other essential components: stability and substantive guarantee'

(continued)

Table 1: *(Continued)*

Author and title	Type	Definition/understanding of legal certainty
SJ Bayern, 'Against Certainty' (2012) 41 *Hofstra Law Review* 53	Article	a rule is 'certain to the extent that it proceeds to a definite legal conclusion without reliance on contextual judgment'
E Paunio, *Legal Certainty in Multilingual EU Law: Language, Discourse and Reasoning at the European Court of Justice* (Farnham, Ashgate, 2013)[10]	Monograph	'interplay of procedural means (procedural certainty) and reasoning (rational acceptability'; 'Rational acceptability aris[ing] from discursive judicial interaction among courts'
H Gribnau, 'Legal Certainty: A Matter of Principle' in H Gribnau and M Pauwels (eds), *Retroactivity of Tax Legislation* (Amsterdam, IBFD, 2013) 72	Book chapter	'fundamental legal value'; 'Predictability of law protects those subject to the law from arbitrary state interference with their lives. Legal certainty enables people to plan their future'
N Chowdhury, *European Regulation of Medical Devices and Pharmaceuticals: Regulatee Expectations of Legal Certainty* (Berlin, Springer, 2014)	Monograph	'function of law is to ensure that the legal structure governing all social relations is predictable, coherent, consistent, and applicable'
R Alexy, 'Legal Certainty and Correctness' (2015) 28 *Ratio Juris* 441	Article	'ability to identify the subject matter as a legal norm' as well as 'certain enforcement of what is identified as law' (with reference to Radbruch)
Civil Law Initiative, Legal Certainty Index—Report (2015)[11]	Report	'laws should be at least accessible, intelligible and stable and have predictable effects'

(continued)

[10] See also Elina Paunio, 'Beyond Predictability—Reflections on Legal Certainty and the Discourse Theory of Law in the EU Legal Order' (2009) 10 *German Law Journal* 1469.

[11] Available at www.fondation-droitcontinental.org/en/wp-content/uploads/2015/06/NS_Rapport-complet-5-juin-2015_EN.pdf.

Table 1: *(Continued)*

Author and title	Type	Definition/understanding of legal certainty
B du Marais and D Marrani (eds), *Legal Certainty in Real Estate Transactions* (Cambridge, Intersentia, 2016)	Collection of articles	'concept defined by a sum of components whose completeness is never postulated: non-retroactivity, accessibility and intelligibility, normativity and quality of the law, consistency of the law and case law, and the need for transitional measures in order to cope with an instability or unpredictability of the law, etc'
M Fenwick and S Wrbka (eds), *Legal Certainty in a Contemporary Context: Private & Criminal Law Perspectives* (Tokyo, Springer, 2016)	Collection of papers	As a conventional concept 'the idea that the law must be sufficiently clear to provide those subject to legal norms with the means to regulate their own conduct and to protect against the arbitrary exercise of public power'
A Portuese, O Gough and J Tanega, 'The Principle of Legal Certainty as a Principle of Economic Efficiency', *European Journal of Law and Economics*, forthcoming (available at DOI 10.1007/s10657-014-9435-2)	Article	a 'feature of the rule of law'. 'Choosing the right legal rules to a factual situation that is predictable.' 'Predictability in terms of those subject to the law'. Idea of 'legitimate expectations'

Some of the statements from Table 1 reflect the specific context of the respective publications (eg Gessner and Budak), but there is also some common ground which can be identified. The most frequently-used term is that of legal certainty as 'predictability': it is seen as important that citizens can *predict* the consequences of their actions (eg Maxeiner, Raban, Bayern, Gribnau). Some of the definitions also refer to the role of lawyers (Raban), and many of them mention elements of the institutional structure of the law more generally (eg Crawford, Popelier). Thus, legal certainty is about legislation, but also about courts and law enforcement (eg Alexy) and therefore everything that matters for the predictable effects that certain actions or inactions may have.

Some of the other elements can be thought of as sub-categories of the requirements of predictability, for example, the consistency (or coherency), accessibility and intelligibility of the law (eg Chowdhury, Braithwaite, Civil Law Initiative). Beyond the current law goes the element of stability, sometimes phrased as reliability or non-retroactivity, as mentioned in many of the definitions (eg du Marais and Marrani, Raynouard and Kerhuel, Braithwaite).

It may be most contentious that some authors not only consider formal criteria but also refer to more substantive elements such as 'acceptability', 'substantive guarantee' or 'legitimate expectations' (eg Paunio, Raynouard and Kerhuel, Portuese et al). Thus, with such definitions, it may be a requirement of legal certainty that its formal elements are balanced with its more substantive ones (as explicitly stated by Raitio). If one disagrees with this extension of the concept of legal certainty, however, the results may often be similar since legal certainty is not a concept that requires an absolute application but has to be balanced and applied in its specific context (as critically noted by Bertea).

Table 2: Legal certainty in French and German-language publications (selection)

Author and title	**Type**	**Definition/ understanding of legal certainty**
Conseil d'État (ed), 'La complexité du droit' (2006)[12]	Report and collection of articles	predictability of the law, clarity and accessibility of norms, stability of the legal situation (*prévisibilité de la loi, clarté et accessibilité de la norme, stabilité des situations juridiques*)
Proceedings of the 'Xe Congrès de l'Association Internationale de Méthodologie Juridique (AIMJ)' (2008) *La Revue du Notariat*	Collection of articles	different definitions used by authors reflecting the position in their respective countries (see Table 4, below)
T Piazzon, *La sécurité juridique* (Paris, Defrénois, 2009)	Monograph	accessibility, stability and predictability as classical criteria (*l'accessibility du droit; la stabilite du droit; la previsibilite du droit*)

(continued)

[12] Available at www.conseil-etat.fr/Decisions-Avis-Publications/Etudes-Publications/Rapports-Etudes/Securite-juridique-et-complexite-du-droit-Rapport-public-2006.

Table 2: *(Continued)*

Author and title	**Type**	**Definition/ understanding of legal certainty**
Groupe de travail présidé par Henri de Castries et Nicolas Molfessis, (2015) 'Sécurité juridique et initiative économique'[13]	Report	laws should be intelligible, stable and predictable (phrased as the problem that today laws tend to be unintelligible etc)
C-W Canaris, *Systemdenken und Systembegriff in der Jurisprudenz* (Berlin, Duncker & Humblot, 1969)	Monograph	legal certainty as an umbrella term for legal determinacy and predictability (*Bestimmtheit and Vorhersehbarkeit*), legislative and judicial stability and continuity (*Stabilität and Kontinuität*) and practicability of the application of law (*Praktikabilität der Rechtsanwendung*)
F Bydlinski, *Fundamentale Rechtsgrundsätze* (Vienna, Springer, 1988)	Monograph	legal certainty as an umbrella term for legal clarity (*Rechtsklarheit*), legal stability (*Rechtsstabilität*), legal accessibility (*Rechtszugänglichkeit*), legal peace (*Rechtsfriede*) and legal enforcement (*Rechtsdurchsetzung*)
A von Arnauld, *Rechtssicherheit: Perspektivische Annäherungen an eine idée directrice des Rechts* (Tübingen, Mohr Siebeck, 2006)	Monograph	main criteria are identifiability, reliability and predictability (*Erkennbarkeit, Verlässlichkeit, Berechenbarkeit*)
JC Schuhr (ed), *Rechtssicherheit durch Rechtswissenschaft* (Tübingen, Mohr Siebeck, 2014)	Collection of papers	determinacy of legal rules, their systematics and generality, legal predictability and commitment (*Bestimmtheit rechtlicher Regeln, ihre Systematik und Allgemeinheit, die Vorhersehbarkeit auf ihnen beruhender Entscheidungen und die Bindung an diese Regeln*)

[13] Available at www.leclubdesjuristes.com/wp-content/uploads/2015/05/S%C3%A9curit%C3%A9-juridique-WEB.pdf.

The French and German terms '*sécurité juridique*' and '*Rechtssicherheit*' have a different connotation than the English term, since these terms could not only be translated as 'certainty'—in the sense of establishing the clear meaning of rules—but also including the 'security' that is provided by the law. Relatedly, it has been suggested that in civil law countries the notion of 'legal certainty' may be wider and deeper than in common law countries. In the latter countries, legal certainty may often be perceived as a mere *means* to promote economic development, while in the civil law world the legal system 'has an inherent value' and legal certainty is seen an 'end in itself'.[14]

This possible difference may be reflected in some of the relatively abstract definitions in Table 2 (eg Piazzon, Canaris, Bydlinski, von Arnauld). Some of the elements mentioned here, for example the emphasis on clarity (Conseil d'État, Bydlinski) and the systematic nature of the law (Schuhr) are also more typical for civil law than for common law countries. Yet, overall, the definitions of Table 2 show that the main criteria are not so different from the ones identified for the English-language literature: predictability is important, including enforcement (eg Canaris, Bydlinski), but also stability, accessibility, intelligibility as well as, more contentiously, substantive criteria such as 'legal peace' (Bydlinski).

This commonality in terminology may be due to a common understanding, but it may also be related to the fact that a good number of the publications cited in Tables 1 and 2 are by authors from both civil and common law countries. Thus, through such common discourse, we may observe some convergence, at least as far as the terminology of legal certainty is concerned. This leads us to an overview of the substance of these publications in the next section.

REVIEW OF FOCUS AND SCOPE OF PREVIOUS LITERATURE

Tables 3 and 4 map the recent literature of legal certainty under the following categories: for each publication, the tables start with the research topic/question which the author explores as regards legal certainty, they then indicate the method of analysis and finally the substantive and geographic scope of the publications.

[14] B Deffains and C Kessedjian (eds), 'Index of Legal Certainty. Report for the Civil Law Initiative' (2015), available at www.fondation-droitcontinental.org/en/index-legal-certainty/, 5 in note 22.

Table 3: Focus and scope in English-language publications (selection)

Authors[15]	Research topic/ question as related to legal certainty	Method of analysis	Substantive scope (eg areas of law)	Geographic scope
Gessner and Budak 1998	Best way to improve legal certainty trans- and cross-border in a globalising society	Comparative and doctrinal	Political science, business law	EU, global, Germany, Netherlands, Austria, Switzerland, Portugal, former Czechoslovakia, Turkey, US
Popelier 2000	The way requirements of legal certainty do and should influence law making	Comparative and doctrinal	Public law requirements to law making	Belgium, France, Germany, EU, ECtHR
Braithwaite 2002	'What are the conditions where rules will deliver us more legal certainty and what are the conditions where principles will do so?' (suggesting that precision of rules can be counter-productive)	Jurisprudential and doctrinal	General with some focus on 'complex domains', eg financial regulation, 'global business regulation'	Universal, although focus on Anglo-American theories
Raitio 2003	Critical analysis of case law of ECJ/CJEU on legal certainty	Jurisprudential and doctrinal	Any area covered by EU case law	EU, some Member States

(continued)

[15] For the precise references, see Table 1, above.

Table 3: *(Continued)*

Authors	Research topic/ question as related to legal certainty	Method of analysis	Substantive scope (eg areas of law)	Geographic scope
Maxeiner 2007	Comparison of 'legal indeterminacy' in US with 'legal certainty' in European context	Jurisprudential and doctrinal	General	Germany, US
Bertea 2008	Relationship between legal certainty and justice according to positivist and argumentation-based theories of legal certainty	Jurisprudential	Legal philosophy, legal theory	General
Raban 2010	Vague standards 'preferable' for capitalism and liberalism	Sociology of law	Contract law, regulating capitalism	General
Crawford 2011	Certainty and effectiveness 'pull in opposite directions'; 'lawmaker must choose one or the other'	Economics, game theory	General	General
Davis 2011	How do we measure certainty/ uncertainty?	Empirical sociology	General	General with example from Africa

(continued)

Table 3: *(Continued)*

Authors	Research topic/ question as related to legal certainty	Method of analysis	Substantive scope (eg areas of law)	Geographic scope
Raynouard and Kerhuel 2011	Relationship between legal certainty and economic development (and whether empirical measurement is possible)	Economics, jurisprudential	General	General with some references to France and other countries
Bayern 2012	'Context-specific evaluations of arguments in favor of certainty' needed: not simply stability but 'certainty of real-world results'	Jurisprudential, economics and doctrinal	Analysis of common law	US
Paunio 2013	How can multilingualism and legal certainty be reconciled in EU law?	Multilingualism	EU law, Legislation	EU and its Member States
Gribnau 2013	Legal principles—such as legal certainty—should function as a constraint on tax law reform, specifically retroactive changes	Jurisprudential	Tax law	General

(continued)

Table 3: *(Continued)*

Authors	Research topic/ question as related to legal certainty	Method of analysis	Substantive scope (eg areas of law)	Geographic scope
Chowdhury 2014	'How do regulatees pursue legal certainty in the context of the multilevel European medical product regulation?' (p 161)	Interdisciplinary and comparative	Law of medical products	General and EU
Alexy 2015	What is the relationship between legal certainty and legal correctness?	Jurisprudential	General considerations	General and some reference to Germany
Civil Law Initiative 2015	How far can a quantitative analysis of legal certainty identify differences between countries (and between areas of law)	Quantitative coding template	Six areas of law (mainly from business law)	13 countries
du Marais and Marrani 2016	How was legal certainty imagined and put in practice in common and civil law, using commercial real estate as a case study	Jurisprudential, practical, economic	Real estate law	France, England

(continued)

Table 3: *(Continued)*

Authors	Research topic/ question as related to legal certainty	Method of analysis	Substantive scope (eg areas of law)	Geographic scope
Fenwick and Wrbka 2016	Shifting meaning of legal certainty: today law needs to be more responsive to rapid economic, social and technological changes, in particular in a transnational law context	Jurisprudential, comparative and doctrinal	Private and criminal law	Japan, Austria, EU, China, Germany, globally
Portuese et al	Forthcoming Partial defence of ECJ/CJEU use of certainty against critics	Doctrinal and economic	EU law, especially case law of Court of Justice	EU

At a general level, the research summarised in Table 3 can be classified in four categories. First, there are some publications which address specific areas of law and provide suggestions on how to improve legal certainty in that field, which may also involve a comparative dimension (for example, Gessner and Budak, Maxeiner, Gribnau). Second, some conceptual publications research the notion of legal certainty from a doctrinal and jurisprudential, and possibly historical and comparative, perspective. In the European context, this often considers the case law of the European courts on matters of legal certainty (eg Popelier, Raitio, Paunio). Third, other conceptual studies criticise the notion of legal certainty as it exists today, with some authors challenging the view that legal certainty is even feasible or beneficial (eg Braitwaite, Raban, Bayern). Fourth, interdisciplinary research often addresses legal certainty from a political and economic perspective. Some of this research also discusses possible measurements of legal certainty, for example, with the aim to examine how far legal certainty may be related to economic development (eg Crawford, Davis, Raynouard and Kerhuel, Civil Law Initiative, du Marais and Marrani).

It is also possible to identify two interconnected trends in the evolution of this literature. The first one is that researchers have a growing interest in the global and transnational dimension and how these socio-economic changes reflect on legal certainty (or, indeed, legal 'uncertainty'). It should, however, also be noted that only a few contributions discuss legal certainty in other parts of the world than Europe and North America (for an exception, see Fenwick and Wrbka, which includes some Asian examples). Second, the question whether we can measure legal certainty is seen as increasingly important (see the references in the previous paragraph). Thus, apparently, the feeling is that some of the doctrinal and jurisprudential debates may go in circles and that an empirical approach may be needed in order to fully understand, and possibly evaluate, legal certainty in an increasingly interconnected world.

Table 4: Focus and scope in French and German-language publications (selection)

Authors[16]	Research topic/ question as related to legal certainty	Method of analysis	Substantive scope (eg areas of law)	Geographic scope
Conseil d'État 2006	Ways to achieve legal certainty given the growing complexity of the law	Jurisprudential and doctrinal	General and public law	France, EU, ECHR with some comparisons
AIMJ 2008	Comparative perspectives on legal certainty, in particular in context of globalisation and Europeanisation of the law	Jurisprudential and doctrinal	General with examples from various areas of law; mainly public law	France, EU, Germany and some further comparisons
Piazzon 2009	Principle of legal certainty in case and statute law, rejecting suggestion that it should be transformed into an individual right	Jurisprudential and doctrinal	General with examples, from public, private and criminal law	France with some references to EU, ECHR, England, Germany, US

(continued)

[16] For the precise references see Table 2, above.

Table 4: *(Continued)*

Authors	Research topic/ question as related to legal certainty	Method of analysis	Substantive scope (eg areas of law)	Geographic scope
Groupe de travail 2015	Growing legal uncertainty in today's world; thus, how legal certainty can be achieved in order to provide a secure economic environment	Doctrinal and policy oriented	General and separate chapters on tax law and labour law	France, EU and ECHR
Canaris 1969	Legal certainty as a fundamental principle of law—can it (and if yes, how can it) be subcategorised?	Jurisprudential	Jurisprudence, general	Germany
Bydlinski 1988	Legal certainty as a fundamental principle of law—can it (and if yes, how can it) be subcategorised?	Jurisprudential	Jurisprudence, general	Austria, Germany
von Arnauld 2006	Aim to identify main principles underlying legal certainty based on inductive reasoning	Historical and jurisprudential	Public law	Germany, EU, ECHR, some comparison with England, France, Italy, Poland, Spain
Schuhr 2014	Contribution of legal academia to legal certainty (in legal dogmatic, legal philosophy etc)	Jurisprudential and interdisciplinary	mainly general considerations with some examples	general and references to Germany

Comparing Tables 3 and 4, it comes as no surprise that the French and German language publications tend to address topics of French and German law more frequently than the English-language ones. In substance, it is noteworthy that the French and German language publications tend to have a stronger conceptual focus, in particular the monographs (Piazzon, Canaris, Bydlinski, von Arnauld). However, considering the two most recent publications (Groupe de travail, Schuhr), there also seems to be some shift in emphasis, as these publications too approach legal certainty from a more interdisciplinary perspective.

As a result, we suggest that the literature shows, on the one hand, some convergence around core themes, for example, the role legal certainty plays in case law and law making, the way it can be conceptualised, and the criticism of focusing only on legal certainty and not on matters of substantive justice. On the other hand, we identify a possible shift in the most recent literature. We also suggest that this is not accidental: the following section will explain that it is indeed justified to talk about a 'shifting meaning of legal certainty' in today's legal world.

THE SHIFTING MEANING OF LEGAL CERTAINTY

The above discussion has highlighted how, in the context of legal modernity, the principle of legal certainty has functioned as a central rule of law value. Even though it has been conceptualised in different ways and has not always been fully realised, concepts of legal certainty have functioned as a core value that has structured normative debates in political and legal modernity, both at the national and international level.[17]

Over recent decades, however, legal certainty has come under increasing pressure from a number of competing demands that are made of law, in particular the demand that the law be more 'flexible' and responsive to an environment characterised by rapid social, economic and technological change. The following sets of developments interest us in particular.

First, in the context of business and market regulation, there has been a tendency across most major jurisdictions towards increasing the degree and scope of discretion afforded to regulators—so-called 'responsive regulation.'[18] This has been justified by a perceived need for more agile and adaptable

[17] See, eg Neil MacCormick, *Rhetoric and the Rule of Law* 7–8 (Oxford, Oxford University Press, 2005) ('Among the values it [the rule of law] can secure, none is more important than legal certainty'); James R Maxeiner, 'Some Realism About Legal Certainty in the Globalization of the Rule of Law' (2008) 31 *Houston Journal of International Law* 27 at 30 ('legal certainty is the international basis of the rule of law').

[18] See, eg John Braithwaite, 'The Essence of Responsive Regulation' (2011) 44 *UBC Law Review* 475; Robert Baldwin and Julia Black, 'Really Responsive Regulation' (2008) 71 *Modern Law Review* 59.

regulation in the context of complex, global markets. Nevertheless, such an approach raises a number of concerns related to the fairness of any framework that is premised on enhancing the flexibility of the regulator when dealing with specific cases.

A risk in any system that adopts flexible regulatory responses to the actions of individual firms is that it creates an unacceptable degree of discretion and a corresponding lack of transparency and accountability. Concerns about consistency of treatment—ie fairness—are also raised. Although rules and guidelines can potentially ameliorate such concerns, the resulting restrictions may end up depriving regulators of the very flexibility that they were pursuing in the first place.

Second, the World Bank's influential *Doing Business* Report[19] had the explicit aim to reduce the 'regulatory burden' of doing business—and, to do so, it applies metric tools in order to rank a country's performance under this benchmark. This report and its impact has been challenged by academic research. But it is particularly interesting to see that it has now also become the target of the so-called 'Civil Law Initiative' that aims to show the virtues of systematically codified legal systems. Specifically, this initiative has recently proposed an 'Index of Legal Certainty' that aims to measure how well legal systems perform under this particular benchmark.[20] Thus, we now observe a 'battle of indices' that not only aims to illustrate but to prove the virtues of their respective models.

Third, there is an expectation that any contemporary regulatory framework needs to regulate wider spheres of social life. This trend has resulted in a proliferation of new forms of law that also impact on understandings of certainty. Increasingly, legal norms have a hybrid quality that does not necessarily originate with the nation state, but is the result of a complex process of interaction between public (local, national and international) and private entities.[21] In this respect, quasi-private ordering increasingly acts as an alternative or supplement to traditional norm-making on the part of the state. The resulting competition between various forms of self-governance, national and international norms adds to the complexity and uncertainties of the contemporary legal landscape for both citizens and regulators. Whatever the virtues of this approach, this development undoubtedly introduces a new degree of uncertainty into the operation of the law, as well as a challenge to conventional conceptions of legal certainty.

These developments all raise difficult, but interesting, questions regarding the meaning, possibility and desirability of legal certainty today. This book

[19] Available at www.doingbusiness.org/.

[20] Available at www.fondation-droitcontinental.org/en/index-legal-certainty/.

[21] This is often phrased as a phenomenon of 'networked governance', see M Fenwick, S Van Uytsel and S Wrbka (eds), *Networked Governance, Transnational Business and the Law* (Berlin, Springer, 2013).

aims to address these issues by bringing together scholars from a wide range of jurisdictions to explore this question of the 'shifting meaning' of legal certainty. In particular, it focuses on unpacking some of the tensions that exist between the demand for legal certainty and the various—and often competing—challenges associated with business regulation, ie regulating a complex, late modern economy characterised by global markets and constant technological innovation.

OVERVIEW OF CONTRIBUTIONS

The 14 substantive chapters of this book address legal certainty from, broadly speaking, four perspectives: theoretical, comparative, transnational and applied. The following provides a brief overview of these contributions.

Part I (Theoretical Perspectives) contains a number of chapters that explore some of the theoretical issues that have arisen in the context of debates around certainty.

Patricia Popelier begins by revisiting the Civil Law Initiative's 'Index of Legal Certainty' discussed above. She notes how the Index adopts a relativist concept of legal certainty, thereby illustrating how legal certainty has been transformed from a conservative device for the maintenance and accumulation of property and vested rights to a more dynamic concept that aims at securing an individual's autonomy when acting in an uncertain environment. At the centre of this concept is a 'standard of reasonableness', enabling a constant process of balancing between stability and flexibility. Hence, the shift in the concept of legal certainty reflects a shift in the meaning of rationality, resulting in a balancing exercise built around the notions of 'accessibility' and 'legitimate expectations'.

Popelier critically analyses how these balancing exercises operate in the case law of both European Courts—the ECJ/CJEU and the ECtHR—laying bare 'principles of proper law-making' that can be used as handles to predict the outcome of judicial reasonability tests, and revealing the economic function that has been inherent to legal certainty since its first conception.

Elina Paunio focuses on the linguistic dimension of legal certainty, namely the inescapeable fact that all law is necessarily trapped in the 'straightjacket' of language. Law is—by necessity—shaped by language, and just like language, indeterminacy is a constitutive feature of all law.

This issue becomes particularly interesting in the context of the European Union. After all, multilingualism constitutes one of the cornerstones of the European project. After successive enlargements, the number of official languages has grown exponentially from the original four to 24 in 2013, after the accession of Croatia. In accordance with the policy of linguistic equality, EU legislation is translated into all official languages. From the principle of equality it also follows that language versions are not considered to be translations at all. Rather, they are *all* regarded as legally authentic versions of legislation. A consequence of this is that in interpreting EU law, no specific language version can take precedence over the others.

Given that there is no 'uncontested' language reference amongst the equally valid official versions, the chapter explores the implications of a situation where certainty can no longer be found 'in' the text. Instead, certainty must be located somewhere 'beyond,' namely in the context or purpose of the law. In line with the communicative view of law, the chapter argues that the effect of this situation is that, in such a situation, certainty operates in a space between the Court's reasoning, on the one hand, and the EU legal community's expectations, on the other. In particular, the chapter emphasises how EU legal provisions have been interpreted on the basis of values and policies that have been deemed to underpin the EU legal system as a whole.

Mark Fenwick examines the issue of the shifting meaning of legal certainty, in the context of criminal law theory, focusing on recent developments in corporate criminal liability. The chapter argues that the scope and reach of corporate criminal law has greatly expanded over the last three decades across multiple jurisdictions, and that this expansion has been paralleled by the introduction of multiple uncertainties into this field of law. A striking feature of recent corporate criminal law is the degree to which the substantive criminal law in this field is plagued by a lack of legal certainty as to the scope of the offence. Examples of this new legal 'uncertainty' are introduced from securities law and anti-corruption law. Moreover, the legal basis for the new corporate criminal law—the doctrine of corporate legal liability—is similarly characterised by uncertainties of various kinds. Finally, various new procedural measures adopted in such cases—notably deferred prosecution agreements—further compound the issue of uncertainty.

The chapter suggests that in the context of regulating corporations the meaning of legal certainty has been subtly transformed from a fundamental principle of criminal justice to one of a number of competing policy considerations that have to be resolved—by regulators—when responding to socially undesirable behaviour on the part of large (often transnational) corporations. The combined effect of net-widening and this new legal 'uncertainty' has been to greatly increase legal risk for companies and to provide a strong incentive to invest in internal governance mechanisms aimed at social enforcement, ie corporate compliance.

Monika Hinteregger explores the theoretical foundations of tort law and examines how the different concepts of tort law (fault liability, no-fault liability, absolute liability) can be brought into a coherent system. In making this argument, Hinteregger draws on the insights of the economic theory of law (Calabresi, Posner et al) and compares them to the concept of the flexible system developed by the Austrian law professor Walter Wilburg.

On this basis, she describes the essential aspects governing the different concepts of tort law and shows how they can be integrated into a coherent system. Such a system can provide legislators (civil law) and courts (common law) with a framework of reference and help them to achieve rational and transparent decisions for the allocation of liability. This systematic approach to tort law thus serves legal certainty but also provides for sufficient flexibility in order to solve individual cases and tackle new societal and technological developments.

Part II (Comparative Perspectives) offers a series of contributions exploring legal certainty in a comparative context, with a focus on how the meaning and function of this concept varies in in different jurisdictions.

Mathias Siems sets out to challenge the widespread view that there is a sharp legal 'family divide' in understandings of legal certainty. In this context, the chapter discusses the traditional position of a 'civil law advantage' over the common law, as well as the challenges to this traditional view. It also shows that much depends on the way legal certainty is understood. For example, the benchmark of legal certainty does not tell us whether one should have a simple codified law that even lay persons can understand or a more elaborate law that can give a clear answer to any legal problem.

The chapter also provides a critical assessment of quantitative research on questions of legal certainty that are based on user surveys, content analysis or expert information. In doing, it suggests that such a measurement should be based on an expert assessment of the actual results to legal problems. Siems also proposes a future indicator that would need to address *both* legal certainty and legal adaptability as the two corresponding aims that lawmakers need to balance.

Stefan Wrbka, in his contribution, suggests that, when taking a closer look at legal certainty debates in different jurisdictions and different geographical contexts, one can see that perceptions of legal certainty often differ. Moreover, this is not only the case between different jurisdictions, but can also be seen within one and the same legal setting.

The chapter explores this question of diversity, focusing on some selected, geographical examples that highlight these underlying differences. In particular, the cases of the EU, Germany, Austria, England and Japan are used to explore different notions of legal certainty, as well as the possible consequences that may result from the actual understanding in given circumstances.

John Linarelli explores the different meanings of the concept of legal certainty in different common law legal systems. He traces the discussion in English law from Lord Mansfield's usage of the concept in the eighteenth century through to its usage today in the fields of English commercial and contract law. Linarelli suggests that the concept of certainty is relatively less important in the United States, for reasons having to do with the fall of conceptualism in American legal thought, the diversity inherent to a federal system, and the influence of law and economics. The result of this very different institutional environment was that predictability and economic efficiency came to substitute for certainty in a US context.

The chapter also describes how the concept of legal certainty in English law has a degree of uncertainty, leading in some cases to unhelpful and even arbitrary conclusions. These difficulties arise because what certainty actually means in particular legal contexts may be unclear and because lawyers sometimes use the concept in imprecise ways, appealing to folk intuitions and unexamined assumptions. As such, it might be better to replace certainty with narrower concepts connecting more closely to human action. In particular, the chapter advocates an alternative approach in which insights from political economy might help us to test whether legal professionals use claims of legal certainty about the law they practise as attempts to steer international legal work to themselves and away from their competitors.

Jonas Knetsch revisits the debate between the Civil Law Initiative and the World Bank's *Doing Business* Report, focusing on some of the challenges that the Index confronted in designing an appropriate framework for studying this issue. In particular, the chapter offers critical feedback about the theoretical and methodological challenges that the working group faced during 18 months of project development. While the group reached swift agreement on the need for questionnaire-based data collection and on the sectors of law particularly affected by considerations of legal certainty, there were lively debates about how to understand the key concept of legal certainty (*sécurité juridique*).

The chapter notes that in the context of late modernity, emerging norm-making phenomena such as responsive regulation or private self-governance have shaken up the traditional criteria of legal certainty, such as accessibility, predictability and reasonable stability. This raises a number of interesting and important issues, including: are comprehensive constitutionality review procedures, developing everywhere across Europe, a positive factor for legal certainty? Or are they instead undermining the stability of law and, simultaneously, the system's legal certainty?

The contributions in Part III (Transnational Perspectives) focus on the transnational aspect of legal uncertainty and the new complexities that arise as a result of the proliferation of transnational and international law.

Mikael Rask Madsen and Henrik Palmer Olsen address the various uncertainties that arise when there is a divergence between the normative contents of EU law and domestic law. In most cases, national courts manage to interpret domestic law in conformity with EU law and thereby avoid such normative contradiction. However, in other cases, it is arguably not possible to interpret domestic law in accordance with EU law. In so-called *contra legem* situations, national courts cannot override clear domestic legislation—in part because it would cause legal uncertainty, as legitimate expectations based on explicit domestic provisions would be jeopardised.

This issue is explored in the context of the recent Danish Supreme Court decision of *Ajos* and the vexed question of Danish participation in the EU more generally. However, the chapter suggests that this type of friction frequently arises in the reception of supranational law by domestic courts. A judicial desire, at the national level, to adhere to a strict textualism and respect for the national legislator can conflict with the very different undertaking most international courts are facing, namely to adjudicate a common law for a group of different Member States. In resolving this tension, the chapter advocates the need for dialogue and legal diplomacy. Otherwise, there is a risk of legal certainty becoming a casuality in 'judicial turf wars'.

Geraint Howells and Mateja Durovic proceed from the suggestion that in the field of consumer law, legal certainty is a highly-praised goal. The achievement of a high degree of legal certainty is in the interest of *all* players in the marketplace. Traders need to be reassured that their commercial activities directed towards consumers are legal, ie in line with all applicable laws, whereas consumers, as weaker parties, need to be comfortable that the rules that secure their confidence and guarantee their rights will be enforced when they are infringed. The chapter focuses on this, last, element of legal certainty, examining the question on how consumers' access to justice has been secured through diverse enforcement mechanisms.

As a regulatory response to this challenging task, different models and mechanisms have been developed in diverse jurisdictions. The idea is to adjust the regulatory design of enforcement to the particularities of different types of consumer transactions. In addition to the regular courts, in a case where their rights have been infringed, consumers may, depending on a legal system, rely on special courts or procedural rules, arbitration, mediation, collective redress, etc. All these mechanisms contribute to access to justice, but in what manner, to what extent and, above all, whether and how successful they are in securing legal certainty to consumers seeking justice, are the key issues that this chapter seeks to address.

Lisa Jost, Gabriel Lentner, Thomas Ratka and Stefan Wrbka address the issue of abuse of rights. In particular, the chapter focuses on a special type of abuse of rights in which there is a circumvention of a piece of legislation by (ab)using norms of international or transnational law.[22] In this chapter, the suggestion that is explored is that EU law has been applied in a way that prevents the domestic legislation of company law from functioning as intended by domestic policy-makers.

This chapter starts with remarks on legal certainty and its significance in the context of EU law, before it comments on international company law

[22] K Schurig, 'Die Gesetzesumgehung im Privatrecht—eine Studie mit kollisionsrechtlichen und rechtsvergleichenden Aspekten' in A Heldrich and HJ Sonnenberger (eds), *Festschrift für Murad Ferid zum 80. Geburtstag* (Frankfurt am Main, Verlag für Standesamtswesen, 1988) 375.

and the issue of shell companies. By doing this the chapter illustrates how legal certainty—a generally highly-valued legal principle—might actually impair the justified interests of stakeholders in certain cases.

The book concludes with a series of contributions in Part IV (Applied Perspectives) that examine how these issues play out in the context of specific fields of contemporary business law and regulation.

Charlotte Villiers explores the tension that exists between certainty and flexibility in the context of corporate governance. Significantly, here it is not the regulators who are granted freedom by more flexibility, but the corporate actors themselves. The flexible and light touch, quasi-private ordering that characterises contemporary corporate governance brings into the spotlight the tensions that exist between self-government and national and international norms. The UK's approach to corporate governance, which is underscored by the 'comply-or-explain' principle, is presented as a way of balancing competing views and so avoiding the process being brought to a halt by people 'digging in around their differences of opinion.'[23]

The result, however, is another legal *un*certainty, a system involving numerous, sometimes rival, regulatory actors, and tensions between mandatory and voluntary are created. The UK corporate governance system operates as a voluntary system but it is underpinned by market enforcement and threats of stronger intervention. From the perspective of legal certainty this can seem unsatisfactory. The voluntariness gives discretion to the corporate actors in deciding for themselves how they should apply the principles. In this way, the power struggles and complexities that have emerged highlight the problems of corporate governance as a neo-liberal regulatory form.

Yo Terakawa discusses the right to withdraw from consumer contracts, ie the so-called 'cooling-off system'. In Japan, the cooling-off system was introduced by the enactment of the Act about Door-step Selling in 1972. Subsequently similar looking concepts have been adopted with respect to distance selling and transactions linked to special marketing situations by the Act on Specified Commercial Transactions. The approach taken therein is commonly known as the 'the goods-return system'.

Although these mechanisms might look similar at first sight, the instruments with respect to door-step selling and distance selling are—unlike in the EU—not coherent. While the right to withdrawal under the door-step selling regime has its parallels to the European system, the goods-return system of the distance selling regime has a different character. The Japanese legislator is not convinced that surprise is an integral constituent of transactions

[23] A Hilton, 'Grudging Acquiescence' in Financial Reporting Council (ed), *Comply or Explain: 20th Anniversary of the UK Corporate Governance Code* (2012) 21, www.frc.org.uk/Our-Work/Publications/Corporate-Governance/Comply-or-Explain-20th-Anniversary-of-the-UK-Corpo.aspx.

concluded via distance sales. The most striking characteristic of the goods-return system is its lack of mandatoriness. Instead of being a mandatory requirement in distance selling contracts, it is rather considered as good commercial practice. In many cases, traders follow the 'recommendation', but in the absence of a binding obligation there is uncertainty and a lack of transparency in consumer contracts. The chapter discusses the practical consequences of this two-tier mechanism and aims to show possible answers that might improve overall legal certainty.

Kunihiro Nakata discusses the regulation of advertising, also focusing on the Japanese experience. He notes how, unlike in many jurisdictions where one can find specially-crafted legal regimes to address the problem of false advertising, a comparable legal tool is still pending in Japan. This does not mean that such practices are allowed, however. With the help of a variety of mechanisms that include competition law, ordinary contract and tort law, criminal sanctions, as well as administrative fines, unwanted business practices can—to a certain degree—be contained. However, none of these mechanisms offer the kind of comprehensive instruments that one can find in Europe or the US.

Against this background, it does not come as a surprise that legal academia in Japan has intensified efforts to propose a better solution. In particular, there are widespread concerns, particularly amongst academics, that a lack of legal certainty—understood as clarity and transparency—has been created by the current fragmented approach. The present analysis aims to take a deeper look at the ongoing debate and to introduce possible answers that might enhance legal certainty and effectiveness in an attempt to regulate unjustifiable advertising and marketing activities.

CONCLUSION

Both the previous literature and the contributions in this book show that there is a considerable degree of diversity in the way legal certainty is understood and discussed. In addition, there is the phenomenon that we refer to as 'the shifting meaning of legal certainty'. This means that, in the context of a rapidly-changing global society, the notion of legal certainty needs to be understood in a more flexible way so as to respond to the new challenges associated with regulating highly-complex, inter-connected economies and societies.

This should not, however, be identified with a relativist perspective, as legal certainty continues to have a profound normative dimension. The principle of legal certainty is of fundamental importance for law and society. It continues to play a vital role in stabilising normative expectations and in providing a framework for social interaction, as well as defining the scope of individual freedom and political power.

It follows from this that the role and design of legal certainty is likely to grow in importance in the future. In order to address the variations in the meaning, possibility and desirability of legal certainty, a future research agenda could specifically explore the relationship between legal certainty and other phenomena. To some extent, this issue has always been a concern for the notion of legal certainty, as it is clear that the benefits of legal certainty need to be balanced with the benefits of a law that is sufficiently flexible in order to be respond to changing circumstances. Thus, the relationship between legal certainty and flexibility (or adaptablity) of the law has always been an important one.

But we suggest that future research can explore many more topics with a 'legal certainty and …' approach. For example, it may consider topics such as 'legal certainty and legitimacy', 'legal certainty and development', 'legal certainty and social justice', 'legal certainty and politics', 'legal certainty and courts', 'legal certainty and legislative reform' and 'legal certainty and language'. Many of these relationships also feature in the contributions to this book, for example, as they critically reflect on the relevance of legal certainty for legislation, the judicial use of the notion of legal certainty and international policy initiatives promoting legal certainty. Thus, we hope that our book will be of core interest for future research in this field.

Part I

Theoretical Perspectives ('Certainty of Law')

1

Legal Certainty and the European Courts: Accessibility and Legitimate Expectations as Standards of Reasonableness

PATRICIA POPELIER

INTRODUCTION

IN ITS REPORT on the 'Index of Legal Certainty', the Civil Law Initiative draws a relativist concept of legal certainty, in search for 'a balance between fixedness and flexibility, certainty and indecision'.[1] In doing so, the authors recognise a shift in the concept of legal certainty from a conservative device for the maintenance and accumulation of property and vested rights to a more dynamic concept that aims at securing an individual's autonomy when acting in an uncertain environment. In this chapter, the jurisprudence of the European Court of Human Rights (ECtHR) is analysed in order to find how this 'balance between fixedness and flexibility' is operationalised. It is organised as follows. First, the shift from a static to a dynamic concept of legal certainty is explained. The next section elaborates on the implications of a dynamic concept of legal certainty. It explains the fundaments and the functions of legal certainty. These functions, one referring to legitimacy of the legal system, the other taking an economic approach, lay bare the underlying portrayal of man. In the last section, the jurisprudence of the ECtHR, as well as the Court of Justice of the European Union (previously the European Court of Justice, ECJ), is analysed against this background. These courts are selected because they cover respectively 47 and 28 national legal systems, and because they are very different types of courts—one a human rights court, the other representative of a European Union (EU) that was built on the foundations of economic freedoms and

[1] B Deffains and C Kessedjian (eds), 'Index of Legal Certainty. Report for the Civil Law Initiative' (2015) 17, available at www.fondation-droitcontinental.org/en/index-legal-certainty/.

an economic market—and are representative of the two approaches to the function of legal certainty: one more principled, the other economic.

THE SHIFT FROM A STATIC TO A DYNAMIC CONCEPT OF LEGAL CERTAINTY

Underlying the traditional, static concept of legal certainty is the nineteenth century view according to which the legal order captures reality in the form of a rational, ie transparent, stable, coherent and predictable system of rules. In this model the legal order is defined in terms of legal certainty, thereby equating legal system and legal certainty.[2] Reality was pictured as stable and immobile, frozen over even longer terms through its transformation into the legal system, eg through codification. Rules were considered rational as they were enacted by Parliament, presumed to be a perfect, all-embracing, rational lawmaker. As a result, the rationality of the law became a paradigm: parliamentary laws were presumed to be clear and accessible, effective and based on an informed decision making process.[3] Complemented with the idea of the sovereign Parliament—supreme and indivisible ruler—the paradigm of the rational lawmaker led to the inviolability of Parliamentary laws. As a result, operationalisation of the principle of legal certainty focused on executive and courts: their task was to interpret and apply laws so as to uphold the image of Parliament as a rational lawmaker. Faithful interpretation and application increases legal certainty, as it makes government action and the outcome of legal disputes predictable. In this model, legal certainty is a conservative device, concerned with stability and the protection of the status quo.[4]

Reality, however, turned out to be far more difficult to grasp. Complexity has become the key term to describe contemporary society, associated with ideas of non-linear dynamic systems, unpredictability, self-organisation, learning networks, change and adaptability.[5] With a new world view came

[2] ibid 5.

[3] For the paradigm of the rational lawmaker, see, amongst others: N Bobbio, 'Le bon législateur' in B Hubien, *Le raisonnement juridique* (Brussels, Bruylant, 1971) 243; L Nowak, 'De la rationnalité du législateur comme élément de l'interprétation juridique' (1969) 12 *Logique et analyse* 65; F Ost, 'L'interprétation logique et systématique et le postulat de rationnalité du législateur' in M Van De Kerchove (ed), *L'interprétation en* droit (Brussels, FUSL, 1978) 97; Z Ziembinski, 'La notion de rationalité du législateur' (1978) 23 *Archives de Philosophie du Droit* 175.

[4] W Leisner, 'L'état de droit—une contradiction?' in M Waline (ed), *Recueil d'études en hommage à Charles Eisenmann* (Paris, Cujas, 1977) 70.

[5] See, amongst many others, JB Ruhl, 'Complexity Theory as Paradigm for the Dynamic Law-and-society System: A Wake-up Call for Legal Reductionism and the Modern Administrative State' (1996) 45 *Duke Law Journal* 875; G Martinico, 'Complexity and Cultural Sources of Law in the EU Context: From the Multilevel Constitutionalism to the Constitutional Synallagma' (2007) 8 *German Law Journal* 205, 209–210.

a paradigm shift, calling into question the very meaning of legal certainty. Scholars pointed out that *un*certainty, not certainty, was inherent to the legal system,[6] leading to the fall of legal certainty and the rule of law as legal concepts in the modern legal order.[7] Instead, uncertainty was valued as a source of innovation and creativity.[8]

This counter-movement, however, did not constitute the death blow for the principle of legal certainty. Instead, the deconstruction of the principle was followed by a reconstruction to adapt it to the requirements of a dynamic and unpredictable environment. This lays bare an interesting paradox. As long as legal certainty was considered such an essential and inherent component of law that it was equated with the legal system itself, it was devoid of practical meaning; in contrast, by putting it into perspective, the principle gained argumentative power in court disputes, increasing the operational import of the principle.

A DYNAMIC CONCEPT OF LEGAL CERTAINTY: FUNDAMENTS, FUNCTIONS AND A PORTRAYAL OF MAN

Fundaments

Sustainability and adaptiveness are key terms to grasp the role of legal certainty within a dynamic, complex environment. The legal system operates in an unpredictable environment, where, unavoidably, external factors emerge with unpredictable impact on the relations regulated by law. Adaptiveness, then, is the key to 'transform disorder into organisation'.[9] It is one of three qualities of *sustainability* that help dynamical and complex systems to survive, along with stability and simplicity.[10]

In legal systems, stability means that relationships remain as close as possible to the way they were. Stability, however, is to be distinguished from immobility. Frictions caused by new evolutions that emerge over time, may call for incremental measures in order to maintain the balance or outcomes that were initially envisaged.[11] Consequently, while lifting or amending a legal rule was considered a threat to a traditional, static concept of legal certainty,[12] it may become a requirement within its dynamic counterpart.

[6] J Frank, *Law and the Modern Mind* (New York, Coward-McCann, 1949) 7; NJ Maden, *L'insécurité inhérente au système juridique* (Dijon, Université de Dijon, 1979).

[7] Leisner, 'L'état de droit' 65–79.

[8] Frank, *Law and the Modern Mind* 7, 118 and 166.

[9] Ruhl, 'Complexity Theory' 892.

[10] ibid 886–87.

[11] ibid 888.

[12] Leisner, 'L'état de droit' 71. See also B Leoni, *Freedom and the Law* (New Jersey, Van Nostrand Co, 1961) 204.

This aligns with Luhmann's idea of 'reflexivity' of trust: in a complex world, we cannot rely on things to remain exactly as they were, but we can expect them to continue their *Selbstdarstellung*.[13] This implies that changes are necessary in order to sustain coherency and to preserve the essence of their identity in changing circumstances.

Simplicity means that relationships—conditions, facts and legal consequences—are easily determined. Again, simplicity does not necessarily call for the least complicated regulation. On the one hand, differentiation is often needed to accommodate different circumstances and avoid complicated implementation rules.[14] On the other, a certain degree of generality or vagueness is required in order to catch unforeseen developments in the situation under regulation.

Adaptability, finally, points to the ability to respond to new challenges.[15] It implies the ability to change the law or its interpretation according to changing circumstances as well as the flexibility granted to private persons to adjust their behaviour under changing circumstances.

Consequently, legal certainty conceived as a tool for sustainability in dynamic and complex legal systems, involves a constant balancing between stability and simplicity on the one hand and adaptability on the other. This is what the Civil Law Initiative means by the 'constant balancing between stability and flexibility',[16] based on the understanding that flexibility is not necessarily a counterbalance, but may constitute an inherent quality to legal certainty. Translated into legal terms, key components of legal certainty are *legitimate expectations* and *accessibility*, with the ability to adapt as a determining operational factor.

The notion 'legitimate expectations' refers to stability: we can expect lawmakers to leave legal consequences unaltered, as long as these expectations are justified despite a dynamic environment, but these expectations are not legitimate if changes are necessary to adapt the law to new challenges or if persons can easily adapt their behaviour to new rules. In other words, if circumstances change (economic) actors may expect rules to adapt so as to keep them efficient; in that case, legal change is predictable, whereas the principle of legal certainty only protects actors against *unpredictable* legal changes.

In turn, 'accessibility' refers to simplicity: we can expect rules to be as simple and comprehensible as possible, taking into account the complexity of the relations subjected to regulation or the environment in which these relations emerge. Accessibility and legitimate expectations are related. If legal rules are difficult to find or unclear as to conditions or legal consequences,

[13] N Luhmann, *Vertrausen. Ein Mechanismus der Reduktion sozialer Komlexität* (Stuttgart, Enke Verlag, 1973) 67.

[14] Leisner, 'L'état de droit' 888.

[15] ibid 887.

[16] Deffains and Kessedjian (eds), 'Index of Legal Certainty' 17.

they cannot create legitimate expectations that certain behaviour will entail certain legal consequences. Since complex environments often require complex sets of rules, it becomes more difficult for governments to make rules simple and make an overload of information readily accessible, and for individuals to find the (different sets of) law and understand its content. Therefore, both government and individuals need to make some efforts. In doctrine, this mutual relation is reflected under the concept of 'access to legislation': the right of the individual to gain effective access to legislative information and the correlative duty of the state to enable and facilitate such access.[17]

The OECD's Sustainable Governance Indicators shows that this is not a mere abstract account for academic debate. In the contemporary environment, 'sustainability' is indeed the key term, in view of which adaptiveness and legal certainty are mutually reinforcing, rather than each other's opposites. 'Sustainable governance' is defined as 'the political management of public affairs that adopts a long term view of societal development, takes into account the interest of future generations, and retains capacities for social change'.[18] One of the criteria to measure sustainability of governments and their ability to adapt to changing circumstances, is legal certainty, defined as the degree to which government and administration act predictably, on the basis of and in accordance with consistent and transparent legal provisions.[19]

Functions

Two functions of legal certainty may explain why strong criticism has led to the reconstruction of legal certainty rather than its destruction. One is a legitimising function, the other is its economic functioning.

Legitimacy

Legal certainty is closely linked to the notions of the rule of law and the *Rechtsstaat*, with origins in respectively British constitutional law and German *Staatsrechtlehre*. Both notions advertise a legal system where a pre-existing and knowable set of general rules, enacted by an elected Parliament, makes government interference predictable and protects individual persons

[17] Y Roznai and M Mordechay, 'Access to Justice 2.0: Access to Legislation and Beyond' (2015) 3 *The Theory and Practice of Legislation* 333, 335.

[18] M Brusis and J Siegmund, *Designing Sustainable Government Indicators 2011: Criteria and Methodology* (Munich, Bertelsmann Stiftung, 2011) 3.

[19] www.sgi-network.org/2015/Democracy/Quality_of_Democracy/Rule_of_Law/Legal_Certainty.

against the arbitrary exercise of power. This generates legitimacy and public trust and it protects individual freedom.

Freedom in the concept of the rule of law is a contextual, socially-bounded freedom: a freedom in restraint, starting from the idea that men can only aspire to autonomy in recognition of social ties as well as biological and technological limitations. Individual freedom, then, is a freedom of choice within a specific context.[20] In essence, it is about a person's self-determination, the ability to determine and realise his or her own life project.[21] Legal certainty furthers individual freedom by enabling persons to construct an adequate decision model.[22] It does so, first, by reducing an infinite number of alternative options to a more limited framework for decision making,[23] and, second, by informing persons of the legal consequences each action will engender.

As mentioned above, one cannot expect rules to be permanent. Considering the complexity of the environment, the possibility that in concrete cases people are disappointed in their expectations arising from a pre-enacted set of rules must be built into the very notion of trust in public power. Changes in the law, then, do not harm public trust if they are justifiable and remain coherent with the overall purpose of the legal framework.

If confidence refers to the system rather than concrete cases, however, this may change as laws explicitly incite persons to take specific actions. If laws become a determining factor for persons to take action, public confidence requires that, in principle, the prospects of legal consequences are redeemed.

Economic Functioning

The importance of legal certainty for economic conduct is illustrated by Fuller's concept of law as developed in *The Morality of Law*. In his definition, the law is 'the enterprise of subjecting human conduct to the governance of rules'.[24] An essential condition of any legal system is the obedience of eight so-called 'principles of morality' which come down to the idea of legal certainty, as they aim at making rules knowable, reliable and enforceable. The purpose of the law is to enable persons to make plans and carry them out, by governing human conduct through the channelling of social relations. Fuller not only equates the legal system with legal certainty, he

[20] L Fuller, 'Freedom—A Suggested Analysis' (1955) 68 *Harvard Law Review*, 1305, 1311; K Hesse, 'Der Rechtsstaat im Verfassungssystem des Grundgesetzes' in E Forsthoff (ed), *Rechtsstaatlichkeit und Sozialstaatlichkeit* (Darmstadt, Wissenschaftliche Buchgesellschaft, 1968) 575; C Starck, *Freiheit und Organisation* (Tübingen, Mohr, 1976) 5.

[21] A Brunner, *Rechtsstaat gegen Totaalstaat* (Zurich, Polygraphischer Verlag, 1948); Starck, *Freiheit und Orgnanisation* 3.

[22] Fuller, 'Freedom—A Suggested Analysis' 1314.

[23] ibid 1311.

[24] L Fuller, *The Morality of Law* (New Haven, Yale University Press, 1973) 106.

also stresses its importance in economic relations. The society where his notions of 'moral and legal duty' can best develop is one 'of economic traders' 'under capitalism'.[25]

From an economic point of view, the legal framework enables trade by making the conduct of other economic partners predictable and by encouraging or discouraging investments in specific activities. From this viewpoint, legal changes produce reliance and opportunity costs, ie 'costs for economic actors to invest in assets given the current positive laws' and costs referring to missed benefits due to the non-realisation of expected legal consequences.[26] When changing legal rules, the lawmaker will have to weigh these costs against the benefits of legal change. The concept of legitimate expectations reflects the search for optimality in the promotion of efficiency in legal changes: reliance and opportunity costs are acknowledged only if reliance is legitimate, ie 'reasonable'; if reliance if reasonable, then these costs are weighed against the social benefits expected to follow from the legal change.[27] This search for optimality reflects the standard of reasonableness, referred to by the Civil Law Initiative.[28]

The Portrayal of Man Underpinning the Concept of Legal Certainty

Underpinning the concept of the rule of law is the notion of autonomous persons: free but socially bounded and therefore responsible for their actions. These persons construct decision models on the basis of specific calculations and expectations, taking into account the societal framework of which they are part. This presupposes a rational person, able to define their own goals and plan their actions, but taking into account socio-economic reality and ready to adapt their plans to a dynamic environment.

This aligns with the notion of the *homo economicus* or the reasonable, prudent person, acting strategically and with self-interest. The assumption is that these persons are well-informed and observant and plan their actions accordingly. They use the law as a guidance system, informing them of which actions are allowed and what the consequences of their actions will be.[29]

Social psychologists and behavioural economics, however, discredited this assumption under the notion of 'bounded rationality'. People's judgments are often biased, especially in a context of uncertainty, and based on shortcuts

[25] ibid 24.

[26] A Portuese, 'The Case for a Principled Approach to Law and Economcs: Efficiency Analysis and General Principles of Law' in K Mathis (ed) *Law and Economics in Europe. Foundations and Applications* (Dordrecht, Springer, 2014) 311.

[27] ibid 314.

[28] Deffains and Kessedjian (eds), 'Index of Legal Certainty' 17.

[29] SJ Morse, 'The Jurisprudence of Craziness' in F Parisi and VL Smith, (eds), *The Law and Economics of Irrational Behavior* (Stanford, Stanford University Press, 2005) 227.

and cognitive errors; simplified strategies are used to avoid decision-making costs and to overcome intellectual or informational deficiencies.[30] Moreover, real people have proved to be less self-interested than the *homo economicus* in the rational choice model.[31]

It is nonetheless claimed that even though a person's action is not always based on reason, action-guiding is still a crucial function of law in human interaction.[32] In the legal system, the *homo economicus* is turned into a responsible agent: an intentional agent who bears the consequences of his or her conduct.[33] This is linked with the concept of liberty: responsible agents have the capacity to act rationally and are therefore required to bear the consequences.[34] The question, then, is how to balance expectations of rationality against empirical findings of boundedness.

According to Morse, the law expects from persons a minimal degree of rationality, defined as some 'coherence between desires, beliefs, and actions', including the ability to reason instrumentally on the basis of facts, to understand the rules, to be flexible, ie responsive to changes in one's situation and environment.[35] The extent to which a person is expected to behave in this way, however, is contextual: the required capacity to act rationally can differ in general or in specific contexts.[36]

The conclusion is that the idea of legal certainty views people as intentional agents who act rationally, guided by legal rules, relying on the legal consequences predicted by law and ready to bear these consequences, but also capable of adapting their behaviour to changing circumstances. As the principle of legal certainty is linked with the idea of the rule of law and personal liberty, persons are, moreover, expected to act responsibly and in good faith. However, it is well understood that the capacities of people to behave rationally are not unlimited. This may be reflected in the government's duty to make rules easily accessible and understandable and to differentiate as regards the degree to which people are expected to inform themselves and to predict the consequences of their actions.

[30] C Jolls, CR Sunstein and R Thaler, 'A Behavioral Approach to Law and Economics' (1998) 50 *Stanford Law Review* 1477–80; RH Frank, 'Departures from Rational Choice: With and Without Regret' in F Parisi and VL Smith (eds), *The Law and Economics of Irrational Behavior* (Stanford, Stanford University Press, 2005) 16–18; CR Sunstein and E Ullman-Margalit, 'Second-Order Decisions' in CR Sunstein (ed), *Behavioral Law and Econnomics* (Cambridge, Cambridge University Press, 2000) 187.

[31] Jolls et al, 'A Behavioral Approach to law and Economics' 1479; Frank, 'Departures from Rational Choice' 18–19.

[32] Morse, 'The Jurisprudence of Craziness' 229.

[33] ibid.

[34] ibid.

[35] ibid 230.

[36] ibid.

Conclusion

From what precedes, the following five threads or general principles can be discerned, that make up a framework for the operation of the principle of legal certainty:

(1) The essential attributes of a dynamic concept of legal certainty, namely stability, simplicity and adaptability, are operationalised in legal systems as requirements of *legal expectations* and *accessibility*. Legal rules are not expected to be absolutely stable or clear. Instead, the rule-maker is expected to amend rules in order to respond to new challenges and unforeseen circumstances, and to catch unforeseen developments through a certain vagueness in the formulation of the rule.

(2) In balancing the benefits of a new rule against individual reliance and opportunity costs resulting from the disappointment of expectations, the latter costs gain weight as:
   (a) rules are explicitly motivational, making governmental action a decisive factor for human behaviour;
   (b) it becomes difficult for persons to adapt their behaviour to new rules without costs or a loss of investments;
   (c) they follow from clear and coherent rules or established practice or jurisdiction;
   (d) legal changes were unpredictable, for example because they do not respond to new challenges, or the former rules were not the object of public debate, or administrative practice or judicial decisions created different expectations;
   (e) persons acted in good faith.

(3) In balancing the benefits of a new rule against individual reliance and opportunity costs resulting from the disappointment of expectations, the latter costs lose weight as:
   (a) the social benefits are so strong that they outweigh individual costs;
   (b) it is easy for persons to adapt their behaviour to new rules without costs or a loss of investments;
   (c) rules were unclear as to which legal consequences could be expected;
   (d) legal changes were predictable, for example because they were announced, or they respond to new challenges or changing circumstances of which persons should be aware, or they do not really bring anything new compared to the situation under the old legal rules, jurisdiction or administrative practice or at least preserve the original intent; or they are a coherent part of a larger reform that gradually takes place;
   (e) persons acted in bad faith.

(4) Government is expected to make efforts in order to make rules accessible and comprehensible, so that they can guide persons in their personal activities. Requirements lessen as rules concern matters that are complex and require flexibility. Instead, while rules should clearly define conditions and legal consequences, they should also be sufficiently general or vague so as to catch new developments without having to amend the rule continuously.

(5) Persons, acting as rational agents, are expected to make efforts in order to find and comprehend the rules applicable to them. More efforts are expected from persons as they are more familiar with the matter, eg if it concerns their professional activities.

In the next section, the case law of the ECtHR and the Court of Justice is analysed in the light of these conclusions.

LEGAL CERTAINTY IN THE CASE LAW OF THE EUROPEAN COURTS

The threads listed above concern: (1) the definition of legal certainty; (2) the operation of legitimate expectations; and (3) the accessibility requirement.

The Definition of Legal Certainty

Both European Courts define the principle of legal certainty in terms of accessibility and legitimate expectations (thread (1)).

Neither the European Convention on Human Rights nor the EU Treaties use the term 'legal certainty', but the European Courts regard it as a general principle implied in the Convention[37] or the EU legal order.[38] The ECtHR links this with the rule of law and public confidence. For example, in *Paduraru v Romania* it considered that the lack of consistency at the legislative level and the conflicting approaches by the domestic courts created uncertainty and reduced the public's confidence in the judicial system.[39]

A recurring definition in the case law of the ECtHR is that government interference 'prescribed by law' should be accessible to the persons concerned and formulated with sufficient precision to enable them—if need

[37] Eg *Mooren v Germany* A no 11364/03 (2009) ECLI:CE:ECHR:2009:0709JUD001136403 para 72.

[38] Eg Case C-181/04–183/04 *Elmeke NE v Ypourgos Oikonomikon* [2006] ECLI:EU:C:2006:563 para 31.

[39] *Paduraru v Romania* A no 63252/00 (2005) ECLI:CE:ECHR:2005:1201JUD006325200 paras 98–99. See also *Beian v Romania* A no 30658/05 (2007) ECLI:CE:ECHR:2007:1206JUD003065805 para 39.

be, with appropriate advice—to foresee, to a degree that is reasonable in the circumstances, the consequences which a given action may engender.[40] The requirement of accessibility is literally inserted in this definition. Foreseeability—or predictability—also appears in this formulation. The term 'legitimate expectations' does not, but it appears in justification tests, mostly to assess the temporal effects of a rule.[41] The idea is that if a person has access to a rule that holds out the prospect of certain legal consequences, he or she may well expect that his or her actions will indeed procure these consequences. At the same time, the definition accentuates the relativeness of the requirements. Laws should be 'sufficiently' precise; and they should be predictable 'to a degree that is reasonable in the circumstances'.

The Court of Justice's definition is put in more absolute terms: the principle of legal certainty requires that EU legislation must be certain and its application foreseeable by those subject to it.[42] The Court adds that the requirement of legal certainty must be observed 'all the more strictly' if rules entail financial consequences: those concerned must know 'precisely' the extent of the obligations imposed on them,[43] and must be able to ascertain 'unequivocally' what their rights and obligations are.[44]

In practice, however, the Court as well conducts a reasonableness test. To that end it very explicitly has in mind 'a reasonably prudent economic agent'. When balancing against legitimate expectations, the Court will first compare the individual's conduct with that of 'reasonably prudent economic agents' for deciding whether an expectation was legitimate.[45]

The strict definition employed by the Court of Justice may find its source in the multi-layered nature of the EU. The Court is especially strict in defining the duty of the Member States to be clear and precise when transposing a directive[46] or, in particular, when derogating from EU provisions.

[40] First formulated in *Sunday Times v United Kingdom (No 1)* A no 30 (1979–80) ECLI:CE:ECHR:1979:0426JUD000653874 para 49.

[41] For an earlier analysis see P Popelier, 'Legitimate Expectations and the Law-Maker in the Case Law of the European Court of Human Rights' (2006) 6 *European Human Rights Law Review* 16.

[42] Case C-325/85 *Ireland v Commission* [1987] ECLI:EU:C:1987:546 para 18; Case C-63/93 *Fintan Duff and Others v Minister for Agriculture and Food und Attorney General* [1996] ECLI:EU:C:1996:51 para 20.

[43] Case C-326/85 *Netherlands v Commission* [1987] ECLI:EU:C:1987:547 para 24; Case C-158/06 *Stichting ROM-projecten v Staatssecretaris van Economische Zaken* [2007] ECLI:EU:C:2007:370 para 26; Case C-201/08 *Plantanol GmbH & Co. KG v Hauptzollamt Darmstadt* [2009] ECLI:EU:C:2009:539 para 46.

[44] *Stichting ROM-projecten v Staatssecretaris van Economische Zaken* para 25.

[45] Joined Cases C-95/74–C-98/74, C-15/75 and C 100/75 *Union nationale des coopératives agricoles de céréales and Others v Commission and Council* [1975] ECLI:EU:C:1975:172 paras 43–45, Case 78/77 *Lührs v Hauptzollamt Hamburg-Jonas* [1978] ECLI:EU:C:1978:20 para 6, Case C-182/03 *Belgium v Commission* [2006] ECLI:EU:C:2006:416 para 147; *Elmeke NE v Ypourgos Oikonomikon* para 32.

[46] Case C-61/05 *Commission v Portuguese Republic* [2006] ECLI:EU:C:2006:467 para 37.

Legitimate Expectations

The European Court of Human Rights

Legitimate expectations may follow from legislation—unless a statutory condition is not fulfilled, even if the petitioner claims that this condition is unconstitutional[47]—administrative practice,[48] a final judgment[49] or established case law (thread (2)(c)).[50] Legitimate expectations can even arise from administrative practice in violation of the law, for example if the government systematically tolerates illegal settlements for a long period of time.[51]

Legitimate expectations come into play especially when new rules have retroactive effect. Although the European Convention on Human Rights only forbids the retroactivity of more stringent penal laws,[52] the Court also treats retroactive laws in non-penal matters with suspicion, and even considers prospective laws, for example if they interfere with existing contracts[53] or in matters of social security. The Court is sensitive in matters such as pensions law, because pension schemes are based on long-term contributions, whereas the benefits are obtained only after reaching the pensionable age. According to the Court,

> the inherent features of the system—stability and reliability—allow for lifelong family and career planning. For these reasons the Court considers that any adjustments of the pension schemes must be carried out in a gradual, cautious and measured manner. Any other approach could endanger social peace, foreseeability of the pension system and legal certainty.[54]

The Court often balances the social benefits of legislative interference with the costs borne by the applicant or her ability to adjust behaviour to the new rule. An example is *Kjartan Ásmundsson v Iceland*, where the Court reasoned that, on the one hand, the applicant was deprived of the entirety of his

[47] *Gratzinger and Gratzingerova v Czech Republic* Series A no 39794/98 (2002) ECLI:CE:ECHR:2004:0928JUD004491298; *Maltzan v Germany* Series A nos 71916/01, 71917/01, 10260/02 (2005).

[48] *Pine Valley Developments Ltd v Ireland* Series A no 12742/87 (1991) ECLI:CE:ECHR:1993:0209JUD001274287.

[49] *Stran Greek Refineries and Stratis Andreadis v Greece* Series A no 13427/87 (1994) ECLI:CE:ECHR:1994:1209JUD001342787; *Teteriny v Russia* Series A no 11931/03 (2005) ECLI:CE:ECHR:2005:0630JUD001193103.

[50] *Stran Greek Refineries and Stratis Andreadis v Greece* para 59; *Pressos Compania Naviera SA v Belgium* Series A no 17849/91 (1995) ECLI:CE:ECHR:1997:0703JUD001784991 para 31; *Draon v France* Series A no 1513/03 (2005) ECLI:CE:ECHR:2006:0621JUD000151303 paras 65–70.

[51] *Öneryildiz v Turkey* Series A no 48939/99 (2004) ECLI:CE:ECHR:2004:1130JUD004893999 paras 127–28.

[52] ECHR, Art 7.

[53] *Bäck v Finland* Series A no 37598/97 (2004) ECLI:CE:ECHR:2004:0720JUD003759897.

[54] *Andrle v Czech Republic* Series A no 6268/08 (2011) ECLI:CE:ECHR:2011:0217JUD000626808 para 51.

disability entitlements, at the time one-third of his gross monthly income, although he was still considered 25 per cent incapacitated to perform work (thread (2)(b)); whereas on the other hand, the new rule did not further the public interest in resolving the Seamen's Pension Fund's financial difficulties, since it only applied to a small minority of disability pensioners (thread (3)(a)).[55] The same considerations played in *Draon v France*: the 'French parliament's determination to put an end to a line of case-law of which it disapproved and to change the legal position on medical liability' was in the public interest (thread (3)(a)), but could not outweigh the absence of a reasonable compensation (thread (2)(b)).[56] In other cases these considerations support legal change. In *Alatulkkila v Finland*, the Court found that the legislator had an important general interest in protecting fish stocks, whereas the applicant's right to fish was not completely extinguished and professional fishermen could apply for compensation for economic losses.[57] In *Maggio v Italy,* the Court decided that a change in pension schemes was justified because it aimed at avoiding unjustified advantages but did not excessively reduce the applicant's pension.[58] Explicit reference to the ability of the applicant to adjust behaviour was made in *NKM v Hungary*, where the Court noted that the applicant bore an excessive and disproportionate burden, whereas 'the legislature did not afford the applicant a transitional period within which to adjust herself to the new scheme' (thread (2)(b)).[59]

The ECtHR confirms that legitimate expectations have special weight if they were created by law, especially to encourage specific behaviour (thread (2)(a)). In *Scoppola v Italy (No 2)* the applicant, tried for murder and attempted murder, opted for a summary procedure involving the waiver of certain procedural safeguard in exchange for a 30 years' imprisonment instead of a life imprisonment. However, a new law deprived him of the advantage that had been the main motivator for choosing the summary procedure. The Grand Chamber stated that on the basis of the legal framework in force when the request for the summary procedure was made, the applicant 'could legitimately expect that, thanks to the procedural choice he had made', he would be liable to a maximum sentence of 30 years' imprisonment, and that this legitimate expectation was frustrated by a new law which was applied not only to defendants making new requests but also to persons who had already made that request and stood trial before the

[55] *Kjartan Ásmundsson v Iceland* Series A no 60669/00 (2004) ECLI:CE:ECHR:2004:1012 JUD006066900 paras 42–44.

[56] *Draon v France* paras 77, 83–84.

[57] *Alatulkkila v Finland* Series A no 33538/96 (2005) ECLI:CE:ECHR:2005:0728 JUD003353896 para 67.

[58] *Maggio v Italy* Series A no 46286/09 (2011) ECLI:CE:ECHR:2011:0531JUD004628609 para 63.

[59] *N.K.M v Hungary* Series A no 66529/11 (2013) ECLI:CE:ECHR:2013:0514JUD0066 52911 para 71.

publication of the new law. The Court added that the state was expected to act in good faith and had acted contrary to the principle of legal certainty and the protection of legitimate trust.[60]

The Court Accepts that the Lawmaker Interferes as a Response to New Developments

In *Affaire Sud Parisienne de Construction v France,* the Court pointed to a strong inflation which changed the monetary conditions (thread (3)(d)). This justified legislative interference, in order to avoid unintended advantages for the applicant (threads (3)(a), (3)(e)).[61] The claim that the legitimacy of expectations decreases if new laws merely adopt a rule that was already applied in practice, only applies if the practice was well-established. This is not the case if the government invokes an interpretation held by a government agency, but not supported by the majority case law (thread (3)(d)).[62] In *Georgian Labour Party v Georgia,* the Court accepted a sudden change in the registration system shortly before repeat parliamentary elections, considering 'the political evolution' and especially 'the challenge of remedying manifest shortcomings in the electoral rolls within very tight deadlines, in a "post-revolutionary" political situation'.[63] Especially if the new law remedies an inadvertent defect of the law, professionals are expected to follow the parliamentary debates so as to understand what the original intent of the law was and to foresee remedying legislation.[64]

The principle of legal certainty may even imply that applicants have legitimate expectations that new law will come into force. In *Centro Europa 7 v Italy,* the Court observed that the applicant, having been granted a licence to operate in the television-broadcasting sector but having been waiting for implementing measures, had been frustrated in performing that activity due to the failure by the state 'to comply with its positive obligation to put in place an appropriate legislative and administrative framework'.[65]

In *Kayriakova v Bulgaria*, the applicants were sanctioned for having occupied property on the basis of a contract that later had been declared void with retroactive effect. The Court ruled that the law on the basis of which the contract was declared void had been a novelty and subjected to 'highly

[60] *Scoppola v Italy (No 2)* Series A no 10249/03 (2009) ECLI:CE:ECHR:2009:0917JUD001024903 paras 137–38.

[61] *Affaire Sud Parisienne de Construction v France* Series A no 33704/04 (2010) ECLI:CE:ECHR:2010:0211JUD003370404 para 43.

[62] *Maggio v Italy* para 48.

[63] *Georgian Labour Party v Georgia* Series A no 9103/04 (2008) ECLI:CE:ECHR:2008:0708JUD000910304 para 89.

[64] *National & Provincial Building Society et al v the United Kingdom* Series A no 21319/93 (1997) ECLI:CE:ECHR:1997:1023JUD002131993 para 81.

[65] *Centro Europa 7 srl and Di Stefano v Italy* Series A no 38433/09 (2012) ECLI:CE:ECHR:2012:0607JUD003843309 para 156.

uncertain interpretation for an initial period of several years' and therefore found that 'the automatic application of retrospective liability for damages to *bona fides* owners' 'squares poorly with the requirements of proportionality, foreseeability and fair balance'.[66] When using the property, the applicant relied on the contract, not on the law. Since the law was unclear, the applicant could not foresee that the contract would be declared void. Hence, while according to thread (3)(d) no legitimate expectations can flow from unclear rules, conversely, it cannot be held against people to not foresee the consequences of an obscure law.

The Court also Takes into Account the Applicant's Good or Bad Faith

In *R Sz v* Hungary, the Court explicitly stated that 'those who act in good faith on the basis of law or contracts should not be frustrated in their expectations without specific and compelling reasons' (thread (2)(e)).[67] In *Scoppola v Italy (No 2)*, the Court even accepted that the applicant, having waived procedural guarantees in exchange for a reduced prison sentence, had not taken the opportunity to return to his decision and opt for the ordinary procedure. The Court took into consideration that the defendant for more than nine months had 'legitimately believed' that the maximum sentence to which he was liable was 30 years' imprisonment and that this 'legitimate expectation was frustrated by factors beyond his control, such as the length of the domestic proceedings and the adoption' of the new law.[68]

By contrast, in *Affaire Sud Parisienne de Construction v France*, the Court disapproved of the applicant taking abnormal advantage of unexpected changes in the monetary environment (thread (3)(e)).[69] This aligns with the general observation that retroactive taxation can ultimately be justified if it aims at remedying technical deficiencies of the law, so as 'to ensure that private entities do not enjoy the benefit of a windfall in a changeover to a new tax-payment regime'.[70]

Retroactive laws are especially treated with suspicion if they interfere with judicial decisions that create legitimate expectations to obtain a financial benefit or compensation. The Court accepts that the general interest may nevertheless justify such interference (thread (3)(a)). However, it

[66] *Kayriakova v Bulgaria* Series A no 30945/04 (2010) ECLI:CE:ECHR:2010:0107JUD003094504 paras 44 and 47.

[67] *RSz v Hungary* Series A no 41838/11 (2013) ECLI:CE:ECHR:2013:0702JUD004183811 para 61. For a few other examples where the Court took into account the applicant's good faith, see *Kjartan Ásmundsson v Iceland* para 44; *Kayriakova v Bulgaria* para 47; *NKM v Hungary* para 75.

[68] *Scoppola v Italy (No 2)* para 144.

[69] *Affaire Sud Parisienne de Construction v France* para 43.

[70] *National & Provincial Building Society et al v United Kingdom* para 81; *R.Sz. v Hungary* para 40.

does not regard a mere financial motive a sufficient reason to interfere.[71] In *Lecarpentier v France,* the Court added that, moreover, assumptions—for example the fear that the absence of legislative interference would put the equilibrium in the banking sector and economic activity in general at risk—must be backed by facts and figures.[72] Likewise, in *Joubert v France*, the Court was not impressed by the French government's fear for an overwhelming number of litigations in the absence of legislative interference, dismissing it as purely hypothetic.[73]

Court of Justice

The threads identified above also appear in the case law of the Court of Justice.

The Court emphasises that the principle of legal certainty does not oppose legislative changes, but 'requires, rather, that the legislator takes account of the particular situations of traders and provides, where appropriate, adaptations to the application of the new legal rules'.[74] The crucial question is whether the addressee was able to comply with the new rules under reasonable conditions.[75] The Court expects EU authorities to take into account the operations and typical calendar in the relevant sector so as to enable companies to adjust to new rules (threads (2) and (3)(b)).[76] For example, if a trader commenced activities under a tax exemption scheme in favour of biofuels and made costly investments, he could see 'his interests considerably affected' by the sudden and unexpected withdrawal of that scheme before the date announced, without leaving enough time for him to adapt to the new situation.[77]

This is in particular relevant if EU rules were explicitly motivational (thread (2)(a)). A landmark case in this respect is *Mulder*. Producers had been encouraged by a Community measure not to deliver milk for a specific

[71] Eg *Zielinski and Pradal & Gonzalez and Others v France* Series A no 24846/94 (1999) ECLI:CE:ECHR:1999:1028JUD002484694 para 59; *Lecarpentier v France* Series A no 67847/01 (2001) ECLI:CE:ECHR:2006:0214JUD006784701 para 47; *Maggio v Italy* para 47; *MC v Italy* Series A no 5376/11 (2013) ECLI:CE:ECHR:2013:0903JUD000537611 para 64. Especially not if the financial risk cannot be considered so important as to put at risk the general interest, *Joubert v France* Series A no 30345/05 (2009) ECLI:CE:ECHR:2009:0723 JUD003034505 para 63.

[72] *Lecarpentier v France* para 47.

[73] *Joubert v France* para 61.

[74] *Plantanol GmbH & Co KG v Hauptzollamt Darmstadt* para 49. See also Case C-330/14 *Gergely Szemerey v Miniszterelnökséget vezető miniszter* [2015] ECLI:EU:C:2015:826 para 48.

[75] *Gergely Szemerey v Miniszterelnökséget vezető miniszter* para 49.

[76] Case C-5/75 *Deuka Deutsche Kraftfutter GmbH BJ Stolp v Einfuhr- und Vorratsstelle für Getreide und Futtermittel* [1975] ECLI:EU:C:1975:88 paras 9–11 and Case C-78/74 *Deuka Deutsche Kraftfutter GmbH BJ Stolp v Einfuhr- und Vorratsstelle für Getreide und Futtermittel* [1975] ECLI:EU:C:1975:44 paras 12–14.

[77] *Plantanol GmbH & Co KG v Hauptzollamt Darmstadt* para 52.

period of time and were later denied a reference quality for milk delivery in the absence of a reference quantity, due to the milk delivery stop. The Court stated that where a producer had been encouraged to suspend marketing for a limited period, he may legitimately expect not to be subject, upon expiry of his undertaking, to restrictions which specifically affect him precisely because he availed himself of the possibilities offered by the Community provisions.[78]

Further, if a new measure requires adjustments that prudent economic operators cannot take in a brief time, these operators have a legitimate expectation that a reasonable transition period is granted.[79] The Court is also critical towards retroactive tax law that deprives tax payers of reimbursement of tax paid but not due for breach of EU law, if the provision is enacted without transitional arrangement and without room for the taxpayers to prepare for the change that adversely affects their situation.[80]

Individuals and enterprises, on the other hand, are expected to keep abreast of evolutions and to predict regulatory amendments on the basis thereof (thread 3d). The Court long ago established that, for example, traders must expect any appreciable change in the monetary situation possibly to entail the extension of the monetary compensatory system to new categories of goods and the fixing of new amounts.[81] In *Plantanol*, the Court, when laying upon the national court the task of examining the legitimacy of expectations, instructed it also to take into account the predictability of the legal change, considering public and parliamentary debates as well as announcements in coalition agreements and draft legislation.[82]

In addition, legal changes do not amount to unpredictable new outcomes if they merely confirm the current situation, for example if an interpretative law explains concepts already contained in the initial version of the provision and defined by the case law of the Court of Justice.[83]

Accessibility

If legitimate expectations are based on the legal framework, this presumes the existence of pre-established, clear and accessible rules. The question

[78] Case C-120/86 *J Mulder v Minister van Landbouw en Visserij* [1988] ECLI:EU:C:1988:213 para 24.

[79] *Belgium v Commission* para 163.

[80] Case C-362/12 *Test Claimants in the Franked Investment Income Group Litigation v Commissioners of Inland Revenue and Commissioners for Her Majesty's Revenue and Customs* [2013] ECLI:EU:C:2013:834 para 44.

[81] Case C-98/78 *A Racke v Hauptzollamt Mainz* [1987] ECLI:EU:C:1979:14 para 20.

[82] *Plantanol GmbH & Co KG v Hauptzollamt Darmstadt* para 63.

[83] Case C-293/04 *Beemsterboer Coldstore Services BV v Inspecteur der Belastingdienst—Douanedistrict Arnhem* [2006] ECLI:EU:C:2006:162 para 22. See also Case C-4/10 and C-27/10 *Bureau national interprofessionel du Cognac v Gust. Ranin Oy* [2011] ECLI:EU:C:2011:484 paras 32–36.

then is how the Courts balance the requirement for clear and accessible rules against the need to grasp unexpected developments and, in other words, what efforts they expect from the government, on the one hand, and individuals, on the other.

The European Court of Human Rights

According to established case law of the ECtHR, the law must be 'sufficiently foreseeable in its terms to give individuals an adequate indication as to the circumstances in which and the conditions on which the authorities are entitled to resort to measures affecting their rights under the Convention'.[84]

A minimum obligation that rests with the government is the publication of the rules. Government interference that relies on a statute that has not been published, is, in principle, not provided by law.[85] The duty to make rules known is easily performed: publication in the official gazette suffices,[86] even though scholars emphasise that to make laws readily accessible, governments should make more effort, for example by managing legislative databases that provide free, consolidated, updated and user-friendly information, including links between various laws and advanced search options.[87]

But even if the rules have not been published in an official gazette, the requirement is still fulfilled if the applicants could or should have known their content, for example if the applicants, by virtue of their office, had access to the unpublished documents in which the relevant rule was inserted.[88]

In *Claes v Belgium*, this was taken a step further. Two applicants, former Ministers, complained that they were convicted by the Supreme Court without pre-established procedural rules. Earlier, the ECtHR found the Belgian state in violation of Article 6 for this very reason.[89] The Court, however, pointed out that this earlier case had provided a precedent, enabling the applicants to know the main traits of the procedure, especially since the

[84] Eg *CG v Bulgaria* Series A no 1365/07 (2008) ECLI:CE:ECHR:2008:0424JUD000136507 para 39; *Oleksandr Volkov v Ukraine* Series A no 21722/11 (2013) ECLI:CE:ECHR:2013:0109JUD002172211 para 170.

[85] Eg *Ciorap v Moldova* Series A no 12066/02 (2006) ECLI:CE:ECHR:2007:0619JUD001206602 para 113.

[86] Eg *Karademirci v Turkey* Series A no 37096/97 (2005) ECLI:CE:ECHR:2005:0125JUD003709697 para 36; *Stefanec v Czech Republic* Series A no 75615/0118 (2006) ECLI:CE:ECHR:2006:0718JUD007561501 para 43; *Piroğlu and Karakaya v Turkey* Series A no 36370/02 (2008) ECLI:CE:ECHR:2008:0318JUD003637002 para 53.

[87] Y Roznai and N Mordechay, 'Access to Justice 2.0: Access to Legislation and Beyond' (2015) 3 *Theory and Practice of Legislation* 339–47.

[88] *Savino v Italy* Series A no 17214/05 (2009) ECLI:CE:ECHR:2009:0428JUD001721405 para 98; *Pasko v Russia* Series A no 69519/01 (2009) ECLI:CE:ECHR:2009:1022JUD006951901 para 82.

[89] *Coëme v Belgium* Series A nos 32492/96, 32547/96, 32548/96, 33209/96, 33210/96 (2000) ECLI:CE:ECHR:2000:0622JUD003249296.

process had been the object of broad media coverage and many doctrinal analyses, and one of the applicants had been a party to this process whereas the other applicant's lawyer had been his representative.[90]

For example, in *Spacek v Czech Republic*, the Court considered the Act that required companies to comply with 'accounting principles'. These principles were contained in rules adopted by the Ministry of Finance and inserted in the Financial Bulletin, not in an official gazette. The Financial Bulletin was distributed to subscribers through the retail units of a state agency. The ECtHR ruled that, 'taking into consideration that the applicant company as a legal entity, contrary to an individual taxpayer, could and should have consulted the competent specialists, the publication of the Regulations in the Financial Bulletin was sufficient'.[91]

In the absence of a knowledgeable source of information, individuals may rely on the information provided by state authorities. The ECtHR stated that

> an individual acting in good faith is, in principle, entitled to rely on statements made by state or public officials who appear to have the requisite authority to do so, and that internal rules and procedures were complied with, unless it clearly follows from publicly accessible documents (including primary or subordinate legislation), or an individual was otherwise aware, or should have been aware, that a certain official lacked the authority to legally bind the State.[92]

Again, the ECtHR takes good faith into consideration on the part of both the applicant and the state authorities. It emphasises that if the authorities fail to observe their own rules of procedure, the risk must be borne by the state authorities and errors must not be remedied at the expense of the individual.

A further question is whether the law was sufficiently clear so as to enable individuals to see the legal consequences of their actions. The Court is aware that it cannot demand absolute precision. It recognises that it may be difficult to frame laws with high precision and, moreover, that 'a certain degree of flexibility' or vagueness may even be desirable to avoid excessive rigidity and to keep pace with changing circumstances.[93] A detailed statute risks constant reviewing and updating to deal with numerous new circumstances

[90] *Claes v Belgium* Series A no 46825/99 (2005) ECLI:CE:ECHR:2005:0602JUD004682599 para 35.

[91] *Špaček sro v Czech Republic* Series A no 26449/95 (1999) ECLI:CE:ECHR:1999:1109 JUD002644995 para 59.

[92] *Lelas v Croatia* Series A no 55555/08 (2010) ECLI:CE:ECHR:2010:0520JUD005555508 para 74.

[93] Eg *Goodwin v United Kingdom*, Series A no 17488/90 (1996) ECLI:CE:ECHR:1996:032 7JUD001748890 para 33; *Soros v France* Series A no 50425/06 (2011) ECLI:CE:ECHR:2011: 1006JUD005042506 para 51; *Oleksandr Volkov v Ukraine* para 175; *Karácsony v Hungary* Series A nos 42461/13 and 44357/13 (2016) ECLI:CE:ECHR:2016:0517JUD004246113 para 124.

arising in practice.[94] The Court is lenient in particular in domains that vary in character and time and are therefore difficult to define in advance, such as national security.[95] By contrast, it is stricter in matters that are sensitive from a human rights point of view. Criminal law is one example, but the Court also stated that, for example, 'a high standard of "foreseeability" must be applied with regard to laws that govern the inspection of the finances of political parties', in order to prevent the abuse of this mechanism for political purposes.[96]

Vague provisions invite other instances to make the rules concrete. The ECtHR refers to 'the existence of specific and consistent interpretational practice' to construe the exact meaning of a term.[97] In the absence of an interpretative community that provides codes and guidelines, responsibility shifts to enforcing and adjudicative bodies. Even in penal matters the legality principle cannot be interpreted as outlawing the gradual clarification of the rules of criminal liability through judicial interpretation from case to case, provided that the resultant development is consistent with the essence of the offence and 'could reasonably be foreseen'[98]—a formulation that calls into mind the idea of 'reflexivity of trust' discussed in the first part of this chapter.

If a wide discretion is granted to the executive in matters affecting human rights, the statute must insert safeguards to protect individuals against unfettered power. These safeguards consist of criteria, procedural guarantees and the establishment of judicial review.[99] Enforcing bodies are required to apply the law in a consistent manner. In *B and L v United Kingdom*, the Court stated that the inconsistency between the aims of a stature and the waiver applied in some cases undermined the rationality and logic of the measure.[100] However, administrative bodies are not required to enforce

[94] *Oleksandr Volkov v Ukraine* para 178.

[95] *Al-Nashif v Bulgaria* Series A no 50963/99 (2002) ECLI:CE:ECHR:2002:0620JUD005096399 para 121; *Lupsa v Romania* Series A no 10337/04 (2006) ECLI:CE:ECHR:2006:0608JUD001033704 para 37.

[96] *Cumhuriyet Halk Partisi v Turkey* Series A no 19920/13 (2016) ECLI:CE:ECHR:2016:0426JUD001992013 para 88.

[97] *Goodwin v United Kingdom* para 33; *Oleksandr Volkov v Ukraine* para 179.

[98] *SW v United Kingdom* Series A no 20166/92 (1995) ECLI:CE:ECHR:1995:1122JUD002016692 para 36, *Streletz, Kessler and Krenz v Germany* Series A nos 34044/96, 35532/97 and 44801/98 (2001) ECLI:CE:ECHR:2001:0322JUD003404496 para 50, *Kafkaris v Cyprus* Series A no 21906/04 (2008) ECLI:CE:ECHR:2008:0212JUD002190604 para 141; *OAO Neftanyanaya Kompaniya Yukos v Russia* Series A no 14902/04 (2011) ECLI:CE:ECHR:2011:0920JUD001490204 para 569.

[99] A vast case-law in this sense is established in particular with respect to secret surveillance matters. Eg *Szabó and Vissy v Hungary* Series A no 37138/14 (2016) ECLI:CE:ECHR:2016:0112JUD003713814.

[100] *B and L v United Kingdom* Series A no 36536/02 (2005) ECLI:CE:ECHR:2005:0913JUD003653602 para 40.

the law with strict rigidity but instead try to adapt to evolving situations through continuous dialogue.[101] The Court also states that if an offence has not been prosecuted for a while, individuals cannot hold that enforcement of the provision was unforeseeable, if in doctrine the Prosecution had been called on to take legal action more systematically and the Prosecution had laid down this intention in a circular published in various specialised journals.[102]

In turn, courts have a responsibility to develop stable and foreseeable interpretative case law. A well-established case law that meets the conditions of accessibility and foreseeability may compensate for vague statutory provisions.[103] This, of course, presupposes that there was any case law at all, and that it was issued before the facts of the case in order to have precedential value.[104] Of course, there must come a time when a vague norm is applied for the first time; in that case the Court seems to rely on common sense, for example to find foreseeable that long-lasting road blocks disrupting ordinary life, traffic and economic activities, were deemed to amount to 'a serious breach of public order'.[105]

By contrast, if the case law is inconsistent, this may render the law unpredictable.[106] This is especially reproachable if a Supreme Court, whose explicit role is to secure uniformity, is the source of divergences.[107] It is equally problematic if the court reverses its case law and retroactively applies a new and unexpected interpretation of the law to previous facts.[108] In this case, the notion of 'legitimate expectations' reappears, allowing the ECtHR to balance the foreseeability of a judicial reversal against other rights and interests, such as the appropriateness of the new case law.[109]

[101] *Leyla Sahin v Turkey* Series A no 44774/98 (2005) ECLI:CE:ECHR:2005:1110 JUD004477498 para 120.

[102] *Tourancheau et July v France* Series A no 53886/00 (2011) ECLI:CE:ECHR:2005:1124 JUD005388600 para 60.

[103] *Hachette Filipacchi Assosies v France* Series A no 71111/01 (2007) ECLI:CE:ECHR:2007:0614JUD007111101 para 33.

[104] *Forminster Enterprises Lmt v Czech Republic* Series A no 38238/04 (2008) ECLI:CE:ECHR:2008:1009JUD003823804 para 67; *Sorvisto v Finland* Series A no 19348/04 (2009) ECLI:CE:ECHR:2009:0113JUD001934804 para 116; *Cumhuriyet Halk Partisi v Turkey* para 94.

[105] *Kudrevičius v Lithuania* Series A no 37553/05 (2015) ECLI:CE:ECHR:2015:1015 JUD003755305 paras 113–14.

[106] *Cleja and Mihalcea v Romania* Series A no 77217/01 (2007) ECLI:CE:ECHR:2007:02 08JUD007721701 para 54; *Guta Tudor Teodorescu v Romania* Series A no 33751/05 (2016) para 48; *Cumhuriyet Halk Partisi v Turkey* para 94.

[107] *Beian v Romania* paras 34–39.

[108] *Fener Rum Erkek Lisesi Vakfi v Turkey* A no 34478/97 (2007) ECLI:CE:ECHR:2007:0109JUD003447897 para 57.

[109] See P Popelier, 'The European Court of Human Rights' Approach to Retrospective Judicial Reversals' in P Popelier et al (eds), *The Effects of Judicial Decisions in Time* (Cambridge, Intersentia, 2014) 276–77 and 279–80 with references to the case law.

The Court not only assesses each individual law or provision, but situates it in a larger complex of legal rules. Laws may become inaccessible because of inconsistencies and contradictions between different statutes.[110]

In assessing whether a provision is sufficiently clear, the ECtHR also takes the government's good faith into consideration. In a series of judgments regarding 'indirect expropriation', the Court concluded that the Italian administration benefited from the absence of stable and complete regulations and inconsistencies between legislative provisions and jurisprudential decisions to find an improper alternative for regular expropriations.[111] In another case, the Court was explicitly harsh, stating that government interference was based on legal rules that, in the light of the rule of law and legal certainty, were of 'questionable quality' and formulated with 'a false appearance of neutrality'.[112]

In turn, individuals are required to obtain 'appropriate' advice. It follows from the above that individuals are not only required to find and read statutes, but to also follow the case law that interprets these laws and to read specialist publications that hold doctrine or administrative circulars. The ECtHR also takes into consideration the applicant's capacity. For example, a judge and a doctor should have been aware that their sadomasochistic activities, consensual but very violent, exceeded the margin of legality;[113] an MP should be able to foresee which conduct violates the disciplinary rules for the orderly functioning of parliamentary activities, especially if (s)he participated in the examination of that provision;[114] a lawyer should be aware that leaving a court hearing to which he was appointed as a defence counsel, because of remuneration disputes, would be considered improper conduct, despite an apparent conflict between the relevant provisions;[115] and a 'doctor of laws and well-informed political figure' should be aware that, although the term 'genocide' lacked precision and despite the absence of ample case law, the public denial of the Armenian genocide was punishable, especially if he already had acknowledged that risk.[116] The Court is

[110] *Sorvisto v Finland* para 119.

[111] eg amongst many others, *Dora Chiro v Italy* Series A no 65272/01 (2005) ECLI:CE:ECHR:2010:0727JUD006527201; *Di Cola v Italy* Series A no 44897/98 (2005) ECLI:CE:ECHR:2010:0518JUD004489798.

[112] *Holy Synod of the Bulgarian Orthodox Church (Metropolitan Inokentiv) v Bulgaria* Series A no 412/03, 35677/04 (2009) ECLI:CE:ECHR:2010:0916JUD000041203 para 157.

[113] *KA and AD v Belgium* Series A no 42758/98 (2005) ECLI:CE:ECHR:2005:0217JUD004275898 paras 57–58.

[114] *Karácsony v Hungary* para 126.

[115] *Konstantin Stefanov v Bulgaria* Series A no 35399/05 (2015) ECLI:CE:ECHR:2015:1027JUD003539905 para 62.

[116] *Perinçek v Switzerland* Series A no 27510/08 (2013) ECLI:CE:ECHR:2015:1015JUD002751008 para 71. The Grand Chamber did not mention the applicant's capacity any more, but referred to a motion adopted by the Swiss Council of which the applicant should have been aware: *Perincek v Switzerland* Series A no 27510/08 (2015) ECLI:CE:ECHR:2015:1015JUD002751008 para 138.

especially strict if the rule addresses professionals, who are expected to carefully assess the risks involved in their professional activities.[117] Professionals are expected to inform themselves, act with due care and seek legal advice so as to familiarise themselves with legislation, administrative practice and case law,[118] and even to read parliamentary proceedings to illuminate the meaning of statutory terms.[119] This is in particular so if the applicant is a large business company that has resource to professional consultants: even if the legislation is vague, and practice and case law are incoherent, the company is expected to carefully assess the risk involved with important transactions.[120]

Court of Justice

As a multi-layered organisation, requirements of accessibility are addressed to both the EU legislator and the Member States. The Court of Justice is particularly worried that Member States, by creating legal uncertainty, harm the unity and uniform application of EU law. This is why, for example, the Court reproaches Member States if they reproduce EU Regulations in national laws, thereby bringing into doubt the legal nature of the provisions as well as the date of their coming into force.[121] This also explains why the Court emphasises that directives must be implemented in a way which fully meets the requirements of clarity and certainty.[122] Therefore implementing measures should, as a rule, be detailed and not rely on administrative practices, which by their nature can easily be changed and which are not publicised widely enough.[123] Exceptions arise where the legal context is sufficiently clear and precise and applied by the national courts in settled case law.[124] Further, the Member States have a duty to remove provisions that are contrary to EU law, even if EU law has primacy and direct effect and even if national case law facilitates the application of the EU provisions,

[117] Cases often concern editors and journalists held liable for the publication of specific contributions, eg *Tourancheau and July v France* Series A no 53886/00 (2005) ECLI:CE:ECHR:2005:1124JUD005388600; *Lindon, Otchakovsky-Laurens and July v France* Series A no 21279/02 and 36448/02 (2007) ECLI:CE:ECHR:2007:1022JUD002127902; *Flinkkilä v Finland* Series A no 25576/04 (2010) ECLI:CE:ECHR:2010:0406JUD002557604.

[118] *Leempoel & sa Ed Cine Revue v Belgium* Series A no 64772/01 (2006) ECLI:CE:ECHR:2006:1109JUD006477201 para 59; *July and Sarl Libération v France* Series A no 20893/03 (2008) ECLI:CE:ECHR:2008:0214JUD002089303 para 55; *Forminster Enterprises Lmt v Czech Republic* Series A no 38238/04 (2008) ECLI:CE:ECHR:2008:1009JUD003823804 para 67.

[119] *Flinkkilä v Finland* para 67.

[120] *Špaček sro v Czech Republic* para 59; *OAO Neftanyanaya Kompaniya Yukos v Russia* Series A no 14902/04 (2011) ECLI:CE:ECHR:2011:0920JUD001490204 para 599.

[121] Case C-39/72 *Commission v Italy* [1973] ECLI:EU:C:1973:13 paras 16–17.

[122] Case C-102/79 *Commission v Belgium* [1980] ECLI:EU:C:1980:120 para 11.

[123] ibid; Case C-384/92 *Commission v Ireland* [1993] ECLI:EU:C:1993:953 para 5.

[124] Case C-233/00 *Commission v France* [2003] ECLI:EU:C:2003:371 para 83.

since the maintenance of such provisions give rise to an ambiguous state of affairs.[125] By contrast, if an EU Framework Decision does not meet requirements of clarity and legality, the EU legislator is not blamed if the Decision does not seek to harmonise offences. Instead, it is the responsibility of the Member States to respect fundamental rights and principles when implementing the Decision.[126]

Publication of the rules is the first requirement arising from the principle of legal certainty. According to the Court of Justice, it is a fundamental principle that a measure adopted by public authorities shall not be applicable to those concerned before they have the opportunity to make themselves acquainted with it.[127] Unlike the ECtHR, the Court of Justice is not satisfied if an EU law was not published in the Official Journal, but the applicant company was familiar with the regulation and the rules were, moreover, published in an electronic version which is more often consulted than the printed form.[128] Likewise, an Act that has not been properly published in the language of a new Member State—Estonia in this case—cannot be applied against individuals and enterprises in that Member State, even if there is evidence that the applicant was aware of the extent of his obligations.[129]

The Court of Justice is especially concerned that the binding force of national provisions implementing an EU Directive is 'unquestionable'. If there is no absolute certainty that, for example, the national courts will accept the binding force of regional and area plans that are not entirely published in the Official Gazette, the implementation is considered defective, even if the plans were published in a much more accessible manner.[130]

If the wording of an EU law is clear, individuals should rely on these provisions, even if the preamble creates ambiguity.[131] By contrast, if an implementing law may leave some doubt as to its coverage, the preamble cannot be relied upon to solve the uncertainty arising from it.[132] All in all, the Court seems less lenient towards the Member States. For example, if the law enables the Minister to grant exemptions from the residence requirement that accompanies the acquisition of agricultural land, the Court demands

[125] Case C-104/86 *Commission v Italy* [1988] ECLI:EU:C:1988:171 para 12.

[126] Case C-303/05 *Advocaten voor de Wereld VZW v Leden van de Ministerraad* [2007] ECLI:EU:C:2007:261 paras 52–3.

[127] *A Racke v Hauptzollamt Mainz* para 15.

[128] Case C-161/06 *Skoma-Lux sro v Celní ředitelství Olomouc* [2007] ECLI:EU:C:2007:773 paras 45–48.

[129] Case C-146/11 *AS Pimix v Maksu- ja Tolliameti Lõuna maksu- ja tollikeskus und Põllumajandusministeerium* [2012] ECLI:EU:C:2012:450 paras 44–47.

[130] Case C-415/01 *Commission v Belgium* [2003] ECLI:EU:C:2003:118 paras 21–24.

[131] Case C-344/04 *IATA and ELFAA v Department for Transport* [2006] ECLI:EU:C:2006:10 para 76.

[132] Case C-143/83 *Commission of the European Communities v Kingdom of Denmark* [1985] ECLI:EU:C:1985:34 para 11.

that the circular inform potential acquirers about 'the specific and objective situations' in which a derogation will be granted or refused.[133]

Like the Strasbourg Court, the Court of Justice takes into account the applicant's good faith. Even if the Court finds that EU rules were not knowable, it is conditional that the applicant acted in good faith. For example, if an applicant-beneficiary of a grant was not informed of a duty imposed upon her, because the EU authorities only communicated this to the Member State and the Member State had neither published it or made it known to the persons or entities concerned, still the applicant is only to be precluded from repayment if (s)he acted 'in good faith'.[134]

Once more, the capacity of the individual is a significant factor in this assessment. Professionals are expected to find, consult and predict EU law, whereas ignorance of EU law is more easily excused where consumers or employees are concerned.[135] Excessive requirements as to the diligence of professionals, however, sometimes disguise the Court of Justice's preference to protect the EU's interest above the individual's.[136]

CONCLUSION

This chapter examined how the European Courts operationalise the 'balance between fixedness and flexibility' that was identified in the Legal Certainty Index as the core of a relativist conception of legal certainty. Both courts endorse a dynamic concept of legal certainty, which no longer prescribes the status quo, but aims at sustainability in a changing environment. In this concept, both 'fixedness' and 'flexibility' are inherent to the concept of legal certainty.

In the case law of both courts, the principle of legal certainty is operationalised as the requirements to respect legitimate expectations and to make the law accessible, with adaptability as an inherent component of both aspects. The Court of Justice is stricter in the formulation of the principle and its requirements where the duty falls upon the Member States, so as to ensure the uniform application of EU law throughout the Union. However, both courts engage in a balancing exercise.

Both courts adhere to the balancing scheme that follows from a dynamic concept of legal certainty. In this scheme, the balancing of individual reliance

[133] Case C-370/05 *Uwe Kay Festersen* [2007] ECLI:EU:C:2007:59 para 43.

[134] *Stichting ROM-projecten v Staatssecretaris van Economische Zaken* paras 31–34.

[135] For this conclusion, see J Van Meerbeeck, *De la certitude à la confiance* (Brussels, Anthemis-Université Saint-Louis, 2014) 620–21.

[136] ibid 623, preferring the Court to refer to the general interest rather than reproach individuals for lack of due diligence.

on legitimate expectations on the one hand and the pursuit of the general good on the other is based upon criteria that measure the extent to which the rule was a decisive factor for human action and the ability of persons to adapt to the new rule, the social benefits of the new rule, the clarity of the old rule, the predictability of legal change, and whether persons acted in good or in bad faith. With regard to accessibility, governments must make efforts to make rules accessible and comprehensible, but rules should also be sufficiently general so as to catch new developments. In turn, persons are expected to make efforts to find and understand the rules applicable to them. Requirements are particularly strict where professionals are concerned.

It follows from the case law that legal certainty is a shared responsibility by lawmakers, enforcing and implementing authorities, the judiciary, as well as the individual acting in good faith. Both the courts expect individuals to read and understand official gazettes, doctrine and case law and to keep abreast of public and parliamentary debates and economic and monetary evolutions. In particular, in the case law of the Court of Justice, the idea of the 'reasonably prudent economic agent' puts a heavy burden upon professional actors.

2

Legal Certainty in the Context of Multilingualism

ELINA PAUNIO

INTRODUCTION

LAW CANNOT ESCAPE the straight-jacket of language. Law is shaped by language, and just like language, law is uncertain and indeterminate. This holds especially true in the multilingual European Union (EU).

Multilingualism constitutes one of the very cornerstones of the European project. After successive enlargements, the number of official languages has grown exponentially from the original four to 24 in 2013 after the accession of Croatia. In accordance with the policy of linguistic equality, EU legislation is translated into all official languages of the Member States. From the principle of equality it also follows that language versions are not considered to be translations at all. Rather, they are regarded as legally authentic versions of legislation. An inevitable consequence of this is that in interpreting EU law, no specific language version is to take precedence over the others.

The extraordinary number of official and at the same time legally authentic languages, together with the linguistic policy of linguistic equality, means that in legal disputes the meaning of EU legal texts is, at least in theory, construed on the basis of and after comparison with all language versions. In case of identified differences, the language versions must be reconciled by way of interpretation at the Court of Justice of the European Union (the Court of Justice or the Court). In that sense, multilingualism and linguistic discrepancies make explicit the fact that the meaning of the law is construed by judicial means. It is not predetermined and stable. That is undoubtedly problematic from the perspective of the principle of legal certainty.

Not only in domestic legal systems, but also in the EU legal system, particular importance is attached to the principle of legal certainty. This volume bears witness to that fact. Despite being the subject of a large body of literature across legal systems and in-depth theoretical enquiry, legal certainty remains an elusive concept. Nevertheless, according to the perhaps most common understanding of legal certainty, that principle requires that the addressees of laws must know the law in order to be able to plan their actions in accordance with it. Put differently, the principle of legal certainty requires certainty in law, a certain degree of predictability so that those concerned are able to know in advance what the legal consequences of their (and others') actions are. That is why a certain degree of clarity and stability is expected of the law. Arguably not wholly without reason, multilingualism could be argued to constitute a risk for those values.

This chapter addresses the question of how multilingualism and legal certainty can be reconciled in a meaningful way. After elucidating how the Court of Justice employs language to construct the meaning of multilingual legislation, the chapter moves on to consider the principle of legal certainty. More particularly, it asks how we should approach legal certainty in the context of multilingualism. It suggests that the answer lies in understanding legal certainty in hermeneutic, interpretative terms. Understood in this way, the focus shifts from predictability and stability to rational acceptability, which evolves in a dynamic manner in judicial decision-making.

MAKING SENSE OF MULTILINGUAL LAW AT THE COURT

In the EU legal system, sources of uncertainty that are present in any legal system are multiplied. The adoption of EU legislation is a mesh of political, linguistic and legal compromise. The final text that is translated in all official languages has been negotiated by 28 Member States and intended to produce the same effect in 28 legal systems.

Translation forms an integral part of the EU law-making process. The omnipresence of translation creates an additional level of uncertainty, as compared to domestic legal systems, with regard to the meaning of the legislative texts adopted in over 20 languages.[1] To be sure, drafting legislation constitutes a collective enterprise also in monolingual contexts. In the context of EU law, collective drafting is mediated by translation. There is a constant interaction between language versions at all levels of the law-making process.

Multilingual EU legislation emerges in a process characterised by multiple interpretations in different directions and at different stages of the law-making process. The final version in each of the official languages carries traces of earlier phases of the process. All the elements of translation and text production are multiplied. Official language versions are usually collective products: the source text does not remain stable throughout the process, but gets rewritten by new authors, then retranslated by the same

[1] See, in more detail, E Paunio, *Legal Certainty in Multilingual EU Law: Language, Discourse and Reasoning at the European Court of Justice* (Farnham, Ashgate Publishing, 2013) 5–50.

translator or someone else, only to be then revised again by someone else. Another particularity is that drafting and translation are inseparably intertwined: rather than constituting a linear process, the source language can change during the legislative process. Texts are translated simultaneously in a 'pendulum like movement' in all official languages.[2] Due to these particularities, no 'original' text exists that could (or should) function as the reference text for judicial interpretation by the Court of Justice.[3]

The fact that EU legislation is expressed in a multiplicity of languages and is, essentially, translated, means that in addition to uncertainties and indeterminacy related to the use of any natural language, the uncertainties engrained in translation are incorporated in the law. Indeed, even assuming that no translation errors occur, there is no such thing as perfect equivalence in translation.[4] In addition, it is by no means unusual that the final text adopted in all the official languages contains mutually irreconcilable provisions that can in certain cases be the consequence of political compromise that has been necessary to adopt a legislative text.[5] In some cases, the text might hide several conflicting interests and objectives. In fact, the final product of the legislative process can be based on different normative assumptions so that fundamental issues of political importance are left undecided and for the Court of Justice to deal with.[6]

In other words, several factors support the proposition that the meaning of EU legal texts is 'potentially ever-changing.'[7] Those factors include

[2] K Koskinen, *Beyond Ambivalence. Postmodernity and the Ethics of Translation* (Tampere, Tampereen yliopistopaino, 2000) 88.

[3] J Bengoetxea, 'Multilingual and Multicultural Legal Reasoning: the European Court of Justice' in AL Kjær and S Adamo (eds) *Linguistic Diversity and European Democracy* (Farnham, Ashgate Publishing, 2011) 106. The Court, although it works with multilingual legislation, remains itself a monolingual actor.

[4] J-C Gémar, *Traduire, ou, L'art d'interpréter: langue, droit et société: éléments de jurilinguistique. Tome 2, Application: traduire le texte juridique* (Quebec, Presses de l'université du Québec, 1995) 154.

[5] See, for example, the treatment of electricity production from waste gases in the context of the EU emission trading scheme, Directive 2003/87/EC, Art 10a, [2003] OJ L275/32 (as amended by Directive 2009/29/EC, [2009] OJ L140/63). In that respect, see Opinion of Advocate General Kokott in Case C-191/14 *Borealis Polyolefine GmbH et al v Bundesminister für Land-, Forst-, Umwelt und Wasserwirtschaft et al* [2016] ECLI:EU:C:2016:311 para 76.

[6] M Maduro, 'Interpreting European Law: Judicial adjudication in a Context of Constitutional Pluralism' (2007) 1 *European Journal of Legal Studies* 137. See on 'incompletely theorised agreements', C Sunstein, *One Case at a Time. Judicial Minimalism on the Supreme Court* (Cambridge, Mass, Harvard University Press, 1999). The Court's recent case law on TFEU, Art 43(2) offers an illustration of a situation where the legislature seems to have left undecided important political issues related to the respective roles of the EU institutions as regards agriculture and fisheries. See Case C-124/13 *European Parliament and European Commission v Council of the European Union* [2015] ECLI:EU:C:2015:790, and Case C-113/14 *Federal Republic of Germany v European Parliament and Council of the European Union* [2016] ECLI:EU:C:2016:635.

[7] T Ojanen, *The European Way. The Structure of National Court Obligation under EC Law* (Saarijärvi, Gummerus, 1998) 25.

the inherent indeterminacy of natural languages, together with problems of translation, the need for political compromise in an EU of 28 Member States, as well as the contextuality of language and adjudication.

This has at least two important consequences. First, EU legislation constitutes an unstable textual basis for interpretation. The multilingual nature of EU law brings to the fore the quagmire of judicial interpretation that not only relates to multilingual legal systems, but to the interpretation and application of law in any legal system: what role does the written text have in judicial interpretation? Even in a monolingual context, where it should, at least in theory, be possible to express legal obligations and rights in relatively precise language, precise linguistic formulations do not necessarily result in precise law. Legal effects depend on the way those linguistic formulations are interpreted in a particular factual situation under the constraints of case law that conditions subsequent interpretations. Inevitably, judges' evaluations concerning the meaning and purpose of the provision in question affect the legal effects of that text.

Second, therefore, the Court of Justice assumes a key role in devising the meaning of EU legislation. As Kjær accurately puts it, the Court's task is to make sense of the 'non-sense' of EU legislation.[8] Given the policy of linguistic equality, the various language versions carry equal weight in judicial interpretation. The Court must, by way of interpretation, reconcile equally authentic language versions. In doing this, it resorts to judicial reasoning based on three primary categories of argument: linguistic, systemic and dynamic arguments.[9]

Given the uncertainties (both linguistic and political) pertaining to the meaning of EU legislative texts, it is understandable that linguistic arguments, including linguistic comparison, are often sidelined in reasoning. This is so notwithstanding the *CILFIT* case law, which requires, as a matter of principle, that language versions are to be compared.[10] Indeed, it is doubtful whether we can discover any uniform 'legislative will' or, indeed, 'ordinary meaning' that would carry across all official languages. Importantly, in addition to linguistic uncertainties that occur in relation to any language taken separately, uncertainty concerning the meaning of a text may become relevant for interpretation when that meaning is considered across several languages. In this context of linguistic plurality, it is not uncommon for the same text to point towards different textual interpretations depending on

[8] AL Kjær, 'Nonsense: the CILFIT Criteria Revisited—From the Perspective of Legal Linguistics' in H Koch, K Hagel-Sørensen, U Haltern and J Weiler, *Europe. The New Legal Realism: Essays in Honour of Hjalte Rasmussen* (Copenhagen, Djøf Publishing, 2010) 315.

[9] For a sophisticated analytical analysis, see J Bengoetxea, *The Legal Reasoning of the European Court of Justice. Towards a European Jurisprudence* (Oxford, Clarendon Press, 1993).

[10] Case C-283/81 *Srl CILFIT and Lanificio di Gavardo SpA v Ministry of Health* [1982] ECLI:EU:C:1982:335 para 16.

which language version we are looking at. Apart from translation errors and syntactical ambiguity, the impossibility of exact translation and the fiction of equivalence of language versions is also due to the fact that languages cannot 'signify identically'.[11]

In *Breitsamer und Ulrich*,[12] the Court of Justice had to decide whether individual portions of honey packaged in cartons supplied to mass caterers fell within the scope of Article 1(3)(b) of Directive 2000/13/EC.[13] To do so it had to pin down the meaning of the concept of 'pre-packaged foodstuff'. With regard to linguistic discrepancies, the Court reasoned as follows:

> 54 In the present case, individual portions of honey such as those at issue in the main proceedings satisfy several of the conditions provided for in Article 1(3)(b) of Directive 2000/13 for being regarded as 'pre-packaged foodstuffs' within the meaning of that provision.
>
> 55 … the individual portions of the honey in question are intended to be offered as such to the ultimate consumer after the mass caterer to whom the carton was delivered has opened the carton and, second, those portions were packed before being offered for sale and their packaging encloses them completely in such a way that their contents cannot be altered without opening or changing the packaging.
>
> 56 However, it should be noted that there are differences between the various language versions of Article 1(3)(b) of Directive 2000/13.
>
> 57 Thus, the versions in English ('any single item') and in Polish ('każd[a] pojedyncz[a] sztuk[a]'), in particular, use terms which refer to a single element, without further qualification. However, other language versions of the same provision, such as the versions in Spanish ('la unidad de venta'), German ('die Verkaufseinheit') or French ('l'unité de vente'), also refer to a single element, but with reference in addition to the concept of a 'sale'.
>
> 58 According to the Court's settled case-law, the wording used in one language version of a provision of EU law cannot serve as the sole basis for the interpretation of that provision or be given priority over the other language versions in that regard. Provisions of EU law must be interpreted and applied uniformly in the light of the versions existing in all EU languages. Where there is divergence between the various language versions of an EU legislative text, the provision in question must be interpreted by reference to the purpose and general scheme of the rules of which it forms part (judgments of 27 March 1990, Cricket St Thomas, C-372/88, EU:C:1990:140, paragraphs 18 and 19; of 15 November 2012, Kurcums Metal, C-558/11, EU:C:2012:721, paragraph 48; and of 17 March 2016, Kødbranchens Fællesråd, C-112/15, EU:C:2016:185, paragraph 36).

[11] S Glanert, 'Speaking Language to Law: the Case of Europe' (2008) 28 *Legal Studies* 161, 164.

[12] Case C-113/15 *Breitsamer und Ulrich GmbH & Co KG v Landeshauptstadt München* [2016] ECLI:EU:C:2016:718.

[13] Directive 2000/13/EC, [2000] OJ L109/29.

59 As regards the general scheme of Directive 2000/13, it should be noted that, although the various language versions of Article 1(3)(b) of that directive differ, that provision, in any event, mentions being offered for 'sale', whether it be in Spanish ('puesto a la venta'), in German ('vor dem Feilbieten'), in English ('being offered for sale'), in French ('présentation à la vente') or in Polish ('oferowanie na sprzedaż').

60 Article 13(1) of the directive, concerning prepackaged foodstuffs, also refers to the 'sale' of foodstuffs. In the same vein, Article 14 of Directive 2000/13 refers to the case where foodstuffs are offered for 'sale' to the ultimate consumer or to mass caterers without prepackaging.

61 Moreover, other provisions of that directive refer to the 'purchaser'. In addition to Article 14, Article 2(1)(a)(i) of the directive states that the labelling and methods used must not be such as could mislead the purchaser to a material degree, particularly as to the characteristics of the foodstuff including its origin or provenance.

62 Consequently, it follows from the general scheme of Directive 2000/13 that, in addition to the other conditions laid down in Article 1(3)(b) of that directive, the labelling obligation under Article 13(1) of the directive concerns foodstuffs intended to be presented as such for sale to the ultimate consumer and mass caterers.

63 That may take the form of the separate sale of individual portions of honey such as those at issue in the main proceedings to the ultimate consumer in a mass catering establishment, such as a restaurant or a canteen.

64 Such a situation also arises where those portions are offered for sale as part of a pre-prepared meal for an all-inclusive price, for instance as part of a set menu prepared in a mass catering establishment or as a component of a hotel buffet.

…

66 That interpretation of Article 1(3)(b) of Directive 2000/13 is supported by the purpose of the directive …

In *Daimler*,[14] the Court was asked to rule on the scope of Article 5 of Directive 2008/95.[15] The crux of the case turned on the reach of the expression 'to use' in the context of trade mark law. It observed:

39 With regard, first, to the wording of Article 5(1), it must be noted, by way of example that, according to its ordinary meaning, the expression 'zu benutzen', 'using', 'faire usage', 'usare', 'het gebruik', 'használ', used respectively in the German, English, French, Italian, Dutch and Hungarian versions of that provision, involves active behaviour and direct or indirect control of the act constituting the

[14] Case C-179/15 *Daimler AG v Együd Garage Gépjárműjavító és Értékesítő Kft* [2016] ECLI:EU:C:2016:134.

[15] Directive 2008/95/EC, [2008] OJ L299/25 (Corrigendum [2009] OJ L11/86).

use. However, that is not the case if that act is carried out by an independent operator without the consent of the advertiser, or even against his express will.

40 Secondly, as regards the scheme of Article 5 of Directive 2008/95, it should be noted that Article 5(3), which lists in a non-exhaustive manner the types of use which the trade mark proprietor may prohibit (see judgment in *Google France et Google*, C-236/08 to C-238/08, EU:C:2010:159, paragraph 65 and the case-law cited), refers exclusively to active behaviour on the part of the third party, such as that of 'affixing' the sign on the goods and their packaging or 'using' it in business papers and advertising, 'offering' the goods, 'putting them on the market' or 'stocking' them for those purposes, 'importing' or 'exporting' them or 'offering' or 'supplying' services under that sign.

41 Finally, with regard to the purpose of Article 5(1) of Directive 2008/95, it is clear from that provision that it is intended to provide the proprietor with a legal instrument allowing him to prohibit, and to prevent, any use of his trade mark by a third party without his consent. However, only a third party who has direct or indirect control of the act constituting the use is effectively able to stop that use and therefore comply with that prohibition.

The above passages could be described as textbook examples of how the Court reasons with language. The Court typically employs linguistic arguments where one of the parties having submitted observations, or indeed the referring court in the preliminary ruling procedure, has evoked the issue. And when it does indeed venture into the vexed issue of 'ordinary meaning' or linguistic comparison, it does so to highlight discrepancies before moving on to systemic and teleological arguments. That seems justified.

The problem with linguistic arguments ties closely to the issue of meaning construction and the indeterminacy of language. The so-called ordinary meaning of words argument generally refers to the meaning that a member of a particular linguistic community would attribute to a word or expression in a given context: it is the ordinary meaning of those words in a particular language in general. The ordinary meaning of a word may also refer to the meaning a lawyer attributes to a word or an expression. In that case, it is the ordinary meaning of those words in a particular legal language.

Ultimately, if language is used as justification, we should, in fact, be able to pin down the 'true' meaning of the text. More importantly, what does clear or ordinary meaning actually refer to in a multilingual legal system comprising a plurality of languages? Where can we find the norm that these language versions are supposed to convey?

Linguistic reasoning is particularly problematic in so far as EU law is concerned because of the multiplicity of official language versions. In a context of linguistic plurality, referring to the ordinary meaning of words as an argument to justify a particular legal outcome means that instead of only two (general and legal) 'ordinary' meanings, it cannot be excluded that several such meanings exist, raising important interpretive questions. The Court must choose among these different possibilities. To avoid the slippery slope of arguing with language, in particular with a plurality of languages, the Court ties, as it did for example in *Breitsamer und Ulrich* and *Daimler*, its interpretations to system and purpose. Indeed, due to the policy of linguistic equality, the Court should not rely on any particular language version of the provisions it interprets. This principle was settled by the Court in *North Kerry Milk v Minister for Agriculture*.[16]

The principle of linguistic equality helps explain why the Court appears to generally favour a more dynamic method of interpretation that not only takes into account the systemic context of the provision in question, but also the purpose of the provision and the piece of legislation at issue. Owing not only to linguistic uncertainties but also to the political compromises that underlie EU legislation, systemic and teleological arguments assume a particularly important role in the interpretation of both the treaties and secondary legislation. That is by no means revolutionary: broad agreement appears to exist today that meaning is context-dependent and is not stable. From that perspective, multilingual or not, construing legal meaning necessarily requires looking into systemic context and purpose. Yet, the risk exists, as the *Röser*[17] and *Euro Tex*[18] cases illustrate, that context and purpose may not always be aligned with the expectations of legal subjects.

In *Röser*, the Court decided, after having compared the then four official languages of the first subparagraph of Article 36(1) of Regulation No 337/79,[19] that the interpretation that was, on the basis of the German language version, the least favourable for Mr Röser should prevail. Mr Röser had been charged in Germany for having increased the alcoholic volume of grape must in fermentation ('Federweißer') before selling it to final consumers. The first subparagraph of Article 36(1) of Regulation No 337/79 only allows the alcoholic volume to be increased where the intermediary product is being turned into wine suitable for yielding table wine or into table wine and in the wine-growing zone where the fresh grapes used have been harvested. Mr Röser argued that the German language version was open to several interpretations. It could be interpreted as meaning that authorisation to increase the alcoholic strength by volume may be granted even where the processing chain does not culminate in the production of table wine or wine suitable for yielding table wine but ends at an earlier stage, such as with the production of 'Federweißer'.

The Court rejected that argument by observing, first, that the other language versions were not ambiguous on that point. Relying, second, on the general scheme of Regulation No 337/79 and the purpose of the

[16] Case C-80/76 *North Kerry Milk Products Ltd v Minister for Agriculture and Fisheries* [1977] ECLI:EU:C:1977:39 para 11.

[17] Case C-238/84 *Criminal proceedings against Hans Röser* [1986] ECLI:EU:C:1986:88.

[18] Case C-56/06 *Euro Tex Textilverwertung GmbH v Hauptzollamt Duisburg* [2007] ECLI:EU:C:2007:347.

[19] Regulation (EEC) 358/1979, [1979] OJ L54/1.

provision to contribute to the regulation's general aim of encouraging the production of quality wines by making it easier to monitor compliance with the regulation, the Court held that an increase in natural alcoholic strength by volume at the time when grape must in fermentation is being processed may not be authorised if the must is not intended to be turned into wine suitable for yielding table wine or into table wine, but is intended for sale to the final consumer.[20]

More recently, in *Euro Tex*, the Court was asked to rule on the concept of 'originating products'. Euro Tex exported, before accession, used textiles to Poland. The German customs authorities withdrew the EUR1 movement certificate from Euro Tex on the grounds that it could not prove the origin of the products. Euro Tex managed an undertaking that collected, transported and processed clothes and other textile products. The articles deposited by the public in street containers were sorted and then subjected to matching operations in several stages. Clothes that could be worn again were progressively separated out according to a series of criteria. Euro Tex's employees responsible for those operations were required to select certain types of garments that corresponded to the customers' requirements. Euro Tex then delivered textile products, which had been sorted and matched, to retailers in Poland. Against that background, the question was whether those operations were sufficient for the purposes of the relevant provisions to confer on goods the status of 'originating products' on the account that they constituted more than 'simple matching operations'.

The Court admitted that some of the language versions could be interpreted as distinguishing between simple and complex matching operations. Yet, it went on to observe that the interpretation advocated by Euro Tex (according to which complex matching operations should be distinguished from simple matching operations that do not confer originating status) would not only be contrary to some language versions; it would also be contrary to the purpose and general scheme of the rules of which the provision in question forms part. For that reason, the Court held that it was not justified to draw a distinction between different matching operations.[21]

These cases show that the meaning of one or more language versions, as understood by the Court, is rarely considered decisive. As Advocate General Kokott observed in *Skoma-Lux*, the Court has not used the consequences of differences in translation for legal subjects as a reason to annul acts or interpret them in line with the version on which a party in the proceedings before the referring court relies. Rather, in consistent case law, the Court has stressed the need for a uniform interpretation of the different language versions in the interest of the effectiveness of EU law. Divergences are dealt

[20] *Criminal proceedings against Hans Röser* paras 22–25.
[21] *Euro Tex Textilverwertung GmbH v Hauptzollamt Duisburg* paras 24–30.

with by reference to the general scheme and purpose of the rules of which it forms a part.[22] In this sense, in pinning down the meaning of EU law, the Court of Justice looks beyond the words of the different language versions.

Seen from this perspective, one could argue that multilingualism is problematic for legal certainty. This would be so because the interpretation arrived at on the basis of the general scheme and purpose may not give priority to the individual's expectations, but to the interpretation that enhances the effectiveness and unity of the EU legal system. The following sections address this issue.

THE UNPREDICTABLE PRINCIPLE OF LEGAL CERTAINTY

The principle of legal certainty has been described as one of 'the most uncertain, ambiguous and unpredictable European norms'.[23] Several explanations exist for why that might be so.

The first explanation is that the Court employs the principle of legal certainty in a variety of manners, as an umbrella principle encompassing other principles.[24] It can be applied as either a rule of interpretation or as a substantive right. It rarely determines a specific outcome in a given case, but is recurrently used as a justification for a particular interpretative solution. As Tridimas observes, it is used as a conceptual aid that must not be viewed in isolation but rather in the context of judicial reasoning taken as a whole.[25]

The second explanation can be found on a more theoretical level. The principle of legal certainty possesses an elusive and multifaceted character. It is generally said to encompass both formal and substantive elements. Sometimes a third, factual element is also included.[26] Formal legal certainty implies that laws and adjudication in particular must be predictable: laws and adjudication must satisfy imperatives of clarity, stability, intelligibility, and predictability so that those concerned can calculate the legal consequences of their actions, and also to a certain extent, the outcome of legal proceedings. Substantive legal certainty, then, is related to rational acceptability of judicial decision-making. On this view, it is not sufficient that laws are predictable; they must also be rationally accepted by the (legal) community in question. The difficulty lies in trying to fit multilingual EU law in this two (or three)-dimensional mould of predictability and acceptability.

[22] Opinion of Advocate General Kokott in Case C-161/06 *Skoma-Lux sro v Celní ředitelství Olomouc* [2007] ECLI:EU:C:2007:525 para 30.

[23] J Van Meerbeck, 'The Principle of Legal Certainty in the Case Law of the European Court of Justice: From Certainty to Trust' (2016) 41 *European Law Review* 275, 275.

[24] X Groussot, *General Principles of Community Law* (Groeningen, Europa Law Publishing, 2006) 190–91.

[25] T Tridimas, *The General Principles of EU Law* 2nd edn (Oxford, Oxford University Press, 2006) 372–76.

[26] For an in-depth analysis of these three aspects in the context of EU law, see J Raitio, *The Principle of Legal Certainty in EC Law* (Dordrecht, Kluwer Academic Publishers, 2003).

Another dichotomy may further help explain the critical description of the principle of legal certainty cited above. Van Meerbeeck argues that in the context of EU law, the principle of legal certainty can be seen as encompassing two conflicting logics. This is particularly visible in the case law of the Court of Justice. On the one hand, the principle of legal certainty can be seen as expressing so-called Cartesian logic, which is based on the requirement of (absolute) certainty. On the other hand, the principle of legal certainty can be understood in terms of fiduciary logic, which is built on the notion of trust. Van Meerbeeck also distinguishes these logics on the basis of the beneficiary of the principle: the political system (Cartesian) and the subject of the law (fiduciary).[27] The problem stems from the tension between the two: in a particular case, they may be mutually incompatible and the Court must choose between one or the other.

As we have seen, in the Court's case law that explicitly deals with linguistic discrepancies arising from multilingual legislation, the focus is on ensuring that the interpretation arrived at does not, at least on the face of it, favour one language version over the others. In that sense, the subject of the law and his or her expectations do not take centre stage in the reasoning of the Court. The importance that the Court places on the need to interpret EU law in a uniform manner to ensure the effectiveness of EU law also suggests that, at least to a certain extent, the unity of the system rather than the expectations of the individual are given priority in the interpretation of EU law. Indeed, the Court has drawn parallels between uniform interpretation and legal certainty, stating that divergent interpretations in domestic courts would not only undermine the effectiveness of EU law, but also legal certainty.[28]

In that sense, the Court places particular emphasis on the need to safeguard the unity of the legal system. Admittedly, a certain tension can be observed between that approach and the emphasis the Court itself places on predictability (for individuals) when describing the rationale of the principle of legal certainty. It has stated that 'rules must enable those concerned to know precisely the extent of the obligations which are imposed on them.'[29] It has also held that 'individuals must be able to ascertain unequivocally what their rights and obligations are and take steps accordingly.'[30]

To the extent that, in construing the meaning of EU law, the Court focuses on the system, rather than the individual, the 'Cartesian' logic seems to override any fiduciary logic. However, it seems plausible to argue that such an approach constitutes an inevitable corollary to the Court's role in the EU

[27] Van Meerbeeck, *The Principle of Legal Certainty*.

[28] Case C-391/05 *Jan De Nul NV v Hauptzollamt Oldenburg* [2007] ECLI:EU:C:2007:126 para 23.

[29] Case C-158/06 *Stichting ROM-projecten v Staatssecretaris van Economische Zaken* [2007] ECLI:EU:C:2007:370 para 25.

[30] Case C-345/06 *Gottfried Heinrich* [2009] ECLI:EU:C:2009:140 para 44.

legal system. In the preliminary ruling procedure, in particular, the Court provides national courts with guidance on the interpretation of EU law. That is why it is by no means surprising that the interpretation suggested by the parties in the main proceedings is only one consideration amongst others when the Court interprets provisions of EU law.

Especially with regard to preliminary rulings, multidirectional dialogue is central to decision-making at the Court. That is because it only interprets EU law, leaving the final decision on the case in question to the referring court. The Court interacts with national courts, the Commission, other institutions, the Member States, the parties to the proceedings, and the broader legal community. It also interprets the law in a continuous internal dialogue that takes into account previous case law and Advocate Generals' Opinions.[31] The meaning of multilingual EU law emerges in judicial decision-making through a complex interplay between text, context, purpose and discourse.

Given that the meaning of EU law is construed in such a complex context of multilingual communication, predictability, understood in the sense of objectivity and predetermined meaning seems no more than a fiction. The question is: What role, if any, can the principle of legal certainty play in multilingual EU law? As it will be argued in more detail below, instead of predictability, what becomes important is that the law, as construed by the Court, is rationally acceptable. To achieve that, reasoning assumes a key role.

TOWARDS DISCURSIVE LEGAL CERTAINTY

Throughout the years, the Court of Justice has faced stark criticism on account of its perceived activist, pro-integrationist approach to interpreting EU law.[32] One recurring criticism in this context is that the Court's decision-making is unpredictable. It has been accused of overstepping the limits of its powers as defined in the Treaties. One reason for this lies in the use of teleological reasoning, rather than linguistic reasoning, which is perceived as leaving less leeway for the Court.[33] Those who express that criticism usually tend to see the EU legal order as international, intergovernmental

[31] On the impact on Advocate General's Opinions: S Sankari and U Sadl, 'The Elusive Influence of the Advocate General on the Court of Justice: The Case of European Citizenship' (2016) *iCourts Working Paper Series No 70* (forthcoming in *Yearbook of European Law*).

[32] For some well-known examples, T Hartley, 'The European Court, Judicial Objectivity and the Constitution of the European Union' (1996) 122 *Law Quarterly Review* 95 and H Rasmussen, *On Law and Policy in the European Court of Justice* (Dordrecht, Martinus Nijhof, 1986).

[33] G Conway, *The Limits of Legal Reasoning and the European Court of Justice* (Cambridge, Cambridge University Press, 2012).

law, as opposed to a sui generis constitutional and supranational legal order.[34] Indeed, depending on the writer's general view on EU law, the same decision may represent itself as either too activist or not activist enough.[35] Given that the view taken on the Court's decision-making can be informed by such an underlying bias, the question arises: how can rational acceptability be achieved?

It is argued that rational acceptability develops in communication between the Court of Justice and its audience. Here, the relevant audience ought to be construed as comprising primarily of national courts, but also more widely of the EU legal community including parties and interveners, that is, the Commission, other EU institutions, as well as Member States, and to a lesser extent, legal scholars. Judicial reasoning that succeeds in convincing the relevant audience about the Court's reading is of particular significance.

From a linguistic viewpoint, (legal) meaning develops in communication. For example, changes occur in the EU law meaning of legal texts as a result of the Court's input. Through judicial reasoning, the Court of Justice can modify the meaning of words, expressions or other textual elements routinely understood in a particular way in Member State legal systems on the basis of the Court's authority in this linguistic community. Change in legal meaning therefore occurs through change in the surrounding systemic framework: change in meaning on a higher institutional level (at the Court) modifies the way national courts interpret statutes when they agree on the acceptability of the proposed interpretation. Similarly, new concepts can be introduced by the Court that bear no resemblance to concepts known in domestic contexts. Change therefore occurs through discourse, in communication with others. Linguistically speaking, to change the way in which the multilingual legal community perceives given words, expressions, or concepts the Court has to convince the legal community of the correctness of its interpretation through judicial reasoning that can be said to mould not only legal concepts but the conceptions that those participating in discourse have about law.[36]

[34] J Bengoetxea, 'Text and Telos in the European Court of Justice: Four Recent Takes on the Legal Reasoning of the ECJ' (2015) 11 *European Constitutional Law Review* 184, 185.

[35] C Kaupa, 'Maybe not Activist Enough? On the Court's Alleged Neoliberal Bias in its Recent Labor Cases' in M Dawson, B De Witte, E Muir (eds), *Judicial Activism at the European Court of Justice* (Cheltenham, Edward Elgar Publishing, 2013). See also S Sankari, *European Court of Justice Legal Reasoning in Context* (Groeningen, Europa Law Publishing, 2013) 61. In her book on legal reasoning at the CJEU, Sankari has shown that, in reality, when one studies a longer line of cases, the Court's case law does not appear particularly revolutionary or unpredictable. In fact, the Court's own case law constitutes an important 'steadying factor' in bringing consistency to a particular field of law. See on such factors G Beck, *The Legal Reasoning of the Court of Justice of the EU* (Oxford, Hart Publishing, 2012). In a manner not dissimilar to Dworkin's famous chain novel of law, the CJEU case law sets the framework and limits to judicial interpretation.

[36] J Engberg, 'Statutory Texts as Instances of Language(s): Consequences and Limitations on Interpretation' (2004) 29 *Brooklyn Journal of International Law* 1135, 1163.

Just as judicial decision-making is discursive, so is substantive legal certainty: rational acceptability arises from discursive judicial interaction among courts. Discourse directs interaction towards achieving mutual understanding with regard to the goals and purposes of the legal system.[37] Linguistically, discourse enables creation of EU law meanings and concepts that may differ from established meanings in the context of national legal systems. As Engberg suggests, this dialogue 'presupposes an open mind on all sides [which includes] the possibility of convincing the Court that their new meaning is not a good solution.'[38]

For example, the Court has gradually 'alimented' the EU legal system with concepts such as primacy and direct effect that have had a profound impact on the evolution of EU law and the EU legal system. Despite varying degrees of resistance from national courts, those and other foundational concepts of EU law have become firmly rooted in the EU legal system and are now accepted as forming part of the very core of the EU legal system.

In this discursive approach, teleological reasoning becomes an inevitable aspect of judicial reasoning, and an important tool for making explicit the interpretative choices made by the Court. Purpose links individual interpretations to a broader systemic context and exposes the value basis of the choice made by the Court to debate within the legal community, and not only to the Court itself. On this understanding, communicative practices of interpretation by courts that are involved in the judicial resolution of disputes in the multilingual EU community harmonise meaning gradually.[39]

Acceptability depends on whether the Court's decisions are subsequently reaffirmed by national judiciaries in other similar cases, or indeed in the case at hand.[40] If further clarification is needed, case law will answer these questions in new preliminary rulings. In this respect, the Court's judicial decision-making helps to stabilise expectations about EU law by means of discourse. To achieve legal certainty through discourse, underlying values and policies guiding judicial decision-making must be expressed in reasoning. Indeed, by expressing these preferences and subjecting them to critical review, multilingual EU law becomes at the same time more predictable and more acceptable, as it can be configured, through discourse, to the expectations of the EU legal community.

[37] J Habermas, *Between Facts and Norms: Contributions to a Discourse Theory of Law and Democracy* (Boston, Blackwell Publishing, 1998).

[38] Engberg, 'Statutory Texts as Instances of Language(s)' 1166.

[39] Bengoetxea, 'Text and Telos in the European Court of Justice' 211.

[40] For a recent example from the Court's case law, see Case C-441/14 *Dansk Industri (DI), acting on behalf of Ajos A/S v Estate of Karsten Eigil Rasmussen* [2016] ECLI:EU:C:2016:278, and the subsequent judgment from the Danish Supreme Court.

CONCLUDING REMARKS

Conceptualising the principle of legal certainty in terms of discourse presupposes that law is seen as a form of communication, and it is itself understood as constituting a basis for communication between the members of a legal community. The preliminary ruling procedure offers an illustrative example of the communicative nature of EU law.

In the multilingual EU legal system, there is no unequivocal language reference amongst the equally valid official language versions in which the multilingual EU law is expressed. That is why it is argued that legal certainty cannot be found in the text, but rather somewhere beyond it, in context, in purpose that is defined in legal reasoning. Accordingly, it is suggested that legal certainty evolves in a dialectic between the reasoning of the Court of Justice, on the one hand, and the EU legal community's expectations, on the other, with regard to how EU legal provisions should be interpreted on the basis of values and policies that underpin the EU legal system.

3

Legal Certainty in the New Corporate Criminal Law

MARK FENWICK

INTRODUCTION

CORPORATE CRIMINAL LAW refers to the body of law that imposes criminal liability on the *corporation*, rather than individual members of the corporation, such as directors, officers, managers or employees. This chapter begins by suggesting that the reach of corporate criminal law has greatly expanded over the last three decades, particularly in the fields of market regulation, anti-corruption, anti-money laundering, and securities laws. In addition to the expansion of the substantive criminal law, various procedural innovations have also occurred, notably the expansion of pre-trial diversion in cases involving corporate suspects. The term—the *new corporate criminal law*—is used to describe the resulting body of substantive and procedural norms.[1]

This expansion in the scope of corporate criminal law has been paralleled by the introduction of multiple uncertainties into this field of law. A striking feature of the new corporate criminal law is the degree to which the substantive criminal law in this field is plagued by a lack of legal certainty as to the scope of the offence. Examples of legal 'uncertainty' are introduced from securities law and anti-corruption law. Moreover, the legal basis for the new corporate criminal law—the doctrine of corporate legal liability—is similarly characterised by uncertainties of various kinds. The various new procedural measures adopted in such cases—notably deferred prosecution agreements and other forms of pre-trial diversion—compound the issue of uncertainty, as legal outcomes become subject to negotiation between regulator-prosecutor and corporate suspect. Broad regulatory discretion means that the results of such negotiations are unpredictable.

[1] See also M Fenwick, 'The New Corporate Criminal Law and Transnational Legal Risk' in M Fenwick and S Wrbka (eds), *Flexibility of Law and its Limits in Contemporary Business Regulation* (Tokyo, Springer, 2016).

The result of these developments? In the context of the new corporate criminal law, certainty no longer seems to function as a fundamental principle of criminal justice that trumps other considerations or, at least, creates a strong presumption for excluding other reasons. Instead, legal certainty seems to have taken on a more modest role as one of a number of competing policy considerations that have to be resolved in addressing the response of the criminal justice system to socially undesirable corporate behaviour. As such, the meaning and character of legal certainty has been transformed, raising important normative questions about the desirability and appropriateness of such a trend.

The law in this area seems to be characterised by a pragmatic recognition of the virtues of a degree of uncertainty. The combined effect of net-widening and greater 'uncertainty' has been to significantly increase legal risk for companies and to provide a strong incentive to invest in internal governance mechanisms aimed at social enforcement, ie corporate compliance.

The focus of this chapter will be examining these issues in the context of US Federal and English law. The decision to focus on these jurisdictions can be justified, in part, by the extensive territorial reach of the new corporate criminal law in these two countries. Companies that issue securities in either the US or UK capital markets or—in the case of UK anti-corruption laws—even conduct a part of their business in the UK, may find themselves exposed to criminal liability. As such, Anglo-American corporate criminal law has taken on a transnational character that creates extensive legal risk for a wide range of firms that operate across national borders.

NET-WIDENING AND THE NEW CORPORATE CRIMINAL LAW

The legal basis of corporate criminal law—the legal doctrine of corporate criminal liability—is not particularly new. In its modern form, it can be traced back to development in English law in the early decades of the nineteenth century.[2] The historical position of most legal systems was that although individual members of a corporation could be criminally liable for offences committed in the course of their occupation, the corporation *itself* could not be liable. Criminal liability lay with members of the corporation—directors, managers or employees—but not with the corporation itself. A corporation fell beyond the domain of criminal liability. From the perspective of the criminal law, a corporation was an incorporeal entity that lacked the necessary degree of fault or blameworthiness that is a necessary condition for the imposition of criminal liability.

[2] For the early history of corporate criminal liability in English law, see especially C Wells, *Corporations and Criminal Responsibility* (Oxford, Oxford University Press, 2001). For the US experience, see especially W Laufer, *Corporate Bodies and Guilty Minds: The Failure of Corporate Criminal Liability* (Chicago, University Chicago Press, 2006) ch 3.

In his *Commentaries*, for example, William Blackstone regarded it as self-evident that criminal liability was confined to natural persons and that any other approach would constitute an anthropomorphic error. According to this view, a corporation is incapable of acting with the requisite moral fault necessary for the criminal law.[3] Moreover, Blackstone identified a number of practical difficulties that would arise in applying criminal law and procedure to corporations. In particular, a corporation cannot appear in court in person to offer a defence (resulting in a trial *in absentia*), a corporation cannot swear an oath, nor can a corporation be arrested, imprisoned or executed. For Blackstone, at least, it seemed fairly obvious that corporations were an impoverished legal subject and could not be subject to the discipline of the criminal law.

The origins of modern corporate criminal liability rules can be traced back to the early decades of the nineteenth century when, in the context of rapid industrialisation, corporations acquired a greater social presence as the scope and impact of their activities expanded dramatically.[4] In response to this socio-economic transformation, English law gradually extended the application of the criminal law to juristic persons, such as municipalities and then corporations. This change was initially a result of judicial rather than legislative action, and involved cases of criminal omission resulting in public nuisance. The scope of this new form of criminal liability gradually expanded, however, to include acts as well as omissions and finally crimes requiring intent and not just absolute liability offences. Within half a century, Blackstone's concerns had been swept away by the pragmatic need to address the pressing issue of misconduct by new industrial corporations.

A similar story can be told about the emergence and development of corporate criminal liability in a US context.[5] The early US history of corporate criminal liability, for instance, culminated in 1909 with the US Supreme Court decision in *New York Central & Hudson River Railroad v United States*. Constitutional concerns about Federal anti-trust legislation that explicitly imposed criminal liability on corporations were set aside in favour of the more pragmatic view that corporate criminal liability represented the 'only means' to 'control' errant corporations.[6]

By the early decades of the twentieth century, the idea of corporate criminal liability was well established in the main jurisdiction of the common law world. Nevertheless, for much of its history, corporate criminal law was marginalised from the mainstream of criminal justice, even in those jurisdictions that embraced the doctrine of corporate criminal liability. In practice,

[3] W Blackstone, *Commentaries on the Laws of England* (Chicago, University of Chicago Press, 1979) 464.

[4] See, eg Wells, *Corporations and Criminal Responsibility* ch 2.

[5] See generally T Bernard, 'The Historical Development of Corporate Criminal Liability' (1984) 22 *Criminology* 3.

[6] *New York Central & Hudson River Railroad v US* (1909) 212 US 481.

criminal prosecution of corporate suspects remained something of an exception, perhaps reflecting both the power of large corporations and a recognition on the part of the state that prosecuting such cases was difficult.

Interestingly, most civilian jurisdictions rejected the doctrine of corporate criminal liability, preferring instead to concentrate attention on personal liability.[7] This approach reflected the view that the liability of *legal* persons, such as a corporation, is properly dealt with as part of public administrative law rather than the criminal law. Many countries in Europe (such as Germany, Italy and Spain) began to confront the growing power of business enterprises by introducing systems of administrative regulation, similar to public welfare offences in the US or regulatory offences in the UK. These infractions are enforced by administrative agencies, do not have the status of criminal sanction and are thought to be morally neutral and lacking the element of condemnation and moral fault associated with criminal liability.

The consequence of these trends in both the common law and civilian worlds was that corporate criminal liability occupied a marginal position in modern criminal justice.[8] As with white-collar offenders more generally, the early history of corporate criminal law is a familiar tale of economically powerful elites being insulated from the gaze of the criminal justice system.[9]

Over the last three decades, however, this situation has changed significantly and corporate criminal law has acquired a new significance in the 'mix' of regulatory strategies for responding to corporate wrongdoing.[10] Across multiple jurisdictions, a process of net-widening has occurred that has significantly expanded the scope of corporate criminal law.[11] Moreover, we have entered a new age of enforcement, as companies routinely find themselves facing the threat of investigation and indictment.

Although we should not be naive in underestimating the capacity of the business community—particularly large firms—to limit the degree of intrusion into their activities, an effect of this new emphasis on corporate criminal law is that business enterprises can no longer afford to ignore corporate criminal law and they are now obliged to incorporate it into their decision-making processes, policies and practices, and organisational structure.

[7] For a discussion of the principles underlying the traditional continental European approach, see eg L Leigh, 'The Criminal Liability of Corporations and Other Groups: A Comparative View' (1977) 9 *Ottawa Law Review* 247.

[8] See, eg A Hamdani and A Klement, 'Corporate Crime and Deterrence' (2008) 61 *Stanford Law Review* 271; VS Khanna, 'Corporate Liability Standards: When Should Corporations Be Held Criminally Liable?' (2000) 37 *American Criminal Law Review* 1239.

[9] See especially E Sutherland, *White Collar Crime* (New York, Holt, Rinehart & Winston, 1949).

[10] See also L Orland, 'The Transformation of Corporate Criminal Law' (2007) 1 *Brooklyn Journal of Corporate Finance and Commercial Law* 45.

[11] See especially S Cohen, *Visions of Social Control* (Cambridge, Polity, 1985).

First, many civilian jurisdictions that did not previously have any provision for corporate criminal liability have now introduced it.[12] From the 1980s, the administrative law approach to corporate wrongdoing has gradually been supplemented by the introduction of corporate criminal liability. In a European context, this seems to have largely been the result of pressure from regional and international organisations that identified a regulatory gap, which—it was believed—corporate criminal responsibility could fill.[13]

The second piece of evidence for net-widening in corporate criminal law has been the expansion in the scope of corporate criminal law and the creation of multiple new categories of criminal offence.[14] Even a cursory list of the main fields of contemporary corporate criminal law highlights the breadth of the law in this area: anti-corruption law; anti-money laundering law; fraud law (including investment fraud, securities fraud, government fraud, mortgage fraud, consumer fraud and false advertising); competition law; tax law (including off-shore tax evasion); accounting standards law; marketing law; export controls and sanctions law; labour law; health and safety law; and environmental law. Moreover, these are just the general fields of law; there are also many industry specific laws that impact upon corporations operating in particular sectors of the economy. These are all areas that have significantly expanded over the last three decades.

A third trend is to apply corporate criminal law extra-territorially or alternatively to apply it to the acts of foreign companies for acts committed in a third state, if such a company issues securities in the home state or conducts a significant part of its business in the home state. This issue will not be explored here, but—as mentioned above—the effect of this trend is to transform domestic criminal law into a form of transnational law, as companies find themselves obliged to meet the legal requirements of multiple jurisdictions.[15]

Paralleling this expansion in the number of criminal offences and extended territorial reach has been a corresponding tendency to weaken the *mens rea* requirements for corporate crimes. The emergence and expansion of strict liability (ie no-fault or public welfare) offences is the most obvious example of this transformation. It is no coincidence that many strict liability offences are concerned with corporate activities, such as pollution and health and

[12] See, eg M Duber, 'The Comparative History and Theory of Corporate Criminal Liability' (2013) 16 *The New Criminal Law Review* 203; G Heine, 'New Developments in Corporate Criminal Liability in Europe: Can Europeans Learn from the American Experience-or Vice Versa?' (1998) 12 *St Louis-Warsaw Transnational Law Review* 173.

[13] See, eg J Gobert and AM Pascal (eds), *European Developments in Corporate Criminal Liability* (London, Routledge, 2011).

[14] See especially J Braithwaite and P Drahos, *Global Business Regulation* (Cambridge, Cambridge University Press, 2000).

[15] See, eg Fenwick, 'New Corporate Criminal Law'.

safety, where there is a clear public interest at stake in halting the proscribed acts. And yet, there has also been a more general trend on the part of legislators to move from relatively high-level *mens rea* requirements, such as intent or knowledge, to relatively low-level requirements, such as recklessness and negligence. As with strict liability, this general trend has also been particularly important in the context of corporate regulation.

The final element in the widening of the criminal justice 'net' is a more aggressive attitude towards enforcement. Enforcement actions have increased substantially, particularly over the past decade. There is a great deal of discussion of a 'new era' of enforcement in multiple fields of corporate criminal law, notably anti-corruption law, anti-money laundering law, securities law and competition law.[16] There has also been a corresponding increase in the size of sanctions. Sentencing guidelines for organisations have been upwardly adjusted and enforcement agencies are more aggressive in pursuing larger penalties.

THE MULTIPLE UNCERTAINTIES OF THE NEW CORPORATE CRIMINAL LAW

The above discussion introduced the new corporate criminal law and suggested that a key feature of this rapidly-developing field of law is that the criminal justice 'net' is widening. Significantly, this widening of the criminal justice net is paralleled by two other trends, namely the outer limits of criminal liability are becoming less certain and various uncertainties surrounding doctrine of corporate criminal justice. The effect of these uncertainties is to obscure the underlying purpose of the law in this field and to raise doubts about the efficacy of the corporate criminal law as a response to corporate wrongdoing.

Uncertainties as to the Scope of the Offence

A key feature of contemporary white collar and corporate criminal law is the degree to which legal certainty has been compromised in this net-widening process. Two examples will be introduced to illustrate what is a more general trend to blur the lines of criminal liability by making the full scope or outer limits of the criminal offence unclear. The examples are taken from US Federal criminal law, but given the territorial reach of these prohibitions they impact business entities from multiple jurisdictions.

[16] See, eg M Koehler, *The Foreign Corrupt Practices Act in a New Era* (London, Edward Elgar, 2014).

First, in the context of securities law there has been a trend to obscure the limits of liability for insider trading. Insider trading law traditionally imposed liability on: (i) corporate 'insiders' who traded on material non-public information in breach of a duty owed to their corporation; or (ii) corporate 'outsiders' who 'misappropriated' and traded on such information in breach of a duty owed to the *source* of the information.[17]

Recently, however, the lines of liability have become increasingly uncertain and liability has been imposed on defendants where it is unclear whether they owe a duty to the corporation or the source of the information.[18] For example, there have been recent convictions where confidential information has been unwillingly thrust on a person, who then trades on that information; cases where the entity whose information was taken and used denied that it was owed a duty; and cases where a duty is found to have arisen where the insider and an inadvertent recipient of that information happen to be friends. In all such cases, neither of the traditional theories seems to apply and the result of this more aggressive enforcement policy is to create ambiguities in the scope of the offence.

Moreover, post-2008 there has been the use of insider trading against hedge funds (the New York Times has spoken of a 'crackdown'). For example, Steve A Cohen's *SAC Capital Advisors* was indicted in July 2013 for securities fraud, which led investors to withdraw from the fund. Many in the financial services sector believe this to be highly controversial. The traders at *SAC* were not corporate insiders, nor outsiders seeking personal gain, rather they were investors looking for information about corporations whose shares they were thinking of buying, selling or shorting. Skeptics asked whether highly aggressive 'diligent' traders should be criminalised in this way? The activity of hedge funds helps speed the flow of information to financial markets, thus enabling more efficient and accurate pricing of the shares of corporations. Uncovering things about corporations that management would rather not disclose is something professional money managers are supposed to do, ie hedge funds perform a valuable public interest function. The key point, however, is that such an enforcement policy seems to expand the scope of the offence to encompass behaviour that was previously thought to fall outside the scope of the norm.

A second example of how uncertainties have been introduced into contemporary white collar and corporate criminal law can be seen in anti-corruption law, particularly anti-corruption laws targeting corporate corruption conducted overseas, such as the US Foreign and Corrupt Practices

[17] See espccially S Green, *Lying, Stealing and Cheating: A Moral Theory of White Collar Crime* (Oxford, Oxford University Press, 2007) ch 18.

[18] See, eg S Crimmins, 'Insider Trading: Where is the Line?' (2013) 2 *Columbia Business Law Review* 330.

Act [FCPA] (1977) or the more recent UK Bribery Act 2010.[19] Multiple uncertainties can be found in these laws. The US law, for instance, prohibits a company of its agents from paying or offering to pay money or anything of value to a foreign official to obtain or retain business. The statute defines a 'foreign official' in part as 'any officer or employee of a foreign government or any department, agency, or instrumentality thereof …'[20]

However, uncertainty surrounds the interpretation of the term, 'instrumentality', which is not defined in the statute. The Department of Justice and SEC have taken advantage of this uncertainty. To take one of a number of controversial cases, in an action against American construction company KBR, the Department of Justice and SEC alleged that KBR made improper payments to employees of Nigeria LNG Limited.[21] The government claimed that these employees were foreign officials under the FCPA despite the fact that the only connection with the Nigerian government was that the Nigerian government held a minority ownership stake in LNG Limited. KBR settled the case to avoid the possibility of a damaging conviction. Given an aggressive enforcement policy, on the one hand, and the uncertainty surrounding the scope of the law on the other, it is extremely difficult for companies to decide ex ante whether companies are sufficiently state-owned or state-controlled to qualify as an instrumentality of a foreign official, that is to say whether the FCPA applies to a particular transaction or business relationship.

In both the example from securities law and anti-corruption law, therefore, the outer limits of the core offence—the boundary between permissible and impermissible conduct—seems to have become increasingly blurred as a result of a combination of executive (ie regulatory), legislative or judicial action.[22] The scope for aggressive enforcement is thus expanded and the legal risk for any company concomitantly increases. From the perspective of a traditional conception of legal certainty in a criminal law context, such a trend would seem to be highly problematic.

Uncertainties Regarding Corporate Criminal Liability

In addition to the uncertainties created by offence-specific developments, multiple uncertainties also surround the legal doctrine that underlies *all*

[19] See, eg M Koehler, 'The Story of the Foreign Corrupt Practices Act' (2012) 5 *Ohio State Law Journal* 930. For the UK law, see E Engle, 'Understanding the UK Bribery Act by Reference to the OECD Convention and the Foreign and Corrupt Practices Act' (2011) 44 *The International Lawyer* 1173.

[20] 15 USC §§ 78dd-1(f)(1)(A).

[21] *United States of America v Kellogg Brown & Root LLC* [2009] United States District Court, Southern District of Texas, Houston Division, Case No H-09-071. See also D Juedes, 'Taming the FCPA Overreach Through an Adequate Procedures Defense' (2013) 4 *William & Mary Business Law Review* 37, 43–47.

[22] See also Orland, 'The Transformation of Corporate Criminal Law'.

corporate criminal law, namely the doctrine of *corporate criminal liability*. These uncertainties will be considered under two headings, namely doctrinal uncertainties and normative uncertainties. It is worth noting from the outset that these uncertainties are not new; critics of corporate criminal liability have pointed to these issues for many years, but these concerns take on a greater significance as the scope of corporate criminal law has continued to expand and greater efforts are devoted to enforcement.

At least in the Anglo-American world, the traditional approach to corporate criminal liability has been variations on so-called imputation doctrines.[23] Such an approach requires the identification of a single human offender whose crime is then imputed (attributed) to the company. By way of introduction to the uncertainty that pervades different forms of imputation, an interesting contrast can be made between the imputation approaches of the US Federal Courts and that employed in English law. In what follows, it will be suggested that both exhibit various doctrinal uncertainties, but that resolving these uncertainties has been accorded much less weight than the competing policy goal to establish a legal standard that can be utilised in tackling corporate wrongdoing.

Since the early twentieth century, US Federal courts have tended to adopt a broad vicarious liability standard whereby the criminal act of any employee 'regardless of rank' that occurs in 'the scope of employment' and which intends, 'at least in part, to benefit the company', can be imputed to the company itself.[24] A company can be convicted for any crime, including crimes of intent, based on this standard.

The rationale for this broad approach is that without the threat of criminal liability there is little incentive for companies to curb illegal but profitable activities that place innocent parties at risk. However, the obvious difficulty with such a standard is that it seems unreasonable to expect a large corporation—particularly one operating transnationally—to take responsibility for the acts of *all* its employees. This is particularly so if the consequences of a criminal conviction for the corporation may cause negative effects that extend to innocent third parties, such as other employees, investors and customers. And even if a particular company adopts all reasonable measures to prevent its staff from committing an offence, it could still be subjected to criminal sanctions under the vicarious liability standard. Stated bluntly, if the company faces the risk of conviction regardless of its actions, what incentive exists to invest heavily in preventive measures and compliance? The legal standard seems to be too open-ended, placing companies in a state of constant non-compliance.

The English approach, therefore, has been to ameliorate the extreme consequences of the vicarious liability standard by limiting the class of employees

[23] See, eg E Lederman, 'Models for Imposing Corporate Criminal Liability' (2000) 4 *Buffalo Criminal Law Review* 641.

[24] See above n 6.

whose criminal acts can be imputed to the company.[25] This results in the so-called identification doctrine. Specifically, only those actions and thought patterns of certain high-ranking individuals within the company—the so-called 'directing mind' of the company—are regarded in law as the acts of the company itself. Criminal acts committed by those individuals are regarded as being committed by the company, ie their acts are 'identified' with the company. In the leading English case, the supermarket company, Tesco, was acquitted of falsely advertising prices, on the ground that the 'brains' of the company were unaware of the wrongdoing even though the store manager had the requisite degree of knowledge.[26] Under the US vicarious liability approach, the company would have been convicted in such a case.

Although the rationale for this more restrictive approach is clear, it has resulted in a number of difficulties. First, it has proven extremely difficult for English courts to arrive at a sufficiently clear and consistent definition of the 'directing mind'. Similar difficulties have occurred in Canada, Hong Kong and Australia in their use of identification standards.[27]

Formalistic definitions of the 'directing mind' that focus on those individuals that occupy particular positions within a company—such as the Board of Directors or CEO—often fails to capture the real distribution of power in complex modern organisations. Moreover, focusing on the name on the door of a particular manager-employee would seem to be easily circumvented by the delegation of criminal activities to lower-ranked employees or those holding no formal title. However, a more substantive approach to defining the 'directing mind' has proven too vague in a criminal law context, as it requires the court to identify various functions or substantive powers—the power to direct company policy, for example—that are not amenable to precise definition. From a conventional view of certainty, both a formalistic and a substantive approach to defining the directing mind of the company seem highly problematic in a criminal law context. The result is that the core concept in the identification approach—namely, the directing mind—is marked by serious ambiguity.

In addition to the definitional challenge, a further problem with identification doctrines is that it has been almost impossible for prosecutors to secure convictions against corporations because high managerial agents—however defined—are going to be relatively well placed to insulate themselves from criminal investigation (ie they are 'judgment proof'). A series of high-profile acquittals—most notably in the case against *P&O* for the sinking of the ferry,

[25] Canada, Australia, Hong Kong and several US states also adopt variations on this approach.

[26] *Tesco Supermarkets Ltd v Natrass* [1972] AC 153.

[27] See generally Department of Justice (Canada), 'Corporate Criminal Liability Discussion Paper' (2002); MJ Lau, 'Director's Criminal Liability in Hong Kong' (2003) 12 *Corporate Practice* 1. Australia is discussed below.

the Herald of Free Enterprise—due to the failure to secure a case against senior management reinforced public perceptions of injustice, and fueled a perception that identification is tantamount to immunity for corporations.[28] This perception of injustice is fueled when low-ranking employees are convicted for their role in the same incident.[29]

Judicial dissatisfaction with the identification standard can also be seen in a 1995 case, *Meridian Global Funds Management Asia Ltd v Securities Commission*, when Lord Hoffmann in an important and influential judgment of the Privy Council suggested that although there is a presumption in favour of identification in English law, vicarious liability may be adopted if the purpose of a statute is better achieved by adopting the broader standard.[30] The *Meridian* formula has been criticised on the grounds that the policy of a statute may be hard to find and it is unlikely that the words of the relevant provisions will provide a clear answer as to *who* constitutes the company. As such, the new approach seems to introduce an enormous amount of uncertainty into the criminal law. The result of *Meridian* seems to pile uncertainty—which standard is going to apply for this particular statute?—onto uncertainty.

Moreover, the more flexible *Meridian* approach does not really address certain fundamental problems with both forms of imputation. First, all imputation standards presume that an individual person has committed a criminal offence. In complex modern organisations where corporate decisions and actions are the result of a combination—or aggregation—of individual acts this may be an unrealistic assumption.

Second, by focusing on the criminal acts of only one person, the *collective* nature of corporate criminal liability is not captured. Stated bluntly, there is no concept of *organisational* fault with imputation doctrines. Criminal liability is derived from the criminal acts of a certain class of employees and this seems a weak basis for the imposition of a criminal sanction against an organisation as a whole. Finally, corporate criminal liability for crimes of intent runs contrary to one of the basic principles of criminal law—punishment of the morally blameworthy—since it relies upon some variation of vicarious guilt rather than direct, personal fault.

A number of jurisdictions have therefore attempted to develop alternatives to imputation. The necessity of this move suggests the limited applicability of the traditional criminal law model to corporations.

[28] *P&O European Ferries Ltd* [1991] 93 Cr App Rep 72.

[29] *Attorney General's Reference (No 2 of 1999)* [2000] QB 796. In this case, a rail company and the driver were both charged for offences connected to a serious rail accident near London. The driver was convicted, but the court dismissed the case against the rail company on the grounds that there was no evidence that any corporate officers had engaged in any criminal act.

[30] *Meridian Global Funds Management Asia Ltd v Securities Commission* [1995] 3 All ER 918. *Meridian* involved the criminal acts of investment managers, therefore the broader US standard was required in order to ensure a conviction against the company.

A first alternative emerged in the US Federal Courts in the late 1980s, so-called 'aggregation doctrine'. The need for aggregation arises when no one individual has committed an offence but the combined effect of several individual actions is criminal. The classic example of this is the *Bank of New England* case from 1987, when a US bank was charged with knowingly violating the federal Currency Transaction Reporting Act.[31] This statute required financial institutions to report to the US Treasury all transactions in excess of $10,000. In this case a customer of a bank withdrew cash from the same account, but from three different branches of the bank. The total sum for the three transactions was greater than $10,000. The bank failed to report the transactions and was subsequently prosecuted. Under imputation doctrines the bank would have been acquitted since no one individual employee had violated the rules. However, the court allowed the three acts to be aggregated in order to establish the corporation's guilt. The rationale behind a doctrine of this kind is clear: it prevents corporations evading criminal liability by compartmentalising their activities.

The principal difficulty with aggregation is that 'the total seems to exceed the sum of the parts'.[32] Two innocent states of mind are being added together to produce a guilty state of mind. Several non-culpable states (the acts of the individual bank tellers in the *Bank of New England* example) are combined to result in a culpable state. Again, this seems to run against basic notions of criminal responsibility. Of course, to those who favour aggregation it is precisely the fact that the conviction of a company does not carry any implication that the workers are guilty of any offence that means this approach is preferable for grounding organisational fault.

However, there is something disturbing about the suggestion that the company committed a crime in the absence of any single criminal act.[33] Another difficulty is deciding which individual acts should be aggregated (any employees? Or just those identified with the company?) and justifying the distinction. As such, we arrive back at earlier debates about which employees are to be identified with the company and the attendant difficulties in such an approach.

Aware of many of the problems in this area, some jurisdictions have sought to develop new models that address the limited ability to stretch, in a fair and legitimate way, familiar criminal law categories (such as personal responsibility) to the very different context of organisational wrongdoing. However, these new approaches also suffer from various difficulties from the perspective of legal certainty.

[31] *United States v Bank of New England* 821 F 2d 844 (1st Cir) (1987).

[32] J Gobert and M Punch, *Rethinking Corporate Crime* (London, Butterworths, 2004) 84ff. See also, J Gobert, 'Four Models of Corporate Fault' (1994) 14 *Journal of Legal Studies* 393.

[33] It is on this basis that aggregation was rejected by English courts; see *Attorney General's Reference (No 2 of 1999)* [2000] QB 796 at 798.

One alternative, for example, is a so-called risk management model of corporate criminal liability. This can be found in various proposals of the English Law Commission to establish a new offence of corporate killing, as well as a 2001 reform in Italian law.[34] In both cases, the issue of criminal responsibility is framed in terms of whether the company's behaviour fell below what could reasonably have been expected in the circumstances. That is to say, criminal liability is imposed on a company if there has been a corporate failure to manage risk in a reasonable manner. Unlike the imputation and aggregation doctrines, the company would be liable not for what its agents had done or thought, but for the organisation of its policies and practices pertaining to risk management.

The draft Involuntary Homicide Bill attached to English Law Commission on corporate criminal liability report illustrates this approach. A company would be liable for the crime of corporate killing if: (i) 'management failure' by the corporation is the cause of a person's death; and (ii) that 'failure constitutes conduct failing far below what can reasonably be expected of the corporation in the circumstances'. Many criticisms have been made of this proposal, but one issue is whether a policy evaluation of the kind envisaged by the draft law is an appropriate task for a criminal court (especially in those jurisdictions with juries or lay-panels).

A similar, but even more radical, example of attempting to re-think the legal basis of corporate criminal liability is found in the Australian Federal Criminal Code of 1995. Under this reform, liability is imposed on the corporation if 'a corporate culture existed within the body corporate that directed, encouraged, or tolerated' criminal acts.[35] The law goes on to define corporate culture expansively as 'an attitude, policy, rule, course of conduct, or practice existing within the body corporate.'[36] Companies are thus prevented from hiding behind codes of conduct or other policy statements if the reality of corporate practice is very different. This approach is not without difficulties. At the very least one is obliged to distort language in ascribing criminal guilt to a corporate body on the ground that it is responsible for the emergence of a morally blameworthy corporate culture.

Even the briefest discussion of the liability standard of companies in a criminal law context reveals how various uncertainties pervade the discussion, and how various competing policy interests need to be resolved in arriving at an appropriate standard. In particular, there is a tension between, on the one hand, finding a fair and workable standard appropriate for dealing with large, modern business organisations and, on the other hand, finding a standard that is sufficiently compatible with traditional notions of

[34] For an extensive discussion of both the English proposals and the Italian law reform, see, eg Gobert and Punch, *Rethinking Corporate Crime* ch 3.

[35] Australian Federal Criminal Code 1995, s 12(c)(2).

[36] ibid s 12(c)(3).

legal certainty, as it has functioned in a criminal law context. Against this background, it is perhaps not surprising that concerns of legal certainty have often taken second place to a more pragmatic desire to find a standard that is going to be workable in complex cases involving highly-motivated and resourced corporate suspects and defendants.

Uncertainties as to the Purpose of Corporate Criminal Law

The uncertainties surrounding these doctrinal questions are further compounded when one considers the uncertainties associated with the policy reasons for adopting corporate criminal liability in the first place. There is a great deal of ambiguity regarding the underlying purpose of corporate criminal liability and how—and whether—it might function to achieve such a purpose.

The normative justification for corporate criminal liability, in general, has conventionally been provided by arguments from deterrence and prevention, rather than retribution.[37] Although there is an academic literature defending retribution as a legitimate aim of corporate criminal law, the dominant approach amongst policy-makers, judges and academics has been to focus on how corporate criminal liability contributes to the deterrence and prevention of corporate wrong doing.[38]

This general unwillingness to advance versions of retribution as a justification for corporate criminal law can be explained by a reluctance to cause economic harm—by punishing a corporation—without some possibility of a clear countervailing social benefit (in the form of a reduction in future wrongdoing). Nevertheless, although retribution has not usually functioned as an independent justification for imposing criminal liability on corporations, it has served as a partial constraint upon the law in this area, in the sense that *some* blameworthiness on the part of the corporate defendant—either in terms of fault or harm—is required for almost all offences.

The main focus of the normative discussion, however, has been on the question of whether and how the goal of reducing corporate wrongdoing might be achieved. In examining this issue, it is helpful to treat deterrence and prevention as separate justifications for corporate criminal liability. In order to avoid terminological confusion, the process whereby a person desists from criminal conduct as a result of the threat of criminal sanction will be referred to as deterrence. In contrast, the process whereby the threat of criminal sanction motivates persons to monitor *other* persons to ensure that crimes do not occur will be termed prevention.

[37] See especially VS Khanna, 'Corporate Criminal Liability' (1996) 199 *Harvard Law Review* 1477.

[38] See, eg WS Laufer, 'Corporate Bodies and Guilty Minds' (1994) 43 *Emory Law Journal* 647.

Taking deterrence first: imposing criminal liability on the corporation might seem incompatible with the aim of deterrence because a corporation is a fictional legal entity that cannot itself be deterred in the way that a natural person can, ie a corporation cannot experience the feeling of being threatened, therefore, it cannot be deterred. This means that corporate criminal liability really aims to deter the unlawful acts or omissions of a corporation's agents.

Although the criminal justice system could focus exclusively on deterring such wrongdoing via *individual* criminal liability, a system of purely personal criminal liability has various limitations from the viewpoint of deterrence. In particular, the state faces significant administrative costs in identifying individual offenders within large, complex organisations and proving, beyond a reasonable doubt, that criminal wrongdoing has, in fact, taken place. Such administrative costs greatly reduce the likelihood of detection—and hence the risks of crime for any prospective offender—and the resulting sense of security might embolden an individual contemplating wrongdoing. Holding the corporation liable therefore represents a cost-effective way to overcome the shortcomings of a system based purely on personal liability. The threat of *corporate* liability deters individual agents of the company from participating in wrongdoing because of the negative outcome that an individual will suffer if the company is convicted and they are implicated in such wrongdoing.

In addition to deterring individual agents of the company from wrongdoing, advocates of corporate criminal liability also argue that is has the additional advantage of preventing wrongdoing by creating a strong incentive for *all* of the stakeholders within a company to monitor one another for wrongdoing and to correct any wrongdoing that is uncovered. In this way, corporate criminal liability motivates a company to reduce its liability exposure by assuming the task of policing the agents of that company.[39] Moreover, companies are particularly well placed to perform this monitoring function. At least, it can be convincingly argued that they are better placed than the state or other third parties negatively affected by corporate wrongdoing to engage in such monitoring. A company can thus introduce internal controls and ex ante measures for detecting agents contemplating wrongdoing. In addition, a company can react to wrongdoing by taking action against those involved in wrongdoing, reporting them to the authorities or implementing reforms to ensure that there is no recurrence of wrongdoing. In this way, corporate criminal liability can contribute to a reduction in corporate crime.

It is worth emphasising the differences between corporate and individual criminal liability on this point. When an individual is punished, or threatened

[39] See, eg S Simpson, *Corporate Crime, Law and Social Control* (Cambridge, Cambridge University Press, 2002).

with punishment, the goal of that punishment or threat of punishment is to inhibit rather than to mobilise. As Brent Fisse noted: 'The message conveyed [to the natural person by the criminal law] is 'refrain from committing that offence', rather than 'refrain from committing that offence and take such steps to improve your physiological and psychological capacity for self-control as are necessary to guard against repetition'. By contrast, when a corporate offender is punished or threatened with punishment, *the message is catalytic as well as inhibitory*. The message conveyed, for corporate offences of commission as well as for those of omission, is 'refrain from committing that offence and take such steps as are necessary organisationally to guard against repetition'.[40]

This reliance on *both* the 'inhibitory' (ie deterrence) and 'catalytic' (ie prevention) functions distinguishes corporate criminal liability from the criminal law as it is applied to natural persons. One of the central aims of the new corporate criminal law has been to bolster this catalytic function of corporate criminal liability and to promote internal efforts at ensuring compliance.

A key premise of both the deterrence and prevention justification for corporate criminal liability is the claim that the *threat* of corporate criminal liability provides a strong behavioural incentive for all individuals to either desist from offending or to monitor others and prevent them from offending. The belief that corporate criminal liability can have this kind of impact on individuals within business entities seems to be widespread among policymakers, judges, prosecutors, regulators and commentators. It is therefore important to look in more detail at the nature of the threat created by the existence of corporate criminal liability and some of the uncertainties that surround the assumption that this threat provides the necessary behavioural incentives.

Both the criminal justice system and society in general impose sanctions on any corporation found criminally liable; the criminal justice system sanctions via the formal sanction imposed (eg a fine) and society sanctions the company in the form of reputational damage caused by a conviction. Moreover, informal sanctions can arise from the fact of an indictment or criminal investigation and are not necessarily contingent on a conviction. It is the *combined* threat of both types of sanction that deters wrongdoing and provides the incentive for corporations to engage in crime prevention. It is, therefore, worth considering the threat that these two types of sanctions pose. The key question is whether this threat is sufficiently severe and certain to have purchase over the behavioural incentives of those individuals contemplating wrongdoing or in a position to engage in crime prevention. In the following, it will be suggested that finding a clear answer to this question is not simple.

[40] 1141, 1160.

Taking formal sanctions first: judges and administrative agencies are empowered to impose a range of formal sanctions if a company is convicted, most obviously fines and loss of licence, although shaming penalties are increasingly used. Traditionally, fines are used as the primary sanction in the context of corporate crime. The rationale for the fine seems fairly simple: the primary goal of all corporate activity is to make money and corporations can thus be deterred from wrongdoing and motivated to invest in prevention by the threat of monetary sanctions that can directly impact upon a company's central purpose. Additional advantages of the fine as a sanction are that they are cheap to administer and there is some (financial) benefit to the state. In general, fines do not extend to allow for compensation for victims, although this may be possible in some circumstances. Further advantages are that fines are flexible and can be calibrated to the specific facts of the case. Finally, in extreme cases a fine can be imposed that is large enough to deprive a corporation of all its assets and drive the company out of business (what can be thought of as a corporate death sentence).

However, many commentators have criticised fines as ineffective in either deterring or preventing corporate wrongdoing.[41] It is often suggested that fines have traditionally been set too low in the case of corporate crime and that, as a consequence, fines are seen as the price of engaging in criminal behaviour. It has also been suggested that fines are ineffective because the company may easily transfer the burden to innocent third parties, such as customers, shareholders, or employees. If the effects of the fine can be reduced, then the threat of the fine is significantly reduced and increasing the level of the fines would merely mean imposing a greater burden on these third parties.

The effect of this kind of consideration is to introduce uncertainty as to the scale of the threat posed by the fine and, in consequence, to drastically reduce the incentive to prevent wrongdoing. A common response to this argument is to suggest that the various third parties who ultimately bear the cost of the fines—eg shareholders or employees, perhaps even consumers—are not innocent parties because they benefited, either directly or indirectly, from the illegal activity in the form of higher share dividends, share price, wages, or product prices. Even though these parties may not be directly responsible for the illegality, it might seem fair to deprive them of these unlawfully-obtained gains, and it is precisely this possibility that is designed to motivate various third parties to engage in social enforcement. The key issue is whether the loss of a job or a decrease in the value of an investment is proportionate, given the lack of direct responsibility and whether this possibility can actually be sufficiently powerful to incentivise these third parties to engage in social enforcement. Moreover, in the case of shareholders the

[41] See eg 'Fine and Punishment' *The Economist* (21 July 2012) www.economist.com/node/21559315.

possibility of such harm may have a chilling effect on investment and reduce the capacity of companies to capitalise via securities markets. Either way, doubts seem to be cast over the capacity of the law to have a clear and predictable impact on behavioural incentives.

Of course, fines are not the only formal sanctions that are available in cases of corporate crime. Other sanctions can be imposed, such as loss of licence or shaming, and, depending on the nature of a corporation's business, these may be equally important: a conviction can have disastrous consequences for a company, even if there is only a small fine imposed.[42]

A consensus amongst most commentators is that informal sanctions constitute a more significant threat to a company than formal sanctions.[43] The ability of any company to succeed is contingent on having and maintaining a reputation for probity. Given the importance that the market attaches to corporate reputation, it is often suggested that large business entities will struggle to survive even an indictment, let alone a trial or conviction. This seems particularly true in some sectors, such as financial services. Even an investigation can be hugely damaging for any firm that depends on public trust as a key element of its business model.

Although it is difficult to verify empirically the claim that the threat to corporate reputation is the primary threat posed by corporate criminal liability, the behaviour of corporate executives in seeking to evade criminal investigation provides strong circumstantial evidence for the claim that executives place a premium on corporate reputation. Corporations that are under criminal investigation will often take drastic measures to avoid indictment, including waiving various legal professional privileges and disclosing the findings of any internal investigation, assisting the investigation of individual employees, and entering into pre-indictment agreements of various kinds (eg deferred prosecution agreements), many of which impose a significant and ongoing burden on the company.

Business leaders clearly regard corporate reputation as a valued asset of a company that both improves profits and facilitates other objectives. The most obvious benefit of corporate reputation is the impact it has on customers. Consumer good will is clearly directly connected to increased corporate profits.

But a positive corporate reputation has a number of other less obvious financial benefits. For example, banks will be more likely to offer credit during financial difficulties to companies with a positive reputation. The reputation of a company also affects the culture within an organisation,

[42] PH Bucy, 'Civil Prosecution of Health Care Fraud' (1995) 30 *Wake Forest Law Review* 720, 693.

[43] See, eg P Bharara, 'Corporations Cry Uncle and Their Employees Cry Foul: Rethinking Prosecutorial Pressure on Corporate Defendants' (2007) 44 *American Criminal Law Review* 53, 73 ('[C]orporate defendants, subject as they are to market pressures, may not be able to survive indictment, much less conviction and sentencing').

which has the potential to boost performance and facilitate attracting the best talent. A positive reputation may also bring benefits in dealing with the state. A company with a positive reputation may have more political influence when lobbying over state action likely to impact upon a company's sphere of business operations.

Adverse publicity may also trigger a variety of other non-financial bad effects for a corporation. Most significantly, negative publicity spotlight may result in further unwanted attention on the corporation and lead to more government or media interest, and potentially private litigation (so-called 'spotlight syndrome').

Reputation thus helps a corporation to achieve a wide range of important corporate goals and the threat posed by corporate criminal liability to that reputation has the potential to alter behavioural incentives in such a way as to deter and prevent corporate crime. However, all of the above seems to depend on various empirical claims and the particular circumstances of a particular company. We can, therefore, see that in addition to the various doctrinal uncertainties discussed above there are various uncertainties about the underlying rationale for corporate criminal liability, in particular relating to the purpose of this form of liability, and the various processes that seem necessary in order to achieve the underlying purpose, however it is defined.

Procedural Uncertainties

Post-2000, a number of new and controversial legal instruments have been used by regulators against corporations suspected of criminal wrongdoing. Notable amongst these are deferred prosecution agreements (DPAs).[44] DPAs are an example of *pre-trial diversion* in which the company avoids prosecution in exchange for fulfilling various obligations contained in an agreement negotiated between the company and regulators. The increased use of this type of instrument since 2000 represents a significant change in how law enforcement deals with corporate crime. It is seen as a response to bankruptcy of Arthur Andersen in 2002, after the firm was convicted of obstruction of justice in the context of the shredding of documents relevant to the *Enron* investigation. Although the conviction was subsequently overturned by the US Supreme Court, the firm went bankrupt, causing many innocent employees to lose their jobs and the market to lose a valuable service provider. In order to avoid so-called collateral damage of this kind, the US

[44] See, eg BL Garrett, *Too Big to Jail: How Prosecutors Compromise with Corporations* (New York, Belknap, 2014); IE Gilbert, *Corporate Crime and the Use of Deferred and Non-Prosecution Agreements* (New York, Nova, 2010); W Kaal, 'The Effect of Deferred and Non-Prosecution Agreements on Corporate Governance' (2014) 70 *Business Lawyer* 1.

government began to look for alternatives, notably some form of pre-trial diversion that sanctions a company, whilst seeking to ensure that the company is not driven out of business and is able to continue operations, albeit in a reformed state.

In a typical DPA, a criminal charge is filed against a corporation and the corporation acknowledges and accepts responsibility for the criminal wrongdoing. The prosecution is deferred for a period of time—usually from one to two years—provided that the corporation fulfils the terms of the DPA and does not engage in further misconduct. If the company fulfils all obligations under the agreement, then the charge is withdrawn. If there is a failure to comply with the terms of the agreement, then the charge can be activated and the case will proceed to trial.

The kind of obligation that is imposed on a company as part of these agreements includes the immediate payment of a 'fine' agreed between the prosecutor and the company; cooperation with any ongoing investigations; waivers of various trial rights and privileges—such as attorney client privilege, work product doctrine and statute of limitation defences; implementation and compliance with corporate governance reform measures (a so-called 'Compliance and Ethics Programme'); and consent to oversight by an 'independent' monitor approved by the government.

The specific terms are negotiated between the government and the particular company. Such agreements have a number of advantages, at least from the perspective of regulators. With a DPA, the company admits to culpability, a change in the company is guaranteed, monitors are placed in the company to avoid future problems, and the cooperation of the company is assured. Moreover, the company is forced to pay a 'fine'. Finally, the company is allowed to continue operating without the possible negative collateral consequences of prosecution—eg suspension or debarment from contracting with government entities, liquidation of the company, loss of jobs for employees not involved in the misconduct, and loss of beneficial products or services in the marketplace.

On the other hand, if the case goes to trial there is the risk of a costly not guilty verdict (and this risk is significant given a jury system and the complex law and facts that characterise most corporate crime cases). And even if the company is convicted it will have cost the taxpayer a significant amount of money for the prosecution, and the net result will be payment of a fine by the company. Since a 'fine' is guaranteed under a DPA, along with other benefits that would not occur if case went to trial, the value added of going to trial is not always clear. Moreover, in the event of a conviction there is a risk of the kind of collateral damage discussed above.

Nevertheless, the increased use of settlement agreements in cases of corporate crime remains subject to criticism. This is not the occasion to examine all criticisms, only those that relate to issues of legal certainty, most significantly, separation of powers and rule of law concerns. Should prosecutors have this kind of discretionary power? Surely, it is for a court ultimately to determine the sanction to be imposed for criminal conduct? In the UK version of the scheme, this criticism was acknowledged and a much greater role for the judiciary was required in permitting the negotiation of a DPA, monitoring such negotiations, and approving the terms of any agreement.[45]

The second related set of concerns relate to the lack of uniformity, transparency and accountability. Until 2007, there were no governing standards or guidance to US attorneys on whether to adopt pre-trial diversion in a particular case. Since 2007, a series of guidelines have been issued, but they afford enormous discretion to the prosecutor. As a result, uncertainty surrounds both whether a particular firm will be offered the opportunity to enter into such an agreement, and the terms of any such agreement.

THE CHANGING MEANING OF LEGAL CERTAINTY, LEGAL RISK AND SOCIAL ENFORCEMENT

One important effect of the increased legal uncertainty created by the new corporate criminal law is to greatly expand the legal risk facing companies. Managing this new legal risk obliges companies—particularly larger companies—to invest heavily in meaningful, flexible and adaptable compliance mechanisms within organisational governance that aim at minimising the liability exposure that has been created by uncertainties as to the scope of the law and liability. In the following, such internal governance mechanisms will be characterised as 'social enforcement'. The suggestion is that social enforcement is a response, at least in part, to the legal uncertainty and the new legal risk that such developments have created.

Social enforcement aims at ensuring that meaningful self-regulatory capacities—a culture of compliance—become firmly embedded in the structure and culture of an organisation. In this context, a culture of compliance can be characterised by a generalised awareness of relevant legal obligations, putting in place incentive structures that encourage compliance with those obligations and establishing institutionalised control mechanisms for monitoring corporate conduct and implementing corrective action in the event of non-compliance.

In this way, the new corporate criminal law transfers much of the responsibility, functions and administrative costs associated with 'policing' compliance from the state to private actors. This approach can be justified on the grounds that the corporation is best placed to monitor for, and—when necessary—correct, wrongdoing at least cost to society. Public enforcement—in the form of indictment, trial and possible conviction—is regarded as a

[45] Deferred Prosecution Agreements: What you Really Need to Know (2013), www.freshfields.com/uploadedFiles/SiteWide/Knowledge/Deferred_Prosecution_Agreements.pdf.

measure of last resort, to be employed in the event of a breakdown or failure in social enforcement mechanisms.

A key organising principle of the new corporate criminal law seems to be to provide corporations with incentives to engage in social enforcement. This is not to suggest that other principles more traditionally associated with criminal justice, such as punishment or deterrence, are irrelevant in the context of the new corporate criminal law. Modern legal systems have a complex character in the sense that they can simultaneously embed multiple, possibly competing, principles and objectives. Nevertheless, the contemporary emphasis on social enforcement gives the new corporate criminal law a distinctive character and this type of account offers a better interpretive and explanatory 'fit' with a wide range of recent developments than the more traditional justifications for imposing criminal liability. The point to be emphasised in this context is that uncertainty as to the legal risk facing a company has the potential to function as a powerful incentive for a company to bolster social enforcement procedures. In this way, uncertainty might be said to contribute to achieving a socially desirable policy objective.

Corporate compliance can be understood as the institutional means adopted by firms to achieve the goal of social enforcement.[46] Stand-alone compliance departments were developed in the early 1960s, initially in the US. Prior to that time, the legal department would have responsibility for compliance functions. However, the legal risks associated with the new corporate criminal law, as well as the proliferation of regulation more generally, has triggered an expanded role for the discourse and practice of compliance in contemporary business enterprises.

Significantly, many legal systems increasingly offer incentives to implement effective compliance programmes. That is to say, the criminal justice system offers 'rewards' for implementing compliance structures in the event that wrongdoing does occur, ie in the event of a breakdown in social enforcement companies will be 'rewarded' for having had compliance in place at the time any offending occurred. Modern corporate criminal law is predicated on a recognition that perfect compliance is impossible and that demanding perfection may be counter-productive. Such an expectation has a potential 'chilling effect' on a firm's willingness to invest in what will often be regarded as a non-revenue generating activity.

There are a number of examples of legal measures designed to 'reward' compliance. First, compliance can function as a justification, that is to say, a full defence against criminal liability. A company that can show it had adequate compliance procedures in place at the time an offence occurred is not criminally liable. The UK Bribery Act 2010, for example, offers a full

[46] See Gobert and Punch, *Rethinking Corporate Crime* ch 10.

defence for the payment of bribes, if—at the time the offence occurred—the corporation had 'adequate' compliance mechanisms in place. Second, compliance can provide mitigation at the sentencing phase.[47] The US Sentencing Guidelines for Organizations include compliance as a key factor in the reduction of sentence. Finally, compliance can provide a company with leverage in any settlement negotiations that take place prior to indictment.

In each of these different ways, therefore, the legal system offers clear and additional incentives for a corporation to implement compliance processes and procedures aimed at social enforcement.

CONCLUSION

The new corporate criminal law seems to be characterised by simultaneous processes of net-widening (ie more offences applied to companies, often with lower *mens rea* requirements) and diminishing legal certainty (ie ambiguity as to the outer limits of these offences). In addition, normative and empirical uncertainties surround the legal doctrine underlying this whole field of law, namely corporate criminal liability. A concern with legal certainty in corporate criminal law constantly seems to run up against other competing policy considerations and resolving the various interests in favour of legal certainty is becoming increasingly difficult. In particular, political pressure to be seen to be doing something about socially undesirable corporate behaviour means that legal certainty is often compromised in the name of some counter-veiling policy argument. Whether such derogation is legitimate or not is a discussion for another occasion.

The point here has been to suggest that, at least in the context of contemporary corporate criminal law, the development of new corporate criminal law seems to have transformed the meaning of legal certainty. Certainty no longer seems to function as a fundamental principle of criminal justice that trumps other considerations or, at least, creates a strong presumption of excluding other reasons. Instead, legal certainty seems to have taken on a more modest role as one of a number of competing considerations that have to be resolved in addressing the response of the criminal justice system to socially undesirable corporate behaviour. Rather, the law in this area seems to be characterised by a pragmatic recognition of—or at least a belief in—the virtues of a certain degree of uncertainty. By introducing additional uncertainty—particularly in terms of the scope of the offence and the likelihood of pre-trial diversion being adopted in a particular

[47] For a comparative perspective on the compliance defence in different jurisdictions, see M Koehler, *The Foreign Corrupt Practices Act in a New Era* (London, Edward Elgar, 2014).

case—corporations are given an additional incentive to invest in internal compliance mechanisms that (ideally) result in a net reduction in offending.

The chapter suggested that one important effect of this change has been to contribute to a significant expansion in the legal risk facing companies, obliging them to invest in meaningful and flexible compliance mechanisms within organisational governance that aim at managing this new legal risk. This trend towards social enforcement—ie transferring much of the responsibility, functions and administrative costs associated with policing compliance from the state to private actors—seems to be a distinctive feature of the new corporate criminal law. This trend towards social enforcement seems to be closely connected to the difficult and ongoing task of managing the complex profile of legal risk that has emerged, partly as a result of the diminishing certainty of the law.

4

Economic Analysis of Law and Wilburg's Flexible System: A Systematic Approach to European Tort Law

MONIKA HINTEREGGER

INTRODUCTION

THIS CHAPTER EXPLORES the theoretical foundations of tort law and examines how the different concepts of tort law can be brought into a coherent system. It draws on the insights of the economic theory of law and compares them to the concept of the flexible system developed by the Austrian law professor, Walter Wilburg.

The chapter first offers a short summary of the status of tort liability in Europe and then describes the essential aspects governing the different concepts of tort law. It continues with comments on Wilburg's 'flexible system' and a discussion of the economic evaluation of tort law. The analysis is rounded off by drawing conclusions about how Wilburg's theory can be used to make European tort law more consistent.

The goal of the chapter is to show how the different concepts of tort law can be put together in a more coherent system. Such a system can provide legislators and courts with a framework of reference and help them to achieve rational and transparent decisions for the allocation of liability. This systematic approach to tort law may not only promote legal certainty but also provides for sufficient flexibility in order to solve individual cases and to tackle new societal and technological developments.

THE STATUS QUO: TORT LIABILITY IN EUROPE

Harmonised and Unified Liability Rules

In Europe, tort law is primarily regulated by national law. Important exceptions exist with respect to product liability, liability of carriers by air and sea and nuclear liability which are to a large extent determined by European Union (EU) rules or international conventions. Product liability is regulated in all the Member States of the EU according to the European Product Liability Directive.[1]

Liability and (compulsory) insurance for the carriage of passengers by sea is regulated by Regulation 392/2009,[2] which is based on the Athens Convention relating to the Carriage of Passengers and their Luggage by Sea from 1974, as amended by the Protocol of 2002 and the IMO Reservation and Guidelines for Implementation of the Athens Convention adopted by the Legal Committee of the IMO on 19 October 2006. Both acts are set out in Annex I and II of the Regulation and constitute an integral part of the Regulation (Regulation, Article 1). The Regulation extends the provisions of the Athens Convention which applies only to international transport, also to certain categories of passenger ships engaged in domestic sea-going voyages (Regulation, Article 1). It adds a specific obligation to compensate for loss of or damage to mobility equipment and obliges the carrier to advance payments in case of death or personal injury of a passenger (Regulation, Articles 4 and 6). For the loss suffered as a result of the death of or personal injury to a passenger caused by a shipping incident (shipwreck, capsizing, collision, stranding of the ship, or explosion, fire or defect in the ship) the carrier is liable for up to 250,000 SDR (Special Drawing Right as defined by the International Monetary Fund) per passenger. For losses that exceed this limit the carrier is liable up to 400,000 SDR, unless he proves that the incident occurred without his fault or neglect (Athens Convention, Article 3 and 7). Compensation of damage to luggage is also limited (cabin luggage 2,250 SDR, other luggage 3,375 SDR, vehicles 12,700 SDR) and subject to fault-based liability of the carrier, who can escape liability by proving that the incident occurred without his fault (Athens Convention, Articles 3 and 8). The Regulation entered into force on 1 January 2013.

Liability of the air carrier for damage caused to passengers is provided by Regulation 889/2002,[3] which is based on the Warsaw Convention of 12 October 1929[4] as amended by the Montreal Convention of 28 May 1999.[5] According to the Warsaw-Montreal regime, the air carrier is obliged to compensate passengers for death and bodily injury for up to 113,100 SDR, subject only to the defence of contributory fault of the victim (Montreal Convention, Articles 20, 21 and 24). For damage exceeding this cap the air

[1] Directive 85/374/EEC, [1999] OJ L141/20.

[2] Regulation (EC) 392/2009, [2009] OJ L131/24.

[3] Regulation (EC) 889/2002, [2002] OJ L140/2.

[4] Convention for the Unification of Certain Rules Relating to International Carriage by Air (signed 12 October 1929) (Warsaw Convention).

[5] Convention for the Unification of Certain Rules for International Carriage by Air (signed 28 May 1999, entered into force 4 November 2003) [2001] OJ L194/39 (Montreal Convention).

carrier is liable according to fault-based liability with a presumption of fault. The air carrier is exonerated if it proves that the damage was not due to the negligence or other wrongful act or omission of the carrier or its servants or agents, or that the damage was solely due to the negligence or other wrongful act or omission of a third party (Montreal Convention, Article 21(2)). With respect to baggage and cargo, special rules and liability caps apply (Montreal Convention, Article 17ff). Regulation 889/2002 extends these rules to all flights, whether domestic or international, operated by Community air carriers and provides some rules favourable to the harmed passenger (advance payments in the event of bodily injury; jurisdiction of the courts of the passenger's principal place of residence; increase of liability limits in the event of delay and damage to baggage). Minimum insurance requirements for air carriers and aircraft operators in respect to passengers, baggage, cargo and third parties, for both commercial and private flights are provided by Regulation 785/2004 on insurance requirements for air carriers and aircraft operators, as amended by Regulation 1137/2008 and 285/2010.[6] The objective of this Regulation is to establish minimum insurance requirements for air carriers and aircraft operators in respect to passengers, baggage, cargo and third parties to cover the risks associated with aviation-specific liability (including acts of war, terrorism, hijacking, acts of sabotage, unlawful seizure of aircraft and civil commotion).

Damage to persons other than passengers is still regulated by the national laws. These rules are not harmonised. Of all the Member States, only Italy and Spain are parties to the 1952 Convention on Damage Caused by Foreign Aircraft to Third Parties on the Surface by the International Civil Aviation Organisation of the ICAO (Rome Convention).[7] Most European countries provide for special strict liability rules for aeroplane accidents.[8]

Nuclear liability is largely regulated by international conventions which, however, divide the EU Member States into two systems. The Convention on Third Party Liability in the Field of Nuclear Energy of 29 July 1960 (Paris Convention)[9] and the Convention Supplementary to the Paris

[6] Regulation (EC) 785/2004, [2004] OJ L138/1; Regulation (EC) 1137/2008, [2008] OJ L311/1; Regulation (EU) 285/2010, [2010] OJ L87/19.

[7] The Convention entered into force on 4 February 1958 and has 49 parties.

[8] Eg Austria: Aviation Act 1957, §§ 148ff; England and Wales: Civil Aviation Act 1982, s 76(2); France: Code of Transports 2010, Arts L6131-1ff; Germany: Civil Aviation Act 2007, §§ 33ff; Poland: Aviation Law 2002, Arts 206–207; Spain: Act of Aeronautical Navigation (LNA) 1960; Sweden: Act on Liability for Damage Caused in the Course of Aviation from 1922. It is interesting to see that Dutch law does not provide for special liability rules for the victims of aeroplane accidents.

[9] Convention on Third Party Liability in the Field of Nuclear Energy of 29 July 1960 (entered into force 1 April 1968) as amended by the Additional Protocol of 28 January 1964 (entered into force 1 April 1968) and by the Protocol of 16 November 1982 (entered into force 7 October 1988).

Convention of 1963 (Brussels Supplementary Convention)[10] constitute the Western European third party liability system in the field of nuclear energy.[11] The Paris Convention provides for the elaboration and harmonisation of third party liability and insurance against nuclear risks. The 1963 Brussels Supplementary Convention, which is only open to members of the Paris Convention, supplements the Paris Convention by providing for additional compensation from public funds. In 2004, the Member States of the Paris Convention signed a new Protocol to the Paris Convention[12] and a new Protocol[13] to the Brussels Supplementary Convention, which are not yet in force. Most Eastern European countries belong to another liability system, the Vienna Convention.[14] The Paris and the Vienna Conventions are linked together by the 1988 Joint Protocol,[15] which mutually extends the benefits of one convention to the members of the other convention.[16]

The nuclear liability conventions establish special rules for the compensation of damage arising from nuclear incidents. All nuclear liability conventions provide for no-fault liability concentrated on the operator of a nuclear installation ('legal channelling') and are limited in amount and time. The operator is obliged to provide financial security ('principle of congruence of liability and coverage'). In order to exclude forum shopping, jurisdiction only lies with the courts of the Member State in whose territory the nuclear

[10] Convention of 31 January 1963 Supplementary to the Paris Convention of 29 July 1960 on Third Party Liability in the Field of Nuclear Energy, as amended by the Additional Protocol of 28 January 1964 and by the Protocol of 16 November 1982 (entered into force 4 December 1974) 2 ILM 685 (Brussels Supplementary Convention).

[11] The following EU Member States are parties to these conventions: Belgium, Denmark, Finland, France, Germany, Greece, Italy, the Netherlands, Portugal, Slovenia, Spain, Sweden and the United Kingdom. All States, except Greece and Portugal, also belong to the Brussels Supplementary Convention.

[12] Protocol to amend the Convention on Third Party Liability in the Field of Nuclear Energy of 29 July 1960, as amended by the Additional Protocol of 28 January 1964 and by the Protocol of 16 November 1982 (signed 12 February 2004).

[13] Protocol to amend the Convention of 31 January 1963 Supplementary to the Paris Convention of 29 July 1960 on Third Party Liability in the Field of Nuclear Energy, as amended by the Additional Protocol of 28 January 1964 and by the Protocol of 16 November 1982 (signed 12 February 2004).

[14] Vienna Convention on Civil Liability for Nuclear Damage (adopted 21 May 1963, entered into force 12 November 1977) IAEA INFCIRC/500 (EU Member States: Bulgaria, Croatia, the Czech Republic, Estonia, Hungary, Latvia, Lithuania, Poland, Romania and Slovakia) and Protocol to Amend the Vienna Convention on Civil Liability for Nuclear Damage (adopted 12 September 1997, entered into force 4 October 2003) IAEA INFCIRC/566 (European Member States: Latvia, Poland and Romania). Since 1997, a further convention has been open for ratification, the Convention on Supplementary Compensation for Nuclear Damage (adopted 12 September 1997) IAEA *INFCIRC/567* which provides for a worldwide liability regime for nuclear damage. It is, however, not yet in effect.

[15] Joint Protocol Relating to the Application of the Vienna Convention and the Paris Convention (adopted 21 September 1988, entered into force 27 April 1992) IAEA INFCIRC/402.

[16] EU Member States which belong to the Joint Protocol: Bulgaria, Croatia, the Czech Republic, Denmark, Estonia, Finland, Germany, Greece, Hungary, Italy, Latvia, Lithuania, the Netherlands, Poland, Romania, Slovakia, Slovenia and Sweden.

incident occurred, or, if the nuclear incident occurs outside the territory of the state, or, if the place of the nuclear incident cannot be determined with certainty, with the courts of the Member State in whose territory the nuclear installation of the liable operator is situated ('exclusive jurisdiction'). Applicable law, both substantive and procedural, that is not specifically governed by the conventions, is the law of the competent court (lex fori). The nature, form and extent of the compensation, as well as distribution matters, are regulated by national law. The Paris Convention, and the national laws implementing it, must be applied without any discrimination based upon nationality, domicile, or residence in order to ensure the equal treatment of victims ('principle of non-discrimination'). Judgments that are enforceable under the jurisdiction of the competent court must be recognised and enforced in all the other Member States. Compensation, insurance and reinsurance premiums, including interest and costs, must be freely transferable between the contracting countries. Many Western European states implemented their obligations under these conventions by way of specific statutes and many of them already provide for the higher liability sums of the 2004 Protocol to the Paris Convention.[17]

The non-nuclear European states Austria, Ireland, Luxembourg, Malta and Cyprus do not belong to any of the nuclear liability conventions. Luxembourg and Austria have only signed the 1960 Paris Convention and the Protocols, as well as the 1963 Brussels Supplementary Convention, but never ratified them.[18] Austria provides for a national nuclear liability

[17] UK: £140 million (Nuclear Installations Act 1965) with the intention to increase the operator liability limit to €1,200 million (Department of Energy and Climate Change, 'Implementation of changes to the Paris and Brussels Conventions on nuclear third party liability' (24 January 2011) www.gov.uk/government/consultations/compensating-victims-of-nuclear-accidents); France: operator liability is capped with €700 million per nuclear incident (Law of 13 June 2006 amending Law no 68-943 of 30 October 1968); Germany: unlimited liability for the operator, with exceptions (Atomic Energy Act 1985); Netherlands: €1,200 million (Nuclear Accidents Liability Act 1979); Spain: €700 million (Act on civil liability for nuclear damage 2011); Sweden: 300 million SDR (Nuclear Liability Act 1968), intention to provide unlimited liability with the obligation insurance coverage up to 1,200 million SDR (*Lag, 2010:950*). The EU Member States belonging to the Vienna Convention provide for the following liability caps for operators: Bulgaria: 96 million BGN (Act on the Safe Use of Nuclear Energy 2002, Art 132); Croatia: 320 million HRK (Act on Liability for Nuclear Damage 1998, Art 8); Czech Republic: 8 billion CZK (Act no 158/2009 Coll); Estonia: no amount specified (Radiation Act 2004, s 64ff); Hungary: 100 million SDR (Act CXVI of 1996 on Atomic Energy, s 52(1)); Latvia: 80 million Ls (Law on Radiation Safety and Nuclear Safety 2000, Chapter VIII s 29); Lithuania: no amount specified (Law on Nuclear Energy of 14 November 1996, no I-1613, Art 58ff); Poland: 300 million SDR (Atomic Law Act 2000, Arts 100–108, consolidated text DzU 2012, at 264); Romania: 300 million RON (Law on Civil Liability for Nuclear Damage, no 703/2001, Art 8); Slovak Republic: up to €300 million (Act of 9 September 2004 on peaceful use of nuclear energy, s 29).

[18] See Nuclear Energy Agency, 'Paris Convention on Nuclear Third Party Liability. Latest status of ratifications or accessions' (30 July 2015) www.oecd-nea.org/law/paris-convention-ratification.html. Switzerland ratified the 1960 Paris Convention and the 1963 Brussels

regime[19] which stands in sharp contrast to the basic principles of international nuclear liability law. Liability is unlimited in amount. Legal channelling is, to a great extent, eliminated and there is no exclusive jurisdiction, as provided by international nuclear liability law. The law ensures that an Austrian court has jurisdiction and that Austrian law is applicable if nuclear damage occurs in Austria, regardless of where it was caused. Further contents of the law are the substantial extension of the definition of nuclear damage and the rules concerning the facilitation of the proof of causality.

In addition, EU law provides for some liability rules in some other legislative acts governing specific fields. Some of these rules are of a quite general character,[20] while others address the issue of liability in a more comprehensive, albeit non-exhaustive, way leaving crucial issues to national law.[21] No harmonisation of laws exists for environmental harm suffered by private persons. Directive 35/2004 on environmental liability with regard to the prevention and remedying of environmental damage,[22] which harmonised the rules on the prevention and restoration of site contamination and on loss of biodiversity in the EU has not interfered with national tort law remedies for the compensation of environmental harm. The picture of private law liability for environmental harm is thus still very heterogeneous in Europe.

National Tort Law Systems

Fault-Based Liability

All European jurisdictions provide for a sort of fault-based liability. In the civil law countries, fault-based liability is regulated in the civil codes. In many civil law jurisdictions, the civil codes provide for a general clause on fault liability.[23] German law is more concrete. Section 823 of the German

Supplementary Convention. As this ratification is effective only with respect to the 1960 Paris Convention and the 1963 Brussels Supplementary Convention as amended by all three Protocols, entry into force for Switzerland will only take place once the 2004 Protocol to either Convention comes into effect.

[19] Federal Law on Civil Liability for Damage caused by Radioactivity 1998.

[20] See Directive 2015/2366/EU, Art 20(2), [2015] OJ L337/35; Regulation (EU) 211/2011, Art 13, [2011] OJ L65/1 and Regulation (EU) 608/2013, Arts 27 and 28, [2013] OJ L181/15.

[21] See Regulation (EU) 679/2016, Art 82 (right to compensation and liability), [2016] OJ L119/1; Directive 2014/104/EU, Arts 3 (right to full compensation) and 11 (joint and several liability), [2014] OJ L349/1; Regulation (EU) 910/2014, Arts 11 (liability) and 13 (burden of proof), [2014] OJ L257/73 and Regulation (EU) 655/2014, Art 13 (liability of the creditor), [2014] OJ L189/59.

[22] Directive 2004/35/EC, [2004] OJ L143/56.

[23] For instance Austrian civil code 1811, § 1295; French civil code 1804, Art 1382ff; Polish civil code 1964, Art 415; Spanish civil code 1889, Art 1902.

civil code (Bürgerliches Gesetzbuch) provides for two heads of liability. According to Bürgerliches Gesetzbuch, § 823(1), a person is liable who, intentionally or negligently, unlawfully injures the life, body, health, freedom, property or another right of another person. Under Bürgerliches Gesetzbuch, § 823(2) liability is provided for the intentional or negligent breach of a statutory duty. The Dutch civil code (Burgerlijk Wetboek) does not provide for a general clause either, and defines fault-based liability even more comprehensively than German law. According to Burgerlijk Wetboek, Article 6:162 § 2, unlawfulness may consist of a violation of someone else's right (entitlement), a violation of a duty imposed by law or by unwritten social rules.

In the civil law jurisdictions, which follow the Germanic law traditions (Austria, Germany, Switzerland, Netherlands) an action under fault-based liability must meet four requirements: actionable damage; unlawfulness; fault; and causation. While the criterion of unlawfulness relates to the assessment of the act of the tortfeasor, the prerequisite of fault deals with the blameworthiness of the concrete actor. In countries following the Romanistic civil law tradition, such as France and Spain, the criterion of unlawfulness is not regarded as a separate requirement but is absorbed by the criterion of fault. In the common law jurisdictions, the most important head of liability is the tort of negligence, the tort most similar to the concept of fault-based liability in civil law. The tort of negligence is comprised of four elements: actionable damage; duty of care; breach of duty; and causation. In most countries, the assessment of fault follows rather an objective standard. Specialists and professionals usually must meet a higher standard according to their special knowledge and abilities.

In all European jurisdictions, the burden for the proof of fault and causation lies with the claimant. Under certain conditions, however, the burden of proof concerning the proof of fault or causation can be lightened or even shifted to the defendant.[24] In this context it is also important to note that there is a fundamental difference with respect to the required standard of

[24] Examples: German civil code, § 831 (product liability); Dutch Code of Civil Procedure, Art 150 allows the court to reverse the burden of proof if this is stipulated by a special statute or if it is seen to be reasonable and fair; Portuguese civil code, Art 492 § 2 explicitly provides for a reversal of proof for dangerous activities establishing a rebuttable presumption that the operator was at fault; Spain: 'theory of risk' according to which the burden of proof lies with the person who profited from the introduction of a risk. In common law the rule of *res ipsa loquitur*, according to which the court may infer negligence from the fact that the accident causing the plaintiff's harm is a type of accident that ordinarily happens as a result of the negligence of a class of actors of which the defendant is the relevant member, may lighten the plaintiff's burden of proof. See M Hinteregger, 'Comparison' in M Hinteregger (ed), *Environmental Liability and Ecological Damage* (Cambridge, Cambridge University Press, 2008) 610ff; M Hinteregger, 'Civil Liability Systems of Seven EU Member States' in L Bergkamp et al, *Civil Liability in Europe for Terrorism-Related Risk* (Cambridge, Cambridge University Press, 2015) 106ff.

proof in the national jurisdictions. Most European countries require that facts are established with high probability, but in some countries (eg UK, Netherlands) the relevant standard of proof is the balance of probabilities.[25]

No-fault liability

With respect to no-fault liability rules, the picture is extremely incoherent. The two poles are marked by English and French law. English law has no general strict liability regime. With respect to damage caused by polluting interference the torts of public and private nuisance that do not require fault are applicable. While public nuisance provides for recovery for personal injuries and property damage as well as pure economic loss, private nuisance requires interference with a proprietary interest in land and covers only property damage. Moreover, the rule in *Rylands v Fletcher*[26] establishes a special form of private nuisance governing property damage caused by the escape of dangerous things. In France (and also in Belgium) a very comprehensive and, in practice, very important no-fault liability regime applies,[27] according to which the custodian of a thing is responsible for the harm caused by the thing ('*responsabilité du fait des choses*'). According to French law, the thing need not be dangerous. In addition, special rules amounting to strict liability apply for damage caused to the neighbourhood ('*troubles de voisinage*').[28]

Some European states have general strict liability regimes for certain activities directly in their civil codes. Portugal has a comprehensive strict liability regime for dangerous activities,[29] and Article 1908 of the Spanish Código Civil provides for strict liability for harm to persons and property caused by toxic fumes. The Dutch civil code comprises several strict liability rules. There is a special strict liability regime for the professional use or possession of dangerous substances (Burgerlijk Wetboek, Articles 6:175ff), for defective objects (movables: Burgerlijk Wetboek, Article 6:173; immovables: Burgerlijk Wetboek, Article 6:174) and for the operator of a dump-site (Burgerlijk Wetboek, Article 6:176) or a bore hole (Burgerlijk Wetboek, Article 6:177). Polish law also has comprehensive strict liability provision in the civil code. According to Article 435 of the Polish civil code, the person who runs an undertaking set into motion by natural forces (steam, gas, electricity, liquid fuel etc) is liable for any damage to persons and property caused through the operation of the enterprise or business. In addition,

[25] Hinteregger, 'Comparison' 609.
[26] *Rylands v Fletcher* [1866] LR 1 Ex 265.
[27] French Code Civil, Art 1384.
[28] P Malaurie and L Aynès, *Les Biens* 6th edn (Issy-les-Moulineaux, Lextenso éditions, 2015) 344f.
[29] Law no 83/95 of 31 August 1995, Art 23.

Polish law provides a special no-fault liability for the organisers of mass events[30] and for genetically modified organisms.[31]

Other European countries only provide for sector-specific strict liability rules outside their civil codes. In Austria, Germany and Sweden there are a number of different statutory strict liability rules for specific activities.[32] Germany, Finland and Sweden also have strict liability statutes concerning environmental harm.[33]

Critical Evaluation

This short overview shows clearly that tort law in the European countries is extremely heterogeneous. One has the impression that many liability rules, especially those that provide for strict liability, are created at random as political answers to the occurrence of a specific problem in the relevant state, rather than being the result of a rational and systematic approach to tort law.

This leads to considerable inconsistencies on the national level, but especially in cross-border cases liability suits are risky, with outcomes difficult to predict. This lack of legal certainty may prevent victims of cross-border damage from pursuing their claims. This is quite surprising, considering the fact that the EU is supposed to provide an internal market in which the free movement of goods, services, capital and persons is assured. Victims who are in a strong economic position may also be induced to engage in strategies of forum shopping in order to seek the jurisdiction most favourable to their claim. EU law is not totally reluctant towards forum shopping for tort claims. Victims of cross-border damage enjoy some flexibility in this regard. The Brussels Ia Regulation,[34] which provides for unified rules concerning jurisdiction and enforcement of court decisions, grants the victim of transboundary damage some discretion to choose the place of jurisdiction.[35] The plaintiff has, according to Brussels Ia Regulation, Article 7(2), the choice to sue the defendant 'either in the courts for the place where the damage occurred or in the courts for the place of the event which gives rise

30 Act on mass events 2009, Art 5.

31 Law on Genetically Modified Organisms 2001.

32 Including aeroplanes, cars, trains, genetically modified organisms and nuclear installations. German law also provides strict liability rules for medical products (pharmaceuticals) and environmental harm.

33 Germany: Law on Environmental Liability 1990; Finland: Environmental Damages Act 1994; Sweden: Environmental Code 1999 c 32.

34 Regulation (EU) 1215/2012, [2012] OJ L351/1. The Brussels Ia Regulation is the successor of the Brussels I Regulation (Regulation (EC) 44/2001, [2001] OJ L12/1).

35 See W Posch, 'Some Observations on the Law Applicable to Transfrontier Environmental Damage' in M Hinteregger (ed), *Environmental Liability and Ecological Damage* 33.

to and is at the origin of the damage.'[36] The same applies to the choice of the applicable law in tort law claims concerning environmental damage. The victim of transboundary environmental damage may also choose between the law of the country in which the damage occurs (Rome II-Regulation, Article 4),[37] and the law of the country 'in which the event giving rise to the damage occurred' (Rome II-Regulation, Article 7).

The heterogenous of the national tort law systems in the EU raises the question whether the different concepts of tort law, particularly the antipodes of fault-based liability and no-fault liability, can be brought into a more coherent system; a system which provides, on the one hand, a high degree of legal certainty, yet allows, on the other hand, sufficient flexibility to solve individual cases and to tackle new societal and technological developments. Legal scholarship offers a theory that can help to promote this goal: the Flexible System of Walter Wilburg. This theory was developed in the first half of the twentieth century[38] and has gained international recognition by legal scholars.[39]

In the following section, I will present this theory and frame it in relation to the economic theory of law, which has important insights for the role and the functioning of tort law. For this comparison, one must bear in mind that the economic theory of tort law[40] has a totally different approach to tort law than the legal doctrine. While the legal doctrine deals with issues of justice concerning the overall fairness and consistency of tort law, economic

[36] See Case C-21/76 *Bier v Mines de Potasse d'Alsace* [1976] ECR 1735 (concerning Brussels Convention on jurisdiction and the enforcement of judgments in civil and commercial matters, Art 5(3), (signed 27 September 1968, entered into force 1 February 1973) [1972] OJ L299/32 (Brussels Convention)).

[37] Regulation (EC) 864/2007, [2007] OJ L199/40.

[38] W Wilburg, *Die Elemente des Schadensrechts* (Marburg an der Lahn, Elwert, 1941); W Wilburg *Entwicklung eines beweglichen Systems im bürgerlichen Recht* (Graz, Kienreich, 1950), translated by H Hausmaninger: W Wilburg, *The development of a flexible system in the area of private law* (Vienna, Manz, 2000).

[39] R Westerhoff, *Die Elemente des beweglichen Systems* (Berlin, Duncker & Humblot, 1991); BA Koch, 'Wilburg's Flexible System in a Nutshell' in H Koziol and BC Steininger (eds), *European Tort Law 2001* (Vienna, Springer, 2002) 545; L Hawthorne, 'Walter Wilburg's "flexible-system approach" projected onto the law of contract by means of the European Draft Common Frame of Reference Principles' (2012) 2 *The Comparative and International Law Journal of Southern Africa* 189; M Lothar, *Der allgemeine Gleichheitssatz als Methodennorm komparativer Systeme: methodenrechtliche Analyse und Fortentwicklung der Theorie der "beweglichen Systeme" (Wilburg)* (Berlin, Duncker & Humblot, 1997).

[40] See eg R Coase, 'The Problem of Social Cost' (1960) 3 *Journal of Law and Economics* 1; G Calabresi, *The Costs of Accidents: A Legal and Economic Analysis* (New Haven, Yale University Press, 1970); S Shavell, *Economic Analysis of Accident Law* (Cambridge, Mass, Harvard University Press, 1987); A Endres, *Ökonomische Grundlagen des Haftungsrechts* (Heidelberg, Physica-Verlag, 1991); M Faure (ed), *Tort Law and Economics* (Cheltenham, Edward Elgar, 2009); RA Posner, *Economic Analysis of Law* 8th edn (New York, Wolters Kluwer, 2011); HB Schäfer and C Ott, *Lehrbuch der ökonomischen Analyse des Zivilrechts* 5th edn (Berlin, Springer, 2012).

theory questions the economic efficiency of the various tort law concepts and instruments. For the economic theory, law is not an instrument to promote justice but an instrument to maximise social welfare. The role of tort law, therefore, lies primarily in the achievement of economic efficiency. According to this theory, the goal of tort law is the minimisation of the total costs of accidents, comprising both the cost of prevention and remediation. An effective system of tort liability must avoid the externalisation of costs. It must therefore ensure that each economic actor takes all the potential costs of his activity into account when performing the activity. Only then will he be induced to conduct a correct cost-benefit-analysis and avoid an activity that is not worth its costs.

THE THEORY OF THE FLEXIBLE SYSTEM AND THE ECONOMIC THEORY OF TORT LAW

The Flexible System

Walter Wilburg, an Austrian law professor based in Graz, developed his theory in order to overcome the confrontation between the rigid traditional order in private law and the increasing tendency towards free decision-making he especially perceived in the field of tort law. Wilburg's main criticism was that the civil law countries provide for the fault principle in their traditional civil codes, but, at the same time, undermine this principle by making numerous exceptions to it. Such exceptions are provided by statutory laws or often by the courts when they see that the fault principle is not appropriate to reach a fair solution in a specific case.

Wilburg thus felt the need for more consistency and flexibility in this regard. As a result of his studies in comparative law he came to the conclusion that the law of damages cannot be based on one idea alone, but must be seen as the interplay of specific aspects. Wilburg found that there are four fundamental aspects for the attribution of liability: (i) a deficiency on the part of the person causing the damage; (ii) a risk created by the person causing the damage through an enterprise or the possession of an object; (iii) the proximity of the causal connection between the causes creating liability and the damage; and (iv) the social balancing of the assets of the victim and those of the person causing the damage. According to Wilburg, all four aspects constitute the elements of private liability law and form the basis of every liability rule. The four elements are not rigid and absolute, but liability is the result of their specific combination and intensity. Accordingly, special intensity of one element alone may suffice to justify liability for damage, but liability may also result from the concurrence of all four elements when occurring only in a weak form.

In order to reach a just decision, the existence and the weight of these four elements must also be assessed with respect to the injured person. These elements have the power to justify liability but, if they burden the harmed person, they may also justify exonerating the tortfeasor. Every liability decision is the result of a comprehensive assessment of the liability elements for both the tortfeasor and the injured person and may, accordingly, lead to full compensation (if they burden only the injurer) or partial compensation (if they burden both parties) or to no compensation at all (if they burden only the harmed person).

The Flexible System allows for a consistent systematisation of tort law. Its main focus is the justification of tort law rules. The perception that the abundance of existing tort law rules can be reduced to four basic principles, and explained as the interplay of these principles, is an important step to rationalise tort law. It has several merits: It helps legal scholarship to describe and analyse an existing tort law system in order to assess the fairness and consistency of the system; it provides legislators with a tool to develop coherent value-orientated solutions for new liability rules; and it gives courts a reliable framework of reference for the allocation of liability in individual cases.

The Flexible System and Economic Analysis of Tort Law: Common Insights and Divergencies

Tort Law as a Consistent System

According to the Flexible System, fault-based liability and no-fault liability are not different liability concepts that exist side by side, but are part of one comprehensive system. The traditional view of the dichotomy of fault-based liability and no-fault liability is replaced by a comprehensive understanding of tort law as a consistent system based on the four elements. In the following paragraphs these elements are further explored and then described in relation to some of the basic findings of the economic theory of law.

The Flexible System tries to explain the tort law system as the interplay of the four elements (deficiency, risk, proximate cause and social balancing). These elements reflect basic concepts that are more or less provided by all national tort law systems. The element of deficiency on the part of the injurer covers all types of fault in a graduated row from intention over gross negligence, light negligence down to the mere defect. The element of risk created by the person causing the damage through an enterprise or the possession of an object is, in most European countries, an important notion for the attribution of strict liability. Many of the existing national liability systems can be categorised according to the level of risk an activity creates, with fault-based liability on the one side and strict liability on the other side.

The element of proximity of the causal connection covers all the considerations in tort law theory to limit liability despite established causation, such as adequacy or the protective scope of the norm or all those restrictions regarding the compensation of pure economic loss provided by the Germanic jurisdictions and the common law. The fourth element, the element of social balancing, is least addressed in legal theory. This is somewhat surprising given that one of the main functions of tort law is to ensure that the victims of a tortious act receive economic restitution.[41] The element of social balancing addresses this compensatory function of tort law and, as will be shown, also plays an important role for the justification of strict liability.

The Flexible System assumes that these four elements stand not in sharp contrast to each other but complement each other. A graduated system according to the Flexible System could, in broad terms, look like this: fault liability for low-risk cases (eg risk of private persons in everyday life); fault liability with reversal of the burden of proof for fault for higher-risk situations (eg risk of animals or buildings); fault liability with reversal of the burden of proof and comprehensive vicarious liability (eg activities that have specific typical risks); strict liability with certain exonerations for dangerous activities (eg traffic or aeroplane accidents); and strict liability without exonerations and combined with compulsory insurance coverage for ultra-hazardous activities (eg the operation of nuclear power plants).

How this graduation is achieved is, of course, a political decision. In the civil law systems, it is primarily the legislator who must set the cornerstones for such a coherent system, but even in the civil law systems much leeway is given to the courts. Courts must decide on the interpretation and application of the general liability rules that have a high degree of abstraction. If necessary, courts must fill the lacunae left by the legislator. In a tort law system that has clear and consistent valuations, courts are in a much better position to fulfil this task. If courts can rely on consistent valuations by the legislator it is also easier for them to react adequately to situations not foreseen by the legislator and to the occurrence of new risks. In common law countries, it would mainly be up to the courts to provide for such consistency in the system.

The insight that the notion of fault is closely connected to the notion of risk is also gained by the economic theory of tort law. Contrary to traditional tort law theory, where fault is a matter of the blameworthiness of the liable person, economic theory sees fault as a purely objective criterion for the attribution of liability. This understanding of fault thus corresponds to

[41] H Koziol, *Basic Questions of Tort Law from a Germanic Perspective* (Salter Townshend Fiona tr, Vienna, Jan Sramek, 2012) 75ff; G Wagner, 'Schadenersatz—Zwecke, Inhalte Grenzen' in E Lorenz (ed), *Karlsruher Forum 2006: Schadenersatz—Zwecke, Inhalte, Grenzen* (Karlsruhe, Verlag Versicherungswirtschaft, 2006) 5; A Tunc (ed), *International Encyclopedia of Comparative Law XI. Torts I* (Mohr, Mouton, Oceana Publications, 1983) para I-164ff.

the notion of unlawfulness in the Germanic tort law doctrine or the purely objective understanding of fault more and more applied in the Romanistic jurisdictions.

In economic theory, the criterion of fault is fulfilled when the injurer does not exercise the optimal level of care. This optimal level of care is defined according to the Learned Hand formula,[42] which provides that an injurer is liable for the victim's damage when the cost of precaution is less than the cost of the expected damage. The term 'expected damage' consists of the amount of the expected loss multiplied by the probability that the loss will occur. In order to define the optimal level of care, this cost-benefit-analysis must relate to marginal cost, as the injurer will only be obliged to take care up to the point where the cost of care becomes equal to or greater that the expected cost of the injury.

The application of the Learned Hand formula leads to a very flexible concept of due level of care, because the due level of care corresponds directly with the expected damage (the amount of the loss multiplied by the probability) and increases with the expected damage. The higher the expected damage, the higher are the costs of precaution the injurer must apply in order to evade liability.

This direct relationship between the level of care and the expected damage leads, however, to the understanding that fault liability can cover all sorts of risk, ranging from the risk of the private person in everyday life to the risk of ultra-hazardous activities. Such an understanding of fault liability does not need a separate concept of strict liability. It is thus not surprising that, for most representatives of the economic theory, the difference between fault liability and no-fault liability lies only in the fact that, under strict liability, the injurer must always compensate the victim, regardless of the extent of his precaution, while under fault-based liability the injurer is only liable for the victim's loss when he violated the socially optimal level of care. For the economic theory, the difference between fault and no-fault liability culminates mainly in the insight that strict liability also affects the injurer's level of activity, because the injurer is forced to internalise the total amount of damage costs (including those not worth preventing from an economic point of view). Strict liability thus may be used to reduce the injurer's level of activity to the socially optimal level.[43]

This economic concept of strict liability, however, does not reflect the legal concept of strict liability. In legal theory, strict liability is not just liability without fault, but a special concept to cope with specific risks. The

[42] Developed by Judge Learned Hand in *United States v Carroll Towing Co* 159 F 2d 169 (2d Cir 1947); see Posner, *Econimic Analysis of Law* 191ff; Schäfer and Ott, *Lehrbuch der ökonomischen Analyse des Zivilrechts* 182f.

[43] See Posner, *Economic Analysis of Law* 205ff; Schäfer and Ott, *Lehrbuch der ökonomischen Analyse des Zivilrechts* 234ff.

decision to put an activity under strict liability is not merely the decision to allocate damage costs unconditionally to an individual who caused harm to another, but the result of a complex assessment. This assessment comprises the following deliberations: (i) the economic argument to burden the person who is in the best position to control the risk; (ii) the moral argument that the person who benefits from the activity shall also bear the costs of this activity; and (iii) the social argument of loss distribution. In economic theory, it is only Calabresi who has a comparable broad understanding of strict liability.[44]

The Justification of Strict Liability

According to legal theory, one of the main arguments for the allocation of liability is the ability of a person, natural or legal, to control the risk of an activity. This applies technically both to fault and no-fault liability. In everyday life, it is the individual person who is in control of his or her acts. That a person is at fault means essentially that the person inflicted harm on another person, despite being mentally and factually able to prevent the harm. For such scenarios, fault-based liability is an adequate solution and, if the assessment of fault is made according to economic standards (in the sense of the Learned Hand-formula), fault liability can also achieve, or at least promote, the overall goal of economic efficiency.

When things become more complex it is not the individual exercising the act (eg the worker on the machine) who is in the best position to control the risk, but, for instance, the principal who gave the orders or organised the sub-optimal operational process. It is a common view in most national tort laws that it makes much more sense to hold principals liable than common workers. This is a matter of risk control and thus of economic efficiency, as well as the consequence of the moral consideration that it is the principal who takes the profits from the worker's activity and the consequence of the social insight that rather the principal than the worker can bear the loss or provide beforehand for insurance coverage. These deliberations, which justify vicarious liability, apply even more to the operator of dangerous activities. If tort law can serve the goal of damage prevention, it is best to allocate liability to the person who is in the best position to control the risk of the activity. This is the person who has sufficient information on the riskiness of the activity and who is able to take effective measures to reduce the risk of the activity (cheapest cost avoider). From an economic point of view, liability hence must be allocated to the operator of the dangerous activity.

[44] G Calabresi, 'Optimal Deterrence and Accidents' (1975) 84 *Yale Law Journal* 656; Calabresi, *The Costs of Accidents*.

For the attribution of liability to the operator of the dangerous activity, two further policy considerations apply. One consideration, usually used by legal doctrine to justify the attribution of strict liability to the operator of risky activities, is the fundamental notion of distributive justice that it is fair to place the liability burden with the person who performs a risky activity in his own interest and to his own benefit. The second consideration refers to the ability of the liable person to spread the loss. This consideration is emphasised both by legal doctrine and economic theory of law alike, because it is neither sensible nor economically efficient to allocate liability to a person who cannot bear the loss. Such a rule would soon be challenged under aspects of social justice and would lead to externalisation of costs and thus lack preventive effect. The effect of loss spreading on prevention is, however, ambiguous, because loss spreading allows the operator of the dangerous activity to externalise costs. Loss spreading hence reduces the preventive effect of liability. As a consequence, effective liability rules must pursue both aims. They must, on the one hand, allocate damage costs as far as possible to the cheapest cost avoider and, on the other, provide for adequate loss spreading in order to make damage costs financially bearable.

With respect to both goals, strict liability of the operator of a dangerous activity is a sensible option. The operator of a dangerous activity who is apparently the cheapest cost avoider with respect to the risks of the activity, also has some ability for loss spreading, since enterprises can pass their liability costs on to their customers and suppliers as far as competition allows.

From a theoretical point of view, strict liability of the operator of an activity that is prone to cause catastrophic harm must be combined with mandatory third party liability insurance. This traditional instrument of loss management ensures the protection of victims by providing secured funds for their compensation and, due to the expertise of insurance companies in this field, it guarantees effective loss settlement. Third party liability insurance also has important effects on the allocation of damage cost. Insurance provides for loss spreading, both temporally by making the insured person pay insurance premiums in order to provide for a possible future loss, and interpersonally by spreading the loss to the collective of insured persons to which the liable person belongs.[45]

[45] See A Endres and R Schwarze, 'Allokationswirkungen einer Umwelthaftpflicht-Versicherung' in A Endres, E Rehbinder and R Schwarze (eds), *Haftung und Versicherung für Umweltschäden aus ökonomischer und juristischer Sicht* (Vienna, Springer, 1992) 58; M Gimpel-Hinteregger, *Theoretische Grundfragen der Umwelthaftung* (Vienna, Manz, 1994) 70ff; G Wagner, 'Versicherungsfragen der Umwelthaftung' in M Ahrens and J Simon (eds), *Umwelthaftung, Risikosteuerung und Versicherung* (Berlin, Schmidt, 1996) 97; MG Faure (ed), *Deterrence, Insurability, and Compensation in Environmental Liability* (Vienna, Springer, 2003) 180ff; M Hinteregger, 'Die Pflichthaftpflichtversicherung im Schadensrecht' in P Jabornegg, F Kerschner and A Riedler, *Haftung und Versicherung: Festschrift für Rudolf Reischauer* (Vienna, Verlag Österreich, 2010) 507ff.

For the victim, strict liability has further advantages. It eases the victim's burden of proof because there is no need to establish fault. As the operator of the activity is comprehensively liable for his employees and agents, the victim need not show vicarious liability either. The second reason, mainly argued by the economic theory of law, is that in cases of technological disasters strict liability can achieve a better internalisation of the cost of the activity than fault-based liability, as the occurrence of damage depends on the operator's rather than the victim's activity level. A further positive effect of strict liability is the fact that strict liability gives the defendant less incentive to cover up mistakes than fault-based liability. If the liability rule does not allow the defendant to escape liability by proving that he could not have known about the danger of his activity by using the scientific or technical knowledge available at the time when the damage was caused, the so called 'state of the art-defence', it will give the operator of a dangerous activity rather an incentive to invest in research in order to reduce his potential liability cost.[46]

CRITICAL ANALYSIS AND CONCLUSIONS

The status quo of tort liability in Europe is quite complex. Tort liability differs from country to country and its rules are closely linked to the legal traditions of the states that belong to three different legal families of private law, the common law, the Romanistic and the Germanic legal family. This already diverse pattern is supplemented by the Middle and Eastern European Reform countries, which, after the fall of the Iron Curtain that separated Eastern Europe from the West, underwent comprehensive tort law reforms. As the heterogeneity of the tort laws in Europe can cause lack of certainty in cross border cases, the EU provides for some harmonisation in this regard. It has enacted harmonised and unified liability rules with respect to jurisdiction and enforcement of court decisions according to the Brussels Ia Regulation and with respect to the choice of the applicable law by way of the Rome II Regulation. Tort law itself, however, has been rather unaffected by the harmonisation efforts of the EU. Harmonisation results comprise primarily product liability and the liability of the air and sea carriers towards passengers. It is quite surprising that the EU has still not taken action to harmonise nuclear liability despite the devastating cross-border risks of nuclear

[46] See G Calabresi, 'Concerning Cause and the Law of Torts' (1975) 43 *University of Chicago Law Review* 69, 88; G Calabresi and AK Klevorick, 'Four Tests for Liability in Torts' (1985) 14 *Journal of Legal Studies* 585, 616 and 621ff; S Shavell, 'Liability and the Incentive to Obtain Information about Risk' (1992) 21 *Journal of Legal Studies* 259; S Panther, *Haftung als Instrument einer präventiven Umweltpolitik* (Frankfurt am Main, Campus-Verlag, 1992) 108ff; Gimpel-Hinteregger, *Umwelthaftung* 80ff.

incidents. Like a remembrance of the former Iron Curtain, Europe is still divided into the western Paris-Brussels nuclear regime and the regime of the Vienna Convention which, with the exception of Slovenia, still applies to the Eastern European Reform countries. Both regimes were established with the intention of protecting the nuclear industry from tort liability and do not provide sufficient protection for victims of nuclear damage.

Tort law is a very flexible legal instrument. Although based on rather general and abstract rules, it provides a very high degree of legal certainty. This is achieved by the courts who decide upon the application of tort liability to the individual cases and thus make it predictable for legal practice. This applies to common law and civil law alike, because even in the civil law countries legislation does not give much guidance to the courts on this issue. Among all tort law instruments, it is fault-based liability that reaches the highest degree of flexibility. It covers all types of activities, all degrees of risks and all types of harm. As is shown both by tort law doctrine and the economic theory of law, it is also very flexible in its application, as the assessment of fault adjusts to the level of risk an activity creates to others.

Fault is, however, not the sole element for the attribution of liability. Tort law is a much broader concept that includes many other deliberations. Wilburg reduced these deliberations to four elements (deficiency, risk, proximate cause and social balancing) and suggested that tort law can be described and graduated according to the occurrence and interplay of these four elements. The graduation starts with simple fault-based liability for the risk of private persons in everyday life and ends with strict liability plus compulsory insurance coverage for ultra-hazardous activities, such as the operation of nuclear power plants. When establishing such a consistent system of tort law one must bear in mind that, according to legal doctrine, strict liability is not just liability without fault, as the economic theory of law sometimes suggests, but the result of a complex assessment of three arguments, namely to burden the person with liability: (i) who is in the best position to control the risk (an economic argument); (ii) who benefits from the activity (a moral argument); and (iii) who can distribute the loss (a social argument). Such a systematic approach to tort law enables legal scholarship to describe and analyse an existing tort law system in order to assess the fairness and consistency of the system. Moreover, it provides legislators, on a national level as well as on EU level, with a tool to develop coherent value-orientated solutions for law reform in the field of tort law.

Part II

Comparative Perspectives

5

Comparative Legal Certainty: Legal Families and Forms of Measurement

MATHIAS SIEMS

INTRODUCTION

CROSS-COUNTRY COMPARISONS of legal certainty are *en vogue* today. Court decisions in Europe frequently refer to the concept of legal certainty, drawing on the experiences from the Member States.[1] The comparison of legal certainty has recently also become the subject of a research initiative, the 'Civil Law Initiative', which aims to show the virtues of systematically codified legal systems. Specifically, this initiative has suggested an Index of Legal Certainty that attempts to measure how well legal systems perform against this benchmark.[2]

But the debate is not an entirely new one. The perhaps earliest comparative statement about legal certainty is from 1827, in a book review of the life of Napoleon (as well as the Napoleonic codes), suggesting that:

> The reader will smile at the expression 'certainty of English law'; it seems a solecism in language, a contradiction in very terms. It is as if one were to talk of the immutability of the English climate, the liveliness of the English character, the discretion of youth, the wisdom of country justices; or the certainty of the lottery.[3]

This position of a common law disadvantage in legal certainty is also widespread today. However, it is also possible to suggest a converging position, as will be discussed in this chapter.

In addition, at least, there is also some common ground as far as the meaning of 'legal certainty' is concerned. The report accompanying the Legal Certainty Index states that legal certainty 'implies that laws should

[1] See the references in nn 6, 27 and 28 below.

[2] B Deffains and C Kessedjian (eds), 'Index of Legal Certainty. Report for the Civil Law Initiative' (2015), available at www.fondation-droitcontinental.org/en/index-legal-certainty/.

[3] NN, 'Certainty of English Law. *The Life of Napoleon Bonaparte, Emperor of the French.* By the Author of Waverley. Edinburgh, 1827 (Vol 6)' (1827) 1 Quarterly Journal of Jurisprudence and Legislation 405 at 405–406.

be at least accessible, intelligible and stable and have predictable effects'.[4] In a decision by the House of Lords, we find the phrase that 'a citizen, before committing himself to any course of action, should be able to know in advance what are the legal consequences that will flow from it';[5] and very similar, according to the European Court of Justice, 'rules should be clear and precise, so that individuals may be able to ascertain unequivocally what their rights and obligations are and may take steps accordingly'.[6]

The structure of the comparative analysis of this chapter will be as follows: to set the scene, the next section outlines why scholarship and practice are interested in country differences in legal certainty as means to explain differences in development. The subsequent sections then turn from the normative to the positive dimension, namely the question how far there are country differences in legal certainty. It starts with the traditional view of a civil law advantage over the common law. The subsequent section deals with the challenges to the traditional view. The penultimate section discusses the quantitative research on this topic, followed by a conclusion.

BACKGROUND: WHY ARE SCHOLARSHIP AND PRACTICE INTERESTED IN COUNTRY DIFFERENCES IN LEGAL CERTAINTY?

It is often suggested that legal differences between countries are one factor that may explain differences in economic prosperity.[7] As far as law is indeed relevant, there is also some support for the position that it is not only the substantive orientation of legal rules but the provision of legal certainty that can be advantageous.

A prominent early proponent of this view is Max Weber. Weber developed a typology of socio-legal systems, distinguishing between two dimensions: on the one hand, formal and substantive (or informal), and, on the other hand, rational and irrational.[8] He saw it as damaging for a society to be

[4] Deffains and Kessedjian (eds), 'Index of Legal Certainty' 9.

[5] *Black-Clawson International Ltd v Papierwerke Waldhof-Aschaffenburg AG* [1975] AC 591 at 638 (HL) per Lord Diplock.

[6] Case C-110/03 *Belgium v Commission* [2005] ECLI:EU:C:2005:223 para 30 with references to further cases. See also J Raitio, *The Principle of Legal Certainty in EC Law* (Dordrecht, Kluwer, 2003); J Van Meerbeck, 'The Principle of Legal Certainty in the Case Law of the European Court of Justice: From Certainty to Trust' (2016) 41 *European Law Review* 275.

[7] Economists often phrase this as showing the importance of 'institutions', see, eg D Acemoglu, S Johnson and JA Robinson, 'Institutions as Long Run Causes of Economic Growth' in P Aghion and SN Durlauf (eds), *Handbook of Economic Growth, vol IA* 385 (Amsterdam, Elsevier, 2005); D Rodrik, A Subramanian and F Trebbi, 'Institutions Rule: The Primacy of Institutions over Geography and Integration in Economic Development' (2004) 9 *Journal of Economic Growth* 131.

[8] The main work is M Weber *Economy and Society* (Berkeley, University of California Press, 1978) (original from 1922).

based on irrationality, be it that it is formal—for example, using oracles—or that it is informal—for example, deciding conflicts in an arbitrary way. With respect to rational regimes, Weber preferred the formality of rules to the informality of principles, values and traditions. This is frequently regarded as an endorsement of the importance of legal certainty, notably the need for 'calculability of economic action.'[9]

Since the 1960s, the movements of 'law and development' have also incorporated 'legal certainty' as one of their policy recommendations. Three examples can be provided: first, policies promoting the 'rule of law' for economic development are relevant in this context. While the precise definition of the rule of law (narrow-formal or wide-substantive) is controversial, it is accepted that it includes core elements of 'legal certainty', such as the need for clear and predictable laws.[10] It is also frequently acknowledged that there is a correlation between the performance of countries in compliance with the 'rule of law' and economic development.[11]

Second, as far as 'law and development' refers to the substance of rules, it is also possible to deduce that those should reflect the need for legal certainty. For example, the Peruvian economist Hernando de Soto emphasises that economic development depends on formal protection of property since informality tends to foster corruption and inefficiencies.[12] Similarly, the line of research associated with 'law and finance' recommends that countries adopt certain rules to stimulate investment, for example as regards shareholder protection in company law: thus, here too, the formality of those legal norms—and not the use of informal substitutes—is seen as crucial for development.[13]

Third, specific examples can be provided to show that a country benefits from a legal system that provides legal certainty. For instance, Singapore is often seen as an example of a well-functioning and secure legal system.[14] Similarly, a general study on the role of law in Asian economic development between 1960 and 1995 found that legal institutions mattered in order to

[9] N Chowdhury, *European Regulation of Medical Devices and Pharmaceuticals: Regualtee Expectations of Legal Certainty* (Cham, Springer 2014) 56.

[10] For a summary of the debate see M Siems, *Comparative Law* (Cambridge, Cambridge University Press, 2014) 265–69.

[11] See S Haggard, A MacIntyre and L Tiede, 'The Rule of Law and Economic Development' (2008) 11 *Annual Review of Political Science* 205.

[12] See, eg H de Soto, *The Other Path: The Invisible Revolution in the Third World* (New York, Harper and Row, 1989); H de Soto, *The Mystery of Capital: Why Capitalism Triumphs in the West and Fails Everywhere Else* (New York, Basic Books, 2000).

[13] For a critical review see M Siems and S Deakin, 'Comparative Law and Finance: Past, Present and Future Research' (2010) 166 *Journal of Institutional and Theoretical Economics* 120.

[14] See A Harding and C Carter, 'The Singapore Model of Law and Development: Cutting Through Complexity' in J Hatchard and A Perry-Kessaris (eds), *Law and Development: Facing Complexity in the 21st Century* (London, Cavendish, 2003) 191.

achieve the respective economic policies these countries were trying to pursue.[15] It is also possible to argue that China's economic growth of the recent decades was at least correlated with a growing emphasis on formal legal rules so as to provide a secure investment climate.[16]

The comparative and normative case for legal certainty already points towards some country differences. The more general positive debate goes further, however, often arguing that there is a civil law advantage over the common law.

TRADITIONAL VIEW: THE CIVIL LAW ADVANTAGE OVER THE COMMON LAW

While legal certainty is, traditionally, seen as a concept alien to the common law,[17] it is frequently used in the civil law tradition, to be precise under corresponding terms such as *sécurité juridique* in French, *Rechtssicherheit* in German and *Rechtszekerheid* in Dutch.[18] The main argument is that this is due to the use of codified law. A brochure by professional associations of French and German lawyers explains this—alleged—advantage as follows:

> Continental law is characterized by statutes and codification. Codification is the systematic and rational collection of rules of law into official compilations, such as civil or commercial codes. Far from being rigid, this ordered compilation, on the contrary, facilitates modernizing the law as needed. Because of such codification, continental law is accessible. It is easy to comprehend: by reading the codes, any person, whether an entrepreneur or a consumer, can learn the rules of law that apply to him. It is also easy to understand because each rule is formulated in simple and general terms. The legal certainty that ensues is a major advantage for citizens, enabling them to anticipate the outcome of litigation and to assess the financial risks of legal action.
>
> In common law countries, the search for the applicable law often requires consulting a long series of court decisions in order to find an appropriate precedent—if one even exists. Understanding all of these court decisions is often difficult for non-lawyers, who therefore must rely on professional legal advisers. The need for such legal assistance greatly increases the costs for those seeking to enforce their rights.[19]

[15] K Pistor and PA Wellons, *The Role of Law and Legal Institutions in Asian Economic Development, 1960–1995* (Oxford, Oxford University Press, 1999).

[16] For further discussion, see Siems, *Comparative Law* 269–71.

[17] See the quote accompanying above n 3.

[18] See, eg T Piazzon, *La sécurité juridique* (Paris, Defrénois, 2009); A von Arnauld, *Rechtssicherheit: Perspektivische Annäherungen an eine idée directrice des Rechts* (Tübingen, Mohr Siebeck, 2006); P Popelier, *Rechtszekerheid als Beginsel van Behoorlijke Regelgeving* (Antwerp, Intersentia, 1997). For many references to the literature see the bibliography of the Deffains and Kessedjian (eds), 'Index of Legal Certainty' 145–61.

[19] Civil Law Initiative, 'Continental law: global, predictable, flexible, cost-effective' (2011), available at www.kontinentalesrecht.de.

In addition, the application of these laws is said to happen in a rational and predictable manner.[20] The typical explanation is that civil law lawyers and judges do not 'simply' reason by analogy with previous cases, but apply deductive reasoning based on syllogism: first, identifying the legal rule and how it should be interpreted; second, subsuming the facts within these legal rules; and, third, applying the consequence of the legal rule.[21] As a result, applying the law becomes something almost mechanical: as famously described by Roscoe Pound, in continental law, the court is 'a sort of judicial slot machine. The necessary machinery had been provided in advance by legislation or by received legal principles and one had but to put in the facts above and take out the decision below'.[22]

As to the role of courts, in civil law countries, previous decisions may be considered in the course of the court's reasoning. However, here too, it may foster legal certainty that the emphasis is on whether there is a clear and consistent judicial practice, for instance, called *jurisprudence constante* in France and *ständige Rechtsprechung* in Germany.[23] It can also be regarded as advantageous that, usually, no dissenting judgments are published, as those may create ambiguity as to the delivered opinion of the court.[24]

A final point to mention in support of a civil law advantage in legal certainty is the role it plays as a specific doctrinal concept. For example, the report accompanying the Legal Certainty Index explains that, in the common law world, law and legal certainty may often be perceived as a mere means to promote economic development, while in the civil law world the legal system 'has an inherent value' and legal certainty is seen an 'end in itself'.[25] Methodologically, this 'transformation of the principle of legal certainty into a legal tool' can be deduced from constitutional principles of the rule of law and human rights.[26] It has frequently been used by courts in civil

[20] J Bell, *Judiciaries within Europe: A Comparative Review* (Cambridge, Cambridge University Press, 2006) 144 and 170 (for Germany).

[21] See K Crawford, 'The Paradoxical Relationship between Econometric Effectiveness and Legal Certainty' (2011) *Research in Law & Political Economy. Research Paper No 5/2011* 5–6, available at digitalcommons.osgoode.yorku.ca/clpe/43; JR Maxeiner et al, *Practical Global Civil Procedure: United States-Germany-Korea* (Durham/NC, Carolina Academic Press, 2010) 33 and 241.

[22] R Pound, *The Spirit of the Common Law* (Boston, Marshall Jones Pound, 1921) 170–71.

[23] See A Portuese, O Gough and J Tanega, 'The Principle of Legal Certainty as a Principle of Economic Efficiency' *European Journal of Law and Economics* forthcoming (early view available at https://dx.doi.org/10.1007/s10657-014-9435-2) at 1.1; Siems, *Comparative Law* 58.

[24] I MacNeil, 'Uncertainty in Commercial Law' (2009) 13 *Edinburgh Law Review* 68, 79 (suggesting to examine dissenting judgments as a test for uncertainty).

[25] Deffains and Kessedjian (eds), 'Index of Legal Certainty' 8 at fn 22.

[26] P Popelier, 'Five Paradoxes on Legal Certainty and the Lawmaker' (2008) 2 *Legisprudence* 47; P Popelier, 'Legal Certainty and Principles of Proper Law Making' (2000) 2 *European Journal of Law Reform* 321, 325–26.

law countries.[27] Based on this civilian approach, it has also been recognised as a general legal principle by both the European Court of Justice and the European Court of Human Rights.[28]

CHALLENGES TO THE TRADITIONAL VIEW

The traditional position is, however, open to a number of counter-arguments. The following starts with the challenge that the alleged civil/common law divide in legal certainty fails to account for varieties within legal families. More fundamentally, it may be said that there could be a common law advantage in legal certainty. Finally, this section discusses challenges due to the general tension between certainty and adaptability and due to convergence in legal (un-)certainty.

Varieties within Legal Families

The previous section indicated that the civil law is sometimes said to have an advantage in legal certainty since its codified laws are easy to understand for its citizens. This aspiration is often explicitly mentioned for the French Civil Code (and much the same applies to the other French Codes): it aims to 'help the layman to understand the law'[29] and the Code followed the precept that it 'should be simple and clear, like the laws of nature'.[30]

However, it may be doubted whether, in reality today, 'just' reading the Civil Code is much help for French citizens who want to find out about their rights and duties in private law. While the language of the Code is clear, it also expresses the law in such a condensed style that in more complex scenarios readers who are not trained in law are unlikely to understand how those would be solved. In addition, as the French Civil Code derives from the year 1804, it contains various phrases and formulations which may not be fully clear to today's readers.

Comparing the French Code Civil with its counterpart in other civil law countries, it deserves an intermediate classification. On the one hand, some

[27] Notably, in Germany, see references in BVerfG (German Federal Constitutional Court) NJW 2013, 2103 para 34, going back to the 1950s. In France, the Conseil d'Etat (Council of State) accepted the principle in the KPMG-judgment, 24 March 2006, no 288460 Rec.

[28] For the CJEU see above n 6; the first case of the ECtHR was *Marckx v Belgique* Series A no 31 (1979) ECLI:CE:ECHR:1979:0613JUD000683374.

[29] JF Gerkens, 'Legal Certainty v Legal Precision: Some Thoughts on Comparative Law' (2010) 16 *Fundamina* 121, 123.

[30] P Sagnac, *La législation civile de la révolution française (1789–1804)* (Paris, Hachette, 1898) 385 ('Le Code civil doit être simple et clair, comme les lois de la nature. Il faut le réduire à un petit nombre d'articles qui découlent logiquement des principes généraux...').

more recent codes may be more easily understood by the common public. The Swiss Civil Code from 1912 is frequently seen as an example of such a 'popular' approach to legislative drafting.[31] On the other hand, the German Civil Code from 1900 is often described as 'professorial'. The main aspiration of the Code was to accurately reflect the complexities of the received Roman law. Thus, it did not have the aim to be readable for lay persons. Rather, the main audience is members of the legal profession who—following an extensive black-letter legal education—have learned to apply these rules in a precise manner.[32]

Turning to the common law, a frequent position is that the US is different from other common law countries. It is possible to argue that US law may be more certain: the codification of US law is extensive, with more statute laws than in many civil law countries. With respect to the interpretation of law, a prominent feature of the US debate is the—contentious—view of a textual interpretation of the US constitution, which, ideally, 'allows people to better predict the consequences of their actions'.[33]

However, it is more plausible to regard US law as putting less emphasis on legal certainty than other common law countries. This position can refer to specific features of US law. For example, while in the common law tradition the doctrine of binding precedents can foster legal certainty (see also the next section), it is said that in the US its importance should not be overemphasised and that it provides judges considerable freedom in legal reasoning.[34] In private international law, the US approach is different from that of most other countries as it does not pursue the goal of policy-neutral legal certainty but uses unilateral rules based on its own domestic interests.[35]

More importantly, it is possible to highlight that US legal thinking is widely dismissive of legal formalism in general and legal certainty in particular. From a legal realist perspective, it is argued that legal certainty is a 'myth' while 'legal indeterminacy' is unavoidable.[36] While legal realism—which peaked in the mid-twentieth century—has now been succeeded by approaches such as law and society, law and economics, and empirical legal

[31] Gerkens, 'Legal Certainty v Legal Precision' 126.

[32] ibid. For a similar assessment of Swiss and German civil law: K Zweigert and H Kötz, *An Introduction to Comparative Law* 3rd edn (Oxford, Clarendon, 1998) 171–77.

[33] O Raban, 'The Fallacy of Legal Certainty: Why Vague Legal Standards May be Better for Capitalism and Liberalism' (2010) 19 *Public Interest Law Journal* 175, 179.

[34] See E Hondius 'Precedent and the Law' (2007) 11(3) *Electronic Journal of Comparative Law*.

[35] See, eg Siems, *Comparative Law* 227.

[36] J Paul, 'Jerome Frank's Attack on the "Myth" of Legal Certainty' (1957) *Nebraska Law Review* 547 referring to J Frank, *Law and the Modern Mind* 4 (New York, Brentano's, 1930) 46; JR Maxeiner, 'Legal Certainty and Legal Methods: A European Alternative to American Legal Indeterminacy?' (2007) 15 *Tulane Journal of International and Comparative Law* 541. See also the discussion in Chapter 7 below, by John Linarelli.

studies, the interdisciplinarity of US legal thinking continues to lead to a distinctive non-formalist approach.[37]

Finally, it is possible to identify many further variations within legal families. Four examples will be provided. First, as 'clear and determinate legal rules' can be linked to free societies,[38] it can be said that liberal societies are likely to be better able to provide legal certainty than illiberal ones. Second, political instability can influence the need for legal certainty, as it may plausibly be argued that in times of crisis citizens have stronger desires for legal certainty than in more stable periods.[39] Third, research in psychology has found that national attitudes are diverse across the world with implications for the amount of law, and by implication the importance of legal certainty. For example, it can be observed that countries with a higher degree of 'uncertainty avoidance' have more laws than others[40] and that countries with a lower degree of trust in other people have more demand for and higher levels of regulation.[41] Fourth, the literature has discussed problems of inter-lingual uncertainty in countries with multiple official languages:[42] thus, there are likely to be differences between such countries and those with a single official language.

Possibility of a Common Law Advantage

Opposing the traditional position, another line of reasoning argues that it is actually common law countries who have an advantage in legal certainty. This counterview is most apparent in two quotes from the 'Jurisdiction of Choice' brochure of the Law Society of England and Wales:

> In ever more complex, sophisticated and inter-related markets, English commercial law provides predictability of outcome, legal certainty and fairness. It is clear and is built upon well-founded principles ... English law gives guidance on almost every issue. Parties (especially commercial parties) can predict, with greater certainty than in many civil law systems, whether a proposed course of action is likely to be lawful or unlawful.[43]

[37] For the debate about 'US exceptionalism' see Siems, *Comparative Law* 65–68.

[38] Raban, 'The Fallacy of Legal Certainty' 178 (with reference to Hayek).

[39] S Ranchordás, 'Sunset Clauses and Experimental Regulations: Blessing or Curse for Legal Certainty?' (2015) 36 *Statute Law Review* 28, 37.

[40] A Perry-Kessaris, 'The Relationship between Legal Systems and Economic Development: Integrating Economic and Cultural Approaches' (2002) 29 *Journal of Law and Society* 282, 294–95.

[41] P Pinotti, 'Trust, Regulation and Market Failures' (2012) 94 *The Review of Economics and Statistics* 650; P Aghion et al, 'Regulation and Distrust' (2010) 125 *Quarterly Journal of Economics* 1015.

[42] D Cao, 'Inter-Lingual Uncertainty in Bilingual and Multilingual Law' (2007) 39 *Journal of Pragmatics* 69.

[43] Law Society of England and Wales, 'England and Wales: The jurisdiction of choice', available at www.eversheds.com/documents/LawSocietyEnglandAndWalesJurisdictionOfChoice.pdf at pp 5, 8.

Specific aspects of the common law may support this position. For example, as far as there is statute law, the traditional preference for a literal interpretation of those rules in common law countries[44] can lead to more certain outcomes than an approach that widely considers the purposes of the law. In contract law, it may speak in favour of the common law—in terms of legal certainty—that contracts are defined and interpreted in an objective way, while civil law countries tend to give more emphasis to the intention of the parties.[45] Also, the concept of good faith—widespread in the civil law world—is generally not followed by the common law as it is said to be too uncertain, or even unworkable in practice, and inconsistent with the values of a market economy, since it gives undefined and unfettered discretion to judges to decide cases with subjective notions of morality and fairness.[46]

But, here too, a plausible response is that there are similar varieties within the groups of both common law and civil law countries. English law has a long history with many legal issues clarified by legal practice and academia, but this is also the situation in many of the established civil law countries such as France and Germany. In those latter countries, then, some of the issues which may, in principle, give rise to uncertainty, such as the principle of good faith, have been specified in a more precise way by courts and scholars. By contrast, younger and smaller jurisdictions of both civil and common law may have more gaps and therefore a lower degree of legal certainty.[47]

The case in favour of the common law is also interesting for the understanding of the notion of legal certainty, as it shows that we can argue about legal certainty at different levels: the orthodox civil law advantage is that there is a simple codified law that even lay persons can understand, while the orthodox common law advantage is that the elaborate case law enables experts to give a clear answer to most legal problems.

A similar ambiguity in the understanding of legal certainty can be seen in the interpretation of Max Weber's position[48] with regard to English law. Sometimes it is said that Weber seems to have had an 'England problem' because English law, being based on case law, may be seen as less 'formally rational' than continental law, while England was at the forefront of economic development in the industrialisation of the eighteenth and nineteenth century. However, it is also possible to reconcile Weber

[44] See Siems, *Comparative Law* 45–46.

[45] See overview in ibid 58–60.

[46] *Walford v Miles* [1992] 2 AC 128 at 138 per Lord Ackner. For further discussion, see Siems, *Comparative Law* 60–61.

[47] See also the finding of the study by Cabrelli and Siems, outlined in text accompanying n 88, below.

[48] Following from text accompanying n 8, above.

with the English case if one places the emphasis on the fact that England did have 'formal justice and guaranteed rights' when it developed economically.[49]

Beyond the discussion about England and the common law, it is worth mentioning that some scholars also understand legal certainty in a way that does not merely focus on a simple law that can easily be understood by lay persons. According to Elina Paunio, for example, a hermeneutic and interpretative conception of legal certainty means that it includes the consideration whether the legal community in question accepts the arguments advanced to support and justify a specific outcome.[50] Thus, according to this position, it is the clarity of the legal process that justifies the rational acceptability, not necessarily the clarity of specific substantive rules.

General Tension between Certainty and Adaptability

The next counter-argument suggests that, broadly speaking, there is a similar degree of legal certainty across both civil and common law countries. To start with, it can be said that, on the one hand, in reality, there *is often* legal certainty:

> Outside the courtroom, we get out of bed each morning performing a dozen actions in the preparation of our breakfast that clearly do not breach any legal rule. As we drive to work and exceed the speed limit we clearly do breach a legal rule and so on through the day it is abundantly clear for nearly all of our actions whether they do or do not breach a legal rule. Most of the things we do in life are simple, stable patterns of action where simple, stable rules can provide us with admirable reliance as to what our legal obligations are.[51]

On the other hand, there is some inevitable uncertainty, again in both civil and common law countries. Law is based on language which leads us to the 'inherent imprecision of language itself'.[52] This applies to both case law and

[49] See Chowdhury, *European Regulation of Medical Devices and Pharmaceuticals* 56; BR Dorbeck-Jung, 'Global Trade: Changes in the Conceptualisation of Legal Certainty?' in V Gessner (ed), *Contractual Certainty in International Trade* (Oxford, Hart Publishing, 2008) 294 n 16.

[50] E Paunio, 'Beyond Predictability—Reflections on Legal Certainty and the Discourse Theory of Law in the EU Legal Order' (2009) 10 *German Law Journal* 1469; E Paunio, *Legal Certainty in Multilingual EU Law: Language, Discourse and Reasoning at the European Court of Justice* (Farnham, Ashgate, 2013).

[51] J Braithwaite, 'Rules and Principles: A Theory of Legal Certainty' (2002) 27 *Australian Journal of Legal Philosophy* 47, 52.

[52] BF Smith, 'Of Truth and Certainty in Law: Reflections on the Legal Method' (1985) 30 *American Journal of Jurisprudence* 97. See also T Endicott, *Vagueness in Law* (Oxford, Oxford University Press, 2000) 7–30 (on linguistic indeterminacy).

statute law, while it may also be noted that there is a world-wide trend to support the use of 'plain language'.[53]

In addition, it is helpful to refer to the idea that law is an aggregate of various 'legal formants'.[54] This means that any analysis of the law has to consider not only legislation but also court decisions and legal scholarship, regardless of whether a particular legal system regards the latter as sources of law, and then aim to explore how these formants interact and compete with each other. Thus, across legal systems, it is rarely the case that there is only one correct solution to a particular problem.

Sometimes such uncertainty is acceptable, again regardless of whether it is in a common or in a civil law country, because it is possible to adjust to uncertainties. In a private dispute, if both parties can make a reliable risk assessment of who may win if it comes to a judgment, they can use this information to settle the case.[55] Even if this is not possible, one party can decide to adjust ex ante by way of getting legal cost insurance. Similarly, in a cross-border context, it may be possible to consider ratings about country risk, as for example published by credit rating agencies.[56]

Going further, it can sometimes be desirable that there is some legal uncertainty. Countries have to balance between certainty and adaptability of the law. While it is clear that law needs to respond to new or changing circumstances, identifying these determinants of 'legal adaptability' is not straightforward. A paper by Thorsten Beck and colleagues used variables on the strictness of judicial legal justification as proxies for legal adaptability.[57] Based on data from 80 countries, this led to the result that the law is more adaptable in common law than in civil law countries. Such a view is shared by other scholars, indicating that the civil law countries' greater reliance on formal legal rules, and the more bureaucratic nature of the judiciary, results in a law that is more insulated from society than in common law countries.[58]

But it is too narrow to focus only on the role of courts. A more meaningful catalogue needs to take into account the legislature, legal practice,

[53] J Barnes, 'Sources of Doubt and the Quest for Legal Certainty' (2008) 2 *Legisprudence* 119, 124. See also the contributions in A Wagner and S Cacciaguidi-Fahy (eds), *Obscurity and Clarity in the Law: Prospects and Challenges* (London, Ashgate, 2008).

[54] R Sacco 'Legal Formants: A Dynamic Approach to Comparative Law' (1991) 39 *American Journal of Comparative Law* 1 and 343 (note: published as two articles).

[55] Settlement bargaining is a frequent topic of law and economics, with further details, such as questions of loss aversion, beyond the scope of this chapter, see eg G Dari-Mattiacci and B Deffains, 'Uncertainty of Law and the Legal Process' (2007) 163 *Journal of Institutional and Theoretical Economics* 627.

[56] See EO Wennerström and Å Valter, 'The Rule of Law in Times of Financial Crises: How EU Rule of Law Correlates with the Market' (2015) 60 *Scandinavian Studies in Law* 367.

[57] T Beck, A Demirguc-Kunt, and R Levine, 'Law and Finance. Why Does Legal Origin Matter?' (2003) 31 *Journal of Comparative Economics* 653.

[58] Eg T Lundmark, *Charting the Divide Between Common and Civil Law* (Oxford, Oxford University Press, 2012) 40 and 101–107.

academics and the general public of a particular place. With a more comprehensive measure, differences between civil and common law countries are bound to be blurred.[59]

Related to this is the debate about the way legal systems strive for a balance between general and precise rules. In the Anglo-Saxon world, this is often phrased as the distinction between rules and principles (or standards). Here, for example, it is suggested that rules work well for simple problems, but that for more complex phenomena a mixture between rules and principles is advisable.[60] Elsewhere too, legal theorists have developed similar variations. For example, it has been said that there is a need for 'openness of law', as law needs to deal with the relationship between conflicting or supplementary rules or simply reflect the 'multifariousness of life'.[61]

Finally, in this balancing between certainty and flexibility, there are bound to be variations according to different areas of law. For example, for laws addressing large business transactions—such as securities regulation and competition law—the parties of a transaction are likely to avoid even small risks deriving from legal uncertainty. There are also likely to be different dynamics in different areas of law as far as the division of powers between parliaments, courts and regulators influences how far any incompleteness of the law leads to an acceptable (or unacceptable) degree of uncertainty.[62]

Recent Convergence in Legal (Un)Certainty

The arguments made in the previous section show that, despite differences between legal families, there are some reasons why levels of legal certainty may not be too dissimilar. Moreover, more recent trends show how countries converge in their degree and approach to legal certainty (as well as legal uncertainty).

Recent research about changes in legal certainty often notes that older approaches face a number of limitations today. For example, as far as legal certainty used to be ensured through a hierarchical system of national legal orders that determined the applicable law, globalisation (however it may be understood) has challenged this country-based clarity.[63] It has also been said that, over recent decades, legal certainty has come under pressure from 'the

[59] See M Siems, 'Legal Adaptability in Elbonia' (2006) 2 *International Journal of Law in Context* 393.

[60] Braithwaite, 'Rules and Principles'.

[61] R Alexy, 'Legal Certainty and Correctness' (2015) 28 *Ratio Juris* 441, 447 (with references to Hart and Kelsen).

[62] K Pistor and C Xu, 'Incomplete Law' (2003) 35 *International Law and Politics* 931. The context specificity of legal certainty is also highlighted in Shawn J Bayern, 'Against Certainty' (2012) 41 *Hofstra Law Review* 53.

[63] Chowdhury, *European Regulation of Medical Devices and Pharmaceuticals* 10.

expectation that the law be more responsive to a social environment characterised by rapid economic, social and technological change'.[64]

In the present context, the core point to note is that it is not only the case that legal certainty has been challenged, but that these trends have transformed legal certainty in a way that is similar across countries of both civil and common law. Conceptually, it can also be helpful to phrase this change as a worldwide trend towards pluralism in law. Legal pluralism refers to the coexistence of legal forms in the same social field.[65] Frequent examples include legal orders where customary law plays an important role, in particular in tribal communities of developing countries, but also in the laws of groups and communities such as the Quakers, Romani, Native Americans and religious organisations.[66] However, even in mainstream Western legal systems, pluralism is ubiquitous as we observe overlapping normative orders of the national legal systems as well as a growing set of rules that derive from private sources, as modern societies 'no longer aspire to one set of apparently solid moral and cultural values'.[67] This trend is also a result of changes in the international and transnational context, with a growing overlap of multiple formal and informal sources.[68]

It follows that today's concerns about legal certainty are not 'simply' about questions such as whether statute law or case law are preferable. Rather, the challenge is to provide solutions on how legal certainty may be achieved in this context. For example, as far as hierarchical orderings are unrealistic, it seems plausible to suggest other structural and procedural mechanisms for the benefit of legal certainty.[69] It has also been argued that new transnational social institutions such as a 'new lex mercatoria' can provide stability without any operative formal and informal sanctions.[70] Another response is that due to the lack of a global private international law, the need for legal certainty is a driving force for the convergence of substantive laws.[71]

All of this leads to converging approaches which further challenge any civil/common law divide in legal certainty. But, of course, none of the arguments

[64] M Fenwick and S Wrbka (eds), *Legal Certainty in a Contemporary Context: Private and Criminal Law Perspectives* 2 (Singapore, Springer, 2016).

[65] References and overview in Siems, *Comparative Law* 107–108.

[66] ibid.

[67] R Banakar, *Normativity in Legal Sociology: Methodological Reflections on Law and Regulation in Late Modernity* 261 (Cham, Springer 2015).

[68] See, eg W Twining, 'Globalisation and Comparative Law' in E Örücü and D Nelken (eds), *Comparative Law: A Handbook* (Oxford, Hart Publishing, 2007) 85; A Griffiths, 'Anthropological Perspectives on Legal Pluralism and Governance in a Transnational World' in M Freeman and D Napier (eds), *Law and Anthropology* (Oxford, Oxford University Press, 2009) 166.

[69] Chowdhury, *European Regulation of Medical Devices and Pharmaceuticals* 15.

[70] V Gessner and AC Budak (eds), *Emerging Legal Certainty: Empirical Studies on the Globalization of Law* (Farnham, Ashgate 1998).

[71] Siems, *Comparative Law* 227.

elaborated in this section mean that all differences have disappeared. Thus, the subsequent section discusses whether and how far quantitative research provides an answer to question of any differences and similarities between countries.

DOES QUANTITATIVE RESEARCH PROVIDE THE ANSWER?

The last two decades have seen a growing use of quantitative methods in comparative law.[72] While some studies have revisited the relevance of legal families,[73] the current quantitative research on topics of legal certainty is somehow limited and problematic, as the following will explain. Three broad approaches will be distinguished: user surveys; content analysis; and expert information.

User Surveys

The prominent indicators that measure the rule of law across countries are an example of data collection usually done by way of user surveys.[74] In these indicators, developed countries of both common and civil law are typically at the top of the rankings.[75] Yet, while legal certainty is part of the rule of law,[76] the indicators do not provide explicit information about quality differences in legal certainty. Thus, they only have indirect relevance for present purposes.

More nuanced data can be found in the business surveys conducted by the World Bank. The World Business Environment Survey (WBES) 2000 included the item 'In resolving business disputes, do you believe your country's court system to be consistent?' with the answer ranging from 1 to 6 (with 1 'never' and 6 'always'). If one aggregates the available data for civil and common law countries, the common law receives a slightly better score: 3.52 (based on 22 countries) versus 2.94 (based on 43 countries).[77] But this result is also rather limited as the question only asks about courts, where the slight common law advantage does not come as a surprise.

[72] See, eg H Spamann, 'Empirical Comparative Law' (2015) 11 *Annual Review of Law and Social Sciences* 131; Siems, *Comparative Law* 146–87.

[73] See, eg M Siems, 'Varieties of Legal Systems: Towards a New Global Taxonomy' (2016) 12 *Journal of Institutional Economics* 579.

[74] But see also text accompanying n 92, below for the indicators by the Bertelsmann Foundation.

[75] See, eg worldjusticeproject.org/rule-of-law-index.

[76] See text accompanying n 10, above.

[77] The country data are from the dataset on 'courts' (discussed in the next section) as available at faculty.tuck.dartmouth.edu/images/uploads/faculty/rafael-laporta/Courts-LuxMundi.xls. The underlying raw data are at go.worldbank.org/RV060VBJU0.

Subsequent World Bank surveys (called BEEPS and Enterprise Surveys) have more but somehow different questions. One of them asks more generally about the evaluation of the issue 'Interpretations of regulations affecting my firm are consistent and predictable'.[78] However, these surveys have only been conducted in a limited number of transition economies and are therefore unsuitable for a general assessment of differences between legal families.

Turning to academic research, a study, though also with a limited number of countries, was conducted by ZEPR, an institute at the University of Bremen in Germany.[79] It dealt with the conveyancing services market in the EU and its survey was answered by 700 respondents from 21 Member States. Amongst others, it asked about the certainty of conveyancing services in their countries (with 6 being the highest score). The average of the 21 countries was 4.08 and the median 4.19. As regards the two common law countries covered, England's average was close to the median (4.26), while Ireland received the third highest score (5.4).[80]

A research project on differences and similarities in European legal cultures by Ase Grodeland and William Miller conducted surveys in five European countries. One of the questions asked whether respondents felt that 'on the whole [...] the law [in your country] is often too complex and too frequently changed to be obeyed?.'[81] This indicator of uncertainty was least frequently supported in Norway (35%), then in England (48%), then in Bulgaria (51%), then in Poland (64%) and then in Ukraine (65%). Again, this information is not comprehensive enough to make a general assessment about civil/common law differences.

Another approach is to use survey answers and then measure the legal disagreement between respondents of each country. Kevin Davis applied this approach to the answers from 18 countries in the Afrobarometer survey 2005 about tax evasion.[82] The average standard deviation, as a measure of disagreement, was 1.0014. If one distinguishes between the average for the

[78] See data.worldbank.org/data-catalog/BEEPS (Question 16a: To what degree do you agree with the statement, 'Interpretations of regulations affecting my firm are consistent and predictable?'); www.enterprisesurveys.org/nada/index.php/catalog (Question j1a: Government officials' interpretations of the laws and regulations affecting this establishment are consistent and predictable).

[79] Study for the European Commission (COMP/2006/D3/003), DG Competition led by the Centre of European Law and Politics (ZERP) at Bremen University (2007), available at ec.europa.eu/competition/sectors/professional_services/studies/studies.html.

[80] ibid 148.

[81] Ase B Grodeland and William L Miller, *European Legal Cultures in Transition* (Cambridge, Cambridge University Press 2015) 35.

[82] KE Davis 'The Concept of Legal Uncertainty' (November 2011), available at ssrn.com/abstract=1990813 (with the question from Afrobarometer: How likely do you think it would be that the authorities could enforce the law if a top official did not pay a tax on some of the income they earned?).

11 common law and 7 civil law countries, the disagreements are very close to the general average (1.0006 and 1.0028).

Overall, it can be seen that these findings are sketchy at best. It is also suggested that user surveys alone do not measure legal uncertainty accurately. For example, assume the scenario that in a particular country the rules of criminal procedure are completely unclear. However, there is widespread popularity of US crime dramas: so when citizens answer a survey about their law, they all wrongly assume that it is just as it is in the US. As a result, according to the user survey the law may be seen as clear and consistent for reasons that have nothing to do with actual law of the country. Thus, more objective criteria, such as content analysis and expert information, may provide a more promising framework.

Content Analysis

Some studies have attempted to count the quantity of codified law across countries. In the 1980s, Heinz Schäffer and Attila Racz led a research project on 'Quantitative Analyses of Law—A Comparative Empirical Study: Sources of Law in Eastern and Western Europe'.[83] This project used questionnaires to estimate the total number of generally binding normative acts, for instance, in terms of pages and the number of single norms. Schäffer and Racz also tried to identify the number of legal changes within a period of ten years, as socialist governments were expected to be less hesitant in changing existing legal orders.

More recently, Tom Ginsburg and colleagues were interested in whether and how legal systems differ in the 'specificity' of codified law. The first paper examined whether in Europe the length of laws implementing EU directives varies systematically across countries.[84] Based on the implementing statutes of directives on product liability, works council, and e-commerce, they constructed a 'statutory specificity index' with the most specific legal system being the UK (ie, having the longest implementing statutes) and the least specific ones being the Scandinavian countries. Ginsburg also examined the specificity of constitutions, using data from most countries of the world.[85] Here too, civil-law countries tend towards shorter texts than common law ones, though, in Latin America, constitutions also tend to be relatively long.

[83] H Schäffer and A Racz (eds), *Quantitative Analyses of Law—A Comparative Empirical Study: Sources of Law in Eastern Western Europe* (Budapest, Akademiai Kiado, 1990).

[84] RD Cooter and T Ginsburg, 'Leximetrics: Why the Same Laws are Longer in Some Countries than Others' (2003), available at ssrn.com/abstract=456520.

[85] T Ginsburg, 'Constitutional Specificity, Unwritten Understandings and Constitutional Agreement' in A Sajo and R Uitz (eds) *Constitutional Topography: Values and Constitutions* (The Hague, Eleven International Publishing, 2010) 69.

These findings may be related to legal certainty since, all things being equal, longer and more specific legal texts should lead to a higher degree of legal certainty. However, such a line of reasoning is also problematic, since variations in the number and length of legal texts may merely reflect the substantive issues that the law of a particular country covers. Thus, it is perfectly possible that a country with few short laws has a higher degree of legal certainty than a country with many long laws if the latter country is keener on restricting certain actions.

A paper by Jan Smits aiming to measure the complexity of laws[86] also uses the length of statutes as one of its criteria. In addition, it includes, amongst others, an evaluation based on the 'Flesch reading ease' score[87] of a country's constitution. Of the 26 countries analysed in Smits' paper, two of the three common law countries (Malta and Cyprus) get the lowest score in terms of readability. But it seems difficult to generalise this finding given the limitations to the texts of constitutions and 26 countries. Moreover, as the analysis was based on the English translations of many of the constitutions, the style of the translations is bound to have influenced the readability of the texts.

Another potentially promising approach may be from a study on comparative company law[88] which analysed the laws of 10 countries in 10 hypothetical case scenarios. The subsequent quantitative evaluation was based on two components for each case; so, in total 20 components. This evaluation scrutinised substantive aspect, not relevant here, but also coded the sources of law cited in the case studies for each of the components. This latter coding also included the option 'none' where the country solution indicated that there was no information available on a particular issue (be it legislation, case law, academic writing or self-regulation). Here, the two countries which had most of these 'none' cases were from Central and Eastern Europe (Poland and Latvia), presumably because they only recently promulgated a new set of company laws, while the other countries of both common and civil law had hardly any 'none' cases.

Of course, this final study too was limited in terms of its scope of countries and topics. Thus, it cannot be used for a general assessment of legal certainty. It can also be suggested that the complexities of legal uncertainty are unlikely to be captured by content analyses—thus, finally, we turn to the use of expert information.

[86] JM Smits, 'Do Small Jurisdictions Have a More Complex Law? A Numerical Experiment in Constitutional and Private Law' in A Albarian and O Moréteau (eds), *Le droit compare et.../Comparative Law and....* (Aix-en-Provence, Presses Universitaires d'Aix-Marseille, 2016) 473.

[87] See flesh.sourceforge.net/.

[88] M Siems and D Cabrelli (eds), *Comparative Law: A Case-Based Approach* (Oxford, Hart Publishing, 2013); D Cabrelli and M Siems, 'Convergence, Legal Origins, and Transplants in Comparative Corporate Law: A Case-Based and Quantitative Analysis' (2015) 63 *American Journal of Comparative Law* 109.

Expert Information

There are different approaches on who to ask as 'experts' about the level of legal certainty in a country. A book by Thomas Lundmark presents the results of a small-scale four country survey where he questioned legal philosophers about the completeness, determinability and certainty of their legal systems.[89] Amongst others, Lundmark asked them to assess whether their legal systems have preference for predictability of the law or individual justice (scored from 1 for a maximum of predictability to 5 for a maximum of individual justice). The average responses from Germany and Sweden were '3' while those from the UK and the US were '4'.[90] A methodological problem with this study is that it does not indicate how many scholars participated in the survey: thus, its validity cannot be scrutinised. In the context of this chapter, it also only re-affirms the traditional view, namely that in academia it is believed that there is indeed a civil law preference for legal certainty.[91]

Coding of legal certainty has also been attempted by political scientists and economists at the Bertelsmann Foundation. Their Sustainable Governance Indicators include a coding of 41 OECD and EU countries in the rule-of-law sub-category of legal certainty.[92] This shows hardly any common/civil law divide: on a scale from 0 to 10, the eight common law countries included in the indicators have the average score of 7.5 while the civil law countries have an average score 7.2. By contrast, the more striking difference is that countries with the lowest rating (4 or less) are economically less wealthy (Mexico, Romania, Turkey, Hungary) than the countries with the top score of 10 (Finland, Germany, New Zealand, Estonia).[93]

Two other studies use practicing lawyers as the source for expert information. In a study on 'courts' by Simeon Djankov and colleagues,[94] one of the criteria can be related to the debate about legal certainty. It coded 'legal justification' of judgments based on the variables '(i) complaint must be legally justified, (ii) judgment must be legally justified, and (iii) judgment must be on law (not on equity)', ranging 'from zero to one, where higher values mean a higher use of legal language or justification'. The data were collected through a network of law firms for 109 countries. Aggregating them according

[89] Lundmark, *Charting the Divide Between Common and Civil Law* 96–130.

[90] ibid 122–26.

[91] See text accompanying nn 17–28, above.

[92] It is defined as: 'Government and administration act predictably, on the basis of and in accordance with legal provisions. Legal regulations are consistent and transparent, ensuring legal certainty', see www.sgi-network.org/2015/Democracy/Quality_of_Democracy/Rule_of_Law/Legal_Certainty.

[93] For possible differences in terms of economic development see also the text accompanying nn 11 and 75 above.

[94] S Djankov et al, 'Courts' (2003) 118 *Quarterly Journal of Economics* 453.

to legal origins, the common law (which Djankov et al call 'English legal origin') has a lower value (0.52) than the civil law groupings (between 0.67 and 0.83).[95] Thus, this confirms the traditional view that legal reasoning in civil law countries is more formalised;[96] yet, it is also a rather limited finding, as it just measures one aspect of legal certainty.

More comprehensive in its ambition, though not yet in its coverage of countries, is the Legal Certainty Index.[97] Based on advice from local legal experts, it coded whether specific legal issues in six areas of law refer to laws that are, for example, based on: legislation or case law; on a rule that is found in one collection or is scattered; on a law that is available on the internet; on a rule that has been consistently interpreted by courts; on a law that has been stable over the last five year etc. For the 13 countries covered in the study, the main finding is that there is no clear common/civil divide while civil law countries are slightly ahead in some of the categories.

This study deserves credit for putting measures of legal certainty on the agenda of scholarship and practice. In substance, it is laudable to cover multiple facets of legal certainty, but it is also not entirely convincing. Its main weakness is that it makes generic assumptions that certain features of the law—such as having codified law and not case law—are universally beneficial for legal certainty. Thus, in this lack of awareness for local context, it shares the problems with the Doing Business Reports that it aims to challenge.[98]

The preferable alternative approach to identify the certainty of the current law[99] would be to measure directly how reliably experts assess particular scenarios in each country.[100] This could also provide further variations that account for the ease of availability of materials. For example, one could develop a research design that would present a legal problem to lawyers, then ask them: (i) to provide a spontaneous answer; (ii) to let them research the topic for 15 minutes using electronic resources; and (iii) to enable them to do further research for another 24 hours, and then evaluate the consistency of the answers for each country. As an extension, as far as it can be

[95] The precise figures are Nordic legal origin: 0.67; socialist legal origin: 0.79; German legal origin: 0.83; French legal origin: 0.83; ibid 478–83.

[96] See text accompanying n 20, above.

[97] See Deffains and Kessedjian (eds), 'Index of Legal Certainty'. A second edition is currently in preparation.

[98] ibid 7; A Raynouard and AJ Kerhuel, 'Measuring the law: Sécurité juridique as a watermark' (2011) 8 *International Journal of Disclosure and Governance* 360. Another problem is that of the subjectivity of its criteria and their weighting, discussed in Chapter 8 below, by Jonas Knetsch.

[99] This should be distinguished from legal stability, for example, the question whether future laws can have a retroactive effect.

[100] This is equivalent to the concept of 'inter-coder reliability'. For an application to legal texts see J Melton et al, 'On the Interpretability of Law: Lessons from the Decoding of National Constitutions' (2013) 43 *British Journal of Political Science* 399.

assumed that citizens would not ask for legal advice for a specific scenario ex ante—say, certain traffic rules such as speeding restrictions—one could ask lay persons for their assessment and then compare their answers (as well as the consistency of those answers) with the answers by the legal experts of each country.

CONCLUSION

The debate about legal families deals with a great variety of topics, such as differences in history, sources of laws, legal mentalities, legal procedure and areas of substantive law. This chapter had the aim to fill the gap in analysing the question whether it is justified to argue that common and civil law countries fundamentally differ in their approach to legal certainty, notably whether it is justified to speak of a civil law advantage in legal certainty.

The main finding is that general statements about a civil-common law divide in legal certainty do not hold up to scrutiny. Neither the conventional comparative analysis of this chapter nor the quantitative research of previous studies point towards a general advantage for either the civil law or the common law. Rather it has been shown that much depends on the way legal certainty is understood. For example, the benchmark of legal certainty does not tell us whether one should have a simple codified law that even lay persons can understand or a more elaborate law that can give a clear answer to any legal problem. The discussion of the quantitative research also shows that any assessment is sensitive to the way legal certainty is measured.

For future research, it is suggested that there is need for a new quantitative approach to measuring legal certainty. In contrast to the use of proxies in the Legal Certainty Index, this should be based on an expert assessment of the actual results to legal problems. Considering the need for a flexible and just law, it is also important to consider that legal certainty is not an absolute aim that lawmakers should pursue. Notably, it is suggested that a future indicator should address both legal certainty and legal adaptability as the two corresponding aims that lawmakers need to balance.

6

The Faces and Implications of Legal Certainty in Contemporary Private Law—A Comparative Law Perspective

STEFAN WRBKA

INTRODUCTION

AT FIRST SIGHT the term 'legal certainty' seems to be clearly definable. It can frequently be found in legal policy-making and academic discourses to discuss, justify and develop legal strategies, doctrine and concepts. The present book is a good example.

However, when taking a closer look at certainty debates in different jurisdictions and different geographical contexts, one will note that legal certainty perceptions differ. Discussing legal certainty in combination with legitimate expectations, Paul Craig and Gráinne de Búrca, for example, stress as follows: 'The connected concepts of legal certainty and legitimate expectations are found in many legal systems, although their content may vary. These concepts are applied in a number of ways'.[1]

The present contribution aims to cast a glance at some selected jurisdictional examples that—although not claiming to draw a definitive picture—highlight some underlying commonalities as well as differences in the use and understanding of legal certainty in the area of private law. The aim of the analysis is to enhance further endeavours to maximise the benefits of legal certainty in all its facets without ignoring the significance of the nuanced conceptualisation of the regime in different jurisdictions.

The contribution will start with a brief general look at legal certainty and selected attempts to define the concept. It will commence with excursions to the private laws of the European Union (EU), Japan, Austria, England and

[1] P Craig and G de Búrca, *EU Law: Text, Cases, and Materials* 6th edn (Oxford, Oxford University Press, 2015) 558.

Germany to exemplify the different notions of legal certainty and possible consequences that may result from their respective uses of it. The covered legal systems were chosen as examples, because they are either undergoing some kind of certainty reform (or at least debate) or have been subject to according efforts in the more recent past. The analysis will be rounded off by an attempt to draw conclusions to facilitate further certainty discussions.

GENERAL REMARKS ON LEGAL CERTAINTY IN A PRIVATE LAW CONTEXT

Over the centuries, legal certainty has evolved to become one of the core legal principles. In modern, developed societies—understood as societies that rest on the rule of law—the degree to which legal certainty exists might be used as a parameter to assess the proper functioning and progressiveness of legal systems.

But what exactly does legal certainty embody? The more conventional view focuses on the foreseeability of legally relevant actions and omissions. John Bell, for example, expounds this concept as follows: 'One of the functions of law is to guide behaviour and to provide frameworks within which individuals can plan.'[2]

Two earlier discourses on legal certainty by two influential continental European commentators in the area of private law, Claus-Wilhelm Canaris and Franz Bydlinski, go beyond this understanding. Canaris distinguishes between three bigger subdivisions. According to him, legal certainty can either be understood as legal firmness and predictability (*Bestimmtheit* and *Vorhersehbarkeit*), legislative and judicial stability and continuity (*Stabilität* and *Kontinuität*) or practicability of the application of law (*Praktikabilität der Rechtsanwendung*).[3] The definitions given by Canaris indicate that legal certainty affects different stakeholder groups and—depending on which group one focuses on—stands for different expressions of the rule of law.

Legal firmness and predictability first and foremost address the wish of the users of law (*Rechtsanwender*) to easily understand their rights and duties. The consequences of legally relevant actions and omissions should be made clearly pre-determinable. To achieve this, one would need clear legal rules. This understanding is complemented by the view that the legal framework should be stable in the sense that—unless necessary—legal rules do not change, at the very least not discretionally. Stability and continuity also imply that law (usually) should not be retrospectively applicable—criminal

[2] J Bell, 'Certainty and Flexibility in Law' in P Cane and J Conaghan (eds), *The New Oxford Companion to Law* (Oxford, Oxford University Press, 2008) 110.

[3] For details, see CW Canaris, *Systemdenken und Systembegriff in der Jurisprudenz* (Berlin, Duncker & Humblot, 1969) 17.

law can be considered as a prime example in this respect.[4] The judicial apparatus adds one more stability layer. It is not only the legislator who should follow the call for continuity, but also courts. The importance of precedents, typically and particularly found in common law countries, can be seen as the prime example of this. Canaris' outline of legal certainty focuses on a more practically relevant issue. His practicability of the application of law concept can be understood in a way that aims to guarantee that legal rules are effective and can actually be used. Making recourse to modern language, one could refer to this idea as the 'user-friendliness' of law.

Bydlinski takes an approach comparable to that of Canaris, in the sense that he comments on legal certainty from different perspectives. He distinguishes, in principle, between five subcategories: legal clarity (*Rechtsklarheit*); legal stability (*Rechtsstabilität*); legal accessibility (*Rechtszugänglichkeit*); peace guaranteed by law (*Rechtsfriede*); and legal enforcement (*Rechtsdurchsetzung*).[5]

The first three expressions relate to Canaris' certainty concepts. The other two categories—peace guaranteed by law and legal enforcement—complement each other and can be considered as a downstream classification of legal certainty. While legal clarity, stability and accessibility aim to provide the users of law with a legal framework that is easily understandable, consistent (in the sense of not being constantly or discretionally altered) and useable in practice, legal enforcement and peace guaranteed by law add a consequent layer. Even the clearest, most stable and best accessible laws can only be of practical relevance if they are enforceable and actually enforced in practice. Legal enforcement thus enshrines a procedural perspective to complete the overall picture. Bydlinski's 'peace guaranteed by law' concept on the other hand refers to the ideal situation, ie to a situation where laws achieve the creation of an environment that is free of (at least bigger, law-relevant) disputes. Understood this way, peace guaranteed by law stands for the possible impact the other four of Bydlinski's certainty layers would ideally result in.

In the following I would like to pick some examples to show how different jurisdictions apply these certainty concepts to their private laws. Following this, I will try to draw a more general, comparative conclusion.

[4] In this sense (in an EU context), eg S Weatherill, *Cases & Material on EU Law* 10th edn (Oxford, Oxford University Press, 2012) 132.

[5] For details, see F Bydlinski, *Fundamentale Rechtsgrundsätze* (Vienna, Springer, 1988) 293; F Bydlinski, *Juristische Methodenlehre und Rechtsbegriff* 2nd edn (Vienna, Springer, 2011) 325.

EXAMPLES OF LEGAL CERTAINTY

Legal Certainty in European Union Private Law

Since the early days of the EU—to be more precise: its predecessors[6]—legal certainty has played an important role in policy- and law-making. Already in the early 1960s the Court of Justice had acknowledged legal certainty as one of the guiding principles of EU law.[7] Within the context of EU law the certainty concept has been usually understood and used primarily in a more conventional certainty sense as referring to clear rules and the foreseeability of legally relevant actions and omissions, ie in the 'clarity' notion defined in the previous section. One of the more recent Court of Justice judgments that explicitly voiced this view was the 2009 decision in *Heinrich*. Here the Court explained that '[Union] rules [shall] enable those concerned to know precisely the extent of the obligations which are imposed on them. Individuals must be able to ascertain unequivocally what their rights and obligations are and take steps accordingly'.[8] This first and foremost relates to the duty to publish EU laws and other relevant EU materials in a freely accessible instrument. In practice this is done with the help of the EU's Official Journal.

The call for clarity, however, goes further and can be understood as an answer to the challenge of providing stakeholders with clear and—to the highest possible extent—standardised legal rules throughout the EU. I will return to this issue several times later in the context of the European domestic examples discussed in this contribution.

Additional expressions of legal certainty can be linked to the Member States' obligation to interpret and implement EU law as easily understandable as possible and in line with the rationale behind the original EU source, to the call for transparent EU laws and to the idea that EU law should principally not be retrospectively applicable.[9]

[6] For the sake of simplicity, I will refer to the EU and its predecessors simply as the 'EU'.

[7] D Chalmers, G Davies and G Monti, *European Union Law* 3rd edn (Cambridge, Cambridge University Press, 2014) 441 with reference to Joined Cases C-32/58 and C-33/58 *SNUPAT v ECSC High Authority* [1959] ECLI:EU:C:1959:18.

[8] Case C-345/06 *Heinrich* [2009] ECLI:EU:C:2009:140 para 44.

[9] For the first one see, eg D Leczykiewicz, 'Effectiveness of EU Law before National Courts' in A Arnull and D Chalmers (eds), *The Oxford Handbook of European Union Law* (Oxford, Oxford University Press, 2015) 224 with reference to Case C-268/06 *Impact v Minister for Agriculture and Food and Others* [2008] ECLI:EU:C:2008:223. For the second one see, eg Chalmers, Davies and Monti, *European Union Law* 412–22. For the latter one see, eg Craig and de Búrca, *EU Law* 558–63, where the authors inter alia refer to Case 98/78 *A. Racke v Hauptzollamt Mainz* [1979] ECLI:EU:C:1979:14. In *Racke* the CJEU explained the retroactivity notion of legal certainty as follows: 'Although in general the principle of legal certainty precludes a Community measure from taking effect from a point in time before its publication, it may exceptionally be otherwise where the purpose to be achieved so demands and where the legitimate expectations of those concerned are duly respected'.

Originally, the underlying consideration behind legal certainty at the EU level rested on the fact that unlike the other, domestic jurisdictions discussed later in this contribution, the EU is subject to different conditions. As a supranational institution, it does not deal with the question of how to best regulate one country's legal system. Rather it focuses on how to best balance the interests of (at the time of writing) 28 Member States to achieve the overall goal of enhancing the EU. This does not mean that EU law should, or even may, ignore domestic legal interests. However, domestic layers are not the sole point to take into consideration in EU policy- and law-making. National positions are undeniably of relevance in an EU context, as EU law-making eventually rests on compromises between national policies. But national interests should be considered as pieces that have to be brought into place to form a bigger picture.

Looking at (one of) the ultimate aim(s) of the EU, ie at the attempt to create an internal market that can function without the hindrance of national borders, one might see why EU policy- and lawmakers consider legal fragmentation as one of the biggest obstacles. At various occasions the EU has expressed the view that the existence of different national legal frameworks could have a negative impact on the creation of a level playing field and the installation of a borderless market. In the early years of the EU it was in particular the area of financial transactions that different national regulations were considered as a hindrance for the smooth flow of money between Member States.

One of the most recent examples, however, is the (not yet adopted) 2011 Proposal for a Regulation on a Common European Sales Law.[10] The proposal aimed to introduce a pan-EU sales law in the form of an Optional Instrument, ie as an alternative set of rules that parties to certain cross-border sales transactions could agree on. Since the CESL Regulation was designed to be chosen regardless of the Member States the parties reside in/operate from, it would—according to the European Commission—have provided the contractual parties with a standardised legal regime that would be the same for any CESL-governed transaction. Leaving the question aside whether the CESL Regulation would really introduce a comprehensive, one-size-fits-all regime,[11] the argumentation of the European Commission on why the CESL Regulation should be considered necessary deserves a slightly closer look in the context of legal certainty.

[10] Proposal for a Regulation on a Common European Sales Law, 11 October 2011, COM(2011) 635 final. Very likely it will never be adopted in its originally proposed way. Policy- and lawmakers have already indicated that—if used at all—it might be changed into a much narrower instrument. For details see, eg S Wrbka, *European Consumer Access to Justice Revisited* (Cambridge, Cambridge University Press, 2015) 255–62.

[11] I commented on this issue in detail elsewhere: ibid 215–54.

According to the Commission, cross-border trade is particularly impaired by the existence of a fragmentation of domestic sales law. Despite the availability of conflicts of law rules, most notably the Rome I Regulation, parties lack the ability to determine in advance the regime ultimately applicable to their envisaged sales contract. The Commission is convinced that the best way to remedy this would be to introduce a uniform set of sales laws to govern cross-border transactions.

According references to legal certainty can be found in the Explanatory Memorandum accompanying the proposal. With respect to consumers the Commission argues as follows: 'One of the important reasons for this situation is that, because of the differences of national laws consumers are often uncertain about their rights in cross-border situations'.[12] With respect to traders, legal certainty is even directly mentioned in the proposal. Article 1(2) of the CESL Regulation Proposal states as follows: 'This Regulation enables traders to rely on a common set of rules and use the same contract terms for all their cross-border transactions thereby reducing unnecessary costs while providing a high degree of legal certainty'. A conceptually important reference to legal certainty is further given (once again) by the CESL Explanatory Memorandum. Explaining why the CESL should take the form of a regulation (and not a directive), the Commission emphasises that 'a Directive … would not be appropriate since it would not achieve the [same] level of legal certainty and the necessary degree of uniformity'.[13]

From these statements, one can note that the Commission uses the legal certainty concept mainly in the more traditional sense of enhanced legal clarity. Parties to sales contracts should enjoy the highest possible level of foreseeability of the legal consequences. The Commission is convinced that a far-reaching standardisation of currently fragmented national provisions would be the most effective strategy by which to achieve this.

Similar thoughts can be found in a variety of other EU instruments. In 2009, for example, the EU legislator adopted a new Timeshare Directive (the 2009 Timeshare Directive) that replaced an older, minimum harmonised directive of 1994. Although the legislator held on to a directive as the basis for the new, revised regime, it sought to increase the level of harmonisation by switching from minimum (1994 Timeshare Directive) to full harmonisation (2009 Timeshare Directive). The alleged need for a move from minimum to full harmonisation is explained by the 2009 Timeshare Directive, Recital 3. Its first two sentences read as follows:

> In order *to enhance legal certainty* and fully achieve the benefits of the internal market for consumers and businesses, the relevant laws of the Member States need

[12] CESL Explanatory Memorandum 3. Comparable references to consumers can be found in CESL Regulation Proposal, Recitals 4, 17 and 34.

[13] CESL Explanatory Memorandum 10.

> to be approximated further. Therefore, certain aspects of the marketing, sale and resale of timeshares ... *should be fully harmonized* (emphasis added).

Full harmonisation—in particular embedded in EU regulations—undeniably has the consequence that affected questions are homogeneously regulated throughout the EU. In this light, it achieves a maximum level of clarity and uniformity at the pan-EU level. However, it also comes at a certain cost for legal certainty at the Member State level. In particular, it can create a situation in which various certainty subcategories, most notably legal clarity and stability, might be at risk at the domestic level. The scope of Member States' concepts might, for example, be broader than the scope of respective EU law. They could cover situations that are not included in the EU counterpart. As a consequence, affected areas at the national level could be split into two different regulatory regimes, if national legislators did not subsume non-directly covered situations under the same rules. Depending on the concrete circumstances, cases might either fall under the new (EU prescribed) rules or the conventional framework, even if the facts were very similar. For the average users of law, being able to foresee the legal consequences in a given situation would clearly pose a challenge (to say the least). From a legal clarity perspective, domestic law could thus suffer.

To avoid this fragmentation at the domestic level, ie to maintain a single-tiered regime, national legislators would have to decide to expand the EU rules to other situations (that are not directly affected by EU law, but traditionally regulated in a similar way at the national level). This would have the positive effect of avoiding friction and safeguarding legal clarity. However, it could unreasonably reduce the level of legal firmness/stability at the national level. This would be the case if the revised frameworks were the results of years and years of national legal evolution and development.[14] Hence, national lawmakers face a certainty dilemma. They have to prioritise one of the two certainty subcategories—clarity or stability—while weakening the other one. I will return to this dilemma in later sections.

It is, however, not only the inter-Member State situation that affects legal certainty at the EU level. As, for example, the Consumer Law Compendium, a comprehensive study of the *consumer acquis* initiated by the Commission showed, incoherent regulations of similar issues by different EU directives and regulations can be detrimental to the overall legal certainty of EU law as well. The authors of said study emphasise that standardising situations at the EU level in a fully harmonised way cannot achieve a sufficiently clear standardisation level unless it is accompanied by a defragmentation of

[14] In this vein, see eg Stefan Grundmann, who argues as follows: 'The more broadly the full harmonization mode is used, the more frustrated become the advantages that the national systems of law have achieved because of centuries of scholarship and practice—advantages in substantive justice and in legal certainty': S Grundmann, 'The EU Consumer Rights Directive: Optimizing, Creating Alternatives, or a Dead End?' (2013) 118 *Uniform Law Review* 98, 126.

substance directly at the EU level. This view basically implies that—for the sake of guaranteeing a high level of consistency—legal regimes should be merged into one single mechanism already at the EU level unless special reasons ask for a different, scattered treatment.[15]

The clarity notion of legal certainty stands arguably at the centre of concern in EU law-making. Over the years, additional certainty expressions have been added. Legal enforceability, for example, has steadily grown into a certainty-relevant area of interest. Ensuring that addressees of substantive duties comply with the rules, civil procedure and administrative law instruments have risen in number. One of the first examples was the Injunctions Directive of 1998 to protect the collective interests of consumers.[16] With a view to improving access to justice, the Tampere Council in 1999 suggested the introduction of further instruments. Several projects have already been realised. Examples include the Legal Aid Directive in 2003, the European Enforcement Order Regulation and the Regulation on Consumer Protection Cooperation in 2004, the European Order for Payment Procedure Regulation in 2006, the European Small Claims Regulation in 2007 and the Alternative Dispute Resolution Directive and Online Dispute Resolution Regulation both in 2013.[17] Some of these instruments have been further refined; additional enforcement projects, such as a possible pan-EU compensatory collective redress mechanism, are being discussed.[18]

One of the most recent attempted enhancements of legal certainty relates to Bydlinski's subdivision of legal accessibility. Finding and identifying case law has traditionally created issues. Although both the EU and the Member States provide the public with freely accessible case law databases, locating, identifying and comparing national case law has always proved difficult. Various (mostly private) initiatives had been launched to simplify the procedure by amalgamating national case law under overarching online umbrellas. However, none of these efforts were comprehensive enough to truly simplify the process. It was not before 2016 that the Commission installed a

[15] H Schulte-Nölke, C Twigg-Flesner and M Ebers (eds), *EC Consumer Law Compendium* (Munich, Sellier, 2008) 504.

[16] Directive 98/27/EC, [1998] OJ L166/51.

[17] Directive 2003/8/EC, [2003] OJ L26/41; Regulation (EC) 805/2004, [2004] OJ L143/15; Regulation 2004/2006/EC, [2004] OJ L364/1; Regulation (EC) 1896/2006, [2006] OJ L399/1; Regulation (EC) 861/2007, [2007] OJ L199/1; Regulation (EU) 524/2013, [2013] OJ L165/1; Directive 2013/11/EU, [2013] OJ L165/63. For details on these instruments see, eg Wrbka, *European Consumer Access to Justice Revisited* chs 4 and 5 with further references.

[18] See most notably the more recent revision of the European Small Claims Regulation and the European Order for Payment Procedure Regulation in late 2015 by Regulation (EU) 2421/2015, [2015] OJ L341/1. For the discussion of compensatory collective redress see, eg S Wrbka, 'European Consumer Protection Law: Quo Vadis?—Thoughts on the Compensatory Collective Redress Debate' in S Wrbka, S Van Uytsel and M Siems (eds), *Collective Actions—Enhancing Access to Justice and Reconciling Multilayer Interests?* (Cambridge, Cambridge University Press, 2012) 21.

device that—so it is hoped—could change the situation. In 2011, the Commission introduced the European Case Law Identifier (ECLI) with the aim to standardise the reference to national and EU case law. To accomplish this, a uniform code—the ECLI code—was introduced that would enable interested parties to identify a court decision with the help of reference to the originating jurisdiction, court and year of decision. After a five-year test phase the Commission implemented a database—the European Case Law Identifier Search Engine—that allows the EU and Member States to feed it with links to ECLI code identified cases. The project was launched in May 2016 and within one month had already more than 3.5 million links to judgments. There are still some flaws—most notably language issues, as most cases are available only in the original language—but at least the identification of case law might be considered easier now.

Legal Certainty in Japanese Private Law

Japanese private law can serve as an interesting example to explain how legal certainty shapes contemporary policy- and law-making. The present Japanese Civil Code dates back to the late nineteenth century. Partly based on German and French models (Books I–III on general issues, Property Law and the Law of Obligations), partly resting on traditional Japanese perceptions (Books IV–V on Family and Inheritance Law), the Japanese Civil Code was introduced in 1896 (Books I–III) and 1898 (Books IV–V).

With the exception of a fundamental revision of the patriarchal Books IV and V to align family and inheritance law with modern, western gender equality standards, the Japanese Civil Code has thus far remained remarkably stable. Although the stability level of the Code is quite high, the clarity, transparency and understandability expressions of legal certainty have been suffering under the restraint and passiveness of the Japanese legislator.

The certainty concerns over the Japanese Civil Code are the result of primarily three facts. First, unlike its German and French models, the Japanese Civil Code opted (in principle) for a considerably shorter catalogue of provisions. Compared with the German Civil Code and the French Code Civil, the number of articles incorporated in the Japanese Civil Code dropped by half. One of the side effects of this is the fact that several practically important questions have remained uncovered, ie unclarified by the Japanese Civil Code.

Second, and further complicating the situation, is the relatively low degree of overall clarity. Many provisions deliberately remained vague to allow courts to respond to individual circumstances and to apply the Japanese Civil Code in a quite flexible way.

Third, private law developments outside the Japanese Civil Code have further worsened the legal certainty situation. Because of the vagueness and incompleteness of the Code (coupled with the legislator's general unwillingness to fundamentally and comprehensively revise it), complementary legislative steps were found necessary to be taken to remedy the Code's shortcomings. Most notably in this respect, it was sectoral law-making that—in addition to case law—aimed to close the lacunae and to clarify the meaning of provisions (where existing).

These attempts, however, led to additional tensions. They were basically twofold. First, the parallel, sectoral regulation of certain private law areas—most notably in the field of the Law of Obligations—made the situation confusing for the users of law. Second, in absence of written rules, ie in cases where not even sectoral legislation existed, one had to additionally resort to case law. The path towards answers to legal problems became even more winding, because some existing Japanese Civil Code rules became obsolete as a consequence of newer case law and specific rules in sectoral acts. Hence, the attempts to counteract the vagueness and incompleteness of the Code were not really successful.

Against this background it becomes quite understandable that the pressure on the legislator to modernise and update the Japanese Civil Code has risen over the years. Relevant initiatives eventually prompted the Japanese Ministry of Justice to install a working group with a focus on Book III of the Code—the Law of Obligations. Since its launch in 2009 the group, ie the 'Working Group on the Civil Code (Law of Obligations)' (法制審議会民法(債権関係); *hōsei shingikai minpō (saiken kankei)*) (referred to henceforth as the JCC Working Group) has produced a remarkable number of materials on a possible revision of the Japanese Law of Obligations.

In particular, considering the slow pace of Japanese law-making it should be noted that the JCC Working Group proceeded quite quickly. Four years after its installation the group presented a first rough draft, the Interim Draft Proposal on the Reform of the Civil Code (law of obligations) (民法（債権関係）の改正に関する中間試案; *minpō (saiken kankei) no kaisei ni kan suru chūkan shian*)[19] ('Interim Draft Proposal'). This was followed by a 'Final Proposal' the 民法（債権関係）の改正に関する要綱案 (*minpō (saiken kankei) no kaisei ni kansuru yōkōan*) in 2015.[20] In the same year the Japanese government declared that it aimed to revise the Japanese Civil Code's Law of Obligations in a timely manner. Further developments are still pending at the time of writing.

[19] The text of the Interim Draft Proposal is available at, eg www.moj.go.jp/content/000112242.pdf. Commented versions are available at, eg www.moj.go.jp/content/000112244.pdf and www.moj.go.jp/content/000112247.pdf (all in Japanese).

[20] For details see www.moj.go.jp/shingi1/shingikai_saiken.html; for the Final Draft Proposal see www.moj.go.jp/content/001136445.pdf (all in Japanese).

Looking at the deliberations of the JCC Working Group, one can see that the central question was how to improve the legal certainty level by enhancing the clarity, understandability and overall transparency of the code's Law of Obligations. Taking the structural characteristics of the Japanese Civil Code (described further above) into consideration, the group basically took a three-tiered approach to achieve this goal. First, to improve the transparency of the Code and its consistency with case law, one suggestion was to complete or (where possible) update the Japanese Civil Code by adding solutions developed by courts. For the sake of simplicity, I will refer to this as the case law implementation method. Second, some outdated provisions had to be revised, although no specific case law had existed (the modernisation method). Third, the JCC Working Group further intended to standardise certain question that had been inconsistently regulated both between and within statutory law and case law (the standardisation method).

Two examples will be used in the context of the case law implementation method to explain how the JCC Working Group planned to revise the Japanese Civil Code with the help of case law. Despite its practical relevance and the relatively high number of relevant court cases, the Code does not contain any explicit regulation on what constitutes usury and what its legal consequences are. The closest provision to solve this issue is Japanese Civil Code, Article 90 on juristic acts that are incompatible with public policy considerations. Pursuant to this article, juristic acts incompatible with public policy considerations should be considered void. One of the central problems, however, is that (unlike several western jurisdictions) Japan has neither introduced a definition nor given any statutory examples of what constitutes an act in conflict with public policy. Moreover, the Japanese Civil Code does not provide a clear link between public policy infringements and usury. It was case law that developed a mechanism by declaring usury as falling under the category of public policy infringements. With its Interim Draft Proposal, the JCC Working Group decided to improve clarity by suggesting the introduction of an explicit link between usury and public policy consideration.[21] This move did not, however, succeed. Very likely having been considered too progressive, an according provision was removed from the final draft version.

A second example proved more successful. The area of mental capacity is only rudimentarily regulated in the Japanese Civil Code. One can find rules relating to the commencement of curatorship, guardianship and assistance for people who constantly lack mental capacity, as well as rules on the consequences of legal acts by people declared as lacking mental capacity by the family court. The Code, however, does not contain general provisions on legal acts by people lacking sufficient mental capacity in cases where

[21] Interim Draft Proposal, Art 1(2)(2).

no respective court decision exists or where the lack of sufficient mental capacity is only temporary. It was again case law that provided an answer. Courts developed the rule that legal acts of that kind should be considered voidable. In line with case law both the Interim Draft Proposal and the Final Draft Proposal included an according solution.[22]

Unlike the case law implementation method, the modernisation method does not (primarily) rest on the courts' shaping of private law. Rather, under this approach the JCC Working Group aimed to get rid of (or at least revise) provisions that were believed to be outdated, overall confusing or practically not very relevant.

A significant yet atypical group of provisions falling under this method is the time limitation catalogue of Japanese Civil Code, Article 166ff. The current regime can be split into two categories: first, the Japanese Civil Code contains a general prescription period of ten years;[23] second, the Code (exceptionally) adds a comparably high number of exemptions from the general rule in subsequent provisions. These special provisions introduce principally shorter prescription periods for special scenarios. Some of these shorter periods are very narrow in their scope and might hardly be justifiable.[24] Examples include special time limitations for claims in relation to certain medical services and construction works.[25] In some cases that include, eg claims against lawyers, there are even subdivisions into different prescription periods with respect to one and the same group of claimants.[26] Finding the right prescription period has remained a difficult task, not only for legally inexperienced stakeholders. Depending on the concrete circumstances, eg in the case of claims against lawyers, different lengths of time come into play. With this and the call for increased transparency, understandability and overall clarity in mind, the Working Group heavily debated a multitude of solutions before agreeing on a two-tiered approach in its Final Draft Proposal. Pursuant to this, in the vast majority of cases exceptions should make room for a combination of a 'subjective' five-year-period (that takes the claimant's concrete knowledge into consideration) and an 'objective' ten-year-period (starting with a clearly determinable event).[27]

The standardisation method relates primarily to attempts to harmonise the legal consequences in cases in which neither concrete statutory law nor consistent case law exists. To improve particularly the predictability of legally-relevant actions and omissions, the JCC Working Group aimed to draft and codify clearer rules to fill the lacuna.

22 Interim Draft Proposal, Art 2 and Final Draft Proposal, Art 2.

23 Japanese Civil Code, Art 167(1).

24 For a critique see, eg N Kano, 'Reform of the Japanese Civil Code—The Interim Draft Proposal of 2013' (2013) 18 *Journal of Japanese Law* 249, 256.

25 Japanese Civil Code, Art 170(i) and 170(ii): three years in both cases.

26 Japanese Civil Code, Arts 171 and 172: two, three or five years.

27 Final Draft Proposal, Art 7(1).

One prime example relates to standard terms that statutorily are only rudimentarily and mostly sectorally regulated.[28] The main problem was twofold: first, neither statutory law nor the courts have developed consistent rules on the requirements for the bindingness of standard terms: courts have traditionally taken a case-by-case approach, leading to inconsistent case law; second, standard terms might contain content that—from a legal perspective—is not acceptable. Statutory law provides for some rules on the permissibility issue, but the system is generally not considered sufficient.[29]

The JCC Working Group discussed the standard terms issue quite extensively and eventually opted for a solution that is known from many Western models. With respect to the general bindingness issue the recommendation follows the 'contract theory model' under which standard terms would form part of a contract if agreed to by the parties.[30] With respect to the question of the permissibility of individual clauses and the legal consequences (if the individual clauses were found impermissible), the Final Draft Proposal (again) lags behind the Interim Draft Proposal, as the Final Draft Proposal contains only a vague definition of what must be considered impermissible. Detailed explanations or examples, eg in the form of black and grey lists, are missing from the final draft version. Generally speaking, the final proposal explains that the permissibility check will occur as a second step, ie after having solved the general bindingness issue. One would have to ask whether the relevant clauses are compatible with the existing statutory (or case law developed) framework. Clauses that are found impermissible would have to be ignored, but (in principle) would have no effect on the validity of the remaining standard terms.[31]

Summarising the (still pending) Japanese Civil Code reform debate, one should note that legal certainty is one of the dominant rationales and parameters in the drafting process of a possible, new Japanese Law of Obligations. The main concern remains the overall understandability of its rules. This relates to aspects discussed above, particularly within the context of legal predictability, legal clarity and legal transparency.[32]

[28] The most relevant provisions are to be found in the Japanese Consumer Contract Law (消費者契約法; *shōhishakeiyakuhō*).

[29] Relevant provisions can be found in the already discussed Japanese Civil Code, Art 90 and—with respect to business-to-consumer contracts—additionally in the general rules of the Japanese Consumer Contract Law, §§ 8–10.

[30] Final Draft Proposal, Art 30(2).

[31] This solution is recommended not only for consumer contracts, but also for contracts in general. It should be noted, though, that the compatibility criteria in consumer contracts are generally stricter.

[32] It should be noted, though, that one can further find some legal accessibility influences, most notably expressed as attempts to make case law more easily accessible for the users of law, eg via enhanced websites.

Legal Certainty in Austrian Private Law

The Japanese example showed that countries, for whatever domestic reason, might deal with legal certainty in multidimensional ways, ie with the aim to respond to several different certainty notions. As we will see in this section, particularly in the case of comparatively old regimes, linguistic considerations can create additional challenges. In an EU context, supranational legislation could introduce one more dare. National policy- and lawmakers often have to balance the interests of preserving the continuity of traditional, domestic rules to secure the highest possible degree in legal stability on the one hand, and of standardising the national framework, ie matters directly affected by EU legislation and similar, yet not directly affected issues, to maximise the overall coherency of domestic solutions.

Our first example—the Austrian sale by dispatch contract regime—relates to the latter of these issues and further shows that the earlier outlined case law implementation method can be found in many different jurisdictions. Until its revision in 2014, the Austrian Civil Code, § 429 (*Allgemeines Bürgerliches Gesetzbuch*) read as follows: 'In principle, sent goods are deemed to be passed, when the transferee receives them; unless the transferee determines or agrees on the method of sending' (my translation). Although this provision (traditionally in combination with § 1064, since the 2014 revision of § 429, additionally in combination with § 905(3) ABGB) seems to give a clear understanding about the moment of the passing of risk in sale by dispatch contracts, courts introduced a (slightly) more complex regime. By the way of re-interpreting the old version of § 429, courts decided that common sending methods—sending by post is arguably the best example—should be understood as automatically agreed upon by the parties. This basically meant that in such cases the passing of risk occurred with the goods being handed over to the carrier, rather than with the receipt of the goods by the buyer.

In the course of implementing the Consumer Rights Directive 2011,[33] Austria had to amend the passing of risk rules with respect to business-to-consumer (B2C) situations. Consumer Rights Directive, Article 20 stated that the risk would generally pass to the consumer when he himself (or any party mandated by him) physically receives the goods. This solution was different from the rule developed by Austrian courts.[34] Austria took a narrow approach and revised its passing of risk regime (only) with respect to B2C

[33] Directive 2011/83/EU, [2011] OJ L304/64.

[34] See also, however, the exception of Consumer Rights Directive, Art 20, sentence 2: 'However, the risk shall pass to the consumer upon delivery to the carrier if the carrier was commissioned by the consumer to carry the goods and that choice was not offered by the trader, without prejudice to the rights of the consumer against the carrier'.

contracts.[35] However, it also took the opportunity to statutorily enshrine the above-mentioned, court-developed concept for non-B2C contracts to answer the call for improved understandability.[36]

The implementation of Consumer Rights Directive, Article 20, in combination with the alignment of the statutory provisions with the case law, led to an interesting shift in (un)certainty. While the codification of the case law-developed passing of risk rule should be considered positive from the viewpoint of enhanced transparency, the new two-tiered regime that differentiates between B2C and non-B2C sale by dispatch contracts might cause mixed feelings. With respect to the decision to retain the traditional rule for non-B2C cases, it should be noted that this might satisfy the wish to treasure legal continuity and the stakeholders' reliance in the existing framework. However, from a consistency perspective it could be regretted that now two conceptually different solutions exist: one for B2C contracts (in line with Consumer Rights Directive, Article 20); and one for non-B2C contracts (in line with existing Austrian case law). I will return to the dilemma of national policy- and law-making in the context of implementing EU law again later.

Linguistic peculiarities add to the legal certainty debate in Austria. The *Allgemeines Bürgerliches Gesetzbuch* is one of the oldest civil codes in the world. Dating back to 1811, it has been partially revised many times, but many of its provisions have stayed in place. This has led to a situation in which various commentators argue that the language used by the Austrian Civil Code has become outdated. Not only is some of the wording old-fashioned and difficult to understand, but some of the still-used expressions are embedded in too complex a context. These shortcomings allegedly impair the transparency, understandability and overall clarity of the code.

Against this background, it might not come as a surprise to discover that initiatives have been launched to linguistically modernise the Austrian

[35] The Austrian Consumer Act (Konsumentenschutzgesetz), § 7b, implements the Consumer Rights Directive, Art 20 nearly word for word: 'In contracts where the trader dispatches the good to the consumer, the risk of loss of or damage to the good shall pass to the consumer only if and at the moment that he or a third party indicated by him and other than the carrier has received the good. If, however, the consumer concluded the transportation contract by himself, without having been offered this transportation method as an option by the trader, the risk shall pass to the consumer already upon delivery to the carrier if the carrier was commissioned by the consumer to carry the goods'. (translation mine)

[36] The new version of Allgemeines Bürgerliches Gesetzbuch, § 429 and the relevant part of § 905 read as follows: § 429: 'If the good—with the transferee's [note: ie the creditor's] consent—is dispatched to a different place than the place of performance, then the good is deemed to be transferred [to the transferee] the moment it is transferred to the person who is mandated with the transfer [note, ie the carrier], if the method of transfer corresponds the agreed—or in its absence: a commonly accepted—method of transportation' (my translation); § 905(3): 'The risk with respect to goods that are—with the transferee's [note: ie the creditor's] consent—dispatched to a different place than the place of performance is passed to the creditor at the moment of transfer (§ 429)' (my translation).

Code in terms of these certainty notions. One of the most ambitious and more recent projects was started in 2015 by an interdisciplinary academic group under the lead of Peter Bydlinski, under the title 'Modernizing the Austrian Civil Code, in particular in linguistic terms (ABGB in clear speech)' (*Modernisierung des ABGB, vor allem in sprachlicher Hinsicht (ABGB in Klarsprache)*), which will be referred to here as the ABGB clear speech project.[37]

The group aims to address two issues. The focus is put on language peculiarities, and the question of how to make the *Allgemeines Bürgerliches Gesetzbuch* linguistically easier to understand for the average user of law. In addition, it includes a more content-related layer by trying to answer to case law and other, non-legislative developments/revision suggestions. The project is quite broad in its approach. Compared with, eg the earlier discussed JCC Working Group endeavours, the scope goes further and basically encompasses the whole code.

Although the ABGB clear speech project is not so much politically driven—at the time of writing, the project is 'merely' an academic project—it might be of practical importance in the future. In particular, the interdisciplinary link between law and linguistics indicates that the focus is put on bringing the law closer to the people and enhancing the comprehensibility of the code. If utilised by lawmakers, the combination of substantive revision and linguistic simplification could be an effective strategy to improve the overall certainty of the Austrian Civil Code. It would answer several of the earlier discussed certainty notions, most notably Franz Bydlinski's concepts of legal clarity and legal accessibility, because it would provide legally-interested stakeholders with an up-to-date framework of significantly more easily understandable legal provisions.

It is to be hoped that the project would further benefit a third certainty concept: peace guaranteed by law. This would be the case if the wording were so clear and unambiguous that the need for time- and money-consuming clarifications would be reduced. The services offered by legal professionals would not be rendered redundant, but one could focus on more complex issues, which could eventually speed up dispute avoidance and resolution at a broader level.

Legal Certainty in English Private Law

English private law (and law in general) has traditionally differed from the other national examples discussed in this contribution. Being a prime representative of common law jurisdictions, English law has conventionally,

[37] For details see abgb-modernisierung.uni-graz.at.

and to a comparatively large extent, relied on precedents and the further development of legal rules by courts. Over the last decades, however, EU law—in particular its fully harmonised portion—has been prompting the UK to implement rules that are new in an English context. This has added an interesting challenge for the legislator. I will also comment on this issue in this section.

In his publication *The Rule of Law* Lord Bingham refers to legal certainty as follows: 'The law must be accessible and, so far as possible, intelligible, clear and predictable', adding that 'Questions of legal right and liability should ordinarily be resolved by the application of the law and not the exercise of discretion'.[38] These statements reflect some ideas already discussed above in the context of central European expertise with the help of Canaris and Bydlinski. Most notably, they directly relate to what was called legal predictability (Canaris) and legal clarity and accessibility (Bydlinski).

Bingham's predictability concept might further be understood as explaining the traditional significance of precedents, ie the principle of *stare decisis*, which asks courts to substantively consider and follow already-existing judgments (by higher courts and to some extent courts of the same level) unless good reasons exist to deviate from them. Without going into details, ie without distinguishing between different forms of precedents, it is fair to say that the *stare decisis* principle has significantly and positively contributed to the overall predictability and clarity of law in common law countries.

In the second half of the twentieth century, however, some criticism had arisen that questioned the merits of precedents from the viewpoint of individual justice. Applying a too-rigid system of bindingness of case law could impair the wish to react to special circumstances. Lord Gardiner's 'Practice Statement' of 1966, in which the House of Lords expressed concerns over the *stare decisis* principle, highlights this. Gardiner explained the possible tension between the precedents' likely biggest advantage—legal certainty—and individual justice as follows:

> Their Lordships regard the *use of precedent* as an indispensable foundation upon which to decide what is the law and its application to individual cases. It *provides at least some degree of certainty* upon which individuals can rely in the conduct of their affairs, as well as a basis for orderly development of legal rules. Their Lordships *nevertheless* recognise that too rigid adherence to precedent *may lead to injustice in a particular case* and also unduly restrict the proper development of the law. They propose therefore, to modify their present practice and, while treating former decisions of this house as normally binding, to depart from a previous decision when it appears right to do so (emphasis added).[39]

[38] Lord Bingham, *The Rule of Law* (London, Penguin Books, 2011) 37 and 48.
[39] Practice Statement [1966] 3 All ER 77.

I discussed the tension between legal certainty and flexibility in more detail elsewhere.[40] What should be noted in the present context is the fact that over time precedents have lost much of their ascendancy. The call for a greater level of flexibility to serve individual justice might have been one reason for this.

Another important factor, however, is the steady, numerical rise of English statutory law. From the viewpoint of interrelation with legal certainty statutory law (in this context) could be seen as primarily connecting to its accessibility layer. Case law had traditionally guaranteed a comparatively high level of stability and predictability. At the same time, however, the increasing number of court decisions had complicated the overall comprehensibility, clarity and accessibility of legal rules. Against this background one might argue that statutory law has aimed to achieve a higher level of certainty by enabling legally-interested stakeholders to access law more easily.

Unlike most civil law jurisdictions, with their private law codifications, English statutory law has become remarkably fragmented and hence has not achieved a level of similar comprehensibility as civil law codifications. A more recent example already touched upon in the previous section—the implementation of the Consumer Rights Directive—explains one strategy by which the English legislator aims to answer the call for maximising legal certainty. It further relates to the dilemma that English policy- and lawmakers have constantly been faced with when implementing EU law. Terms often used in this context are 'copying out' and 'gold plating'.

Unlike Austria, the UK was relatively fast in implementing the Consumer Rights Directive. This was realised in two steps, with the Consumer Rights (Payment Surcharges) Regulations 2012 (Consumer Rights Regulations 2012) and the Consumer Contracts (Information, Cancellation and Additional Charges) Regulations 2013 (Consumer Rights Regulations 2013).[41] Belonging to the group of Member States that are principally quite skeptical of EU private law-making,[42] England implemented the Consumer Rights Directive (in line with the traditional English approach) relatively narrowly and almost verbatim.[43] Narrowly, because the UK focused on the directly-affected areas and principally did not extend the provisions to matters not regulated by the Consumer Rights Directive. This basically means that

[40] S Wrbka, 'The Potential and Limits of Teleological Reduction Shown with the Example of the Austrian Warranty Regime' in M Fenwick and S Wrbka (eds), *Flexibility in Modern Business Law—A Comparative Assessment* (Singapore, Springer, 2016) 15.

[41] SI 2012/3110 and SI 2013/3134 respectively.

[42] In the case of the UK this is usually explained with the argument that EU private lawmaking would be heavily influenced by continental European legal doctrine.

[43] For details see in principle P Giliker, 'The Transposition of the Consumer Rights Directive into UK Law: Implementing a Maximum Harmonization Directive' (2015) 23 *European Review of Private Law* 5.

sometimes similar-looking scenarios are now regulated in different ways, depending on whether the facts are covered by the Consumer Rights Directive or not. The copying out technique is further reflected in the vastly word-for-word, ie verbatim, implementation of EU law, also applied in the present case of the Consumer Rights Directive transposition. Copying out achieves a maximum level of stability, as only those matters that are covered by EU law are subsumed under a new regime. It further minimises the risk of breaching EU law. But it could also negatively affect legal certainty. From the viewpoint of improved understandability, the increasingly scattered and incoherent domestic system can be considered as a retrograde step. The verbatim implementation of EU law additionally leads to a tension between the overall readability of English law and EU law-congruency.

The copying out technique, in combination with the rejection of gold plating, ie the 'no' to the equal regulation of similar matters, has been criticised in the literature. Certainty concerns, in particular, have remained strong. Hugh Beale, for example, argues that the coexistence of different rules for similar matters leads to a significantly high degree of fragmentation and incoherence. In combination with the relatively verbatim implementation this is further characterised by a quite vague and 'technical' language.[44] From the viewpoint of enhancing the transparency, clarity and comprehensibility of private law, this trend should be counteracted. To improve legal certainty, Beale asks for a simplification of the language—something we already saw in the Austrian context above—and a better standardisation, if not codification, of private law at the domestic level.[45]

The debate to consolidate English consumer law for the sake of increased clarity and comprehensibility gained further momentum in late 2013 and early 2014 when the plan to craft an updated and more comprehensive instrument materialised. The result of this, the Consumer Rights Bill 2014,[46] was considered a big move in English consumer law.[47]

A year later the project was finalised with the passing of the Consumer Rights Act 2015.[48] It replaced several older sectoral laws, including the

[44] H Beale, 'The Draft Directive on Consumer Rights and UK Consumer Law—Where now?' in G Howells and R Schulze (eds), *Modernising and Harmonising Consumer Contract Law* (Munich, Sellier, 2009) 298; H Beale, 'English Law Reform and the Impact of European Private Law' in S Vogenauer and S Weatherill (eds), *The Harmonisation of European Contract Law* (Oxford, Hart Publishing, 2006) 31.

[45] Beale, 'The Draft Directive on Consumer Rights and UK Consumer Law' 299ff.

[46] For details on it and its interplay with the earlier discussed Consumer Rights Regulations 2012 and 2013 see, in particular, Giliker, 'The Transposition of the Consumer Rights Directive'.

[47] Lorraine Conway, for example, calls it 'the biggest overhaul of consumer law for decades'—see L Conway, 'Draft Consumer Rights Bill', *position paper* (2013) 1 (copy with the author).

[48] SI 2015/1630. For details and background information see services.parliament.uk/bills/2013-14/consumerrights.html. For a summary of the Consumer Rights Act 2015 see,

Unfair Contract Terms Act 1977, the Sale of Goods Act 1979, the Supply of Goods and Services Act 1982, and the Unfair Terms in Consumer Contracts Regulations 1999. It further contains a couple of references and addendums to the Consumer Rights Regulations 2012 and 2013.

Overall, the Consumer Rights Act 2015 can be considered as the most comprehensive and integrated piece of English consumer law to date, and arguably as one of the most consolidated English private laws in general. From a certainty perspective, it has to be noted that it clearly aims to answer some of the earlier outlined certainty layers, most notably transparency, clarity and comprehensibility. It further seeks to achieve a balance between reflecting EU law and maintaining more traditional English ideas. With the Brexit *ante portas* it will be interesting to see which path future private law-making and legal certainty will take in English law.

Legal Certainty in German Private Law

I would like to conclude with a brief view of German private law. Legal certainty traditionally carries great weight in Germany. Together with securing justice and promoting the common good, Gustav Radbruch, for example, listed it as one of three principal legal concepts.[49] The long tradition of legal certainty debates in Germany might be one reason to explain the efforts to optimise its domestic private law. Unlike the other civil law jurisdictions discussed in this chapter, Germany has relatively recently undergone a more comprehensive, yet partial revision of its civil code to incorporate legal certainty considerations in its core private law, the German Civil Code or *Deutsches Bürgerliches Gesetzbuch*.

As pointed out earlier, legal certainty can manifest itself in different forms. Law should be as precise, determinable, understandable, stable, coherent, predictable, practicable and transparent as possible to be of service to its users. In the context of contract law, for example, the concept of protection of trust and legitimate expectation (*Vertrauensschutz*) demands that contractual provisions be clear and intelligible, and further mandates the contractual parties to abide by the agreement. This idea aims to implement the earlier-mentioned 'peace guaranteed by law' concept, by preventing disputes from arising. Legal certainty in its complexity does not, of course, only relate to contractual agreements. It goes further, as it dictates the legislator

eg L Conway, 'Consumer Rights Act 2015' (2015) *Briefing Paper Number SN 6588*, www.parliament.uk/briefing-papers/SN06588.pdf. Conway uses (nearly) the same words to highlight the importance of the act in terms of comprehensibility, calling it 'the biggest overhaul of consumer law for many decades': ibid 3.

[49] G Radbruch, *Der Geist des englischen Rechts* (Heidelberg, Adolf Rausch, 1947) 51.

to craft legislation that meets the certainty parameters as expressed above at a more general level.

One of the biggest German certainty projects in the field of private law thus far was the attempt to enhance the German Law of Obligations by revising, aligning and merging sectoral legislation with the relevant, more general rules of the German Civil Code in the early 2000s. With its 'modernisation of the law of obligations' (*Schuldrechtsmodernisierung*) in 2001/2002, Germany opted for an integrated approach that differs, for example, from the civil law jurisdictional approaches discussed earlier in this chapter. In Germany, the main emphasis was put on the consolidation of private law, while Austria, for example, largely followed a more fragmented approach by differentiating between the core provisions of the *Allgemeines Bürgerliches Gesetzbuch* and ancillary, more specific issues of special, sectoral legislation. The situation in Japan was—until recently (at the very least)—not much different, and basically resembled the Austrian development.

In the course of implementing the Consumer Sales Directive 1999[50] the German legislator took the opportunity to reconsider the (previously fragmented) structure and allegedly outdated and occasionally incoherent—hence confusing—substance of the German Law of Obligations. One of the key points was whether an incorporation of more specific issues into the *Deutsches Bürgerliches Gesetzbuch* (commonly referred to as the 'big solution'; *große Lösung*) was desirable, or whether one should rather distinguish between general issues (regulated in the *Deutsches Bürgerliches Gesetzbuch*) and more specific questions (regulated in sectoral laws; commonly referred to as the 'small solution'; *kleine Lösung*).

After intense discussion, the German legislator eventually arrived at the conclusion that integrating subconcepts into the German Civil Code would best serve an enhancement of legal certainty. With the 2001/2002 law of obligations modernisation Germany accordingly strove for a relatively high level of integration. From a completeness perspective, the revision project has to be considered successful, as it managed to combine previously fragmented regulations into one single set of rules. Yet, at least in the first years after the modernisation process, certainty-centered criticism remained strong. The complex and ramified structure of the new provisions was sometimes found detrimental to the understandability of the revised regime. However, over the last couple of years the situation has further improved, as most stakeholders have become increasingly familiar with it.

Germany is also a good example with which to explain some of the criticism towards a higher degree of centralisation and standardisation of private law at the EU level. In the context of the crafting process of the Consumer Rights Directive, for example, several German commentators heavily

[50] Directive 1999/44/EC, [1999] OJ L171/12.

criticised the plan to maximise full harmonisation (at least) with respect to core contract law issues.

One of the advocates against the EU plans was Michael Stürner, who, in a commentary on the 2008 Consumer Rights Directive Proposal, took the opportunity to elaborate on the tension between full harmonisation and domestic rules. Stürner based his certainty censure on those parts of the *Deutsches Bürgerliches Gesetzbuch* that would have been directly affected had the Consumer Rights Directive Proposal been adopted without changes. Since EU law, according to Stürner, would necessarily be the product of a compromise between different Member State policies and (additionally) between domestic and pan-EU interests, EU law could hardly ever meet exactly the same standards as used in every single Member State.[51]

This could manifest in various ways. Concepts used at the EU level would often differ from those used in older, domestic regimes. The material scopes might also be set apart. In most cases, national regimes take a broader approach. This, according to Stürner, is usually also the case in Germany.

In the case of the relatively narrow Consumer Rights Directive, the German legislator (again) had to choose between two unsatisfying solutions, seen from a certainty perspective. It could have subsumed those similar situations under the EU rules that would not have been covered by the directive. From a stability perspective, this would, however, have been counterproductive, in particular if one considers that the German rules have been developed and strengthened over decades. The alternative would have been treating quite similar-looking situations in different ways: one group under the already-existing law; the other one in accordance with the relevant EU rules.[52] This narrow approach could have impaired the overall clarity of the affected areas, because determining the correct set of rules in a concrete case might prove difficult.

The certainty dilemma of full harmonisation might have been the biggest reason why Germany and most other Member States who faced a similar situation strongly opposed the Consumer Rights Directive Proposal. In the end the resistance was, from a Member State perspective, successful, as the Consumer Rights Directive in its final version had a much narrower scope and did not absolutely follow full harmonisation. Some of the more controversial yet kept areas became subject to a different treatment, either via minimum harmonisation or regulatory options, giving Member States the opportunity to maintain their own, traditional approaches for the sake of legal stability and continuity.[53]

[51] Stürner notes as follows: 'It is obvious that different stakeholders pursue different, sometimes opposing interests, which obviously makes it difficult to reach a reasonable compromise' (my translation): see M Stürner, 'Das Konzept der Vollharmonisierung' in M Stürner (ed), *Vollharmonisierung im Europäischen Verbraucherrecht?* (Munich, Sellier, 2010) 3.

[52] Stürner, 'Das Konzept der Vollharmonisierung' 7.

[53] For details on this see, eg Wrbka, *European Consumer Access to Justice Revisited* 184 with further references.

CONCLUDING REMARKS

The examples discussed in this contribution underline the fact that no one-size-fits-all definition of legal certainty exists. The legal certainty concept shows elements of Wittgenstein's notion of a 'family resemblance', since it can be broken down into a multitude of smaller subcategories that, to a certain extent, possess some similarities.

What does this mean in practice? As pointed out elsewhere, the certainty sub-layers could be classified into two bigger categories.[54] Legal clarity, stability, predictability and transparency could, for example, be merged into the broader concept of 'legal clarification'. Here the focus is put on the question of how to conceptualise legal rules to simplify the legal framework without impairing the overall quality of law. In this context, legislators deal primarily with linguistic and comprehensibility challenges. Two examples discussed in this chapter are the more recent Austrian and Japanese efforts to create norms that can be easily understood by laypeople. Trends in Austria go towards more interdisciplinary research, merging purely legal questions with input from psychology and linguistics. Japan, instead, aims to modernise its private law with the help of comparative legal research to assess whether foreign developments should be incorporated into Japanese law.

In contrast to this, a second group of certainty notions, most notably legal accessibility, legal enforcement and the practicability of the application of law, can be grouped together under the umbrella of 'legal rationalisation'. This concept breathes more life into law by adding value considerations to the legal framework. Here it is not so much a question of improving the understandability of law: it is rather the issue of suitability that determines whether a particular legal rule is certain enough. Attempts to strive for a practical, well-working legal apparatus can be seen as a prime example.

Although the legal certainty expressions met in this chapter highlight different faces of certainty, it should be noted that all of them are bound together by a common thread. Eventually, they all can be used to explain efforts to maximise the potential of law for the sake of society, be it understood in a collective sense or as benefiting each individual. In this respect, legal certainty can be considered as a parameter by which one can determine the appropriateness of legal policy decisions to enhance the stakeholders' well-being with the help of law. Different as the approaches look in practice, it is this connecting idea that provides for some kind of common denominator and criteria for assessment.

[54] For details see S Wrbka, 'Comments on Legal Certainty from the Perspective of European, Austrian and Japanese Private Law' in M Fenwick and S Wrbka (eds), *Legal Certainty in a Contemporary Context: Private and Criminal Law Perspectives* (Singapore, Springer, 2016) 13.

7

Legal Certainty: A Common Law View and a Critique

JOHN LINARELLI

INTRODUCTION

ONE OF THE most fundamental principles of English contract and commercial law is that the law needs to be 'certain'. The principle of certainty is widely accepted as an important working concept, even a standard of legitimacy, in active operation in English private law and indeed in English law more generally. If one were to peruse any standard treatise on the English law of contract, for example, one would find use of the concept to support legal doctrines and case outcomes.[1] In October 2011, Lord Mance, a Justice of the UK Supreme Court, gave the Oxford Shrieval Lecture on 'Should the Law be Certain?'[2] Going back to the founding generation of modern English commercial law, Lord Mansfield's pronouncement in *Vallejo v Wheeler* can be found in leading contemporary texts on English contract and commercial law: 'in all mercantile transactions the great object should be certainty. And therefore, it is of more consequence that a rule should be certain than whether the rule is established one way or the other: because speculators in trade then know which ground to go upon'.[3] In the 2007 House of Lords judgment of *Golden Straight Corpn v Nippon YKK*, Lord Bingham asserted in his dissenting speech that 'the quality of certainty' is 'a traditional strength and major selling point of English commercial law'.[4]

[1] Treitel's classic text refers to 'certainty' 75 times: E Peel, *Treitel on the Law of Contracts* 14th edn (London, Sweet & Maxwell, 2015).

[2] Lord Mance concluded that certainty is desirable but 'not the ultimate aim of the law'. He was referring generally to the role of judges in a society. Lord Mance, 'Should the law be certain?' (The Oxford Shrieval Lecture given at the University Church of St Mary the Virgin, Oxford, on 11 October 2011).

[3] *Vallejo v Wheeler* (1774) 1 Cowp 143, 153.

[4] (The 'Golden Victory') *Golden Straight Corpn v Nippon YKK* [2007] UKHL 12 para 1. I refer throughout this chapter to 'English law', which in the United Kingdom is the law of the jurisdiction of England and Wales.

Yet, in contrast, one would be hard pressed to find any such emphasis or pronouncements by American lawyers or judges. Hardly do we hear the word 'certainty' uttered in an American law school classroom or in an American courtroom. There are, of course, institutional differences in the structure of court systems in the two countries that lead American Supreme Court justices to give lectures on federalism and public law issues. Private law, is generally state and not federal law.[5] But should not legal certainty be as important to American private and commercial lawyers as it is to their English counterparts?

What is going on here? The aim of this chapter is to aid us in understanding the meaning of the concept of certainty in the common law tradition and the role of the concept in that tradition. To strive for clarity, we need to explore some relatively recent intellectual history about how the common law tradition diverged in approach between England and the US in the twentieth century. The first section provides that intellectual history. It outlines in brief the split in the common law tradition that occurred in the early twentieth century between English conceptualists and American legal realists. The result is a now a demarcation between two sub-traditions within the common law tradition itself, one English and the other American. At the centre of this divergence was a dispute about the meaning of legal certainty. The second section goes over how the more contemporary and tractable concept is predictability, but the divergence in traditions has resulted in two different versions of predictability, one conceptual and about the logical form of legal rules, and the other instrumental, about the move of legal rules towards meeting standards of economic efficiency. English and American lawyers appear to agree that the law should be predictable, though they marly give predictability a different meaning depending on the context.

CONCEPTUALISM VERSUS REALISM

In their influential *Introduction to Comparative Law*, Konrad Zwiegert and Hein Kötz classify legal systems around the notion of legal families. Comparativists are well-familiar with their classifications of 'Romanistic,' 'Germanic,' and 'Anglo-American' legal families, among others. While Zwiegert and Kötz classify civilian traditions in separate families, they classify all common law traditions within a single legal family, though they acknowledge that 'though England is unquestionably the parent system, the law of the US, while staying in the family', has developed a 'distinctive style'.[6] Others go further and classify the differences between American and

[5] See *Erie Railroad Co v Tompkins* (1938) 304 US 64.

[6] K Zweigert and H Kötz, *An Introduction to Comparative Law* (Oxford, Oxford University Press, 1998) 41.

English law as more fundamental.[7] Still others question these distinctions and whether the US really is a set of mixed jurisdictions.[8] These issues are beyond our scope here and I will stipulate for purposes of getting the argument out that American law is broadly within the common law tradition with some exceptions. It is certainly true that lawyers and judges in the early American Republic saw as one of their roles to adapt English common law to American conditions and that ancestral imprint still probably remains on American law. Because of differing political, economic, social, and geographical conditions between the two countries, differences have always existed since the very beginning of the American Republic and even before during the colonial period.

In the eighteenth and nineteenth centuries, American law and legal thought diverged from English law but was still a net borrower of ideas and legislative innovations from Britain. The first wave of commercial legislation in the US borrowed substantially from British legislation.[9] In the nineteenth and early twentieth centuries, the US was in its 'classical' stage of legal thought, which emphasised formal and conceptual reasoning about positive sources of law and supported a wholly individualist approach to the organisation of society.[10] The individualistic ethics that law was supposed to represent in its rules has been overlooked; it can be seen as forming the most important pillar of support for any legal system grounded in formal and conceptual reasoning. It is reflected in law when the law's focus is primarily on the rights and duties of individual actors. For example, classical legal thought supported a tort law whose purpose was only to correct injustice in a binary relationship between tortfeasor and victim. It could not support a tort law serving social ends beyond corrective justice, such as in getting right the distribution of the risk of accidents. So too, contract and commercial law would focus on the will of the parties and so certainty in the law of market transacting would serve the needs of individuals to engage in voluntary exchange, however these concepts might be understood at the time. In such a society, certainty in the law takes on great importance because society has no real aims other than to support the individual in whatever they choose to do in market transactions. If we conceive of private

[7] See PS Atiyah and Robert S Summer, *Form and Substance in Anglo-American Law: A Comparative Study in Legal Reasoning, Legal Theory, and Legal Institutions* (Oxford, Oxford University Press, 1991).

[8] See N Garoupa and CI Gómez Ligüerre, 'The Evolution of the Common Law and Efficiency' (2012) 40 *Georgia Journal of International and Comparative Law* 307.

[9] See, eg S Williston, 'The Law of Sales in the Proposed Uniform Commercial Code' (1950) 64 *Harvard Law Review* 561; KN Llewellyn, 'Why a Commercial Code?' (1951) 22 *Tennessee Law Review* 779.

[10] A definitive of source on this period is WM Wiecek, *The Lost World of Classical Legal Thought* (Oxford, Oxford University Press, 1998).

law in these bilateral and individualist ways, then certainty of course will have an important rank in the order of values a legal system purports to serve. Conceptualism offers a very important framework for thinking about the law in such a legal system.

Conceptualism, in the sense used here, refers to a way of thinking about the law that places primary importance on the logical features of legal rules.[11] A lawyer uses conceptual analysis to understand the meaning of legal concepts and to search for logical coherence among legal concepts. The idea is that we should strive to understand the meaning of, say, legal obligation, right, duty, justice, and so on as those concepts are used by lawyers and judges. A conceptualist understanding of the law relies on a presupposition that law is, in Richard Posner's words, an 'autonomous discipline'.[12]

Differences in how to think about the law as between the US and England became apparent in the early twentieth century, leading to modes of legal thought in the US focusing more on the social ends of law and in trying to understand the effects of law in society. While such a move made inroads in the UK generally sometime later in the twentieth century, conceptualists still have relatively greater influence in English private and commercial law. For example, legal scholarship in commercial and corporate law in the US is substantially in the law and economics school of thought, but less so in the UK. How did this happen? The answer partly (but clearly not wholly) lies in understanding jurisprudential movements in the two countries from the late nineteenth century until the early 1960s. The brief excursion into intellectual history to follow is disputed by some[13] but it is likely to represent the 'mainstream' view.

In the US, sociological jurisprudence and then American legal realism brought an end to conceptualism as the most influential way of understanding the law. We can begin to comprehend the divergence in legal thought in the common law tradition by starting with Oliver Wendell Holmes Jr's lecture for the dedication of a new law building at Boston University, 'The Path of the Law', published in the Harvard Law Review in 1897.[14] Thomas Grey describes Holmes as '[t]he greatest oracle of American legal thought.'[15]

[11] See J Raz, *Practical Reason and Norms* (Oxford, Oxford University Press, 1999) 10.

[12] RA Posner, 'The Decline of Law as an Autonomous Discipline: 1962–1987' (1987) 100 *Harvard Law Review* 761.

[13] This is not the place to investigate competing interpretations, but it may but it may be well worth reading BZ Tamanaha, *Beyond the Formalist-Realist Divide* (Princeton, Princeton University Press, 2010) and perhaps also investigating some of the recent literature on historical jurisprudence. See DM Rabban, *Law's History: American Legal Thought and the Transatlantic Turn to History* (Cambridge, Cambridge University Press, 2013); KM Parker, *Common Law, History, and Democracy in America, 1790–1900: Legal Thought Before Modernism* (Cambridge, Cambridge University Press, 2011).

[14] OW Holmes Jr, 'The Path of the Law' (1897) 10 *Harvard Law Review* 457.

[15] TC Grey, 'Holmes and Legal Pragmatism' (1989) 41 *Stanford Law Review* 787.

Sanford Levinson describes 'The Path of the Law' as 'the single most important essay ever written by an American on the law'.[16] Morton Horwitz argues that in 'The Path of the Law' Holmes 'pushed American legal thought into the twentieth century.'[17] Richard Posner argues that it 'may be the best article-length work on law ever written.'[18]

In 'The Path of the Law', Holmes offered his clearest criticism of the 'fallacy ... that the only force at work in the development of the law is logic.'[19] In 'The Path of the Law', he offered a direct attack on certainty:

> [T]he logical method and form flatter that longing for certainty and for repose which is in every human mind. But certainty generally is illusion, and repose is not the destiny of man. Behind the logical form lies a judgment as to the relative worth and importance of competing legislative grounds, often an inarticulate and unconscious judgment, it is true, and yet the very root and nerve of the whole proceeding.[20]

In his dissenting opinion in the famous case of *Lochner v New York*, Holmes stated his famous aphorism that '[g]eneral propositions do not decide concrete cases'.[21] Legal rules will only take us so far. They will 'run out' and other more policy-oriented considerations will have to be deployed to solve the particular 'legal' problem at hand.

We must combine Holmes' criticism of the notion of legal certainty with his support for a prediction theory of law. Holmes thought certainty impractical, but prediction to be central to the role of law. Holmes offered what is widely considered to be a precursor account to contemporary law and economics.[22] Holmes argued: 'a legal duty so called is nothing but a prediction that if a man does or omits certain things he will be made to suffer in this or that way by judgment of the court; and so, of a legal right.'[23] His famous 'bad man' quote is worth repeating here:

> If you want to know the law and nothing else, you must look at it as a bad man, who cares only for the material consequences which such knowledge enables him

[16] S Levinson, 'Strolling Down the Path of the Law (and Toward Critical Legal Studies?) The Jurisprudence of Richard Posner' (1991) 91 *Columbia Law Review* 1221.

[17] M Horwitz, *The Transformation of American Law, 1870–1960: The Crisis of Legal Orthodoxy* (Oxford, Oxford University Press, 1994) 142.

[18] RA Posner, 'Introduction' in RA Posner (ed), *The Essential Holmes* (Chicago, University of Chicago Press, 1990) x. I do not want to paint too rosy a picture of Holmes. I rely on him here for the limited purpose of elucidating how the concept of certainty has worked its way into legal thought. For thoroughgoing critiques of Holmes, see SJ Burton (ed), *The Path of the Law and its Influence: The Legacy of Oliver Wendell Holmes, Jr* (Cambridge, Cambridge University Press, 2000).

[19] Holmes, 'The Path of the Law' 465.

[20] ibid 466.

[21] *Lochner v New York* (1905) 198 US 45, 76 (Holmes J dissenting).

[22] Many have so asserted. See G Minda, *Postmodern Legal Movements: Law and Jurisprudence at Century's End* (New York, New York University Press, 1995) 86.

[23] Holmes, 'The Path of the Law' 458.

> to predict, not as a good one, who finds his reasons for conduct, whether inside the law or outside of it, in the vaguer sanctions of conscience.[24]

He continues:

> But if we take the view of our friend the bad man we shall find that he does not care two straws for the axioms or deductions, but that he does want to know what the Massachusetts or English courts are likely to do in fact. I am much of his mind. The prophecies of what the courts will do in fact, and nothing more pretentious, are what I mean by the law.[25]

In the prediction theory set forth in 'The Path of the Law' we find the origins of the efficient breach doctrine in the economics of contract law: 'The duty to keep a contract at common law means a prediction that you must pay damages if you do not keep it,—and nothing else.'[26]

We need to combine Holmes' argument for law as serving the role of prediction with his argument that inquiry about law must move towards a focus on social ends, using the tools of the social sciences. Holmes said in 'The Path of the Law':

> For the rational study of the law the black-letter man may be the man of the present, but the man of the future is the man of statistics and the master of economics. It is revolting to have no better reason for a rule of law than that so it was laid down in the time of Henry IV.[27]

Holmes's approach is a forerunner to American legal realism. Let us now move forward in time to the apex of the legal realist movement in the US. Karl Llewellyn was the principal architect of the Uniform Commercial Code in the US and the Code is widely seen as the most important achievement of the legal realists. Llewellyn was commercial lawyer and the most influential figure in the first school of jurisprudence (broadly understood) indigenous to the US. The Code drafters, led by Llewellyn, seem to have agreed with Llewellyn's view that uniformity of language was no guarantee of uniformity of interpretation. Rather, what was needed were clear statements of reason and purpose in the Code, which would prompt courts to justify decisions according to these statements of reason and purpose.[28] This approach to drafting the Code led to disquiet among practicing lawyers, who were accustomed to placing the integrity of a commercial statute on the notion of certainty. Llewellyn was aware of this worry and turned the argument

[24] ibid 459.

[25] ibid 460–61.

[26] ibid 462.

[27] Beyond our scope here is an investigation of how the economics of Holmes' day differ from contemporary economics. See H Hovenkamp, *The Opening of American Law: Neoclassical Legal Thought, 1870–1970* (Oxford, Oxford University Press, 2015) 75–90.

[28] See ZB Wiseman, 'The Limits of Vision: Karl Llewellyn and the Merchant Rules' (1987) 100 *Harvard Law Review* 465, 495.

on its head in his promotion of the newly-drafted Code by arguing that it improved the certainty of the law:

> It costs the business man first because of the uncertainty. There are fields in which no man, before the case has been brought up to the supreme court of the particular state in the particular instance, has any assurance as to what the law is. There are fields, therefore, in which the counselor is without a sound foundation for effective counseling.[29]

The historical evidence suggests, however, that Llewellyn may have held a different and much more nuanced view of the role of certainty than what he offered during the drafting stages of the Uniform Commercial Code. We of course do not know his motives when he was deep in the process of drafting the Code, and he may have been assuaging the fears of the bar to promote the success of the Code, or he may have simply changed his views at various stages in his professional life. His writings both before and after the Code project tell us something different about his views on the role of certainty in the law, and perhaps are closer to his true convictions, though we will never know.

Llewellyn's work early in his career, *Präjudizienrecht und Rechtsprechung in Amerika*, published in German in 1933 and not translated into English until 1989, offers perhaps his most sophisticated insights on legal certainty.[30] This book, in English, *The Case Law System in America*, was written for a series of lectures that Llewellyn gave at the University of Leipzig Faculty of Law. It can be difficult to segregate legal certainty as a notion from other arguments the legal realists made about law and legal interpretation because a good deal of what they said was an attack on legal conceptualism more generally, which places great value on certainty. Llewellyn's German scholarship reflects a set of themes that he pursued more generally in his work. At least three claims come out of that work, two of which relate indirectly to legal certainty and one of which is directly about legal certainty. First, Llewellyn argued that the methods of judges and lawyers, which he characterised as the lawyer's craft and 'feel,' are significant sources of certainty about the law. Second, the 'situation sense' of cases and not the legal rules are what lead to the predictability of judicial decisions. In other words, a judge's 'sense of justice' is normatively relevant. Third, while legal certainty refers to predictability of judicial decision-making for the lawyer, for the layperson it means consistency of legal rules with social norms. It is this layperson sense of certainty that will make him write an Article 2 of the

[29] Llewellyn, 'Why a Commercial Code?' 779–80.

[30] KN Llewellyn, *The Case Law System in America* (Chicago, University of Chicago Press, 1989) (translated by M Ansaldi; edited and with an introduction by P Gewirtz).

Uniform Commercial Code, on the sale of goods that places great importance on merchant custom.[31]

Llewellyn's later work dealt with what William Twining has described as the myth of uncertainty, which was really a way to say that the concept of certainty was unhelpful in understanding the quality of law.[32] In his book, *The Common Law Tradition*, published in 1960, Llewellyn took the following position on legal certainty:

> I reject as useless and misleading the dichotomy which infected so much writing of the '20s and '30s: absolute or 100 per cent certainty versus anything else at all as being 'uncertainty.' I see no absolute certainty of outcome in any aspect of legal life, and think that no man should ever have imagined that any such thing could be, or could be worth serious consideration. Instead I see degrees of lessening certainty of outcome ranging from what to the observer or participant seems pure chance, into a situation where a skilled, experienced guess (though only a guess) is yet a better bet than the guess of the ignorant, through a situation where the odds run plainly a little one way, through one where skilled counsel can be expected to materially increase the odds, and on through the situation which is a business gamble or better into the one which is for human living 'safe'.[33]

And also in *The Common Law Tradition*:

> [T]he ideal is not 'certainty' at all, in any way of the senses in which that term is commonly applied to matters legal. The true ideal is reasonable regularity of decision. If there is regularity, there is continuity enough. ... The reasonable aspect of the regularity ... holds out full room to adjust any complex of tension to the hugely variant needs of whatever the relevant type-situations may be. ...[34]

Llewellyn connected these claims to the idea of 'reasonable reckonability' in appellate judging. For Llewellyn, reasonable reckonability rather than certainty was the appropriate focus, which connects to his idea of law as a craft and with judges sharing deeply-ingrained professional habits of thought, beliefs, and attitudes. He catalogued 14 'steadying factors' at work in litigation that underwrite what could be expected from judicial decision-making.[35] Reasonable reckonability shares substantial similarities with the notion of legitimate expectations that one finds in English and European public law.[36]

Llewellyn was not in the 'radical' wing of legal realism and his approach to critiquing the concept of certainty was to substitute what he considered to be more useful concepts that more closely connected to being able to

[31] Wiseman, 'The Limits of Vision'.

[32] See W Twining, *Karl Llewellyn and the Realist Movement* 2nd edn (Cambridge, Cambridge University Press, 2012) 207.

[33] KN Llewellyn, *The Common Law Tradition: Deciding Appeals* (Boston, Little Brown, 1960) 17.

[34] ibid 216 (footnotes omitted).

[35] ibid 19–61.

[36] P Craig, 'Legal Certainty and Legitimate Expectations' in P Craig, *EU Administrative Law* (Oxford, Oxford University Press, 2012) ch 18.

evaluate the behaviour and action of judges for those limited to elucidating the logical form of the law. The radical wing of legal realism was more critical and less reconstructive. Jerome Frank, for example, argued that there was a value to legal uncertainty, in that a person has a 'positive delight' for the 'hazardous, incalculable character of life' and sees 'life's very insecurity' as offering its 'most inviting aspect'.[37] One must wonder whether Frank's attempt at a psychology of judging was more fanciful than serious.[38] Still, regardless of which wing of legal realism we examine, taking the influence of legal realism as a whole on American legal thought, along with some of its successor movements such as Critical Legal Studies, we can say with some confidence that the concept of legal certainty has received less emphasis in American legal education and in American law more generally after the rise and fall of the legal realists.

Llewellyn's approach to certainty did seem to prevail on the drafting style of the Uniform Commercial Code. Homer Kripke, a key member of the drafting team of the original Code and a practitioner, summarises the tensions between the academics and the practitioners about legal certainty in Code drafting as follows:

> The extent to which the draftsmen left commercial law without rules operating with certainty made some of the practicing members of the sponsor organizations very unhappy. Here again, the draftsmen's academic orientation was apparent. They could view with more equanimity than the practicing lawyers the fact that a question of commercial reasonableness or good faith is uncertain and unpredictable, a question of fact, ie a jury question, an invitation to litigation. Where the practitioners wanted problems answered in the statute, the draftsmen were content to leave the answers to the judicial process. The draftsmen pointed out that the fear of jury decisions applies only to the man who practices brinkmanship in his application of the nonautomatic standards. One who keeps himself well within commercial standards, or who acts in unquestionable good faith, has no problem. This was scant comfort to the practicing lawyers who envisioned specific close problems.
>
> The academicians rightly prevailed. In these days of airway bills and forwarders' receipts, of computers, of magnetic tapes and magnetic inks, of communication satellites, the only rule that will not become obsolete is the rule that automatically adjusts to change. In the long run, the Code's efforts to restore the vitality of the law merchant will prove to have been well conceived.[39]

[37] LL Fuller, 'American Legal Realism' (1934) 82 *University of Pennsylvania Law Review* 429, 433; J Frank, *Law and the Modern Mind* (Paris, Brentano 1930) 17: Frank dedicated significant parts of his book to the 'myth of certainty'; J Paul, 'Jerome Frank's Attack on the 'Myth' of Legal Certainty' (1957) 36 *Nebraska Law Review* 547.

[38] See Roscoe Pound's critique. R Pound, *The Ideal Element in Law* (Calcutta, University of Calcutta Press, 1958).

[39] H Kripke, 'The Principles Underlying the Drafting of the Uniform Commercial Code' (1962) *University of Illinois Law Forum* 321 (footnotes omitted).

Much later, these views about trade-offs between flexibility or adaptability and certainty will be challenged[40] but the challenge has probably not stuck and still the basic characteristics associated with the decline of conceptualism in the US continues to be influential in law and legal thought in that country.

From Holmes onward we can see a clear trend in American legal thought away from the conceptualism of certainty and towards an instrumental form of predictability about the law. American legal realism left its imprint on American commercial law, and American law more generally, even as the legal realist movement receded into history. The school of American legal thought that attempted a middle ground between conceptualism and realism—the legal process school—did nothing to bring back the notion of certainty to prominence. In fact, it perpetuated the decline of the concept in American legal thought, with its focus on statutory interpretation that relies on statutory purpose rather than a literal interpretation of the language of statutes and its allowance for moral principles and social aims to inform the law.[41] The familiar refrain in the American legal academy has been that 'we are all legal realists now,' which we should not interpret literally but as a way of saying that legal realism has left its influence on American law.[42] That refrain will be less heard as legal realism recedes to a more distant history for succeeding generations, but to the extent that the history of ideas matters the influence of legal realism will persist.

While conceptual analysis still remains important in American law, as it does more or less in any legal system, there is far more of what Joseph Singer calls 'line drawing' in the US than in the search for certain answers grounded in the immanence and internal logic of immutable and abstract legal concepts.[43] A lawyer engaged in line drawing must necessarily think of law as an attempt at balancing competing sets of interests along the broader lines of the policies and purposes underlying legal rules, in search of how

[40] A Schwartz and RE Scott, 'Contract Theory and the Limits of Contract Law' (2003) 113 *Yale Law Journal* 541; D Charny, 'The New Formalism in Contract' (1999) 66 *University of Chicago Law Review* 842; RA Hillman, 'The 'New Conservatism' in Contract Law and the Process of Legal Change' (1999) 40 *Boston College Law Review* 879; RJ Mooney, 'The New Conceptualism in Contract Law' (1995) 74 *Oregon Law Review* 1131.

[41] The canonical text in the Legal Process School is HM Hart and AM Sacks, *The Legal Process: Basic Problems in the Making and Application of Law*, initially published in mimeo form for use by students but in current form is a casebook published by Foundation Press, and edited by WN Eskridge, Jr and PP Frickey. The latest edition is as of 2006.

[42] See J Singer, 'Legal Realism Now' (1988) 76 *California Law Review* 465: 'Legal realism has fundamentally altered our conceptions of legal reasoning and of the relationship between law and society. The legal realists were remarkably successful both in changing the terms of legal discourse and in undermining the idea of a self-regulating market system. All major current schools of thought are, in significant ways, products of legal realism. To some extent, we are all realists now.'

[43] ibid.

law might achieve social ends such as those associated with efficiency or fairness. In such an approach, certainty will necessarily have less importance. More generally, the trend of legal thought in the US moved in the early to mid-twentieth century towards placing high importance on understanding the social ends of law and began to place a lower-order emphasis on the logical features of the law and legal concepts. Doing so-called 'doctrinal' analysis has never lost its significance in the US, but it is just not considered all that high-powered any more as a tool for the development of the law.

In the early to mid-twentieth century, legal thought in England, and Britain more generally, took a different course. The period in the history of legal thought when Holmes wrote the 'Path of the Law' in 1897 and in which the legal realists were ascendant in America, from about 1930 to 1955, compare approximately to the period from when John Austin resigned as Professor of Jurisprudence from University College London in 1834 to when HLA Hart began his appointment as Professor of Jurisprudence at Oxford in 1952. Of course, legal thought then was not monolithic and even the realists had influential critics in America.[44] I can only suggest general trends.[45] There will be counterexamples. I offer a brief sketch of intellectual history here to show that there has indeed been a divergence in the common law tradition in ways to approach legal certainty, that this divergence connects more basically to differing ways of thinking about the law generally, and that the divergence remains influential to this day, though, as I explain below, both the English and the American traditions within the common law world have retrenched somewhat in the contemporary period from more extreme positions when legal realism was ascendant.

When the history of legal thought is explored, rarely is anything said about the period between Austin and Hart, expect perhaps about Maine's historical jurisprudence, which seems to have had little lasting influence.[46] Neil Duxbury offers a critique: 'It would be wrong to assume that nothing happened in English jurisprudence between Austin's era and Hart's. It is just that nothing much happened that would be remembered' and '[i]t seems fair to say … that English jurisprudence after Austin lacked imagination and direction'.[47]

English 'jurisprudes' of the day did not write jurisprudence as we know it today, though neither did the legal realists.[48] We can narrow our scope of

[44] Lon Fuller among them. See Fuller, 'American Legal Realism'.

[45] My approach is like that of Atiyah and Summers, *Form and Substance in Anglo-American Law*.

[46] But see Rabban, *Law's History*, which suggests a reinterpretation.

[47] N Duxbury, 'English Jurisprudence Between Austin and Hart' (2005) 91 *Virginia Law Review* 1, 3 and 15.

[48] 'Jurisprudes' was a term that Llwellyn often used to describe legal realists and others who investigated questions about the role of law and its operation in society. Beyond our scope here are the internecine debates about what constitutes 'jurisprudence'. Most legal scholars

discussion to a grouping of legal scholars on both sides of the Atlantic who asked questions about the law generally and about the preferred methods for inquiring about law, and who pitted themselves against each other in ways that have affected the way that legal certainty is understood in the common law tradition today.

Says Duxbury, 'Americans who travel the neglected path that is English jurisprudence from the 1830s to the 1950s will soon find themselves in a world very different from their own. …'[49] English jurisprudence focused on the analysis of legal concepts in this period.[50] Duxbury explains that the English legal scholars of the day that are the focus of our discussion wrote 'essays about stare decisis, the relationship between law and equity, statutory interpretation, the English court system, the growth of negligence liability, the divisions between the various branches of the law, and other basic legal themes'.[51] The influence of focusing on the analysis of legal concepts remains a stronger influence in England (and Britain more severally) than in the US. Hart's analytical jurisprudence did nothing to dispel it and indeed could be said to have promoted the analysis of legal concepts. The analysis of concepts of course occurred in the US, where its most influential proponent of the time under investigation was probably Wesley Newcomb Hohfeld.[52] But Hohfeld's work was not as influential as legal realism (which followed later) or even Pound's sociological jurisprudence.

One of the more influential figures of the time in Britain was Arthur Goodhart, who held the Chair in Jurisprudence that Hart would eventually hold for 20 years before Hart, from 1932–52.[53] Though Goodhart was careful to balance competing considerations in his inaugural lecture in 1932,[54] Harold Laski, who chaired the lecture, wrote to Holmes that Goodhart 'thought clearly, that the realists … were just wicked'.[55] Goodhart argued that the common law doctrine of precedent gives the common law its certainty and that 'when a precedent is created the law becomes rigid'.[56] In a stunning display of ignorance or naivete (or a combination of the two) of

today think of American legal realism as some form of proto-social science about the law. Brian Leiter argues that it is a naturalised version of jurisprudence: B Leiter, *Naturalizing Jurisprudence: Essays on American Legal Realism and Naturalism in Legal Philosophy* (Oxford, Oxford University Press, 2007).

49 Duxbury, 'English Jurisprudence Between Austin and Hart' 5.

50 ibid 6.

51 ibid 14.

52 ibid 7; WN Hohfeld, *Fundamental Legal Conceptions as Applied in Judicial Reasoning* (New Haven, Yale University Press, 1919).

53 ibid 58.

54 So says Duxbury, 'English Jurisprudence Between Austin and Hart' 58.

55 ibid quoting letter from Harold J Laski to Justice Oliver Wendell Holmes Jr (20 January 1932) in M DeWolfe Howe (ed), *Holmes-Laski Letters* vol 2 (Cambridge, Mass, Harvard University Press 1953) 1358.

56 AL Goodhart, 'Precedent in English and Continental Law' (1934) 50 *Law Quarterly Review* 40, 64, quoted in Duxbury, 'English Jurisprudence Between Austin and Hart' 58–59.

civilian legal methods, Goodhart argued in his inaugural lecture that '[i]t is in its claim to certainty and rigidity that the English method has a marked advantage over the Continental one. …'[57] Goodhart was also critical of the legal realist focus on uncertainty in the law. He argued that 'the most striking feature of this school is the stress they place upon the uncertainty of law'.[58] This emphasis, said Goodhart, 'may lead to juristic pessimism on the part of students, and, what is even more dangerous, that it will induce an emotional rather than rational approach to legal problems'.[59] His criticism of Frank in his inaugural lecture was tautological, relying on an odd analogy to military orders to make the point that '[i]t is of course possible to point to exceptional cases, but we do know that in practice English Courts recognise that they are bound by precedents, and that no attempt is made to escape from them if they are clearly on point'.[60]

CK Allen, Goodhart's colleague at Oxford, described attempts to evaluate law using the social sciences as 'Megalomaniac Jurisprudence.'[61] Says Duxbury, he considered Pound's sociological jurisprudence to be 'inappropriately normative' and that that 'legal realism filled him with feelings approximating disgust'.[62] Said Allen: 'It was perhaps appropriate that the age of jazz should produce a Jazz Jurisprudence.'[63] Others at Oxford and particularly at the London universities of the time were more receptive,[64] but remember there were few academic law schools at the time in Britain and scholarship from the medieval universities such as Oxford carried great weight, not only in England but in the British sphere of influence in what was to become the Commonwealth family of nations.

One could suggest a number of related reasons for the divergence in the common law tradition between realists and conceptualists. Ultimately the explanation will depend on the discipline in which the person offering it operates. The most compelling is perhaps a sociological explanation.[65] American legal realism may have been a response to social and political events

[57] ibid 59.

[58] AL Goodhart, 'Some American Interpretations of Law' in I Jennings (ed), *Modern Theories of Law* (London, Wildy, 1933) 11, quoted in Duxbury, 'English Jurisprudence Between Austin and Hart' 58.

[59] ibid 20.

[60] Goodhart, 'Precedent in English and Continental Law' 59.

[61] CK Allen, *Law in the Making* 3rd edn (Oxford, Oxford University Press, 1939) 35, quoted in Duxbury, 'English Jurisprudence Between Austin and Hart' 61.

[62] Duxbury, 'English Jurisprudence Between Austin and Hart' 61.

[63] Allen, *Law in the Making* 45, quoted in Duxbury, 'English Jurisprudence Between Austin and Hart' 62.

[64] Duxbury, 'English Jurisprudence Between Austin and Hart' 63–69.

[65] See ibid 55–56: 'It would be a mistake to expect English jurisprudence to take much from the lessons that were being learned in the United States. American legal realism, after all, was a jurisprudential response to the dominance of Langdellianism in the law schools, the initiatives of the American Law Institute, the perceived and some of the legal problems posed by the New Deal' (footnote omitted).

in the US in the early twentieth century, in which classical legal thought was associated with a 'laissez faire' ideology of the US Supreme Court of the time, which used its powers of judicial review to enforce freedom of contract doctrines that obstructed early attempts at regulating the economy and made difficult the implementation of New Deal policies.[66] It may also have been an attempt to undo so-called Langdellian approaches to the study of law in American law schools, associated with classical legal thought.[67] Add to all of this that federalism in a large country that was undergoing significant social change made it impossible to maintain consistency of case law across many jurisdictions and so American versions of the common law necessarily would lead to contradictions in the case law. The Supreme Court in *Erie Railroad Co v Tompkins*[68] is widely understood to have settled the point that the common law resided in the states, and this lead eventually to the common law comprising essentially only private law in the US. Duxbury concludes:

> North American commentators were concluding by the 1960s that English jurisprudence and American jurisprudence were each motivated by different concerns, and that the English had but the flimsiest understanding of realist legal thought. It is difficult to argue that this conclusion is wrong.[69]

It is difficult to draw clear lines in this divergence of thought in the common law tradition. Legal realism was not a coherent body of thought and legal realists can be said to form different wings or variants.[70] Many legal realists were 'hard core' lawyers and took legal doctrine seriously. Many American legal scholars and lawyers of the time were not legal realists and were avid critics of legal realism. The folklore around Llewellyn, for example, was that he had an encyclopaedic knowledge of sales law and a review of his challenging Sales Law casebook reveals it.[71] Paradoxically, the study of law in the US must necessarily be on the concepts of law and their logical form because there is really no way in a large and diverse federal system of many jurisdictions to study 'the' cases for many categories of law, except perhaps for American federal constitutional and administrative law.

The debate about certainty between American and English lawyers transformed in the latter part of the twentieth century into a discussion of the predictability of the law. Predictability is the more sensible concept because it allows for the consideration of probabilities and to be able to say with

[66] For a summary, see E Chemerinsky, 'Substantive Dues Process' (1999) 15 *Touro Law Review* 1501.

[67] Duxbury, 'English Jurisprudence Between Austin and Hart' 55–56.

[68] See n 5 above.

[69] Duxbury, 'English Jurisprudence Between Austin and Hart' (footnote omitted).

[70] Leiter, *Naturalizing Jurisprudence*.

[71] KN Llewellyn, *Cases and Materials on the Law of Sales* (Chicago, Callaghan & Co, 1930).

something less than 100 per cent accuracy what the law will be or a court will decide.

If we were to take certainty at its word it would be difficult to find it except for very simple rules that specify simple concepts like durations of time. Lawyers in the common law tradition, English or American, broadly agree that predictability is important, but what predictability means to them depends at least to some extent on how the debate between the conceptualists and the realists played out as outlined above. It is to the divergent meanings of predictability in the common law tradition to where I now turn.

CONCEPTUAL VERSUS INSTRUMENTAL PREDICTABILITY

In his 1988 Memorial Lecture at Monash University, the preeminent English commercial law scholar Sir Roy Goode outlined eight principles for a 'philosophy and concepts of commercial law'.[72] The second principle after party autonomy is predictability. Nowhere does Goode identify certainty as a principle. In a footnote to his discussion of predictability, Goode asserts that predictability is 'also termed "certainty", a term I dislike as nothing in life is certain except uncertainty, and this is particularly true of litigation'.[73] Goode continues:

> A reasonable degree of predictability is needed in the commercial world because so much planning and so many transactions, standardised or high in value, are undertaken on the basis that the courts will continue to follow the rules laid down in preceding cases.[74]

We can term Goode's idea of predictability as conceptual predictability. It is predictability about the text of the law itself, a matter of whether the law can be used to plan transactions or other human activity. Conceptual predictability is predictability in the form of the law, grounded in the law's logical features and the features of the language of the law in offering guidance to business planners and legal professionals.

Conceptual predictability is a value sought in both the English and the American versions of the common law. Legal realism did not change this basic feature about American law. For example, the American Revised Uniform Partnership Act, a uniform model law that the Uniform Law

[72] R Goode, 'The Codification of Commercial Law' (1988) 14 *Monash University Law Review* 135, 148–55. I will not rehash the many arguments about the problems with a prediction theory about law. For extended discussions, see MS Green, 'Legal Realism as a Theory About Law' (2005) 46 *William and Mary Law Review* 1915 and select papers in Burton, *The Path of the Law and its Influence*.

[73] ibid 150 at n 36.

[74] ibid 150.

Commission in the US has produced for consideration by state legislatures, contains Section 404, designed to clarify on what precisely are the fiduciary duties of partners to each other.[75] Section 404(a) specifies that '[t]he only fiduciary duties a partner owes to the partnership and the other partners are the duty of loyalty and the duty of care' as specified in subsections (b) and (c).[76] Subsection (b) states that a partner's duty of loyalty 'is limited to' a discrete list of duties.[77] Subsection (c) does the same for the duty of care.[78] Other subsections of section 404 provide that while partners owe each other a duty of good faith, '[a] partner does not violate a duty or obligation under this [Act] or under the partnership agreement merely because the partner's conduct furthers the partner's own interest' and'[a] partner may lend money to and transact other business with the partnership, and as to each loan or transaction, the rights and obligations of the partners are the same as those of a person who is not a partner, subject to other applicable law'.[79] These concrete provisions were meant to clarify open textured statements in the case law on the fiduciary duties of partners. Other examples of conceptual predictability in action are the many 'safe harbour' provisions found in American securities regulation and other fields, including in some areas of EU law.[80] Though the law will differ in some substantial respects, similar techniques are at work in English law.

There is another version of predictability at work, probably more in American law than in English law. I shall call this version of predictability instrumental predictability. The idea of instrumental predictability is this: the law is predictable or 'certain' to the extent that it conforms reliably to some criterion independent of or external to the coherence of the legal rules themselves as legal rules. We can develop two versions of instrumental predictability. One is the positive version that the law in fact tends to comply with the designated external normative criterion. The other is the normative version that the law ought to comply with the designated criterion. The idea here is not to construct legal concepts that reliably produce predictable

[75] Uniform Partnership Act (1997).
[76] ibid § 404(a).
[77] ibid § 404(b).
[78] ibid § 404(c).
[79] ibid § 404 (e) and (f).
[80] The Legal Information Institute at Cornell University defines a 'safe harbour' as a 'provision granting protection from liability or penalty if certain conditions are met. A safe harbor provision may be included in statutes or regulations to give peace of mind to good-faith actors who might otherwise violate the law on technicalities beyond their reasonable control' (www.law.cornell.edu/wex/safe_harbor). An example of a safe harbour can be found in the agreement between the European Commission and the US Government that US companies could self-certify with a set of conditions that ensured compliance with EU data privacy protections. The CJEU declared the safe harbour invalid under EU law: Case C-362/114 *Maximillian Schrems v Data Protection Commissioner* [2015] ECLI:EU:C:2015:650.

consequences in a logical or formal sense, but that if we use an external criterion as a guide for making and interpreting legal rules, then predictability will result from the use of this criterion in developing the content of legal rules around it.

In the American context, the most prominent external criterion, at least for commercial and private law, is economic efficiency.[81] So, the positive version of instrumental predictability is that the law does comply with the dictates of economic efficiency, a claim made in the very early law and economics literature about the efficiency of the common law.[82] The normative version of instrumental predictability is that legal doctrines that fail to comply with standards of economic efficiency should be made to comply, either through evolution of case law or through legislation, though of course any such efforts should be examined with the tools of public choice theory or political economy.[83] The positive version may be true or false. The normative version offers a set of prescriptions to promote a form of predictability in the law centred around the substance of the law but not its form.

Instrumental predictability may not be in the minds of lawyers when they read cases or interpret statutes. It is unlikely to be something that practicing lawyers and judges actually reflect on when engaging with the law. With its connections to the social science of economics, it is a theoretical notion independent of what lawyers actually do. It is a theory about how people behave, reducible to economics. An analogy would be that Hank Aaron did not have to know about the physics of hitting a baseball to hit home runs in American baseball. In its positive form, it is a prediction about the law's direction. It is more likely that legal academics take an active approach to implementing instrumental predictability when they critically examine the law and critique it to determine whether it is efficient and argue that it should meet efficiency standards. While it is difficult to generalise about the path of legal thought, it is probably true that such activity by American legal academics is accepted at least partly because their intellectual ancestors, the American legal realists, were among the first legal thinkers to approach law from social science perspectives. To the extent that the idea of instrumental predictability has traction with American legal academics, either

[81] It seems well accepted in American law schools that economics is the prevalent methodology for private and commercial law, while normative political theory maintains some currency at least for the constitutional aspects of public law. These arguments can be seen in the contentious L Kaplow and S Shavell, *Fairness Versus Welfare* (Cambridge, Mass, Harvard University Press, 2006).

[82] See GL Priest, 'The Common Law Process and the Selection of Legal Rules' (1977) 6 *The Journal of Legal Studies* 65; PH Rubin, 'Why is the Common Law Efficient?' (1977) 6 *The Journal of Legal Studies* 51.

[83] See J Linarelli, 'The Economics of Uniform Laws and Uniform Law Making' (2003) 48 *Wayne Law Review* 1387.

consciously or not, it will have crept into American legal scholarship and ultimately into ways of understanding the law from an American point of view more generally.

CONCLUSION

Legal certainty remains one of the more important concepts about the law, yet there has been little serious reflection about it. Its presence tends to be taken for granted in mature legal systems. This chapter has traced the origins of the concept in the common law tradition from its eighteenth century pronouncements by Lord Mansfield on the King's Bench in England to the present day. Along the way, I have tried to show that there are actually two somewhat divergent traditions within the common law tradition itself, which came to a sharp point of departure in the early twentieth century in the differences in approaches to the law as evidenced by English conceptualist and American legal realist traditions. In that divergence, the concept of certainty changed in the common law tradition. English lawyers and judges still articulate the concept to evaluate the merits of English commercial law. American lawyers and judges do so far less, but the concept of certainty is still important in American law. In both traditions predictability is the more modern and tractable concept. I outlined two versions of predictability: a conceptual version that looks for predictability in the form and structure of the law itself; and instrumental predictability, which looks for predictability in the law's compliance with economic efficiency. Conceptual predictability is important in both the American and the English versions of the common law, though it is more explicitly stressed in English law. Instrumental predictability is probably more important in American than in English law, though English law probably conforms no more or less to it than American law.

8

Measuring Legal Certainty? Critical Feedback about the Development of an Index of Legal Certainty

JONAS KNETSCH

INTRODUCTION

SINCE 2004, THE World Bank Group has published annual reports called 'Doing Business', which measure the costs of business regulations all over the world. The first issues of these reports harshly criticised countries with a civil law tradition because their regulatory environments were not conducive to business operations.[1] Much to the surprise of the French legal community, France was ranked 44th in the 2006 report, just behind Jamaica and right before Kiribati—still in the first third of the ranking, but far below the United States (3rd) or the United Kingdom (9th), which were towards the top of the list.[2]

As one can imagine, this outcome did not go down very well with French legal scholars, who felt that the World Bank did not treat their legal system fairly.[3] Most commentators noted that it should not be up to a team of lawyers in partnership with an American consulting firm[4] and backed-up by a

[1] See, eg World Bank, *Doing Business in 2004. Understanding Regulation* (Washington, World Bank, 2004) xiv: 'Common law countries regulate the least. Countries in the French civil law tradition the most. ... Heavier regulation is generally associated with more inefficiency in public institutions ... and more unemployed people, corruption, less productivity and investment, but not with better quality of private or public goods.'

[2] World Bank, *Doing Business in 2006. Creating Jobs* (Washington, World Bank, 2006) 92.

[3] See M Haravon, 'Le rapport Doing Business et la Banque mondiale: mythes et réalités d'un rapport sans nuances' (2005) *La Semaine Juridique. Edition Entreprise* 1680; B du Marais, 'Entre la Jamaïque et le Kiribati. Quelques réflexions sur l'attractivité du Droit français dans la compétition économique internationale' (2006) *Rapport annuel du Conseil d'Etat* 377; J Berg and S Cazes, 'Comparer et classer les droits du travail nationaux: les limites des indicateurs Doing Business' (2008) *Revue droit du travail* 264; L Usunier, 'Le rapport DB 2012, la concurrence des systèmes juridiques et l'attractivité du droit français des contrats' (2012) *Revue des contrats* 575.

[4] World Bank, *Doing Business in 2006* 85: 'The [Paying Taxes] project is developed and implemented in cooperation with PricewaterhouseCoopers.'

small group of 'law and economics' academics to measure the efficiency of legal systems.[5]

In a collective response to the 2004 and 2005 reports, a group of six eminent professors from France's leading law school in Paris raised detailed arguments against the methods used by the Doing Business working group.[6] The target was not only the benchmarking methodology, but also the poor work on the legal background. They considered the research on each legal system to be so superficial that the result was merely a 'Da Vinci Code of comparative law' littered with inaccuracies and approximations.[7]

Wishing to contribute to a constructive dialogue, in 2012, the Civil Law Initiative (*Fondation pour le droit continental*), a private institution headquartered in Paris and promoting the radiation of civil law around the world, announced a call for interest on a project on legal certainty. The aim was to develop a research method to measure the level of legal certainty in response to the World Bank's 'Doing Business' programme.

At the same time, the Panthéon-Assas University in Paris established a new centre for 'law and economics' (*Centre de Recherches en Economie et Droit*),[8] one of the few places of research in this field in France. Thanks to the funding of the Civil Law Initiative, a working group led by Bruno Deffains, one of the leading 'Law and Economics' professors in France, and Catherine Kessedjian, law professor and specialist in international arbitration and private international law,[9] was able to initiate its work on an Index of Legal Certainty (*Index de la sécurité juridique*) in May 2013.

The objective of this chapter is to present how the research project on the Legal Certainty Index operated and the difficulties the working group encountered during the development of the first version of this index.[10] This chapter does not intend to provide an in-depth analysis of the concept of legal certainty or to assess the econometric methods used during the research. In fact, as the title indicates, this chapter is confined to personal,

[5] In addition to the references cited in n 3, see also B du Marais, 'De Koror à Palikir: à la recherche du paradis du droit des affaires' (2006) *Recueil Dalloz* 1110.

[6] Association Henri Capitant (ed), *Les droits de tradition civiliste en question. A propos des rapports Doing Business de la Banque Mondiale* (Paris, Société de législation comparée, 2006). See also G Canivet, M-A Frison-Roche and M Klein (eds), *Mesurer l'efficacité économique du droit* (Paris, LGDJ, 2005); F Rouvillois (ed), *Le modèle juridique français: un obstacle au développement économique?* (Paris, Dalloz, 2005).

[7] Association Henri Capitant (ed), *Les droits de tradition civiliste en question* 33.

[8] Further information is available on the centre's website (cred.u-paris2.fr).

[9] The working group was composed of doctoral students, both in law and in economics, postdoctoral researchers, research assistants and assistant professors (such as the author at that time).

[10] The index presented an explanatory report. An English version is available on the Civil Law Initiative's website (www.fondation-droitcontinental.org/fr/wp-content/uploads/2015/04/ILC-Report-june-2015_EN.pdf).

critical feedback and an outlook on the ongoing work on the second version of the index.[11]

IMPLEMENTATION OF THE PROJECT

The working group started research by trying to gain an overview of the literature available on legal certainty in different countries. As is well known, the literature on this topic is overwhelming, and it is nearly impossible to read every book or paper ever published on legal certainty in the major languages.[12] Yet the advantage of the working group was its dual skills in law and economics, which is rare for a research team in France, if not in continental Europe. The result of this first phase was a bibliographic database, which continues to be useful for the working group.

Once this preparatory work was completed, in a second phase the group developed a comprehensive glossary to gain an accurate picture of what legal certainty means in the major legal systems and in different branches of the law. This glossary is appended as an annex to the final report available on the website of the Civil Law Initiative[13] and compiles more than 150 key words and ideas, revealing the difficulties with which the working group were faced when trying to grasp the concept of legal certainty. The author remembers very stormy discussions about whether, for instance, the idea of 'trade union negotiations' was connected to legal certainty, and if yes, in what way.

The third phase was devoted to the choice of the methodology. For the team, composed of legal scholars and economists, it was clear from the beginning that the working group would adopt the classical 'case method'. This consisted of defining several model cases with questions relative to legal certainty that would be sent out to legal practitioners in 13 countries. Since the aim of the study was to evaluate legal certainty for a foreign investor (as in the 'Doing Business' reports), the group defined six key sectors that are of particular importance in this context.

For each of those six sectors—contract law, property law, liability law, corporate law, labour law and dispute settlement—the group designed two model cases with both general questions on the applicable rules and questions

[11] The second edition of the index will integrate four new areas of law (law of public contracts, environmental law, intellectual property law and insolvency law) and add at least five new countries. Further information is available on the Civil Law Initiative's website (www.fondation-droitcontinental.org/en/our_action/index-legal-certainty-ilc/) and at isj.u-paris2.fr/repondants.php.

[12] See B Deffains and C Kessedjian (eds), 'Index of Legal Certainty. Report for the Civil Law Initiative' (2015) 145–71.

[13] ibid 133–44.

that were more specific.[14] The group decided to conduct a 'crash-test', during which the cases and their questions were submitted to an international group of academics who were asked to give critical feedback on the phrasing and content.

Finally, during the fourth phase, which lasted more than six months, the case-based questionnaires were sent out to more than 300 national correspondents,[15] and their responses were reviewed by the group's economists. In order to fully exploit the survey responses, they had previously worked on the scoring of the different answers available. The ultimate aggregation of the scores obtained by the selected legal systems in each sector led to a final ranking.

Unlike in the 'Doing Business' reports, the French legal system did very well on this survey. Without weighting the general part of the questionnaire,[16] France ranked first out of 13; after a weighting, it still was in third place.[17]

MAJOR CHALLENGES FOR THE WORKING GROUP

In spite of its thorough and rigorous scientific approach, there has been criticism of the results of this survey. It comes as no surprise that the good performance of France and other civil law countries and the relatively poor ranking of US law were suspect to some observers, who challenged the representativeness of the results. As a former member of the working group, the author will not take a position on the seriousness of the first version of the Index of Legal Certainty. Instead, this section will outline two major challenges the team faced during the project. The first one was of a methodological nature, and the second was a substantive one.

Methodological Issues

A questionnaire-based enquiry depends heavily on the quality of the cohort of its respondents. Attached to the report, one can find the list of all the practitioners who submitted a reply to the questionnaires.[18] Most of them

[14] The cases are included in the final version of the report: see ibid 73–257.

[15] ibid 123–31.

[16] ibid 93: 'Each case … contains general and specific questions. As explained above, the general questions are identical from one sector to another. These questions therefore have very important relative weight both in the score per sector and the final score. It is therefore appropriate to weight these general questions in order to limit their influence compared to the specific questions.'

[17] ibid 93 and 103.

[18] ibid 123–31.

are lawyers at important, multi-national law firms. Initially, the group fixed the minimum number of respondents to two for each sector in each of the 13 countries. However, for certain sectors and in certain countries (like Senegal), it was impossible to find available practitioners. In such cases, the group called on academics who are specialists in the legal system of those countries and whose work focuses mainly on the sector in question.[19]

One of the major challenges in this project was to phrase the questions in such a way that the respondent could only give objective and factual answers about his or her legal system. The group tried to avoid, as far as possible, appealing to the subjective perceptions of legal certainty in a given country. Here is just one example of the type of questions the group decided to rule out for fear of receiving subjective impressions or mere opinions rather than neutral feedback. It was the unanimous opinion that this kind of question left too much scope for the respondent's subjectivity.

Is the [applicable] rule controversial and are there plans to modify it?
— Not controversial and no plans to modify it
— Controversial and no plans to modify it
— Not controversial and plans to modify it
— Controversial and plans to modify it

Figure 1

However, with the benefit of hindsight, the author wonders if the working group did not act somewhat precipitately.[20] In fact, one must ask whether one really can ignore the subjective dimension of legal certainty. Does not an Index of Legal Certainty necessarily reflect people's trust in their own legal system and, through it, their personal judgement of it? If this is so, to what extent should we incorporate this subjective bias in the rating method?

Directly related to this subjectivity issue, the group also faced the problem of respondents who obviously overrated the qualities of their own legal system, out of either national pride or embarrassment. Then, some of the respondents seemed to have an opposite attitude, judging their own national law too harshly, perhaps out of a political sentiment. Under the cloak of objective answers to the questions, some respondents clearly tried

[19] ibid 84 and 131.

[20] See also the Foreword of the Civil Law Initiative's then President Jean-François Dubos in Deffains and Kessedjian (eds), *Index of Legal Certainty* vi: 'The present case is our first exercise and the methods used can certainly be improved for future editions of this Index to include new countries and new legal sectors.'

to sell 'their' legal system as a particularly good one, or on the contrary, to denigrate it.

Probably, those methodological issues are quite trivial in any sociological survey. However, for legal research in Europe, those issues are not well known, and it would be helpful for the current research working group to involve sociologists in the preparatory work and to pay greater attention to social science methods.

Substantive Issues

Had there only been those methodological problems, the expectations for the new version of the Index would be very high. However, more substantive issues are still unresolved and cause speculation about the outcome of the ongoing project.

If you take a closer look at the scoring process, ie the allocation of a certain number of points for each answer chosen by the respondent, it is impossible to evade the issue of neutrality. As pointed out at the beginning, French scholars criticised the 'Doing Business' reports of the World Bank for promoting common law systems due to its excessively one-sided approach. Since civil law countries came out much better in the Index of Legal Certainty, the question arises, and it is a pressing one, of whether the project of the Civil Law Initiative has been designed—deliberately or unconsciously—to give more favourable treatment to the legal systems of continental Europe.

The mere fact of raising suspicion of such a bias may seem somewhat surprising, especially coming from a former member of the working group. But to bring a critical perspective to the results of the research project, it seems essential to provide insight into the scoring of the two most controversial questions of the survey.

One of the questions was about the origin of the applicable rule in the case: 'Is the rule of legislative or case-law origin?' The research team considered that the origin of the rule was not, as such, a source of more or less legal certainty, but only that ease of access to this rule was the fundamental point. The team therefore suggested identical scoring be used for rules of statutory and case-law origin, only taking into consideration the fact of whether or not they were easily available, for example, in a code or a case-law collection.[21]

[21] Deffains and Kessedjian (eds), 'Index of Legal Certainty' 80.

Is the rule of legislative or case-law origin?		
—	Legislative, available in a collection, interpreted by case-law also present in a collection	10
—	Case-law, available in a collection	10
—	Legislative, scattered throughout multiple sources, and the case-law is important in order to understand it	0
—	Case-law, scattered throughout multiple sources	0

Figure 2

Another question focused on constitutional review. As is well known, in some countries, constitutional courts may invalidate legal provisions on the grounds that they violate a fundamental right or any other provision of the Constitution.[22] Those reviews may take the form of a control prior to enactment or an ex post verification, ie after the enactment of the rule.

The working group considered that checking constitutionality before legislation comes into force provided more legal certainty than a control ex post or the possibility of a control both before and after the provision. The following scoring was therefore proposed:

Is the [applicable] rule checked to ensure it complies with the Constitution?		
—	Yes, before the rule is included in the legal system	10
—	Yes, after the rule comes into force	5
—	Yes, both before and after the rule comes into force	5
—	No	0

Figure 3

At that time, one of the funders of the project reminded the working group that reasonable legal certainty means that the rule of law—published in a comprehensive and validated collection—has to be foreseeable due to the hierarchy of norms and predefined competences of the legislative and the judicial branch of power.[23] The working group was explicitly urged to review the phrasing and the scoring of some of the questions.

[22] ibid 81.

[23] Dubos, 'Foreword' vi: '[Legal certainty] presupposes the accessibility of the applicable law—contained in fully inclusive, validated, published form—its predictability, achieved through the *ranking of the norms* and the *predefined competencies of lawmakers and judges*, reasonable stability over time, and lastly a balance between economic interests and the parties concerned'.

Some of the members of the group, including the author, were highly critical of this interference by the main funder of this project. However, both the questions mentioned above were rescored: the case-law origin of an applicable rule was awarded half the points a legislative rule would receive.

Is the rule of legislative or case-law origin?	
— Legislative, available in a collection, interpreted by case-law also present in a collection	10
— Case-law, available in a collection	5
— Legislative, scattered throughout multiple sources, and the case-law is important in order to understand it	0
— Case-law, scattered throughout multiple sources	0

Figure 4

As for the constitutionality review, the new scoring now appeared as follows:

Is the [applicable] rule checked to ensure it complies with the Constitution?	
— Yes, before the rule is included in the legal system	5
— Yes, after the rule comes into force	5
— Yes, both before and after the rule comes into force	10
— No	0

Figure 5

Those last-minute changes were not neutral, and in particular, they were not favourable to the common law systems. Let there be no mistake. It is entirely arguable that the hierarchy of norms, the codification of the rule of law and even a balancing of competing interests contributes to the concept of legal certainty. However, the author doubts that such a vision would represent the only valid concept of legal certainty.

CONCLUSION

As mentioned in the introduction, this chapter is not intended to give the author's understanding of legal certainty. Despite 18 months of work on the Legal Certainty Index, the author still ignores the precise limits of this concept, and several unresolved issues affect the quality of each research project on legal certainty.

Can we really elaborate precise scientific methods in order to make legal certainty measurable, when we do not know the exact outlines of the concept? To what extent do we have to integrate subjective and even substantive variables? Should we not first make clear whether an Index of Legal Certainty only reflects the point of view of investors, or whether we must take the perspective of their contractual partners or of consumers, employers and local authorities into account?

This much is certain: for now, the concept of legal certainty remains as elusive as ever, and somehow, everyone seems to see what he or she wants to see in it.

Part III

Transnational Perspectives

9

Clashing Legal Certainties: The Danish Supreme Court's Ruling in AJOS *and the Collision between Domestic Rules and EU Principles*

MIKAEL RASK MADSEN AND HENRIK PALMER OLSEN*

INTRODUCTION

THE EUROPEAN CONSTRUCTION, and particularly the European Union (EU), has in large part been built by developing supranational principles of law. Since the EU landmark decisions of the 1960s, it has been argued that European society has developed as a post-national society, marked by a highly distinctive, and increasingly autonomous, sui-generis legal system.[1] Although the many principles underpinning the contemporary EU legal order assume supremacy, they continuously collide with how national courts construct the interface of domestic law and EU law. This is documented in a steady flow of cases from both the Court of Justice of the EU (previously the ECJ) and its national counterparts. This chapter explores a very recent example of such a clash, the *Ajos* judgment of the Supreme Court of Denmark (SCDK), in which the Danish court defied clear guidelines from the Court of Justice by reconstructing EU law through the lens of Danish law.[2]

These collisions are typically the result of divergent normative contents of EU law and domestic law. In most cases, national courts manage to interpret

* This research is funded by the Danish National Research Foundation Grant no DNRF105 and conducted under the auspices of iCourts.

[1] MR Madsen and C Thornhill (eds), *Law and the Formation of Modern Europe: Perspectives from the Historical Sociology of Law* (Cambridge, Cambridge University Press, 2014) 2.

[2] The case-study of the *Ajos* case included in this article repeats the analysis found in MR Madsen, HP Olsen and U Sadl, 'Competing Supremacies and Clashing Institutional Rationalities: The Danish Supreme Court's Decision in the Ajos Case and the National Limits of Judicial Cooperation' (forthcoming) 23 *European Law Journal*.

domestic law in conformity with EU law and thereby avoid normative contradictions. But in other cases, it is arguably not possible to interpret domestic law in accordance with EU law. In so-called *contra legem* situations, national courts cannot override clear domestic legislation—in part because it would cause legal uncertainty, as legitimate expectations based on explicit domestic provisions would be jeopardised. In the *Ajos* case analysed below, the SCDK argues that if they were to follow general principles of EU law that would not only jeopardise legal certainty and legitimate expectations of Danish citizens, but it would also put the court in the position of legislator and thereby violate the principle of separation of powers as set out in Article 3 of the Danish Constitution.

Part of the problem witnessed in the *Ajos* case is the inherent institutional friction between regulating by rules and regulating by principles, and the corresponding different notions of legal certainty of each of these approaches. On the one hand, most domestic European legal systems are marked by an intense and detailed regulation by statutory law—what is known as the civil law tradition in comparative law. On the other hand, EU law is marked by a more general approach to legislation, often using open formulations as a result of political compromises necessary to achieve majority or unaninimity between the Member States. Moreover, it is differentiated by the prominent role played by the Court of Justice and its tradition of both seeking concrete meaning in its adjudication of openly-formulated EU provisions and by formulating general principles in its adjudication of EU law. Comparatively, a very similar debate is found in the United States on rules and standards.[3] In both Europe and the US, the two approaches differ most fundamentally with regard to the precision of prescription: rules are assumed to be precise and principles or standards are assumed to be more general, even vague.

In terms of legal certainty, the one approach cannot a priori be assumed to be better than the other, at least not in the context of complex societies. The EU undoubtedly regulates highly complex issues of securing open and equal market access across many different sovereign states, and the interrelationship between the EU, and specifically EU law, and its national counterparts is undoubtedly a case of legal complexity. It is, moreover, a case of contested legal hierarchies in which both European and national courts assume supremacy in each of their own domains. Our goal in this chapter is not to attempt to solve the dilemma of competing legal certainties. Rather we aim at making intelligible the fundamental collisions of law and legal culture, including cultures of legal certainty, that animate the broader European legal system and its particular dynamics.

[3] J Braithwaite, 'Rules and Principles: A Theory of Legal Certainty' (2002) 27 *Australian Journal of Legal Philosophy* 47, 47.

The analysis is structured as follows. We first provide an overview of the *Ajos* case, both as presented before the Danish court and the response from the Court of Justice to the case. We then analyse the constitutional limits influencing the Danish participation in the EU. We highlight how those limits have been tightened in recent years and how this has influenced the judgment in the *Ajos* case. Against this background, we provide three interpretations of the case. In conclusion, we situate the case in the broader context of competing legal certainties of EU law.

THE *AJOS* CASE

On 6 December 2016, the SCDK took the European legal community by surprise. In its decision in the *Ajos* case[4] the SCDK disregarded the guidelines of the Court of Justice of the EU, which had been set out in a preliminary ruling earlier in the year.[5] More notably still, the SCDK used the occasion to set new boundaries to the applicability of the Court of Justice's rulings in Denmark. It did so in two steps: first, the SCDK delimited the competences of the EU through the lens of its interpretation of the Danish Accession Act.[6] Second, the SCDK delimited its own power within the Danish Constitution. In regard to the first point, it concluded that the judge-made principles of EU law developed after the latest amendments of the Accession Act, such as the general principle of non-discrimination on grounds of age, were not binding. This conclusion was of consequence since the case at hand concerned such a principle developed by the Court of Justice after an amendment. With regard to the second step, the SCDK argued that it would in fact exceed its own judicial mandate within the Danish constitutional framework if it interpreted a national law, which violated the principle in question, in conformity with EU law in a dispute between private parties, or dis-applied it.[7]

The *Ajos* case appears trivial at first glance: it concerns a minor pecuniary claim, a legal provision which was later amended, and a claimant who

[4] Case no 15/2014 *Dansk Industri (DI) acting for Ajos A/S v The estate left by A*, available at www.hoejesteret.dk/hoejesteret/nyheder/Afgorelser/Documents/15-2014.pdf. An informal translation is available at www.supremecourt.dk/supremecourt/nyheder/pressemeddelelser/Documents/Judgment%2015-2014.pdf.

[5] Case C-441/14 *Dansk Industri (DI), acting on behalf of Ajos A/S v Estate of Karsten Eigil Rasmussen* [2016] ECLI:EU:C:2016:278.

[6] Act of Parliament no 321 of 30 April 2008, available at www.retsinformation.dk/pdfPrint.aspx?id=116752.

[7] It is important to note that the relevant EU Directive had been implemented by the Danish Parliament which had deemed it compatible with existing legal regulation and court practice in Denmark (this included the provision under dispute in *Dansk Industri (DI) v Rasmussen*). See Act of Parliament no 1417 of 22 December 2004, available at www.retsinformation.dk/Forms/R0710.aspx?id=30191. The Act has subsequently been amended multiple times.

is deceased. Nonetheless, it has substantial importance at the level of principle. It highlights institutional frictions that have been building for some time, and it provides an example of irreconcilable judicial perceptions of the relationship between national law and EU law. The SCDK, which has not been known for disturbing the operation of EU law,[8] makes a clear statement in favour of Danish law and legal culture. The question is whether this SCDK judgment inverts the logic of EU law, making the determination of the conferred powers ultimately a national legal matter?

This was a rare show of force and Danish legal experts were quick to analyse the case in the Danish media. Though analyses varied, they formed a pattern of neo-sovereigntist versus Europeanist interpretations. Neo-sovereigntists contended that the Court of Justice cornered the SCDK and forced it into an unpopular decision. The Court provided no way out for its Danish counterpart in its response to the preliminary reference. The same camp applauded the extent to which the case offered the SCDK a chance to draw a line in the sand and to remind the Court of Justice of the national constitutional limits it must respect—now and in the future. For the Europeanist camp, the case was primarily deemed a damaging rebellion against the Court of Justice and its method. It was an explicit product of the long-disputed use of dynamic interpretation of EU law from the viewpoint of the Danish perception of legitimate judicial action, and legal culture more broadly. This camp also noted that the SCDK's attempt to push through a different and new institutional order rests on a misconception of EU law that is entirely inadequate for regulating the contemporary and future Danish-European legal interaction.

The central legal question in the *Ajos* case concerns the horizontal effect of general principles of EU law. More specifically, the case raises the question of whether a private party who is engaged in a dispute against another private party can rely on an unwritten principle of EU law prohibiting discrimination on grounds of age. In addition, should the national court give effect to an unwritten general principle of EU law—by interpreting the conflicting national law in conformity with EU law or by dis-applying it—even if this means reversing the Court's long-standing interpretive position and its ensuing case law related to this provision?

These issues arose in the context of a private employee who was laid off at the age of 60. Under the then-applicable national law—Danish Salaried Employees Act (*funktionærloven*), section 2a(3)—he was not entitled to a severance allowance. The reason for this was that the employee was entitled to receive an old-age pension from the employer, as he had joined the

[8] See, however, JE Rytter and M Wind, 'In Need of Juristocracy? The Silence of Denmark in the Development of European Legal Norms' (2011) 9 *International Journal of Constitutional Law* 470.

pension scheme before turning 50. This, the applicant argued, constituted discrimination based on age and, thus, a violation of EU law.[9]

According to a prior Court of Justice ruling, the Danish rule was contrary to the Employment Directive, and it constituted unjustified discrimination on grounds of age.[10] The Court ruled that individuals could rely directly on the Directive in disputes against public employees if the relevant Danish law could not bear the interpretation that was in conformity with EU law. Notwithstanding this clear position with regard to Article 2a(3) in vertical situations, the SCDK continued to apply Article 2a(3) in disputes between private parties (horizontal situations). The Danish Parliament eventually amended the contested section of the Danish Act to bring it in line with EU law, but only with effect to situations arising after 1 February 2015. The *Ajos* case thus arose at a time where the existing case law of the Danish courts concerning Article 2a(3), which was contrary to the Directive, continued to apply to disputes between private parties (prior to legislative amendment). Meanwhile, public sector employees could—in situations otherwise factually comparable—rely directly on the Directive to claim severance allowance under Article 2a(3).

BETWEEN CONFORMITY AND LEGAL CERTAINTY

For the SCDK, this resulted in an obvious dilemma: how, when confronted with the *Ajos* case, was it to balance the general principle prohibiting discrimination on the grounds of age with the principle of legal certainty and the principle of legitimate expectations grounded in the Danish Act applicable in its old formulation? Additional complication arose out of an established perception in Danish legal culture by which Parliament is and shall be the supreme author of the law. Alluding to the traditionally rather constricted role of the SCDK in the constitutional framework, the SCDK argued that it would possibly overstep the limits of its judicial role under the Danish Constitution (Article 3 on the separation of powers) if it dis-applied the national law. In effect, this would be to enter the realm of politics. Hence, the court sought guidance from the Court of Justice; but it did so by asking a question whose answer was practically a foregone conclusion. This

[9] Prior to the insertion of the 50-year rule, everyone who was entitled to a pension was denied access to a severance allowance. The 50-year rule was introduced to allow persons employed after their 50th birthday the right to severance payment. The rationale was that because the pensions received by such persons would usually be small (due to their brief employment), the general denial of a severance allowance would hit this group harder. Notwithstanding its positive intentions, there is no denying that the rule introduced arbitrary differential treatment between people employed before or after their 50th birthday.

[10] Case C-499/08 *Ingeniørforeningen i Danmark v Region Syddanmark* [2010] ECLI:EU:C:2010:600.

inevitably prompted conflict. Simply put, the Danish court posed the question through the lens of national law.

Advocate General Bot offered a legally modest solution: the SCDK could interpret the relevant Danish law in conformity with the Directive. The Advocate General relied on the *Ingeniørforeningen* case, and especially on the opinion of Advocate General Kokott, delivered in that case. She argued that the Danish law could bear a conforming interpretation of Article 2a(3), notably because the Danish law was ambiguous in this respect.[11] The Commission, which submitted observations, also argued that the case law of the SCDK did not necessarily follow the wording of Article 2a(3) of the Danish law. Nor did the Danish government seem to believe, according to the Advocate General, that it would be impossible to interpret the Danish law in conformity with the Directive.[12] In fact, Advocate General Bot reasoned that the SCDK would *not* have to override the national legislator in this case, and that the reversal of its *own* previous case law to give the Directive full effect was in no way akin to overstepping its judicial powers.[13]

The Court of Justice reminded the SCDK of the essential role that it played in 'providing the legal protection which individuals derive from the rules of EU law and (ensuring) that those rules are fully effective.'[14] It simply stated that the SCDK could either try to interpret the Danish law in conformity with the Directive or dis-apply it.[15] The Court then invoked its settled case law (citing only Wroclaw),[16] which in situations where the Court of Justice defines the meaning of EU law, and where that law has been interpreted differently, requires that a national court adopts a correct interpretation even to situations that were established before the Court of Justice laid down a correct interpretation. The protection of legitimate expectations could not, according to the Court, change this conclusion.

None of this was likely to be helpful or surprising to the SCDK. The SCDK could not directly transpose the solution from the *Ingeniørforeningen* case because, according to long-standing Court of Justice case law, directives cannot impose obligations on private individuals.[17] It could, however,

[11] *Dansk Industri (DI) v Rasmussen*, Opinion of AG Bot, ECLI:EU:C:2010:248 para 61.

[12] *Ingeniørforeningen v Syddanmark*, Opinion of AG Kokott, ECLI:EU:C:2010:248 para 84 and *Dansk Industri (DI) v Rasmussen*, Opinion of AG Bot para 63.

[13] *Dansk Industri (DI) v Rasmussen*, Opinion of AG Bot para 71. It should be noted that the Directive in question was implemented in Danish Law through Act no 1417 of 22 December 2004, available at www.retsinformation.dk/Forms/R0710.aspx?id=30191.

[14] With reference to Case C-555/07 *Seda Kücükdeveci v Swedex GmbH & Co KG* [2010] ECLI:EU:C:2010:21 para 47, and the case law cited.

[15] *Dansk Industri (DI) v Rasmussen* para 34 and repeated in para 37. It refers to *Kücükdeveci v Swedex* para 51 (para 35 of the judgment).

[16] Case C-276/14 *Gmina Wrocław v Minister Finansów* [2015] ECLI:EU:C:2015:635.

[17] Case C-91/92 *Paola Faccini Dori v Recreb Srl* [1994] ECLI:EU:C:1994:292, and Case C-152/84 *M. H. Marshall v Southampton and South-West Hampshire Area Health Authority* [1986] ECLI:EU:C:1986:84. Exceptionally, Directives can have a so-called incidental effect (see in particular Case C-194/94 *CIA Security International SA v Signalson SA and Securitel SPRL* [1996] ECLI:EU:C:1996:172).

apply an unwritten principle of non-discrimination on grounds of age which had the force of primary law and could have such effect. Alternatively, the SCDK could give the Directive a so-called indirect effect, by adopting an interpretation of national law in conformity with the Directive.[18] In fact, the obligation of the SCDK under EU law to adopt any of those solutions stemmed from a well-established principle that national courts had the duty to ensure the effectiveness of rights that individuals derived from EU law and to give EU law full effect.[19]

Thus, it can be argued that the SCDK retained the option of following a set of clear, if controversial, precedents. As such, national courts can apply written and unwritten principles of EU law (*Defrenne*,[20] *Internationale Handelsgesellschaft*),[21] including the principle of non-discrimination on grounds of age (*Mangold*,[22] *Kücükdeveci*).[23] According to the Court of Justice, the latter is a general principle of EU law to which the Employment Directive gives a 'specific expression'.[24] If necessary, national courts must dis-apply any provision of national legislation contrary to that principle.[25]

Setting aside constitutional provisions to give effect to secondary EU law has proved challenging in the past. Setting aside national legislation to apply primary EU law, should, at least prima facie and from a strictly legal point of view, be less of a problem. To proceed in this way, though, the SCDK would have to reverse its own long-standing practice in order to ensure individual rights and give full effect to EU law.[26] In principle, and as per the above discussion, there is no question that it should do precisely that. Moreover, the legislation in question could bear conform interpretation in the concrete case according to two Advocates General, the Court of Justice, the Commission and even the Danish government—based on the government's submissions in the case.[27] In practice, however, the question of jurisprudential reversal is far from trivial, even if it is triggered from the inside. Needless to add, when prompted from the outside, it can be controversial.

[18] Case C-14/83 *Sabine von Colson and Elisabeth Kamann v Land Nordrhein-Westfalen* [1984] ECLI:EU:C:1984:153; Case C-106/89 *Marleasing SA v La Comercial Internacional de Alimentacion SA* [1990] ECLI:EU:C:1990:395.

[19] Case C-106/77 *Amministrazione delle Finanze dello Stato v Simmenthal SpA* [1978] ECLI:EU:C:1978:49 and Case C-213/89 *R v Secretary of State for Transport, ex p Factortame Ltd and others* [1990] ECLI:EU:C:1990:257.

[20] Case C-43/75 *Gabrielle Defrenne v Société anonyme belge de navigation aérienne Sabena* [1976] ECLI:EU:C:1976:56.

[21] Case C-11/70 *Internationale Handelsgesellschaft mbH v Einfuhr- und Vorratsstelle für Getreide und Futtermittel* [1970] ECLI:EU:C:1970:114.

[22] Case C 144/04 *Werner Mangold v Rüdiger Helm* [2005] ECLI:EU:C:2005:709.

[23] *Kücükdeveci v Swedex.*

[24] ibid para 21.

[25] ibid paras 51 and 53.

[26] This is why the national court considers the principles of legitimate expectations and legal certainty, and this is why the Advocate General is completely unburdened by them.

[27] These are referenced by AG Bot in paras 61–64.

The Court of Justice's assumption was probably that the SCDK would follow the lead of the German Federal Constitutional Court, notably its *Honeywell* jurisprudence.[28] Considering the generally collaborative approach of the SCDK over the years, this seemed a fair assumption. The only problem was that the SCDK opted for a path that collided directly with this assumption and thereby the guidelines provided by the Court of Justice and EU law. To reach such a conclusion, the SCDK had to reconstruct the case as being mainly a matter of Danish constitutional law, from where the Danish Accession Act to the EU draws its authority and sets the limits for the EU, including the Court of Justice and its interpretative power. It had, in other words, to break away from a broad European judicial consensus, and to operate in a less collaborative manner with the Court of Justice than had so far been the legal standard.

DOMESTICATING THE EUROPEAN QUESTION: DANISH CONSTITUTIONAL LIMITS

The decision reached in the *Ajos* case ultimately relies on an interpretation of Danish constitutional law, as well as on taking the high road in the protection of legal certainty and legitimate interests in Danish law. EU law plays a surprisingly secondary role in the reasoning of the SCDK. In reaching its conclusion, the SCDK states:

> [W]e accordingly find that the Law on Accession does not provide the legal basis to allow the unwritten principle prohibiting discrimination on grounds of age to take precedence over Paragraph 2a(3) of the Law on salaried employees in so far as the provision is contrary to the prohibition.
>
> The Supreme Court would be acting outside the scope of its powers as a judicial authority if it were to disapply the provision in this situation.
>
> As a result of the foregoing, Danish courts cannot disapply Paragraph 2a(3) of the Law on salaried employees as then in force and Ajos can thus rely on the provision.

In the process of explaining this striking conclusion more fully, we will now scrutinise and evaluate some 40 years of Danish participation in the EU. The conflicts that were exposed by this decision have in fact been simmering below the surface for quite some time.

Denmark acceded to the European Community in 1972, but the legal pathway for acceding was paved 20 years earlier. Amid a constitutional amendment process, Max Sørensen, a professor of law and later judge at the Court of Justice, wrote a report on what was considered a new legal

[28] BVerfG, BvR 2661/06 of 6 July 2010 available at www.bverfg.de/e/rs20100706_2bvr266106en.html.

phenomenon: supranational organisations with the power to issue acts which were immediately applicable in national law in the same way as domestic legislative acts.[29] As there was sufficient political support for creating a constitutional vehicle for allowing Denmark to participate in such organisations, Max Sørensen drafted what became Article 20 of the 1953 Danish Constitution. The provision is similar to provisions found in other constitutions from the period. See, for example, the Swedish Constitution's Chapter 10, Article 5, and the German Constitution's Articles 23 and 24. The wording of Article 20 of the Danish 1953 Constitution reads as follows:

> (1) Powers vested in the authorities of the Realm under this Constitutional Act may, by statute to a certain specified extent, be delegated to international authorities set up by mutual agreement with other states for the promotion of international rules of law and cooperation.
>
> (2) For the enactment of a Bill dealing with the above, a majority of five-sixths of the members of the Folketing shall be required. If this majority is not obtained, whereas the majority required for the passing of ordinary Bills is obtained, and if the Government maintains it, the Bill shall be submitted to the electorate for approval or rejection in accordance with the rules for referenda laid down in section 42.[30]

This central provision has been applied only a few times since 1953: first in 1972 and then subsequently when the EC/EU's competences have been extended. Article 20 has also been used for Danish participation in the European Patent Convention (1989) and most recently for Danish participation in the not yet active European Patent Court (2014).

As is well-known, Danish membership in the EC/EU has from the very beginning been marked by reluctance, if not scepticism. In the 1972 referendum, more than 35% of votes cast were 'no' votes (90% participation). Leftist political parties, including a significant number of MPs from the Social Democratic Party, conspicuously supported a 'no' vote. A new movement, The Peoples' Movement against EC, was formed at this precise moment.

The reluctance was, however, not limited to this decisive moment. Well into the 1980s Danish participation in the EC was marked by 'limited engagement, fragmentation and pragmatism' as described by some scholars.[31] After the end of the Cold War, though, the degree of engagement did change, and a notable sign of this was the broader acceptance of the

[29] Danish Constitutional Commission, *Betænkning afgivet af Forfatningskommissionen af 1946* (Valby, JH Schultz A/S, 1953) 124–26. See also H Zahle, *Dansk Forfatningsret, bd. 2: Regering, forvaltning og dom* (Copenhagen, Christian Ejlers Forlag, 2001).

[30] The English translations of the Danish Constitution used here can be found at legislationline.org/documents/section/constitutions.

[31] M Kelstrup, D Martinsen and M Wind, *Europa i forandring: En grundbog om EU's politiske og retlige system* (Copenhagen, Hans Reitzels Forlag, 2012) 417.

European project exhibited by the Social Democratic Party. Yet, in 1992, a referendum on the Maastricht Treaty ended in a narrow win for those opposed to EU collaboration, whereby 50.7 per cent voted against the proposed Treaty.[32] This shocked the political establishment, which was, by and large, in favour of the Maastricht Treaty. Only some complex diplomatic manoeuvrings and the resulting Edinburgh Agreement allowed for a new but controversial referendum on the Maastricht Treaty—now in a significantly watered down version introducing four reservations to the Treaty. The vote was 56.7 per cent in favour of entering the Edinburgh Agreement. In the bigger picture, Denmark thereby became a conditional member of the European project and this has been the status quo ever since. Recently, a referendum was held over Danish participation in police and judicial collaboration (elements of the Edinburgh Agreement), which resulted in another no-vote, further side-lining Denmark in matters such as police collaboration in Europol.

From the very beginning, such popular and political resistance also entered the realm of law. In fact, even prior to the original accession, attempts were made to get the SCDK to rule that Denmark could only accede to the EC through a constitutional amendment. However, the case was not admitted as there is no access to ex ante review in Denmark.[33] Another attempt was made immediately following accession, but that case was also refused on the ground that there was no locus standi. The SCDK did not find that the citizens seeking review had a sufficiently concrete and immediate interest in a ruling.[34] Twenty more years would pass before the Supreme Court, in what was considered a landmark ruling at the time, allowed the EU question to go to court. Following the referenda on the Maastricht Treaty in 1992 and 1993 (the latter over the Edinburgh Agreement), the SCDK found that EU law now so profoundly affected the lives of ordinary citizens that the conditions for locus standi were met.[35]

The SCDK thereby created a chance to adjudicate on the constitutional relationship between the Danish Accession Act and EU law. In their 1998 Maastricht Judgment,[36] a key question concerned the wording 'to a certain specified extent' in Article 20 of the Danish Constitution and what

[32] ibid 418.

[33] See Ugeskrift for Retsvæsen (Danish law reports; UfR) 72.903H.

[34] See UfR 73.694H.

[35] See UfR 96.1300H, which introduced a new standard of access to court specifically designed to allow for a review of the constitutionality of EU law. Indicative of the attention this ruling received is the fact that Professor Hjalte Rasmussen published an entire book about the issues at stake in the Supreme Court. See H Rasmussen, *Folkestyre, Grundlov og Højesteret. Grundlovens § 20 på prøve* (Copenhagen, Christian Ejlers Forlag, 1996).

[36] See UfR 1998.800H, often referred to as the Maastricht case or the Maastricht ruling. For a commentary, see HP Olsen and S Harck, 'Decision concerning the Maastricht Treaty' (1999) 93 *American Journal of International Law* 209.

it entailed precisely with respect to the delegation of powers to an international/supranational organisation. The Court, however, suggested a very pragmatic solution to the question:[37]

> The fields of responsibility may be described in broad categories, and there is no requirement for the extent of the delegation of sovereignty to be stated so precisely that there is no room left for discretion or interpretation. The powers delegated may be indicated by means of reference to a treaty.

This wording certainly contains an indication of a genuine openness towards the necessity of not treating a novel supranational community like a static state-like organisation, but rather as something more open-ended and dynamic. Importantly, the SCDK also noted that the requirement of specification should not lead Danish courts to generally police the applicability of EU law. On the contrary, there was a spirit of collaboration with the Court of Justice that echoed the German Federal Constitutional Court's *Solange* doctrine, which at the time of the decision had been further refined in the *Brunner* case. The SCDK stated:[38]

> … Danish courts must [only] rule that an EC act is inapplicable in Denmark if the *extraordinary situation* should arise that *with the required certainty* it can be *established* that an EC act which has been upheld by the EC Court of Justice is based on an application of the Treaty which lies beyond the surrender of sovereignty according to the Accession Act. Similarly, this applies with regard to community-law rules and legal principles which are based on the practice of the EC Court of Justice. (emphasis added)

Another 15 years would pass before the SCDK adjudicated again on the constitutional relationship between EU law and the Accession Act(s), and this time with much less openness towards the EU. The background for the 2013 ruling was the adoption of the Lisbon Treaty and a complaint by a group of citizens that the Danish government had decided to ratify the treaty without using the procedure in Article 20, which the government had considered unnecessary as no new powers were transferred. The Supreme Court, following their 1996 ruling on locus standi, issued a decision in 2011, allowing the citizens access to hear the case in Court.[39]

After re-affirming, as per UfR 1998.800H, that the EU's political bodies may only adopt acts which fall *within* the framework created by

[37] There is no official English translation of the decision published in UfR 1998.800H. However, a subsequent Supreme Court ruling in the so-called *Lisbon* case (UfR 2013.1451H) does exist in a formal English translation, see www.hoejesteret.dk/hoejesteret/nyheder/ovrigenyheder/Documents/199-12engelsk.pdf. This ruling quotes most of the important passages from UfR 1998.800H *in extenso*. The quoted passages from UfR1998.800H are in our analysis derived from the translation of UfR 2013.1451H.

[38] UfR 1998.800H.

[39] See UfR 2011.984H.

the Treaty, the SCDK noted in the *Lisbon* ruling[40] that although the Court of Justice is charged with settling any disputes on the interpretation of EU law: '… this must not result in a widening of the scope of Union powers …'. The Court further emphasised that since Denmark's implementation of the Lisbon Treaty was based on the government's constitutional assessment that no new powers were transferred to the EU: '… Danish authorities are obliged to ensure that this is observed.'

But the Court went an important step further in that it added what looks like an open invitation to anyone not happy with EU law to bring their case to court:[41]

> If an act or a judicial decision which has a specific and real impact on Danish citizens etc. *raises doubts* as to whether it is based on an application of the Treaties which lies beyond the surrender of sovereignty according to the Accession Act, as amended, this may be made subject to a judicial review, as stated in paragraph 9.6 of the Maastricht judgment.[42] (emphasis added)

While extensive reference is made to the 1998 ruling, there is no repetition here of the reconciling language used in that decision. There is no mention here of 'extraordinary situation' or 'required certainty'. Instead, there is a plain affirmation of competence to carry out ultra vires review of decisions made by either the legislative or judicial authorities within the EU, if any such decision 'raises doubts.'

This development towards what seems like a stricter standard of review runs contrary to the simultaneous developments in the German Federal Constitutional Court as per their *Honeywell* judgment issued a few years earlier.[43] While the SCDK's 1998 ruling on the Maastricht Treaty[44] followed the German Federal Constitutional Court's decision in the *Brunner* case,[45] the SCDK seems to have changed its course thereafter. In *Honeywell*, the German Federal Constitutional Court elaborated on the long-lasting doctrine of collaboration between the Court of Justice and Member State Supreme Courts by introducing the notion that EU law can only be deemed inapplicable when a transgression of the limited competences of an EU body is considered to be 'structurally significant'. The SCDK, however, took a much less conciliatory approach.[46]

[40] See UfR 2013.1451H. For a commentary, see HP Olsen 'The SCDK's decision on the constitutionality of Denmark's ratification of the Lisbon Treaty' (2013) 50 *Common Market Law Review* 1489.

[41] ibid.

[42] Para 9.6 of the Maastricht judgment is quoted in Joined Cases C-199/12 to C-201/12 *Minister voor Immigratie en Asiel v X and Y and Z v Minister voor Immigratie en Asiel* [2013] ECLI:EU:C:2013:720 paras 1–13.

[43] BVerfG, BvR 2661/06 of 6 July 2010.

[44] Højesteret [Supreme Court] case 361/1997 of 6 April 1998. For a commentary, see Olsen and Harck, 'Decision concerning the Maastricht Treaty'.

[45] BVerfG 89, 155 of 12 October 1993.

[46] The position is in fact closer to Judge Landau's dissenting opinion on the 'structurally significant' requirement, BVerfG, BvR 2661/06 of 6 July 2010, 102–103.

The *Ajos* case arose only a few years after this hardening occurred in the Court's stance on EU law. The way the SCDK constructs its argument in the case follows very much in the slipstream of the previous decision. In *Ajos*, the SCDK crystallises an approach that it had been working towards in its 2013 decision. In essence, the case is illustrative of a turn towards a greater national patrolling of the limited mandate given to the EU, including its judicial organ. Yet such an amplified role for the domestic court is bound to create frictions with the EU, both because it creates a collision between a rather static national understanding of the law and the inherent dynamism of the European project of integration through law, and because it unavoidably invites litigants to test out the avenues and their colliding understandings. Although the SCDK inter alia justifies its decision with arguments concerning legal certainty and legitimate expectations, the longer-term result is likely to be increased legal uncertainty and less clear expectations.

EXPLAINING *AJOS*

There are multiple possible explanations for the turn of events witnessed here at the highest echelons of the Danish judiciary. A more structural explanation would be that political trends have changed towards a renewed affirmation of national sovereignty. This is the result of a number of disintegrative processes, notably the refugee crisis, Brexit, and the 2008 financial crisis. Political momentum existed, in other words, for a push-back response when the case appeared before the SCDK; and if the time was right, the case at hand was certainly also conducive. The *Ajos* case offered in many ways a perfect springboard for a 'push-back strategy', as it concerned an area of EU law that is both controversial and weakly-founded, according to many commentators. By pushing the case to its extreme, the SCDK eventually forced itself into a *contra legem* situation—and Danish law needed to prevail by necessity if the SCDK was to stay within its domestic constitutional mandate. The SCDK was probably fully aware that although this would upset certain Europeanist milieus, including those at the Court of Justice and those working in Brussels, it would be welcomed in many other quarters, both nationally and across Europe. In this sense there was a low cost attached to issuing a high-profile decision challenging the perceived wisdom of the hierarchy of EU law.

A second explanation for the marked change in the behaviour of the SCDK involves changes on the bench in Copenhagen. From 1991 to 2000, Niels Pontoppidan presided in the SCDK. He was a figure who worked towards a pragmatic but genuinely open approach towards international law as evidenced in the constitutional jurisprudence during his tenure as president. The current bench of 19 judges only includes three judges from that period, one of whom wrote the only dissent in the *Ajos* case. In recent years, the bench has been increasingly occupied by a new and more diverse group of jurists. This differs from the preceding era in which the golden path to the SCDK was via the central state administration, notably the Ministry of Justice. The original recruitment pattern ensured what has been described as a high degree of alignment between government positions and the SCDK.[47] The recent changes on the bench are, in part, the result of a reform of the governance of the Court designed to create a more autonomous court. In theory, this has contributed to a court readier to deviate from government policy. This remains, however, speculative and it is beyond the scope of this chapter to firmly link changes on the bench to changes in SCDK legal practices.

A third explanation posits that the *Ajos* case is a product of what might best be described as a growing irritation with international courts over their perceived legal micromanagement. In this view, the expansive tendencies of international courts via dynamic interpretation essentially collide with Danish legal culture and its focus on textual interpretation. A former president of the SCDK (from 2010 to 2014), Børge Dahl, openly states the latter in a recent *Festschrift* to a colleague from the SCDK, drily noting that 'Danish judges work on the basis of the law and view creative judicial activism as something that puts legal certainty under pressure and which may over time encumber the trust in courts and their legitimacy.'[48] He reminds the reader that Danish courts, and notably the SCDK, should maintain their particular pragmatic and textual approach and not succumb to the push from international courts:

> In the cooperation with international courts and other countries' supreme courts, the Danish side does not need to come cap in hand. Denmark is number one on the global list of legal certainty. … In the annual EU survey of trust in the courts of the Member States, Denmark comes out as number one.[49]

Dahl, though, is not alone in arguing along these (hardened) lines. There is a growing choir extolling the virtues of taking a hard stance against the perceived intrusions of international tribunals and their dynamic legal approaches, notably the Court of Justice but also the European Court of Human Rights.[50] What the *Ajos* case adds to this picture of a growing 'sovereigntism' in Danish law—at times even plain nationalism—is that it does not stop short of implementing the viewpoint into legal practice.

[47] See for example MR Madsen, *La genèse de l'Europe des droits de l'homme: enjeux juridiques et stratégies d'état: France, Grande-Bretagne et pays scandinaves, 1945–1970* (Strasbourg, Presses universitaires de Strasbourg, 2010).

[48] B Dahl, 'Hvad skal vi med Højesteret?' in MH Jensen, SH Mørup and B Dahl (eds), *Festskrift til Jens Peter Christensen* (Copenhagen, DJØF, 2016) 632 (translated by the authors).

[49] ibid 632 (translated by the authors).

[50] Examples of Danish critiques of the European Court of Human Rights are included in J Christoffersen and MR Madsen (eds), *Menneskerettighedsdomstolen—50 års samspil med dansk ret og politik* (Copenhagen, Thomson Reuters, 2009).

The conclusion of the *Ajos* case makes two clear assertions, with both elements becoming fully visible through the narrow lens of Danish law. First, that the Accession Act does not provide the legal basis for a general unwritten principle to be unfolded in specific rulings by the Court of Justice in a way that takes precedence over national legislation. Second, that the SCDK would be violating its own constitutional mandate were it to dis-apply Danish legal provisions, even when they are contrary to EU law. In both cases the argument gathers intensity by reference to legal certainty and legitimate expectations. The result of the approach is effectively a domestication of the question of the effect of EU law—now essentially a question of the limits of the Danish Accession Act.

Using this approach, the legal status of the contested principle of non-discrimination is that of an unwritten principle without a clear legal basis in the Treaty. As such, it is not deemed to be covered by the Accession Act. Instead, the SCDK views it as judge-made and thus belonging to a quasi-legal realm outside the constitutionally binding sphere of EU law in Denmark. This reconstruction of the validity of EU law is obviously deeply troubling when seen from a supranational perspective. The consequence is that every single national constitution of Member States creates its own variation of EU law. That transforms EU law from an autonomous order into a residual order, the latter contingent on national legal practice and specific constitutional provisions. The game is, of course, not completely over yet. The Danish government might well be facing suits from Danish citizens over incorrect implementation of the Directive. Meanwhile, determining whether the EU will act remains speculative at this stage.

Yet by far the most striking issue arising from the SCDK's actions concerns the defective decision to stay strictly within the (domestic) law, and to stay out of (national) politics by violating obligations under (EU) law. Although the decision is drafted in the spirit of Scandinavian legal pragmatism and textualism upon which the SCDK prides itself, it is likely to be viewed and received in very different terms. Judicial self-restraint simply fails to materialise as the guiding logic of the decision. The approach of supposedly avoiding politics, the formal *leitmotif* of the decision and its formalism, comes across as political. The main reason for this is that EU law simply cannot be reduced to an exterior phenomenon. Rather, it is part and parcel of the Danish law. It follows that switching it off, as is done in the *Ajos* case, even when justified under an interpretation of national law, necessarily entails applying one law by breaking another. That is not a viable path for any legal system taking supranational obligations seriously.

CONCLUSION

What does the path taken by the highest Danish court mean for EU law? And what are the implications for the EU more generally? The most conservative reading is that it is simply a singular case, highly specific to a now-amended provision in Danish law. In that optic, it has no broader implications beyond the specific case. A second—and more expansive—reading is that the case is a kind of warning issued to the Court of Justice on the need for a two-way judicial collaboration. By mobilising the heavy artillery of constitutional law, the SCDK raises its own standing and re-asserts some measure of equality into the partnership. This implies that the Court will have to exercise more restraint when it reaches the boundaries of its conferred competences. A more expansive reading still would maintain that the SCDK is pursuing a neo-sovereigntist agenda, seeking to rebalance the institutional order in favour of national legal institutions. If the basic legal logic of the decision were to apply systematically across Europe, it would fragment the concept of the EU legal order. That would be legally problematic in terms of coherence, and most likely undermine the broader project of European integration through law.

But what does the *Ajos* case mean for legal certainty? The decision's rationale resembles classic dualist theories of public international law. In the SCDK's conceptual realm, the application of EU law is primarily a matter of national law. Even the powers of the Court of Justice are revisited (and revised) through the lens of Danish constitutional law. The EU is basically treated as entirely residual to Danish law. At first glance that seems to enhance legal certainty: Danish law prevails and so does the SCDK. The problem is, however, that such an understanding is strangely at odds with the legal reality of the EU project. Since its formative years in the 1960s, the project of European integration through law has been anchored in the notions of the supremacy and direct effect of European law. This clashes fundamentally with the position crafted by the SCDK that seeks to domesticate the question of supremacy in Danish constitutional law. As a result, the at first glance enhanced legal certainty at the domestic level is not likely to create any certainty at the supranational level. Paradoxically, the strict positioning of the SCDK might well augment legal uncertainty, as it will be unclear what to expect from European law at large as different venues will provide different answers.

The legal stand-off between the SCDK and Court of Justice is not unique, however. There have been many instances of frictions between the Court of Justice and the highest national courts in Europe. A broader analysis of the reception of supranational law by domestic courts across the globe reveals similar conflicts. A perhaps particularly striking case of the conflict between dualism and supranational law is found in integration law under the Caribbean Community Caricom. Most Caricom Member States are staunch dualists and reluctant travellers with regard to giving effect to supranational law by any other means than national incorporation. As a result, Caricom law exists today in a parallel supranational system adjudicated almost entirely at the supranational level.[51] Supranational rights are in practice almost exclusively claimed before the Caribbean Court of Justice and not domestic courts.

The essential conflict that can be observed in the Caribbean, Europe, as well as elsewhere, is also about different ways of exercising the judicial function and associated cultures. The Danish case is particularly illustrative of a culture of strict textualism and respect for Parliament's intention. This clashes with the very different undertaking most international courts are facing, namely to adjudicate a common law for a group of different Member States. While the former relies mainly on statutory law with precise prescriptions, the latter is governed by broader principles, applicable across different national legal traditions and cultures. The fundamental challenge is not to choose one approach over the over. Instead, and this remains a challenge in many places, it concerns developing ways of integrating the specific with the general—the national with the supranational. This calls for dialogue and even legal diplomacy on the part of both national and international courts.[52] Legal certainty is otherwise lost in unproductive judicial turf wars.

[51] S Caserta and MR Madsen, 'Consolidating Supranational Authority: the Caribbean Court of Justice Decisions in the Tomlinson Cases' (2016) 110 *American Journal of International Law* 533.

[52] On the notion of legal diplomacy, see MR Madsen, 'Legal Diplomacy—Law, Politics and the Genesis of Postwar European Human Rights' in SL Hoffmann (ed), *Human Rights in the Twentieth Century: A Critical History* (Cambridge, Cambridge University Press, 2011).

10

Towards Appropriate Legal Certainty for Consumers Seeking Justice in a Globalised World

GERAINT HOWELLS AND MATEJA DUROVIC

INTRODUCTION

LEGAL CERTAINTY IS a prized goal. The rule of law debate has at its core the predictability of the legal system.[1] A Chinese judge was recently honoured for passing down thousands of judgments that were always right—the evidence being that they had not been successfully appealed. Yet such an idealistic belief in legal certainty does not match the reality. Of course, in rule of law societies the uncertainty comes from the problems inherent in administering the law, rather than any arbitrariness that is inherent in totalitarian or more primitive forms of justice. However, it would be delusional to think that legal uncertainty is not a phenomenon that is omnipresent in all jurisdictions in relation to all areas of law, including consumer law.[2]

Legal rules can never cover every circumstance. Even the Civil Law Codes that aimed to be complete legal texts have gaps or concepts that are open-textured and subject to interpretation, in particular regarding diverse standard and principles. Most famously, we have the discussions around the concept of good faith.[3] In the common law world some may believe that there is a right answer to legal questions based on natural law principles, but even those who believe the true common law should always be discoverable accept that few humans have the capacity of Dworkin's Herculean judges.[4]

[1] A Scalia, 'The Rule of Law as a Law of Rules' (1989) 56 *University of Chicago Law Review* 1175, 1179.
[2] I Benöhr, *EU Consumer Law and Human Rights* (Oxford, Oxford University Press, 2013) 209.
[3] R Zimmermann and S Whittaker, *Good Faith in European Contract Law* (Cambridge, Cambridge University Press, 2000).
[4] R Dworkin, *Law's Empire* (Cambridge, Mass, Belknap Press, 1986).

At best judges approach perfection, but being human they will always have some weaknesses and many judges are in practice less than perfect. Even if the law can be correctly stated, there will be issues in applying it. Vague judgements leave a lot of room for different interpretation.

Equally the process of establishing the facts depends upon the rules of evidence and procedure and how much resources by parties, lawyers and the courts can be devoted to fact-finding. Again, there is also the human element in evaluating the facts and applying them to the law. These are the problems Rawls describes as imperfect procedural justice.[5] Legal uncertainty is an undesirable state of affairs, which needs to be avoided as far as prudent. However, a certain level of legal uncertainty can never be completely avoided. Strong efforts need to be made in order to secure that this level is as low as possible.

However, there are diminishing returns. If every situation could be totally covered by a legal rule, the cost in terms of drafting and opaqueness would be high. Equally, the resources needed to establish every fact or consider every angle of the case might be so significant that law and economics would tell us that this is an inefficient use of scarce societal resources. These costs are particularly high in the consumer context. As soon as one recognises consumer disputes as different from general commercial transactions because the law introduces the element of ensuring fairness for the weaker party, and this is more complicated to assess than simply applying traditional legal principles. There are many examples of the law seeking to modify its principles to introduce fairness, but often the concepts are open-textured, leaving a lot of discretion to the decision-maker. Ironically, justice may be more expensive to deliver in cases that have an intrinsic low value, making them difficult to run in traditional legal form.

This has led to simplified regimes being set up, that indeed emphasise fairness alongside legal principles. Normally, this is seen as adavantageous to consumers, who benefit from decisions based on a sense of justice, rather than a mechanical application of the law. However, protection of consumers through the principles of fairness, as might be the case of small claims, instead of law might not be always in the interest of the consumer. This is because judges may consider that reasons of fairness should favour the trader in a particular dispute instead of the consumer. They might, for instance, not consider a prohibition of exclusion clauses fair in particular circumstances.[6] As a result, one should always be cautious when applying the principle of fairness of consumer dispute and the decision on the ground of law, enabling consumers to protect their infringed rights, should be always left to secure legal certainty for consumers.

[5] J Rawls, *A Theory of Justice* (Cambridge, Mass, Belknap Press, 1971).

[6] On the position in New Zealand see K Tokely, 'Disputes Tribunals: should the monetary limit be increased?' (1999) 5 *New Zealand Business Law Quarterly* 13.

Discretion-based decisions are normally more expensive to make than those that simply apply the rules. Rawls describes this as the problem of quasi-pure procedural justice, where there are no clear right answers and the need is to structure the law so that the results are within acceptable limits. In the consumer context, there is an irony that consumer cases are usually of rather small value. Law and economics tells us that we should have a limit on how much we invest in resolving such cases. Yet process and fairness is a hallmark of the rule of law society and the extent to which it is worth investing in assuring minimum access to justice rights must be assessed. Equally, authors like Rawls and Habermas have underlined the need to ensure weaker parties are able to have their case heard fairly, even when against a stronger party.[7]

Consumer-trader disputes call out for such protection because consumers typically represent significantly weaker parties in comparison to traders.[8] Securing a consumer's access to justice is one of the most challenging tasks for any regulatory regime of consumer protection.[9] However, there is a noticeable and constant struggle regarding how consumer access to justice is to be designed and improved.[10] A particular challenge is how to set up a coherent and efficient justice system among all possible enforcement options that are given to consumers, and which may be developed and run by different entities with a clear lack of any cooperation mechanism.[11] This is the context in which legal certainty in consumer law needs to be understood: as securing the consumer's access to justice and the existence of an appropriate enforcement mechanism that will guarantee that consumers' rights are protected when they are infringed in an effective and efficient manner.

There is also the broader issue that whilst some consumer disputes may be for small amounts and/or based on individualised circumstances, many others will reflect deeper issues that affect larger numbers of consumers and even threaten to undermine confidence in the market and injure good traders. The question is how to design an efficient system of consumer redress that would secure consumers' access to justice?

Consumer justice may be a Morris Minor rather than a Rolls Royce, but consumer law itself teaches us that even the Morris Minor must meet some basic standards. The question is what trade-offs can be safely made? Our

[7] J Rawls, *Justice as Fairness: A Restatement* (Cambridge, Mass, Belknap Press, 2001); J *Habermas, Faktizität und Geltung. Beiträge zur Diskurstheorie des Rechts und des demokratischen Rechtsstaats* (Frankfurt am Main, Suhrkamp, 1992).

[8] AJ Belohlávek, *B2C Arbitration: Consumer Protection in Arbitration* (Huntington, Juris Publishing, 2012) 38.

[9] H-W Micklitz, 'Social Justice and Access Justice in Private Law' in H-W Micklitz (ed), *The Many Faces of Social Justice in Private Law* (Cheltenham, Edward Elgar, 2011) 3, 59.

[10] S Wrbka, *European Consumer Access to Justice Revisited* (Cambridge, Cambridge University Press, 2015).

[11] See P Cortes (ed), *The Regulatory Framework for Consumer Dispute Resolution* (Oxford, Oxford University Press, 2016).

approach is to accept that consumer law does in reality demand a slimmed down form of justice—be it small claims or any form of consumer alternative dispute resolution mechanism. The nature of consumer disputes lends itself to this in many respects. Most consumer disputes are fairly straightforward: the goods did not arrive; the goods did not work or the goods did not do what was claimed. The same happens with the provision of services.

These are cases that are fairly easily resolved by almost any decision-maker. Indeed, we shall see that many online schemes take advantage of this to try to find cost-efficient solutions. It seems right then to sacrifice some aspects of procedure to ensure access, as otherwise justice will be denied by placing redress practically out of reach. Safeguards are needed. In small claims courts this is usually achieved by having a ceiling on claims dealt with under expedited procedures. The alternative dispute resolution (ADR) procedure is more complicated as it tends to deviate more from traditional court procedures. Here we favour systems that are formally only binding on traders, leaving consumers at least the option of pursuing the claim through the ordinary courts. Moreover, the points of general interest need to be addressed through a class action system of reporting regimes that allow these more informal procedures to have an information loop back into the regulatory structure.

In the context of enforcement, two issues seem to be particularly complex. On the one hand, there is the question of transnational enforcement. Transnational enforcement is a rising phenomenon tightly connected with globalisation. Economies and trade also results in an increasing number of cross-border transactions. Law needs to follow that trend, which is particularly difficult in the case of securing access to justice to consumers for problems that have arisen from cross-border transactions.[12]

On the other hand, the internet is becoming as an increasingly popular forum for performance of cross-border transactions. That requires an adequate regulatory answer when it comes to the protection of consumer rights that have been infringed in this kind of transaction, preferably also online. The application of traditional means for the resolution of internet-originated consumer disputes faces numerous problems and difficulties. As a result, it is possible to observe attempts to provide diverse forms of online means for resolution of consumer disputes.[13]

From the perspective of transnational consumer law, legal certainty is today primarily understood in the context of familiarity of traders and consumers with the rules on consumer protection of another jurisdiction than

[12] See C Twigg-Flesner, *A Cross-Border-Only Regulation for Consumer Transactions in the EU* (New York, Springer, 2012).

[13] Eg Regulation (EU) 524/2013, [2013] OJ L165/1.

the home jurisdiction or the site of business operations, and whether these rules are enforced in practice.[14]

In the context of transnational consumer law, the argument of legal certainty is thus used as a justification for the promotion of unification of the rules of consumer protection among different legal regimes as an argument to support cross-border trade. Traders need to know that their business activities, such as standard contract terms or commercial practices, are fully in compliance with the legal requirements of the state or territory where they operate. Legal certainty is, in that aspect, tightly connected with planning, as all business activities require planning. Equally, consumers need to be sure that they are protected also when they perform commercial transactions outside of their jurisdiction. In that sense, legal certainty is especially relevant in a transnational consumer law setting.

Significant efforts have been invested in harmonising consumer rules in different regions or even on a global level. The question is always the level of harmonisation that is aimed to be achieved.[15] For instance, during the latest decades in the EU, it is possible to follow constant efforts to harmonise consumer rules among its 28 Member States.[16] Similarly, some leading international organisations, such as the United Nations, World Bank or the OECD, have also called for more uniform consumer rules globally.[17] Recently, the focus of these harmonisation efforts is on enforcement. However, the question is whether the harmonisation of the rules contributes to legal certainty from the perspective of consumers' access to justice.

In that sense, superficial or fake harmonisation, which means harmonisation only on the paper of black letter law but which leaves material differences untouched, is particularly dangerous. The model of the EU also demonstrates well that harmonisation of substantial consumer rules, without harmonisation of the procedural rules, leads to different levels of protection in diverse Member States, resulting in further uncertainty. The example in the case of consumers against Apple, which took place in 11 Member States, clearly demonstrates how different enforcement mechanisms can result in diverse outcomes.[18]

[14] H Collins, 'Transaction Costs and Subsidiarity in European Contract Law' in S Grundmann and J Stuyck (eds), *An Academic Green Paper on European Contract Law* (The Hague, Kluwer Law International, 2002) 270.

[15] G Howells, 'European Consumer Law—The Minimal and Maximal Harmonisation Debate and Pro Independent Consumer Law Competence' in Grundmann and Stuyck, *An Academic Green Paper on European Contract Law*.

[16] See J Stuyck, *1993—Twenty Years Later. The Evolution of Consumer Law in the European Union* (Cambridge, Intersentia, 2013).

[17] H-W Micklitz and M Durovic, *Internationalisation of Consumer Law* (Abingdon, Routledge, 2017) 5.

[18] M Durovic, '*The Apple Case:* The Commencement of Pan-European Battle against Unfair Commercial Practices' (2013) 9 *European Review of Contract Law* 253.

TRANSNATIONAL CONSUMER LAW

Legal uncertainty is, in particular, present in the case of the procedural rules of consumer law. However, legal uncertainty is also a factor that affects the development of substantive rules of consumer law, particularly in a transnational context. From a transnational perspective, the presence of diverse regulatory regimes of consumer protection among different states is typically seen as a form of non-tariff obstacle for cross-border trade.[19] The existence of this diversity among consumer law regimes in a globalised world is also seen as one of the causes of legal uncertainty, as market players (both the traders and the consumers) are not familiar with the rules at the market that regulate their commercial transactions.

In that sense, legal uncertainty is tightly connected with additional costs of trade, and thus there is a strong incentive to decrease the level of the present legal certainty. The argument is that not only traders would profit from such a state of affairs, but also consumers—to whom, in reality, traders pass the burden of these costs. Globalisation of trade is thus supposed to be followed by globalisation of law, including the rules of consumer protection.[20]

However, very few rules on consumer protection on a global level have been adopted. Countries materially differ in their approaches towards the regulation of consumer protection, which negatively affects cross-border commerce. The most successful example of internationalisation and codification of commercial contract law, The United Nations Convention on Contracts for the International Sale of Goods of 1980 (CISG), which today has 84 contracting parties, explicitly excludes business-to-consumer transactions from its scope.[21] The UN Guidelines on Consumer Protection of 1985 (as revised in 1999 and 2016) are also of too general and vague a character and, being soft law, do not represent a binding piece of legislation. The UN Guidelines only envisage that the 'Governments should establish or maintain legal and/or administrative measures to enable consumers or, as appropriate, relevant organisations to obtain redress through formal or informal procedures that are expeditious, fair, inexpensive and accessible'.[22]

[19] A Grainger, 'Trade Facilitation: A Conceptual Review' (2011) 45 *Journal of World Trade* 39.

[20] R Michaels, 'Globalization and Law: Law Beyond the State' in R Banakar and M Travers (eds), *Law and Social Theory* (Oxford, Hart Publishing, 2013) 288.

[21] CISG, Art 2.

[22] United Nations/Department of Economic and Social Affairs, 'United Nations Guidelines for Consumer Protection' (2003) 32, available at www.un.org/esa/sustdev/publications/consumption_en.pdf.

ENFORCEMENT OF CONSUMER LAW

A particularly relevant element of legal certainty in a consumer law context is the issue of enforcement. Enforcement of consumer law is something that really matters to any consumer. This is why consumer law is only as good as its enforcement. In order to achieve a higher level of legal certainty, it is not sufficient only to provide unified consumer rules, but also to ensure that consumer law is applied in practice and that consumer shopping from another jurisdiction will always be effectively protected. In other words, consumers need to be certain that their rights will be effectively protected, in an easily accessible and affordable manner, in cases when they are infringed.[23] This is a necessary prerequisite for legal certainty.

However, the establishment of an adequate and functional regulatory regime of enforcement has become one of the most challenging tasks in consumer law and policy. For many different reasons, the enforcement before state institutions, such as courts or administrative authorities, through diverse judicial and administrative (rather formal and strict) mechanisms, has demonstrated that it is not fully capable of providing effective protection to consumers whose rights have been breached.

Likewise, the authorities in charge of the enforcement of consumer law always need to fulfil certain criteria. These criteria mean that these authorities have to be impartial, accountable, transparent, and operate in the interest of consumers. These are the necessary conditions that any enforcement mechanism must fulfil.[24]

Consumer law disputes are typically disputes of low value. That is one their main differences from classical commercial disputes between merchants. Therefore, financial incentives for consumers to initiate this kind of dispute are very low, unless the procedure is simple and fast. This has led to the development in different models of collective redress whose aim is to unite the claims of a number of individuals and seek justice.

Today, throughout the world it is possible to observe the development of less formal, cheaper and more accessible mechanisms that consumers may use to resolve their disputes with the traders.[25] These include the establishment of special courts and courts procedure for consumer disputes, aggregation of consumer claims into one in case of collective redress, as well as alternative methods for resolution of consumer disputes. All these are imagined to secure a high level of certainty for consumers when it comes to enforcement if their consumer rights have been breached.

[23] CJ Miller, BW Harvey and DL Parry, *Consumer and Trading Law: Text, Cases and Materials* (Oxford, Oxford University Press, 1998) 393.

[24] G Howells and H-W Micklitz, 'Guidelines for Consumer Organisations on Enforcement and Collective Redress and Collective Redress' (2009) *Consumer Law Enforcement Forum Project* 17, www.cojef-project.eu/IMG/pdf/d_CLEFfinalguidelines_76647.pdf.

[25] Cortes (ed), *The Regulatory Framework for Consumer Dispute Resolution.*

SMALL CLAIM COURTS/PROCEDURES

Small claim courts and small claim procedures are means for the resolution of consumer disputes that are imagined to secure a cheaper and faster procedure than the regular courts and regular court procedure. The rationale behind such measures is to offer a litigation opportunity to consumers at a reduced cost and with the promise of a faster resolution of the dispute. Of course, the question of 'how small is really small?' remains, and this is something that needs to be addressed when defining the legal framework for small claims procedures.

However, the small claims court and procedure is a good idea that, unfortunately, seems to be insufficiently developed in practice. This is the case with, at least, the EU and its 28 Member States, where special rules exist in cases of small claim procedure. Harmonised European rules on small claim procedure have been introduced through the provisions of Regulation No 861/2007.[26]

Regulation No 861/2007 on small claim procedure has developed a special procedure for consumer disputes based on simplicity, speed and proportionality.[27] The main problem with this Regulation is that it is not really applied in practice. Specifically, very few of the national authorities implement small claim procedure measures. One of the principal reasons for this failure is the lack of familiarity of the lawyers and general public about its existence and content. For instance, empirical data demonstrates that around three quarters of surveyed consumers have never heard of such a procedure. Also, only a few Member States offered practical assistance in filling in the form, as required by the Regulation.

In relation to Regulation No 861/2007 on small claim procedure, special problems occur in the case of transnational consumer disputes. The cause of these problems is the fact that the national procedures vary. Moreover, these procedures are often still based on traditional and general procedural rules and evidence, which do not take into consideration the particularities of consumer disputes. Time allowed for small claims is usually less than for other claims.

COLLECTIVE REDRESS/CLASS ACTIONS

Class actions and other forms of collective redress are becoming an increasingly popular method of resolution of consumer disputes.[28] The development

[26] Regulation (EC) 861/2007, [2007] OJ L199/1.

[27] XE Kramer, 'Small Claim, Simple Recovery? The European Small Claims Procedure and Its Implementation in the Member States' (2011) 1 *ERA Forum: Journal of European Law* 119.

[28] C Hodges, 'Collective Redress in Europe: The New Model' (2010) 7 *Civil Justice Quarterly* 370.

of mechanisms for the protection of the collective interests of consumers certainly contributes to the achievement of legal certainty. This is primarily because they unite the claims of individual consumers that would never be pursued unless they are brought together. Claims become of viable size for lawyers to invest and, where needed, the costs of expert witnesses can be shared. The choices concerning group actions, and accordingly representative actions, reflect the objectives and core values of each legal system.[29]

However, among the existing models of collective redress, several shortcomings may be observed. First, in certain jurisdictions, class actions are not used as a means of protecting consumers, but rather as an instrument to increase the profit of the lawyers. This is particularly true with the US model of class action. That factor represents the main obstacle, and is why so many jurisdictions are reluctant to adopt any kind of model of collective redress that would resemble the US model. Legal certainty may even be diminished if class actions simply become tools for extracting settlements. Second, in the case of models of collective redress that have not followed the US model, but have adopted different ones, not based on the lucrative desires of lawyers, the problem which arises relates to the funding of these actions, as it is difficult to obtain adequate resources to financially support such an action on behalf of consumers.

The class action originates from the US, but over the time it has inspired the development of a similar model in a number of jurisdictions worldwide.[30] In the EU, for example, the legal framework for collective redress has been established through Directive 2009/22/EC on injunctions[31] and Recommendation 2013/396/EU on collective redress.[32] The idea behind the introduction of such a mechanism is to improve the enforcement of consumer law in all EU Member States. Contrary to the US model, the principal goal of the common European consumer policy when it comes to collective redress is the deterrence of wrongdoing by stopping bad practices, rather than providing compensation.[33]

In addition, an interesting development has been the emergence of claim management companies (for example, Flightright or EUClaim). There is a very high rate of success in practice of the claims managed by these companies. The reason for this success is that they typically only deal with claims where they believe they have a very high probability of success.

[29] G Calabresi and KS Schwartz, 'The Costs of Class Actions: Allocations and Collective Redress in the US Experience' (2011) *European Journal of Law and Economics* 169, 171.

[30] Micklitz and Durovic, *Internationalisation of Consumer Law* 69.

[31] Directive 2009/22/EC, [2009] OJ L110/30.

[32] Commission Recommendation of 11 June 2013, [2013] OJ L201/60.

[33] G Wagner, 'Collective Redress—Categories of Loss and Legislative Options' (2011) 127 *Law Quarterly Review* 55, 60.

ALTERNATIVE METHODS FOR THE RESOLUTION OF CONSUMER DISPUTES

Consumer alternative dispute resolution (ADR) mechanisms are developed in such a manner as to provide more effective protection to consumers. The idea behind the development of alternative methods for the resolution of consumer disputes is to contribute to improving consumer's access to justice and thus providing a higher level of legal certainty to consumers that their infringed rights will be protected in an effective manner. Currently, the increasing presence of ADR as means for resolution of consumer disputes may be noticed throughout the world.

One of the most challenging tasks in relation to consumer ADR is how to design a regulatory framework that will suit the needs and particularities of the market, traders and consumers. A regulatory design that does not fit with the needs of all these three categories will not work in practice and thus will not secure consumer access to justice. For that purpose, consumer ADR needs always to fulfil certain requirements,[34] for example, the legality of consumer ADR is a particularly important element—the consumer must always have access to the court.

Examples of existing consumer ADR mechanisms are: mediation, complaint boards, ombudsmen, arbitration or conciliation. In other words, there is not one unique model, but many different forms of consumer ADR mechanism, each with its own particularities. However, what unites all of these models is that they all typically offer to consumers less formal, more discrete, less expensive, faster, more accessible, simpler, less time consuming, easier mechanisms for the resolution of consumer disputes than those offered before different judicial and administrative bodies. Their relationship with legal certainty is interesting. They all seek to ensure more access to justice, and therefore to make it more certain that some justice is done. However, mediation and conciliation place more emphasis on reaching a solution with which the parties are content, rather than strictly enforcing legal rights. Equally, some forms of ADR seek to adjudicate according to justice standards that extend protection beyond the formal law.

The development of the internet in the twenty-first century as a forum for consumer cross-border shopping has also inspired the development of diverse alternative methods for the resolution of disputes. Such dispute resolution is performed in the same manner as the disputed transactions, namely online. Online shopping automatically also requires the development of online methods for the resolution of consumer disputes which have arisen from this kind of transaction.

[34] M Doyle, K Ritters and S Brooker, *Seeking Resolution: The availability and usage of consumer-to-business alternative dispute resolution in the UK* (London, National Consumer Council, 2004) 5–6.

All such ADR mechanims aim to secure a higher level of certainty to consumers. The remaining question is whether they offer certainty or a chance of some sort of justice. They certainly do, but, in order to avoid conflict with the requirements of legal certainty, the possibility for consumers to access the court to ask for more formal protection of their infringed consumer rights, needs always to be maintained. That is essential. In addition, in the case of consumer ADR, there is always the uncertainty of whether the case will be won or not.

Again, in the case of consumer ADR, the consumer is in a significantly worse position than the trader. The regulatory framework needs to be designed in such a manner to avoid this kind of situation. Also, the problem might be a lack of consistency, as well as unclear costs that the consumer will eventually have to pay. In the case of the EU, this is all tightly connected with the consumer's right to effective legal protection: access to justice is, under EU law, a fundamental right of any consumer. This is why the EU has been particularly focused on developing a common European regulatory framework for consumer arbitration.

In order to provide an adequate regulatory framework that would provide an appropriate level of protection to consumers throughout the EU, Directive 2013/11/EU on alternative resolution of consumer disputes was adopted (the Consumer ADR Directive).[35]

Member States are obliged to secure that the ADR entities in charge of running consumer ADR mechanisms, as well as the consumer ADR procedure itself, fulfil the following characteristics: expertise, independence, impartiality, transparency, effectiveness, fairness, liberty and legality. The Consumer ADR Directive is, in particular, focused on the consumer ADR mechanisms in cases of cross-border consumer disputes.

ONLINE RESOLUTION OF ORDINARY DISPUTES

Together with the Consumer ADR Directive, Regulation 524/2013 on online resolution of consumer disputes was passed (th Consumer ODR Regulation).[36] It came into effect in January 2016. The Consumer ODR Regulation is focused on a particular form of consumer ADR, online ADR, the so-called ODR. Online ADR is to be applied in consumer disputes that have arisen from online transactions, in particular cross-border online transactions. In an era when the internet has become one of the most important and common marketplaces, and when an increasing number of consumers decide to purchase products online, it has become necessary to establish an online mechanism for the resolution of disputes that arise from online shopping.

[35] Directive 2013/11/EU, [2013] OJ L87/19.
[36] See above n 13.

It is, somehow, expected that consumers who perform their economic activities online should also have the possibility to pursue the online resolution of disputes that arise from those online activities. Online resolution of consumer disputes is thus seen as an excellent and efficient way to resolve consumer disputes that have arisen from online commercial transactions. In such a manner, the development of online platforms contributes to the level of legal certainty, as it secures an additional means by which consumers may address their consumer problems arising from online transactions.

The Consumer ODR Regulation applies to the disputes initiated by consumers who are residents of one of 28 Member States, against traders who also have a residence or are established in one of the Member States. Its scope of application is not limited only to cross-border online shopping, but also applies to domestic commerce. It is designed to cover business-to-consumer disputes. In line with the scope of application of EU consumer law, it applies to disputes arising solely from business-to-consumer relations, and not to disputes arising from consumer-to-consumer relations or business-to-business relations. The Consumer ODR Regulation applies to disputes related to contractual obligations arising from online sales and services contracts.

The existence of an online platform for resolution of consumer disputes is also encouraged since the presence of such a platform stimulates consumers to perform more cross-border online shopping, knowing that there is an easily accessible and unified manner to resolve disputes online, should any dispute occur. The Consumer ODR Regulation provides a legislative framework aimed at ensuring a certain level of quality of ODR mechanisms and independence, impartiality and transparency of the ODR schemes.[37] This approach is fully in line with the common EU policy of strengthening of the digital Single Market and this is why the Consumer ODR Regulation was adopted. Under EU law, the ODR mechanism is very advantageous for consumers, since it offers a simple, efficient, fast and low-cost way for consumers to resolve disputes that arise from online commercial transactions. This is why the online mechanism is particularly important when it comes to legal certainty in the case of cross border online transactions.

For the resolution of online disputes, the establishment and functionality of the common European ODR platform is of essential importance. Accordingly, the Consumer ODR Regulation establishes a legal framework for a common European ODR platform and secures an independent, impartial, transparent, effective, fast and fair out-of-court resolution of disputes between consumers and traders online. However, in line with the approach of the Consumer ADR Directive, before submission of a claim to the ODR platform, consumers are encouraged to try to contact traders to resolve disputes in an amicable manner.

[37] Wrbka, *European Consumer Access to Justice Revisited* 97.

The idea is to establish the ODR platform, which will link all of the national ADR entities of the Member States. The practical results of the platform are still to be seen, as operation started only in 2016. In reality, it remains to be seen to what extent the ODR will contribute to the achievement of a higher level of legal certainty. It might appear that it only provides a standardised solution and less informed evidence-gathering.

The Regulation founds the legal basis for the establishment of an ODR platform for the entire EU. The ODR platform is imagined to be an interactive website that offers a single point of entry to consumers and traders who are willing to resolve consumer disputes in an out-of-court manner when disputes have arisen from online commercial transactions.

The ODR platform's aim is to ensure that consumer and traders can submit complaints arising from online contractual disputes, by completing a simple electronic complaint form. The form is to be accessible in all official languages of the EU, so that it can be accessed and used in all Member States. The platform is linked to an ADR entity that is supposed to be competent to deal with the dispute concerned, fulfilling all the conditions of the Consumer ADR Directive. A free-of-charge, electronic case management tool that secures that ADR entities may conduct the dispute resolution procedure through the ODR platform also needs to be made available.

A very important requirement of the ODR platform is that it be user friendly and thus accessible to all potential users. A particular concern is in ensuring that it is useable by vulnerable consumers, which clearly demonstrates the continuity of EU consumer policy towards the protection and securing of access to justice of vulnerable consumers.

Secrecy and confidentiality are essential when it comes to any form of alternative resolution of consumer disputes. This is why the Consumer ODR Regulation imposes the obligation of professional secrecy or a related confidentiality obligation, in line with the applicable national legislation of the Member State to all ODR points.

In order to secure the effective use of the online mechanism for resolution of consumer disputes, the submission of the complaint needs to be easy and user friendly. This is why the Consumer ODR Regulation envisages that an electronic complaint form should be made available on the ODR platform. The complaint form must contain certain information. The ODR platform will automatically, and without delay, transmit the complaint to the ADR entity that the parties have agreed to use. The ADR entity to which the complaint has been transmitted will, without delay, inform the parties about whether it agrees or refuses to deal with the dispute, in accordance with the Consumer ADR Directive. The ADR entity that has agreed to deal with the dispute will also inform the parties of its procedural rules and, if applicable, of the costs of the dispute resolution procedure concerned.

It is essential that consumers be informed about the existence of the possibility of resolving their disputes in an alternative manner, since consumers are not always aware of such an opportunity. Moreover, the easy access and usage of the online mechanism for the resolution of consumer disputes needs to be secured. This is why, under EU law, Member States are obliged to inform consumers about the existence of the ODR platform and about the possibility of using the ODR platform as a medium for the resolution of consumer disputes. However, this obligation does not apply to all traders—only to traders that are established in the territory of the EU, who engage in online sales or service contracts and who are committed or obliged to use one or more ADR entities.

The traders are, accordingly, obliged to have on their websites an electronic link to the ODR platform, as well as information about the ODR platform provided in the general terms and conditions that apply to online sales and services contracts. In addition, in cases when the offer is made by e-mail, that e-mail must also include an electronic link to the ODR platform. The link must be easily accessible to consumers. Moreover, the list of the ADR entities must always be published in the ODR platform.

In addition to the obligation on traders to inform consumers about the existence of the ODR platform, this obligation also relates to the ADR entities, the centres of the European Consumer Centres Network, who must also provide electronic links to the ODR platform.[38] Consumer organisations and traders' associations are to be encouraged to provide the links to the ODR platform, though there is no obligation on them to do so.

Alongside the European model, another important set of rules for online resolution of disputes is being proposed by a UN agency, the UNCITRAL. The United Nations has traditionally played an important role in the development of consumer law worldwide.[39] UNCITRAL is certainly the most important UN body when it comes to regulatory activities in the area of international trade law.

UNCITRAL published its Model Law on International Commercial Arbitration in 1985.[40] These principles are based on fairness, transparency, due process and accountability. These rules apply only in commercial arbitration, but they are designed as a model to cover all types of commercial transactions. The UNCITRAL rules are seen as a regulatory response towards an increasing number of cross-border commercial transactions concluded via the internet. The idea is to provide a set of rules that are a simple, fast, flexible and effective option for resolution of consumer disputes.

The rules are supposed to apply both to disputes arising from the sale of goods and provision of services. These rules are of a general character, rather than being adapted specifically to business-to-consumer commercial

[38] For details see ec.europa.eu/consumers/ecc/.

[39] Micklitz and Durovic, *Internationalisation of Consumer Law*.

[40] Available at www.uncitral.org/uncitral/en/uncitral_texts/arbitration/1985Model_arbitration.html.

transactions and the particularities of disputes arising from such transactions. Thus, criticism of the UNCITRAL rules comes from the fact that they are not designed in a 'consumer friendly' manner. Parties in consumer disputes are not of equal strength, and that must always be taken into consideration.

The provisions of the UNCITRAL model law do not provide a high level of legal certainty to consumers, as these provisions are not designed to fit with the particularities of business-to-consumer transactions, where the consumer is a weaker party, and thus they do not provide an adequate level of protection to consumers. The example of UNCITRAL demonstrates how important it is that rules for an online resolution of disputes should take into consideration the particularities of business-to-consumer relations.

In practice, many of the schemes work well for standardised problems. For example, Square Trade operated a scheme for ebay until 2008, by which software matched solutions to problems. It also provided an online mediator, with asynchronous e-mail and web communications. However, if the matters become contested then the schemes have the same issues about assessing evidence and applying legal rules as exist in the offline world. Other schemes simply offer blind bidding schemes and again, as in general ADR, the issue is that legal certainty is less important than finding a solution that is satisfactory to both parties.

CONCLUSIONS

The chapter examined different legal mechanisms for the enforcement of consumer law in order to assess the level of legal certainty that these diverse mechanisms offer to consumers when they use them. It was possible to observe that different legal mechanisms have been developed worldwide in order to secure and facilitate consumers' access to justice. In the context of consumer law, legal certainty is to be understood as a guarantee that a consumer will have the possibility of effective, fair and fast protection whenever any of their consumer rights have been infringed.

Besides the regular judicial and administrative possibilities, the innovative, consumer specific and sensitive mechanisms for protection of consumer rights include small claim courts and small claims court procedures, different designs of collective redress mechanisms and the alternative methods for the resolution of consumer disputes. Among all these methods, the latest one is the online mechanism for the resolution of consumer disputes. All of these mechanisms contribute, to a different extent, to the achievement of legal certainty, especially in cross-border commercial transactions, where legal certainty in the enforcement of consumer law is especially problematic, complex and difficult.

11

Legal Certainty and Abuse of Loopholes in the Context of Transnational EU Company Law

LISA JOST, GABRIEL M LENTNER, THOMAS RATKA AND STEFAN WRBKA*

INTRODUCTION

THE MAIN FUNCTIONS of law are regulation, protection, certainty, predictability and reliability.[1] According to Hobbes, these elements, in particular, help to maintain public peace.[2] Additionally, law also has a number of other functions that should be considered, including education, justice and fairness.[3] Unfortunately, however, tensions may arise between these different functions. For instance, the function of certainty might be in a conflicting position with the justice function of law (safeguarding overall fairness; for the purpose of simplification we will refer to this scenario as 'abuse').[4]

How these tensions are resolved depends on the general concept of law. For example, legal positivism would answer that a 'sense of justice is not a criterion of a norm' (Hans Kelsen).[5] This view is shared by the Anglo-American tradition as expressed by Lord Halsbury in 1895: 'If it was a lawful act, however ill the motive, he had the right to do it!'[6]

* The authors wish to thank Kristina Mizzi who assisted in the proof-reading of the manuscript.

[1] H Pötzsch, *Die Deutsche Demokratie* 5th edn (Bonn, Bundeszentrale für politische Bildung, 2009) 131–33.

[2] J Hampton, *Hobbes and the Social Contract Tradition* (Cambridge, Cambridge University Press, 1988).

[3] Pötzsch, *Die Deutsche Demokratie*.

[4] A Chelidonis, 'Legalität und Legitimation—Gedanken zum Verhältnis von subjektivem Recht und Rechtsmissbrauch' (2010) 32 *JURA* 726, 727.

[5] H Kelsen, *Eine politikwissenschaftliche Einführung* (Baden-Baden, Nomos, 2009) (edited by T Ehs) 47–65.

[6] *Bradford Corpn v Pickles* [1895] AC 587.

Referring to the issue of 'shell companies' (which will be used in this chapter to explain the relationship between legal certainty and the risk of abuse of the law), this means that although we might consider a shell company as a vehicle for tax evasion, creditor deception or money laundering and the result of the EU's freedom rights, it remains the sole competence of the lawmaker (and not of the judge) to declare them void as a whole.

Generally, these arguments and considerations can predominantly be found in public law.[7] Peter Bülow, for example, has argued that

> in private law we can, to a certain extent, interpret an unsatisfactory law or we have case law; the judges have a much better understanding of justice than the lawmaker. On the other hand, however, in public law the civil servant is—unfortunately—not entitled to correct the 'stupidity' of the lawmaker.[8]

In private law, the possibility of combating abuse by (teleological) interpretation and so-called 'general clauses' (blanket clauses/comprehensive clauses)[9] is more often found and, in principle, more comprehensively available, whereas public law is characterised by legal positivism and constitutional formalism.[10]

When it comes to the issue of 'abusing the law', a distinction must be made between different types: First, the 'abuse of law', where a norm is improperly applied; second, the 'circumvention of law', where an existing norm, which would have to be applied in principle, is not applied due to artificial construction of facts; and finally, a third and special type of abuse of rights, ie the circumvention of a piece of legislation by (ab)using norms of international or transnational law.[11] The latter refers to our topic: EU law—in this case, the freedom of establishment as guaranteed by EU law. The suggestion that is explored is that EU law has been applied in a way that prevents the domestic legislation of company law from functioning as intended by domestic policy-makers.

Due to different legal trends, an increase in these types of abuse of rights can, as we will see in this chapter with respect to the third category, be witnessed.

[7] P Mader, *Rechtsmissbrauch und unzulässige Rechtsausübung* (Vienna, LexisNexis, 1994) 157ff.

[8] K Siehr, 'Gesetzesumgehung' in J Basedow, KJ Hopt and R Zimmermann (eds), *Handwörterbuch des Europäischen Privatrechts* (Tübingen, Mohr Siebeck, 2009) 742 (translated by the authors).

[9] W-H Roth, 'Generalklauseln im Europäischen Privatrecht' in J Basedow, KJ Hopt and H Kötz (eds), *Festschrift für Ulrich Drobnig zum 70. Geburtstag* (Tübingen, Mohr Siebeck, 1998) 135.

[10] HLA Hart, 'Der Positivismus und die Trennung von Recht und Moral' in N Hoerster (ed), *Recht und Moral* (Göttingen, Vandenhoeck & Ruprecht, 1971) (translated by N Hoerster) 14ff.

[11] K Schurig, 'Die Gesetzesumgehung im Privatrecht—eine Studie mit kollisionsrechtlichen und rechtsvergleichenden Aspekten' in A Heldrich and HJ Sonnenberger (eds), *Festschrift für Murad Ferid zum 80. Geburtstag* (Frankfurt am Main, Verlag für Standesamtswesen, 1988) 375.

First, the increase in juridification in national and international law raises the possibility for abuse of rights.[12] Second, European integration, which introduced the freedoms of the internal market, facilitates the circumvention of domestic law. Finally, there has been a global 'race to the bottom' amongst lawmakers in so-called 'havens' that are known for their excessively liberal tax law, labour law, environmental law, capital market laws etc.[13]

This chapter will start with some remarks on legal certainty in general and its significance for EU law, in particular. We will then comment on international company law and the emergence of shell companies before turning to the Court of Justice and pertinent case law. The chapter will conclude with a brief discussion of legal certainty in the context of EU company law and the likely tension between EU law goals, on the one hand, and fairness considerations, on the other.

REMARKS ON LEGAL CERTAINTY IN THE CONTEXT OF EU LAW

Legal Certainty in General and Its Interplay with Legal Flexibility

As shown by the more dogmatic contributions to the present book, legal certainty is a core, yet relatively vague, concept that can be split into different pillars. As explained in an earlier chapter, more prominent certainty expressions include legal predictability, stability and overall clarity.[14]

Unlike legal flexibility, which allows for different solutions in individual cases, legal certainty can basically be understood as the idea of creating a level playing field that treats similar cases alike and hence aims to guarantee a certain degree of equality and *general* fairness. Flexibility, on the other hand, strives for *individual* fairness in the sense that it allows for a case-by-case specific application of general legal norms. In this sense, one could refer to Claus-Wilhelm Canaris, who concludes as follows: '[I]n addition to the value of legal certainty it is the concept of [general] fairness that could contradict a flexible system'.[15] Against this background, one can argue that legal certainty and legal flexibility are two opposing regulatory mechanisms that necessarily create a certain degree of tension.

[12] C Jabloner, 'Verrechtlichung und Rechtsdynamik' (1999) *Zeitschrift für öffentliches Recht* 261; N Dimmel, 'Nutzen und Grenzen der Verrechtlichung' (1999) *Journal für Rechtspolitik* 64.

[13] C Joerges, 'The Market without the State? The 'Economic Constitution' of the European Community and the Rebirth of Regulatory Politics' (1997) 1 *European Integration Online Papers*, available at www.eiop.or.at/eiop/pdf/1997-019.pdf; R Hahn, *Multinationale Unternehmen und die 'Base of the Pyramid'—Neue Perspektiven von Corporate Citizenship und Nachhaltiger Entwicklung* (Wiesbaden, Gabler, 2009) 118–26.

[14] See the contribution by Stefan Wrbka in this book.

[15] C-W Canaris, *Systemdenken und Systembegriff in der Jurisprudenz* (Berlin, Duncker & Humblot, 1969) 83 (translated by the authors).

Although legal flexibility can be considered as an increasingly popular argument in lawmaking and the practical application of law, legal certainty has remained a strong, fundamental legal principle.[16] One can argue that it is one of the central expressions of the rule of law.[17]

Legal Certainty in EU Law and Its Tension with Domestic Law

The principle of legal certainty can be regarded as one of the main dogmatic features of EU law. Dating back to case law of the early 1960s, it has gained importance over the decades to evolve as one of the main goals of the approximation of the laws of the Member States. Nowadays, the term legal certainty can be found in numerous EU regulations and directives to justify the need for the introduction of the respective instruments.

The central role of legal certainty can be noticed not only when it comes to direct law-making by the EU legislator, but also when one takes a look at the clarification tasks carried out by the Court of Justice.[18] The latter is, in practice, primarily realised with the help of preliminary rulings by the Court (TFEU, Article 267). From the viewpoint of the consistent application of EU law, in and by the Member States, ie both in cross-border and (where applicable) purely domestic situations, the legal certainty establishing function of the Court of Justice has to be considered as very important.

Overall, legal certainty might indeed be an invaluable legal principle (also) in an EU law context. However, there are downsides to it, as we will explore in the following in the context of EU company law and the relationship between EU and domestic legal interests and policy-making.

A lot has been written about the tension between EU law and domestic laws. This tension is best explained with attempts by EU policy-makers to approximate the laws of the Member States with the help of EU legislation, most commonly with EU regulations and directives. Arguably the most prominent areas in this respect are the debates between proponents of full harmonisation and advocates of minimum harmonisation.[19]

In the present context, of particular relevance is the possible clash of interests of centralised policy-making, ie drafting legislation at the EU level, and domestic regulatory approaches. Consisting of 28 Member States, the EU has to meet the challenge of striking an appropriate balance between

[16] For a contemporary discussion of the significance of legal flexibility in business law see, for example, the contributions in M Fenwick and S Wrbka (eds), *Flexibility in Modern Business Law—A Comparative Assessment* (Tokyo, Springer, 2016).

[17] See, eg M Fenwick and S Wrbka, 'The Shifting Meaning of Legal Certainty' in M Fenwick and S Wrbka (eds), *Legal Certainty in a Contemporary Context—Private and Criminal Law Perspectives* (Tokyo, Springer, 2016) 1.

[18] One could refer to this as 'indirect' law-making.

[19] See, for example, S Wrbka, *European Consumer Access to Justice Revisited* (Cambridge, Cambridge University Press, 2015) 324–28 (with further references).

different, sometimes opposing, state interests, potentially intensified by additionally different, genuine EU interests. Addressees of this challenge are not only the primary stakeholders involved in EU lawmaking, ie the European Commission as the motor and the European Parliament together with the Council of the EU as the prime decision making bodies. For this chapter, the role of the Court of Justice and its indirect lawmaking competences is of primary interest.

The core tasks of the Court of Justice include inter alia interpreting and clarifying EU law passed by the Parliament and the Council. Hence the Court plays a central role in maximising the legal certainty of EU law. In principle, this task should be treasured, as it contributes to solving pending disputes and avoiding post-legislative disputes over the meaning and application of supranational law in the EU by monitoring the 'correct' use of EU laws. In this way, it is guaranteed that legal principles are applied equally throughout the EU.

One result of the supranational character of EU law is that it approximates—or overrides—domestic laws, even if the latter are important in responding to justified domestic issues. Stated differently, under normal circumstances pan-EU interests would trump domestic concerns if they contradict EU interests. Hence, the certainty character of EU law—either as introduced by the direct legislator or via the indirect legislator, the Court of Justice—comes at a certain cost for addressing domestic (and sometimes regional, multi-jurisdictional) interests.

In most cases, this fact would still be acceptable if it could be justified with the help of overarching, inter- or transnational arguments that could lead to a win-win-situation for all affected stakeholders. It could, however (and this is often neglected), result in a situation where domestic laws and domestic solutions are levered out by EU law. This becomes particularly worrisome if loopholes are non-intentionally created that allow certain stakeholders to abuse EU law and the freedoms guaranteed by it to circumvent protection offered by domestic legal rules (checkmated by EU law). In the following, we explore a concrete example that can be found in transnational company law, namely the phenomenon of shell companies and how EU law and EU institutions—more precisely the Court of Justice—deals with them.

'LAW EVASION' IN TRANSNATIONAL EU COMPANY LAW—THE EXAMPLE OF SHELL COMPANIES

A prominent example of abuse of rights in company law is related to so-called 'shell companies'. Shell companies could arguably be considered as a plague in the global economy. According to the NGO 'Tax Justice Network',[20]

[20] G Zucman, *Steueroasen—Wo der Wohlstand der Nationen versteckt wird* (Berlin, Suhrkamp 2014) 21ff.

approximately 12 per cent of the revenue of the world's capital is hidden in so-called 'offshore-paradises,' while most states face increasing difficulties with national debt. Most investor fraud cases are related to shell companies established overseas.

For example, in Austria two particular cases, both involving leading domestic business banks, have recently hit the headlines. One shell company—a real estate investing fund—was established in Jersey, where it secretly 'invested' in its own stocks, (ab)using over 50 per cent of the whole amount to be invested with the aim of 'overcoming' the subprime crisis (not surprisingly the investors lost all of their money). The second case concerned one of Austria's oldest banks, which sold the investment certificates of notorious fraudster Bernie Madoff via a 'sub-subsidiary' letterbox vehicle established on the Cayman Islands. The result was the same: investors (most of whom were 'small' investors) lost everything. The parent companies, however, were not found liable for any wrongdoing.

These two cases show dramatically that the lawful formation of shell companies is, on the one hand, used to bypass national legislation through an abusive application of a company law's framework (especially limited liability) and the freedoms of the EU's internal market. On the other hand, the mentioned functions of law—especially legal certainty—permitted some of these practices. Unlike under EU Directives,[21] the clandestine buying of one's own stocks is legal on Jersey, and the possibility of establishing shell companies on the Cayman Islands was even granted by a contractual extension to the EU freedom of settlement (dicussed further below). A look at the latter illustrates the unusual 'landscape': the Cayman Islands have around 50,000 inhabitants, 400 banks and 10,000 investment fund companies. The world's largest hedge funds, almost all big European commercial banks, insurances and auditing companies, have branches there. No taxes have to be paid and no foreign exchange control is established. It appears that there are only two viable options to fight shell companies' paradises: Either the investors bear the consequences of such practices (in other words, they should not invest in foreign jurisdictions if they do not agree with the laws there) or one pushes for changes in the legislation.

THE COURT OF JUSTICE'S APPROACH TOWARDS THE FREEDOM OF ESTABLISHMENT AND SHELL COMPANIES

In continental Europe and its former colonies, the 'real seat' theory is prevailing.[22] This means that shell companies are to be declared as void.

[21] See Directive 2012/30/EU, [2012] OJ L315/74.

[22] M Brombach, *Das Internationale Gesellschaftsrecht im Spannungsfeld von Sitztheorie und Niederlassungsfreiheit* (Munich, Sellier, 2006).

However, because of the burden of proof in civil proceedings, classifying a company as a shell company can be difficult to prove. In contrast, the UK and its former colonies tend to apply versions of 'incorporation' theory.[23] This leads to the so-called 'Delaware effect', which potentially turns forum shopping into a principle and results in a 'competition between lawmakers'.[24] The underlying basis for this approach is the principle of autonomy in private law, ie 'If you contract with an offshore company, it is your own fault'.

According to the Court of Justice, the real seat theory is in conflict with the freedom of establishment.[25] In the *Centros* decision,[26] the court held that a company may register a branch from a foreign shell company of an EU Member State, even if it runs 100 per cent of its business in the host state and despite the fact that the incorporators clearly stated that they had established the shell company (in the UK) solely to avoid the minimum capitalisation requirement (for Danish limited liability companies). Through this decision, the risk of a Delaware-type effect was established throughout Europe, despite the great diversity in national company laws (compare, for example, the ultra-liberal UK 'Limited' with the heavily regulated German or Austrian 'GmbH').[27] The *Centros*-decision suggests that this unsatisfactory result must be accepted on the basis of the principle of the freedom of establishment.

This raises the question as to whether the freedom of establishment applies to 'overseas companies'. In 1993, the Austrian Bank A established a shell company ('P Ltd') on the Cayman Islands. P Ltd sold stocks of 'Madoff funds' (and nothing else) to Austrian Investors. Its directors were all Austrian

[23] F Streiber, *Gläubigerschutz bei Auslandsgesellschaften—Eine Untersuchung zur Reichweite des Gesellschaftsstatuts unter Geltung der Gründungstheorie* (PhD thesis, University of Freiburg, 2008).

[24] SR Göthel, 'Delaware bestätigt Gründungstheorie und schützt Pseudo-Foreign Corporations' (2006) *Recht der Internationalen Wirtschaft* 41; DJH Greenwood, 'Democracy and Delaware: The Mysterious Race to the Bottom/Top' (2005) 23 *Yale Law & Policy Review* 381.

[25] TFEU, Art 49 states that '[...] restrictions on the freedom of establishment of nationals of a Member State in the territory of another Member State shall be prohibited. Such prohibition shall also apply to restrictions on the setting-up of agencies, branches or subsidiaries by nationals of any Member State established in the territory of any Member State.' Furthermore, TFEU, Art 54 states that 'Companies or firms formed in accordance with the law of a Member State and having their registered office, central administration or principal place of business within the Union shall [...] be treated in the same way as natural persons who are nationals of Member States.'

[26] G Hoor, 'Das Centros-Urteil des EuGH und seine Auswirkungen auf die Anknüpfung des Gesellschaftsstatuts' (1999) *Neue Zeitschrift für Gesellschaftsrecht* 984; P Kindler, 'Niederlassungsfreiheit für Scheinauslandsgesellschaften?—Die Centros—Entscheidung des EuGH und das internationale Privatrecht' (1999) *Neue Juristische Wochenschrift* 1993.

[27] Critically on the effects of *Centros*, see, eg V Habersack, *Europäisches Gesellschaftsrecht* 2nd edn (Munich, CH Beck, 2003) paras 15ff; E-M Kieninger, 'Internationales Gesellschaftsrecht nach "Centros", "Überseering" und "Inspire Art": Antworten, Zweifel und offene Fragen' (2004) *Zeitschrift für Europäisches Privatrecht* 685, 692ff.

citizens and the company was only active in the Austrian market. Then, when the ponzi scheme of Madoff collapsed in 2009, the investors sued Bank A for compensation. They argued that the real seat theory was applicable and therefore P Ltd was void. Consequentially, Bank A would be liable for the debts as a parent company, piercing the corporate veil. On the other hand, the argument was put forward that the EU's freedom of establishment was applicable and the now insolvent P Ltd was solely liable, not Bank A. If the latter was true, ie if the Court of Justice arrived at the conclusion that the *Centros* principle of freedom of establishment was applicable also in the case at hand, one could argue that the legal certainty construct created by *Centros* would stand in tension with common-sense fairness, ie with the chance of the investors—who have fallen victim to serious fraud—to see any compensation. In the following we would like to take a brief look at the general background regarding how EU law applies to overseas companies before commenting on how the Madoff case was—and should have been—solved.

APPLICATION OF THE EU LEGAL FRAMEWORK TO 'OVERSEAS COMPANIES'

One crucial preliminary question is: in which situations is there 'freedom of establishment' for companies under EU law? More specifically, in the context of a discussion of shell companies, one needs to have a closer look at the different categories of overseas territories where the rules apply.

The first group comprises overseas territories where the TFEU fully applies. This refers to the Azores, Madeira and the Canary Islands.

The second group of overseas territories consists of those overseas territories that are part of the EU, but do not form part of the Internal Market (Customs Union). Helgoland and Büsingen am Hochrhein, Guayana, Guadeloupe, Martinique and Réunion, Ceuta and Melilla, Athos, Livigno and Campione d'Italia, Åland and Gibraltar all fall into this category.

Finally, there is one final group of overseas territories—the so-called 'Overseas Countries and Territories' (OCT), which have a special relationship to Member States, but which are not part of the EU itself. TFEU, Article 198 deals with this issue:

> The Member States agree to associate with the Union the non-European countries and territories which have special relations with Denmark, France, the Netherlands and the United Kingdom. These countries and territories (hereinafter called the 'countries and territories') are listed in Annex II. The purpose of association shall be to promote the economic and social development of the countries and territories and to establish close economic relations between them and the Union as a whole. In accordance with the principles set out in the preamble to this Treaty, association shall serve primarily to further the interests and prosperity of the inhabitants of these countries and territories in order to lead them to the economic, social and cultural development to which they aspire.

According to the Annex II of the TFEU, these territories are Greenland, New Caledonia and Dependencies, French Polynesia, French Southern and Antarctic Territories, Wallis and Futuna Islands, Mayotte, Saint Pierre and Miquelon, Aruba, Netherlands Antilles, Bonaire, Curaçao, Saba, Sint Eustatius, Sint Maarten, Anguilla, Cayman Islands, Falkland Islands, South Georgia and the South Sandwich Islands, Montserrat, Pitcairn, Saint Helena and Dependencies, British Antarctic Territory, British Indian Ocean Territory, Turks and Caicos Islands, British Virgin Islands, and Bermuda.

According to Gabriel Zucman,[28] three of the world's worst tax and company law havens—the Cayman Islands,[29] British Virgin Islands[30] and Bermuda[31]—are part of this territory list granted special freedoms by the EU.

This means, that the OCTs are to a certaint extent 'associated' with the EU, but are not part of the Union and are exempted from the application of EU law. The reason for the removal of the OCTs from the application of EU law and its fundamental freedoms, according to the EU governments, lies in the, at times, significantly lower state of development in these territories compared to the European continent.[32] In this context, it should be noted that the resulting 'protection against EU law' works both ways: not only are the former colonies protected from the application of law that they had no legislative role in formulating, but it also prevents the (ab)use of the EU's fundamental freedoms.[33] Otherwise, this would open the possibility of abuse and potentially create a 'race to the bottom', where stakeholders could 'escape' to such territories to make use of local legislation that is not approximated, or otherwise touched upon, by EU law.[34]

Having these various categories of overseas territories in mind, this raises the question as to whether the freedom of establishment—important for shell companies—is applicable to OCTs or not; or, put differently,

[28] See Zucman, *Steueroasen.*

[29] Bernie Madoff is a prime example for understanding the status of the Cayman Islands as an 'offshore-paradise'. He caused the biggest loss to investors in history, which amounted to approximately €51 billion. Many EU commercial banks established mailbox subsidiaries to sell 'Madoff-shares' to EU-investors, which led to an evasion of EU capital market and company law regulations.

[30] The Virgin Islands' population amounts to only 32,000, but 450,000 shell companies have their residence there. Many convicted tax evaders from the EU and the US have established their domicile on the Virgin Islands. Banks tend to establish 'management companies' there, as managers cannot be held liable under its jurisdiction.

[31] A strict banking secrecy law was introduced and tax fraud is not an offence in that jurisdiction.

[32] See 36th Declaration annexed to the Final Act of the Intergovernmental Conference which adopted the Treaty of Lisbon.

[33] See also P Troberg and C Tiedje, 'Vor Art. 43–48 EG' in Hans von der Groeben and Jürgen Schwarze (eds) *EGV/EUV* (Baden-Baden, Nomos, 2003) para 33.

[34] See also M-P Weller, *Europäische Rechtsformwahlfreiheit und Gesellschafterhaftung* (Cologne, Carl Heymanns, 2004) 74ff.

to what extent the exemption from EU law reaches in the context of OCTs. Here, TFEU, Art 199(5) is relevant, which states:

> In relations between Member States and the countries and territories the right of establishment of nationals and companies or firms shall be regulated in accordance with the provisions and procedures laid down in the Chapter relating to the right of establishment and on a non-discriminatory basis, subject to any special provisions laid down pursuant to Article 203.

In conclusion, it follows that the freedom of establishment is—as an exception—applicable to the OCTs, but its application is subject to 'special provisions' provided for in TFEU, Article 203. This leads to an interesting situation.

These 'special provisions', ie the TFEU, Article 203 provisions, did not exist until 1997. On 29 November 1997, the Council Decision on the association of the overseas countries and territories with the European Economic Community (EG/97/803) amended Article 232 in a way that established only the prohibition of discrimination of companies in accordance with the General Agreement on Trade in Services (GATS).[35]

The latest decision was the 'Overseas Association Decision' of 27 November 2001 (EG/2001/822), where Article 45(1) of the Decision stated, that 'OCT companies or enterprises' are those formed in accordance with the law applicable in a given OCT and whose registered office, central administration or principal place of business is in that OCT. However, a company or enterprise having only its registered office in a country or territory must be engaged in an activity which has an actual and continuous link with the economy of that country or territory.

Thereby, the 'genuine link'[36] principle was established. Such a link will generally not be present in the case of shell companies that do not perform any business activities in the OCT.[37] In fact, this is an amalgamation of the real seat and incorporation theory. As a result, shell companies incorporated in the OCT cannot enjoy freedom of establishment.[38] One might argue that

[35] For the substantive reasoning on this conclusion see eg OLG Graz 2 R 151/05a; Konrad Lachmayer and L Bauer, *Praxiswörterbuch Europarecht* (Berlin, Springer, 2008) 59 (with further references); C Tietje, 'Art 183' in E Grabitz and M Hilf (eds), *EU-Kommentar* vol III (Munich, CH Beck, 2016) para 5; R Süß, '§ 1' in R Süß and T Wachter (eds), *Handbuch des internationalen GmbH-Rechts* (Basel, Helbing & Lichtenhahn, 2006) para 22 (with further references).

[36] On the content of this genuine link requirement, see 'General Programme of the European Council for the abolition of restrictions on freedom of establishment' (18 December 1961) section I, OJ 4/1962, 36; see also Case C-221/89 *Factortame* II [1991] ECR I-3056, recital 20; A Scheuer 'Art. 48' in CO Lenz (ed), *EG-Vertrag Kommentar* 2nd edn (Cologne, Bundesanzeiger Verlag, 2006) para 4.

[37] Süß, '§ 1' para 22; U Thölke, 'Kapitalgesellschaft liechtensteinischen Rechts mit tatsächlichem Verwaltungssitz in Deutschland ist rechts- und parteifähig BGH, Urt. v. 19. 9. 2005' (2006) *Deutsche Notar-Zeitschrift* 143, 146.

[38] See also M Straube and T Ratka, 'Das "Herkunftslandprinzip" im EU-Gesellschaftsrecht nach der "Überseering"-Entscheidung' (2003) *Österreichische Zeitschrift für Wirtschaftsrecht* 34;

the GATS agreement could be interpreted as allowing an interpretation of national laws that would result in the application of the freedom of establishment. However, this cannot be the case, due to the fact that the GATS does not contain any provisions for such an interpretation.[39] Any other conclusion would mean that the GATS introduced the incorporation theory to all WTO members, which cannot be the case.[40]

From the above discussion, it follows that, on the one hand, no full freedom of establishment, in relation to the incorporation theory (*Centros*), can be applied to the OTCs from 1997 onwards. One the other hand, before 1997, the freedom of establishment was fully applicable for the OCT.

With the change in the applicability of the freedom of establishment in the OCT, the question arises as to whether a company established before 1997 may still invoke the freedom of establishment.

Three interpretations are possible. First, when considered as an economic freedom right, the freedom of establishment may be granted, but at the same time, it may also be revoked. In the present case, the decision to withdraw the right to the freedom of establishment was up to the EU; and the freedom was abrogated in 1997. Therefore, a company cannot invoke the freedom of establishment after this decision, regardless of when the company was established.

A second interpretation could be that, although the freedom of establishment is an economic freedom right, it is an established right, and so the company has a vested interest in keeping this status (German: '*wohlerworbenes Recht*', 'bona fide'). According to such an interpretation of the freedom of establishment, a company would retain the right to invoke it, despite the restriction of the freedom of establishment from 1997 onwards. However, this interpretation should be rejected on several grounds. The Council Decision does not in any way affect the legal capacity of the OCT incorporated companies. Also, the provisional applicability of the EU's fundamental freedoms

T Bachner and M Winner, 'Das österreichische internationale Gesellschaftsrecht nach Centros' (2000) *Der Gesellschafter* 73, 161ff; S Korn and C Thaler, 'Das Urteil des EuGH in der Rs Centros: Ein Meilenstein für das europäische Gesellschaftskollisionsrecht?' (1999) *Wirtschaftsrechtliche Blätter* 247; for Germany see H Eidenmüller, 'Wettbewerb der Gesellschaftsrechte in Europa' (2002) *Zeitschrift für Wirtschaftsrecht* 2233ff; S Leible and J Hoffmann, '"Überseering" und das (vermeintliche) Ende der Sitztheorie' (2002) *Recht der internationalen Wirtschaft* 925, 930ff; D Zimmer, 'Grenzüberschreitende Rechtspersönlichkeit' (2004) *Zeitschrift für das gesamte Handelsrecht und Wirtschaftsrecht* 355.

[39] See M Lehmann, 'Fällt die Sitztheorie jetzt auch international?' (2004) *Recht der internationalen Wirtschaft* 816; P Jung, 'Anwendung der Gründungstheorie auf Gesellschaften schweizerischen Rechts? Zugleich eine Anmerkung zu den beim BGH anhängigen Revisionsverfahren II ZR 158/06 und II ZR 290/07' (2008) *Neue Zeitschrift für Gesellschaftsrecht* 683; Tietje, 'Art 183' para 5; see further the decision by the German Supreme Court in *Trabrennbahn* (2008) BGH II ZR 158/06.

[40] See P Troberg and C Tiedje 'Vor Art. 43-48 EG' in H von der Groeben and J Schwarze (eds), *EGV/EUV* (Baden-Baden, Nomos, 2003) para 63.

via association agreements with third states (before their EU membership) are in the same way revocable.[41] There is no apparent reason as to why the same would not apply to the OCT. Otherwise, the decision to revoke these rights would have no actual effect on juridical persons established before that date, nor natural persons born before the decision was taken. Nevertheless, in the above-mentioned Cayman Islands case, it seems that the court eventually allowed for a differentiating approach that would—under certain circumstances—extend the freedom of establishment.

A third and final interpretation—that would lead to a similar substantive result as the first interpretation—could refer to the 'freedom of establishment' not as an economic *freedom right*, but as a rule of private international law. As a rule, it regulates which jurisdiction(s) apply to the issue at hand. Within the context of the rule, at least since the decision of the Court of Justice in the *Centros* case, the incorporation theory has to be applied within the EU. For the OCT, the rules of private international law apply, which means that a change of the rules (relating to the application of the freedom of establishment for the OCT) has no effect on contracts concluded or previously established rights (see Austrian Private International Law Act, § 7).[42] However, this only applies to rules relating to the conflict of law, and the freedom of establishment is not a rule of the conflict of laws because it is a material norm that grants certain rights and, as such, does not determine the applicable law.[43] In conclusion, the freedom of establishment would not be applicable to the OTCs from 1997 onwards.

CONCLUSIONS

This brief excursion into transnational EU company law reveals a paradox. Can shell companies, established in jurisdictions that can be counted as members of the 'axis of evil' in international tax evasion, investor fraud

[41] Decision No 1/80 of the EEC-Turkish Association Council of 19 September 1980 on the development of the Association; see also the association agreements of the then EU accession candidates Bulgaria, Estonia, Lithuania, Latvia, Malta, Poland, Romania, Slovenia, Hungary, Cyprus, Slovakia and the Czech Republic; on this see Troberg and Tiedje, 'Vor Art. 43–48 EG' para 50f.

[42] B Verschragen, '§ 5 IPRG' in P Rummel (ed) *Kommentar zum ABGB* 3rd edn (Vienna, Manz, 2004) para 3.

[43] F Rüffler, 'Gläubigerschutz durch Mindestkapital und Kapitalerhaltung in der GmbH—Überholtes oder sinnvolles Konzept?' (2005) *Zeitschrift für Gesellschaftsrecht* 411; D Schnichels, *Reichweite der Niederlassungsfreiheit* (Baden-Baden, Nomos, 1995) 171ff (with further references); W-H Roth, 'Grundregeln' in Manfred Dauses (ed), *Handbuch des EG-Wirtschaftsrechts* (Munich, CH Beck, 2016) para 91; P Kindler, 'Internationales Handels- und Gesellschaftsrecht' in FJ Säcker, R Rixecker, H Oetker, B Limperg (eds), *Münchener Kommentar zum Bürgerlichen Gesetzbuch, Band 11*, 6th edn (Munich, CH Beck, 2015) paras 116ff and 343ff (with further references).

and money laundering, enjoy the benefits of EU freedom of establishment and avoid liability under EU law? This would—if one follows pertinent case law—be the case in situations where the shell company was established prior to November 1997. This becomes even more problematic when one considers that—with the exception of the freedom of establishment—EU law would, in principle, not apply to many such overseas companies and that they could be subject to (only) their own, EU law-detached jurisdiction.

While this conclusion might be the consequence of the 'legal certainty' case law of the Court of Justice, which has sought to clarify the conditions for granting companies the freedom of establishment, the outcome is—from a fairness point of view—unsatisfactory. In contrast to post-November 1997 shell companies, older institutions would fall through the liability net, leaving harmed investors stranded.

In modern, rule of law based societies, legal certainty provides the backbone of a well-functioning legal framework. However, one must not neglect the fact that lawmakers and policy-makers might—for whatever reason—not be in a position where they can properly incorporate the certainty principle. In the present analysis, we highlight the possible tensions that exist between the decisions of the Court of Justice and EU law. Legal certainty, as enshrined by the Court's case law, might lead to the necessity for legislative action by the EU legislator to appropriately address and incorporate desired outcomes, in this case a safety-net for fraud-struck investors.

Stated differently, rather than letting shell companies enjoy the freedom of establishment (as a consequence of upholding legal certainty), actions need to be taken to restrict this freedom in situations in which there is no argument to justify the application of such freedom. One way is to rectify this with revised 'direct' legislation. The other way might be to rely on 'indirect' lawmaking and to reinterpret the 'seat' concept. Such a new understanding would reflect the 'genuine link principle' in cases of likely abuse.

Part IV

Applied Perspectives ('Certainty through Law')

12

Legal Ambiguity in Corporate Governance

CHARLOTTE VILLIERS*

INTRODUCTION

THE THESIS OF this book is that legal certainty is a virtue in that it increases fairness through consistency of treatment, transparency and accountability. Without sufficient levels of certainty, regulators may enjoy too much discretion. The counterclaim to this argument is that flexibility is necessary for addressing different circumstances and changing contexts. The field of corporate governance provides a lens for observing the problems of a more flexible and responsive regulatory framework. However, in the corporate governance context it is not so much the regulators who are granted freedom by this flexibility but the corporate actors. The flexible and light touch, quasi-private ordering that characterises corporate governance brings into the spotlight the tensions between self-government and national and international norms. The UK's approach to corporate governance, which is underscored by the 'comply or explain' principle, is presented as a way of balancing competing views and so avoiding the process being brought to a halt by people 'digging in around their differences of opinion.'[1] The result, however, is another legal *un*certainty, a system involving numerous, sometimes rival, regulatory actors, and tensions between mandatory and voluntary approaches.

The UK corporate governance system operates superficially as a voluntary system but it is underpinned by market enforcement and threats of stronger legislative intervention. From the perspective of legal certainty this is not

* I wish to thank my colleagues at the University of Bristol Law School, to whom I presented this chapter in November 2016, for their inspiring comments. Errors remain my own.

[1] A Hilton, 'Grudging Acquiescence' in Financial Reporting Council (ed), *Comply or Explain: 20th Anniversary of the UK Corporate Governance Code* (2012) 21, www.frc.org.uk/Our-Work/Publications/Corporate-Governance/Comply-or-Explain-20th-Anniversary-of-the-UK-Corpo.aspx.

satisfactory. The voluntariness gives discretion to the corporate actors in deciding for themselves how they should apply the principles. Moreover, the power struggles and complexities that have emerged highlight the problems of corporate governance as a neo-liberal regulatory form. The UK's corporate governance system comprises a 'co-existence of voluntary charter provisions, legal backing and full legal provisions with dividing lines that are unclear and continuously shifting.'[2] Indeed, this hybridised mishmash of self-governance, national and international norms has created so much ambiguity that the firms being regulated, are not so much at risk of regulators' discretionary actions but, instead, appear free to do as they please. Despite multiple layers of regulations and standards on many different issues,[3] the inconsistencies and contradictions among them result in company boardrooms having *carte blanche* in the use of corporate governance practices[4] to the extent that so much regulation has the effect of being no regulation at all because it lacks the vigour needed to achieve the behavioural modifications intended.[5] This experience fits in with what has been observed as 'a perverse legacy of the global crisis', which has been 'a further entrenchment of neoliberal rationalities and disciplines' and 'a further entrenchment of market-disciplinary modes of governance.'[6]

This chapter presents the argument by highlighting the ambiguities in the corporate governance system in the UK, conceptually and in practice. For example, despite repeated appeals for long-term goals, the system permits, in practice, more short-term strategies with respect to profit maximisation. Such inconsistencies are augmented by the adjustments and adaptations that have occurred in response to crises and corporate failures.[7] The roles of the actors are then also blurred.[8]

[2] E Wymeersch, 'Enforcement of Corporate Governance Codes' (2005) *ECGI Law Working Paper No 46/2005* 20.

[3] D Kingsford Smith, 'Governing the Corporation: The Role of "Soft Regulation"' (2012) 35 *University of New South Wales Law Journal* 378.

[4] I Haxhi, H van Ees and A Sorge, 'A Political Perspective on Business Elites and Institutional Embeddedness in the UK Code-Issuing Process' (2013) 21 *Corporate Governance: an International Review* 535.

[5] Julia Black reminds us of the three elements that can help us to identify regulation: 'regulation is the sustained and focused attempt to alter the behaviour of others according to defined standards or purposes with the intention of producing a broadly identified outcome or outcomes, which may involve mechanisms of standard-setting, information-gathering and behaviour-modification' in J Black, 'Critical Reflections on Regulation' (2002) 27 *Australian Journal of Legal Philosophy* 1, 26, quoted in Kingsford Smith, 'Governing the Corporation' 387.

[6] J Peck, N Theodore and N Brenner, 'Neoliberal Resurgent: Market Rule after the Great Recession' (2012) 111 *The South Atlantic Quarterly* 265, 265.

[7] D Nordberg, 'Reasonably Good Corporate Governance' (2014), available at eprints.bournemouth.ac.uk/21213.

[8] See eg Z Ahmad and D Taylor, 'Commitment to Independence by Internal Auditors: the Effects of Role Ambiguity and Role Conflict' (2009) 24 *Managerial Auditing Journal* 899 and CA de Kluyver, *A Primer on Corporate Governance* 2nd edn (New York, Business Expert Press, 2013).

The main regulatory instrument is the UK Corporate Governance Code, long praised for the flexibility it grants to corporations.[9] The Code, however, embodies some of the problems that are the focus of this book. The Code is characterised by principles rather than prescriptive rules, giving flexibility and encouraging compliance with the spirit rather than with the letter of its provisions. In addition, the comply or explain principle, in particular, lends recognition to the individual character and needs of each company and encourages an individualised 'best practice' approach to corporate governance. However, uncertainties arise: around companies' compliance and around explanations for non-compliance and, in turn, around monitoring processes.[10] Ultimately, such uncertainties drive companies to comply with the Code purely to avoid allegations of wrongdoing and reputational damage for non-compliance.[11] The effect then is to lose the desired flexibility and the Code becomes a more fixed, harder form of regulation.

The Code, amended frequently, seeks to adapt to the changing marketplace. Being developed under a neoliberal, market-oriented influence, the aim has been to grant to the business actors freedom from burdensome state-imposed rules and to limit the role of regulation to enabling the market to operate and discipline efficiently. The one consistency around Cadbury and since is deference to the market and to the business actors, in particular, the institutional investors and the boardroom members. From a regulatory perspective, despite claims that the UK has 'some of the highest standards of corporate governance in the world'[12] the regulations have not accomplished their stated goals of developing trust and accountability. Despite such regulations being developed in response to corporate failures and scandals, such events have not abated. We are still observing the fall-out from the global financial crisis for which the corporate governance systems have been partly blamed; in the UK excessive remuneration payments for corporate executives continue to receive public outrage;[13] and recently UK household name companies have fallen, such as BHS,[14] or been criticised for their poor-quality processes and human resources practices, such as Sports Direct,[15] compelling the Conservative government to initiate

[9] Financial Reporting Council, 'Corporate Governance and Stewardship', www.frc.org.uk.

[10] A Keay, 'Comply or Explain in Corporate Governance Codes: In Need of Greater Regulatory Oversight?' (2014) 34 *Legal Studies* 279; K Sergakis, 'EU Corporate Governance: A New Supervisory Mechanism for the "Comply or Explain" Principle?' (2013) 10 *European Company and Financial Law Review* 394.

[11] M Becht, 'Comply or just explain?' in Financial Reporting Council, *Comply or Explain* 13.

[12] Financial Reporting Council, 'Corporate Governance and Stewardship'.

[13] See C Villiers, 'Executive Pay: A Socially Oriented Distributive Justice Framework' (2016) 37 *Company Lawyer* 139.

[14] See eg J Tapper, 'All BHS Stores to Shut down by 20 August' *The Guardian* (23 July 2016).

[15] S Martin, 'Sports Direct and BHS: Everything Must Go' (20 November 2016), Chartered Management Institute, www.managers.org.uk/insights/news/2016/november/sports-direct-and-bhs-everything-must-go.

an inquiry and Green Paper on corporate governance reform in the UK.[16] In addition, social and economic problems persist, including increasingly stark levels of wealth inequality,[17] poor productivity,[18] worker exploitation[19] and depleted tax revenues.[20] Yet, rather than seek a complete paradigm shift in light of these failures, such experiences have led to demands for more and stronger but similar regulatory responses. This increasingly overloaded corporate governance system is characterised by repeated attempts at reform that do not really change behaviours because they do not seek to alter the corporate structures or shift the focus from the boardroom-investor relationship. Ultimately, the legal ambiguities that plague the corporate governance system lead to frequent further ambiguities and to the power contests that come with lack of legal certainty. These repeated failures also lead to the suspicion that in fact there is satisfaction with the system among those who are benefiting from it, and so there is no will to change the dynamics or the structures that it shields.

The piecemeal and messy development of the corporate governance system is symptomatic of its inherent ambiguity but also of its confined scope that concentrates on satisfying the shareholders' pursuit of wealth. Like all neoliberal experiments, this approach to corporate governance will continue to fail in any quest to attain a free society or economy that is unrealisable. As Peck et al remark, 'beneath the mythology of market progress lies the turgid reality of neo-liberalisation processes variously flailing and failing forward.'[21] More cogently, Peck et al note that

> real world experiments in neoliberalization routinely—indeed, predictably—fail. But they typically fail in such a way as to engender new rounds of experimentation, generally oriented toward the same market-disciplinary agendas that underpinned earlier forms of policy reform—and associated policy failure(s).[22]

These same market-oriented experiments do not fit with the goal of achieving a trustful, long-term oriented system but they do perhaps fit the pursuit of short-term profits and continuation of power preserved for political and

[16] Department for Business, Energy and Industrial Strategy, Corporate Governance Inquiry, launched September 2016: see House of Commons, www.parliament.uk. See also Department for Business, Energy & Industrial Strategy, *Corporate Governance Reform: Green Paper* (November 2016), www.gov.uk/government/uploads/system/uploads/attachment_data/file/573438/beis-16-56-corporate-governance-reform-green-paper-final.pdf.

[17] T Piketty, *Capital in the Twenty First Century* (Cambridge, Mass, Harvard University Press, 2014).

[18] A Valero and I Roland, 'Productivity and Business Policies' (2015), available at cep.lse.ac.uk/pubs/download/ea021.pdf.

[19] See eg AM Barry and R Palmer, 'Forced Labour, Human Trafficking and the FTSE 100' (October 2015) Finance Against Trafficking, available at www.uspg.org.uk/docstore/112.pdf.

[20] A Bird and SA Karolyi, 'Governance and Taxes: Evidence from Regression Discontinuity' (2015), www.sbs.ox.ac.uk/sites/default/files/Business_Taxation/.

[21] Peck et al, 'Neoliberal Resurgent' 274.

[22] ibid 274.

business elites.[23] A successful legal or regulatory system requires not just clarity, but also effectiveness in achieving the intended goal, and consistency with other regulations and involving a range of parties in their promulgation and application. The regulatory controls require greater clarity and more effective enforcement possibilities rather than reliance on the threat of a questionable market discipline. Not only is lack of legal certainty or legal ambiguity problematic, but more disturbing is the neoliberal agenda in which corporate governance has a key role, because it is found to be 'a crisis-induced, crisis inducing form of market-disciplinary regulatory restructuring',[24] but one which benefits some with special privileges.[25]

This chapter explores the problem of legal ambiguity in corporate governance in three parts. The first part identifies the conceptual ambiguities that arise in a corporate governance system that is developed in a reactive fashion. The second part highlights the ambiguities and practical impact of the Corporate Governance Code under the comply or explain principle. The third part places these ambiguities within their neoliberal frame and considers the implications. Finally, this chapter concludes with tentative suggestions for some remedies.

CONCEPTUAL AND DEVELOPMENTAL AMBIGUITIES IN THE CORPORATE GOVERNANCE SYSTEM

The UK's corporate governance system presents real challenges from a legal certainty perspective. In the UK Corporate Governance Code corporate governance is defined and described as follows:

> the system by which companies are directed and controlled. Boards of directors are responsible for the governance of their companies. The shareholders' role in governance is to appoint the directors and the auditors and to satisfy themselves that an appropriate governance structure is in place. The responsibilities of the board include setting the company's strategic aims, providing the leadership to put them into effect, supervising the management of the business and reporting to shareholders on their stewardship. The board's actions are subject to laws, regulations and the shareholders in general meeting.[26]

[23] Haxhi et al, 'A Political Perspective on Business Elites and Institutional Embeddedness'.

[24] Peck et al, 'Neoliberal Resurgent' 268.

[25] Piketty, talks about 'supermanagers' (see Piketty, *Capital in the Twenty First Century* 302–303) and Streeck talks about the 'strong' beginning 'to exit from the encompassing risk pools of the postwar era in the name of individual freedom and a new liberal-voluntaristic order': see W Streeck, 'Corporate Governance: The Decline of Germany Inc' in W Streeck (ed), *Re-Forming Capitalism: Institutional Change in the German Political Economy* (Oxford, Oxford University Press, 2009) ch 6.

[26] Cadbury Code on the Financial Aspects of Corporate Governance, 1992, para 2.5, adopted in subsequent UK Corporate Governance Codes, latest version 2016, at para 2.

The Code clarifies this description by stating that

> Corporate governance is therefore about what the board of a company does and how it sets the values of the company. It is to be distinguished from the day to day operational management of the company by full-time executives.[27]

The focus is on the internal relationships between the board and the managers and shareholders. The OECD Principles, similarly narrow, tell us that

> Corporate governance involves a set of relationships between a company's management, its board, its shareholders and other stakeholders. Corporate governance also provides the structure through which the objectives of the company are set, and the means of attaining those objectives and monitoring performance are determined.[28]

The Principles also state that good governance 'is a means to create market confidence and business integrity, which in turn is essential for companies that need access to equity capital for long term investment.'[29] Most definitions and policies on corporate governance in the Anglo-Saxon models focus more on internal governance than on the external constraints on corporate behaviour[30] and any relationships are instrumentalised towards pursuit of private profit. Influential academics in the field such as Shleifer and Vishny define corporate governance as 'the ways in which suppliers of finance to the corporations assure themselves of getting a return on their investment.'[31]

Other conceptual uncertainties in corporate governance are found in key terms such as 'accountability', 'capital', 'control', 'manage', 'regulate', 'stakeholder'. All of these terms remain conceptually vague and without a single established definition. Accountability, for example, is a term highlighted in the Code but it is not defined anywhere in the Code.[32] We can see that the required accountability is to shareholders and the market, but this itself is problematic because, as Kingsford Smith reminds us, 'accountability through the market is more hidden, informal and fragmented' than that seen in 'more formal, open and institutionalised versions' that are found 'in curial review or formal regulatory action.'[33] Nordberg and McNulty trace the evolutionary development of the concept of accountability and note that as newer versions of the Code were created the emphasis changed from control to trust and openness and dialogue. Thus, shifts between versions of

[27] UK Corporate Governance Code, 2016, section on Governance and the Code, para 3.

[28] OECD, 'G20/OECD Principles of Corporate Governance' (September 2015), www.oecd.org/daf/ca/Corporate-Governance-Principles-ENG.pdf.

[29] ibid 3.

[30] M Pargendler, 'The Corporate Governance Obsession' (2015) *Stanford Law and Economics Olin Working Paper no 470* 2, ssrn.com/abstract=2491088.

[31] A Shleifer and R Vishny, 'A Survey of Corporate Governance' (1977) 52 *The Journal of Finance* 737, 737, quoted in Pargendler, 'The Corporate Governance Obsession' 2.

[32] A Keay, *Board Accountability in Corporate Governance* (Abingdon, Routledge, 2015).

[33] Kingsford Smith, 'Governing the Corporation' 402.

the code alter the meaning of accountability and how it may be achieved.[34] Such ambiguities arise in part from the involvement of different disciplines and their different literatures on the subject, including economics, organisation theory, law, politics, management, finance, sociology and psychology.[35]

Corporate governance is also a territory in which competing interests lead to different understandings and different claims and goals. Thus, the term and scope of corporate governance may be determined by the viewpoint from which it is considered. A stakeholder-oriented view, for example, would see the firm as a place in which the different constituents—investors, managers, employees, suppliers, customers and broader stakeholders—contribute to and receive benefits from the enterprise. An alternative view might be that the firm is an organisation that obtains resources from its investors, employees and suppliers to produce goods and services for its customers. In the UK the concept of enlightened shareholder value has been criticised for its lack of precision because it fails to provide a way of balancing the interests of conflicting shareholders, and also because stakeholders have no way of enforcing any failure to consider their interests appropriately.[36]

The corporate governance system, as currently constructed, because of its lack of clarity and its limited conceptual basis, struggles to keep up with and respond to the fast political, social and economic changes and dynamics.[37] While corporate governance and corporate social responsibility are increasingly intertwined, it is still not clear how each relates to the other and how their relationship should shape the regulatory landscape, nor how different corporate governance actors are supposed to behave as circumstances change. Similarly, the contested terrain of corporate social responsibility comprises a lack of definitional precision and poor measurement, to the extent that some critics have been moved to suggest discarding the concept altogether.[38]

As corporate governance develops, the problem of role ambiguity for the different actors increases. Auditors, for example, must check and report against the financial reports but their role in the verification of non-financial reports is unclear. In addition, auditors frequently offer multiple services,

[34] D Nordberg and T McNulty, 'Creating Better Boards through Codification: Possibilities and limitations in UK Corporate Governance, 1992–2010' (2013) 55 *Business History* 348, 366.

[35] S Turnbull, 'Corporate Governance: Its Scope, Concerns and Theories' (1997) 5 *Corporate Governance: An International Review* 180, 180.

[36] A Keay, 'Tackling the Issue of the Corporate Objective: An Analysis of the United Kingdom's "Enlightened Shareholder Value Approach"' (2007) 29 *Sydney Law Review* 577.

[37] M Mason and J O'Mahoney, 'Post-traditional Corporate Governance' (2008) 31 *Journal of Corporate Citizenship* 1.

[38] J Van Oosterhout and PPMAR Heugens, 'Much Ado About Nothing: A Conceptual Critique of CSR' (2006) *ERIM Report Series Reference No ERS-2006-040-ORG*, papers.ssrn.com/sol3/papers.cfm?abstract_id=924505.

leading to problems of independence as well as failures in fully carrying out specific tasks.[39] Auditors appear not to be checking the compliance with all the provisions they should be reviewing and when they report they are using almost identical wording and resorting to symbolic ceremonial exercises rather than real reviews.[40] Similarly, an ongoing debate envelops the role of non-executive directors: should they be monitors or strategic advisers or both?[41] A further ambiguity surrounds the role of shareholders. The discussion of ownership continues to cause controversy.[42] Increasingly, attempts are made by policy actors and regulators to encourage greater levels of engagement by shareholders. Such measures as the Stewardship Code, adopted by the Financial Reporting Council in 2010, sit uneasily with the corporate law structures that really only grant shareholders limited mechanisms for intervention through voting rights and opportunity to sell their shares, and in rare cases a chance to challenge by way of a derivative action.[43] Moreover, the Stewardship Code only targets a limited group within a heterogeneous shareholder constituency, and is extremely light touch, being regarded by one commentator as 'trivial'.[44] For some investors, greater levels of engagement are impracticable and conflict with their other roles and activities.

These narrow, internal focuses restrict the development of corporate governance, which is increasingly identified as being linked to broader economic and social problems such as poor economic growth and increasing wealth inequality.[45] Thus, structural deficiencies limit the potential to deal with these external challenges. This is especially problematic as we see corporate governance rise in prominence and demands are made for this system to tackle and respond to bigger problems, and increasingly to substitute for government.[46] In the next section, the main regulatory device, the Corporate

[39] See below.

[40] PJ Shrives and N Brennan, 'A Typology for Exploring the Quality of Explanations for Non-compliance with UK Corporate Governance Regulations' (2015) 47 *The British Accounting Review* 85, 21.

[41] See eg: E Mahmoud and R Watson, 'Wearing Two Hats: The Conflicting Control and Management Roles of Non-Executive Directors' in K Keasey, S Thompson and M Wright (eds), *Corporate Governance* (Oxford, Oxford University Press, 1997) 54; D Higgs, *Review of the Role and Effectiveness of Non-Executive Directors* (London, Stationery Office, 2003); A Alcock, 'Higgs—the Wrong Answer?' (2003) 24 *Company Lawyer* 161.

[42] See eg P Ireland, 'Company Law and the Myth of Shareholder Ownership' (1999) 62 *Modern Law Review* 32, and J Velasco, 'Shareholder Ownership and Primacy' (2008) 2010 *Illinois Law Review* 897.

[43] See eg J Velasco, 'Taking Shareholder Rights Seriously' (2007) 41 *UC Davis Law Review* 605.

[44] A Reisberg, 'The UK Stewardship Code: On the Road to Nowhere?' (2015) 15 *Journal of Corporate Law Studies* 217.

[45] Piketty, *Capital in the Twenty First Century*.

[46] Pargendler, 'The Corporate Governance Obsession' 5.

Governance Code, is considered, demonstrating fundamental deficiencies in light of legal certainty goals and other important regulatory features.

THE UK CORPORATE GOVERNANCE CODE

General Remarks

In the wake of the corporate governance scandals that afflicted the UK in the late 1980s and early 1990s, including the collapses of Coloroll and Polly Peck, the Financial Reporting Council, the London Stock Exchange and the accountancy bodies initiated the establishment of the Cadbury Committee on the Financial Aspects of Corporate Governance in 1991.[47] On that Committee there were representatives from industry, shareholder groups and the accountancy profession. They were given the remit of examining the financial aspects of corporate governance. Further shocks occurred with the collapse of Bank of Credit and Commerce International and then of the Maxwell Group. The Committee, alongside its final Report in 1992, introduced a new voluntary Code of Best Practice, which comprised of a set of recommendations on issues such as division of responsibilities between the Chairman and the Chief Executive, the majority of the board to be comprised of independent directors, appointment of an audit committee including at least three non-executive directors, strengthened control systems and improved disclosure. Since 1992, the recommendations in the Cadbury Report have been amended and added to at regular intervals. In 1995 the Greenbury Report set out specific recommendations on the remuneration of directors,[48] and in 1998 the Hampel Report[49] brought the two earlier reports together into a single code, known as the Combined Code. Since the Financial Reporting Council, as the UK's independent regulator for corporate governance and reporting, took over responsibility for publishing and maintaining the Code in 2003, it has regularly updated the Code, in response to events and developments in the business world. In 2010 the Code was renamed as the UK Corporate Governance Code and its latest version was published in 2016.

The current Code, building on its predecessors, sets standards of good practice in relation to board leadership and effectiveness, remuneration, accountability and relations with shareholders. Numerous ambiguities remain,

[47] See The Cadbury Archive, University of Cambridge, Judge Business School, available at www.cadbury.cjbs.archios.info.

[48] Greenbury Study Group, *Final Report on Directors' Remuneration* (London, Gee Publishing, 1995).

[49] Hampel Committee, *Final Report of the Committee on Corporate Governance* (London, Gee Publishing, 1998).

including the conceptual ones noted above. Thus, in the section on remuneration, the Code does not provide guidance on some aspects relating to clawback provisions, such as how long any clawbacks should apply to awards paid out, or whether remuneration schemes should cover clawback and/or malus provisions.[50] Another uncertainty is found in the requirement for companies, when appointing new directors, to have a formal, rigorous and transparent procedure; they should ensure they give due regard for the benefits of diversity on the board, including gender. This does not tie up with the Preface, which in paragraph 3 states that diversity 'includes, but is not limited to, gender and race.' Thus it seems inconsistent to limit expressly the supporting principle for main principle B.2 to a reference to gender. Companies are clearly still free to determine their own boardroom appointments, so long as they follow a process which shows their policy. Apart from having 'objective' criteria and giving due regard to diversity, no more guidance is given in the Code. In that same supporting provision the Code does not offer guidance for what might comprise 'an appropriate balance of skills and experience within the company and on the board.' This is left to be evaluated by the nomination committee, under provision B.2.2. A further vague provision is main principle B.3, which states that 'all directors should be able to allocate sufficient time to the company to discharge their responsibilities effectively.' Yet no guidance is offered on what would be a sufficient time allocation, although the Walker Review had recommended that non-executive directors should have a minimum time commitment of 30–36 days a year to be stated in the terms of appointment of 'several NEDs'. The view was that directors and chairman on each company board should determine the appropriate time commitment.[51] This flexibility allows room for discretion, but it does not help to clarify what time commitment would suffice, at least as a minimum.

The Comply or Explain Principle

The UK Corporate Governance Code's modus operandi is the principle of comply or explain. This principle underlines the Code's support for flexibility and avoidance of a one-size-fits-all approach. The Code identifies good governance practices relating to, for example, the board and its committees and risk management and internal control, but companies can choose to adopt different practices if they would be more appropriate to their circumstances.

[50] See Freshfields Bruckhaus Deringer, 'Pay Aspects of the New Corporate Governance Code' (2014), communications.freshfields.com.

[51] Walker Review, 'A Review of Corporate Governance in UK Banks and Other Financial Industry Entities, Final Recommendations' (2009) 47–48, available at webarchive.nationalarchives.gov.uk/+/http:/www.hm-treasury.gov.uk/d/walker_review_261109.pdf.

They do not have to comply with the Code's recommendations, but where they depart from the Code, companies must explain the reason for that departure to their shareholders, who will then decide whether they are content with the approach that has been taken. At the time of the Cadbury Report, this 'cooperative route' was favoured over legislation, which the Cadbury Committee 'thought would stifle innovation and enterprise'.[52] Comply or explain might also have been viewed as 'a bolt hole' to accommodate opposing views.[53] In any event, this comply or explain approach is widely regarded as 'the single most important feature of this form of soft law.'[54]

The Code tells us that

> an alternative to following a provision may be justified in particular circumstances if good governance can be achieved by other means. A condition of doing so is that the reasons for it should be explained clearly and carefully to shareholders, who may wish to discuss the position with the company and whose voting intentions may be influenced as a result.[55]

Compliance with the Code is not compulsory but disclosing non-compliance *is* mandatory. Moreover, as Seidl explains, 'where individual rules do not fit the particular organisational setting, companies are *expected* to deviate'.[56] Thus, in providing an explanation, the company should demonstrate how, while differing from the code provision, the company is behaving in a way that is consistent with the relevant principle and how its own practices are, in fact, contributing to good governance and achieving its business objectives.

If the company provides an adequate explanation for its non-compliance with a Code provision the company have conformed with the Code because it is showing through that explanation that the company is well managed, is likely to perform well and is therefore meeting the overall aims of the Code—best practice and good performance. The aim of this soft law approach, designed to avoid box ticking, is for common sense to apply and to accommodate the individual circumstances of each company. Companies are, in this way, encouraged to adopt the spirit of the Code rather than

[52] P Stiles and B Taylor, 'Benchmarking Corporate Governance: The Impact of the Cadbury Code' (1993) 26 *Long Range Planning* 61, 69.

[53] Hilton, 'Grudging Acquiescence' 21.

[54] R Hooghiemstra and H van Ees, 'Uniformity as Response to Soft Law: Evidence from Compliance and Non-compliance with the Dutch Corporate Governance Code' (2011) 5 *Regulation & Governance* 480, 481; RV Aguilera and A Cuervo-Cazurra, 'Codes of Good Governance' (2009) 17 *Corporate Governance: An International Review* 376.

[55] UK Corporate Governance Code, 2016, 4.

[56] D Seidl, P Sanderson and J Roberts, 'Applying "Comply-or-explain": Conformance with Codes of Corporate Governance in the UK and Germany' (2009) *Centre for Business Research, University of Cambridge Working Paper No 389*, www.cbr.cam.ac.uk/fileadmin/user_upload/centre-for-business-research/downloads/working-papers/wp389.pdf.

the letter.[57] Parallels might be drawn with the true and fair view approach in accounting regulation, which is designed to avoid a mechanistic following of the accounting standards but looks for objective and professional judgement.[58]

Shareholders have an important role in this process, at least in theory. They are required to respond to the statements from companies and engage in a dialogue with the managers. Thus, companies and shareholders both have responsibility for ensuring that 'comply or explain' remains an effective alternative to a rules-based system. The aim of comply or explain is shareholder empowerment, giving to them the chance to make an informed evaluation as to whether non-compliance is justified, given the company's circumstances. Moore has suggested that comply or explain could be viewed as a managerial 'bonding' mechanism in the eyes of institutional investors, preserving a level of trust enough to encourage them to continue providing equity capital to the company.[59] Through this process, the market is expected to enforce the code where the company has failed to explain adequately, by penalising such non-compliance through assigning a lower share value. The market mechanism relies on reputational sanctions, which depend on proper disclosure and effective evaluation by the market participants.[60]

Is Comply or Explain Successful?

The claim in the Code is that comply or explain is 'strongly supported by both companies and shareholders and we see a high level of code compliance'. Thus, the Financial Reporting Council states, in its response to the European Recommendation on the quality of corporate governance reporting, 26 June 2015,

> The 'comply or explain' method of adherence has given companies flexibility and made it possible to set more demanding standards than can be done through

[57] S Arcot, V Bruno and A Fuare-Grimaud, 'Corporate Governance in the UK: Is the Comply or Explain Approach Working?' (2010) 30 *International Review of Law and Economics* 193, 193.

[58] See Financial Reporting Council, 'True and Fair' (2014) 1, www.frc.org.uk/FRC-Documents/Accounting-and-Reporting/True-and-Fair-June-2014.pdf. Note also the recognition of the problem of creative compliance by report preparers who might interpret standards in ways that suit their own self interests rather than representing good accounting and where they use the regulations to escape regulatory control without actually violating the regulations. See eg BA Rutherford, 'Creative Compliance and Behaviour in Response to Mandatory Changes in Accounting Policy: Three Cases from Pre-Dearing Britain' (1999) 4 *Accounting History* 31, and D McBarnet and C Whelan, 'The Elusive Spirit of the Law: Formalism and the Struggle for Control' (1991) 54 *Modern Law Review* 848.

[59] MT Moore, '"Whispering Sweet Nothings": The Limitations of Informal Conformance in UK Corporate Governance' (2009) 9 *Journal of Corporate Law Studies* 95, 116.

[60] M Bianchi et al, 'Comply or Explain? Investor protection through Corporate Governance Codes' (2010) *ECGI Finance Working Paper No 278/2010* 6, papers.ssrn.com/sol3/papers.cfm?abstract_id=1581350.

hard rules. Experience has shown that the vast majority of companies attain these standards.[61]

However, despite this claim, the comply or explain principle has limitations. There is growing evidence that whilst there are departures from the Code, which are allowed, such departures are not always accompanied with adequate explanations, which is not allowed. Researchers have found that companies' explanations are 'remarkably similar'[62] and often the explanations are 'uninformative', providing no justification for departure from the Code.[63] Arcot et al, for example, found that whilst there were more than half of firms in the FTSE 350 who were fully compliant with the Code, those firms that were not compliant 'did a very poor job of providing explanations' and in one in five cases firms gave no explanation for their non-compliances at all. Similarly, the ABI, in 2012, found that 17 per cent of explanations did not meet the Code explanation criteria.[64] The Financial Reporting Council has also documented inadequate explanations.[65] In 2015 the Financial Reporting Council noted that overall explanations in relation to non-compliance with some provisions were of poorer quality than the previous year, with little real information provided in a number of cases.

Additionally, outside of the UK, the comply or explain principle does not seem to fare better. A European Commission research project in 2009, echoed in the 2011 Green Paper,[66] expressed concerns over the level of monitoring of compliance statements and on the quality of non-compliance explanations.[67] The adoption of best practices is 'markedly weaker and much more differentiated than what is formally declared in company reports.'[68] Indeed, even when a company declares compliance this might

[61] Grant Thornton surveys have confirmed this: see G Thornton, 'UK Corporate Governance Review and Trends 2015' (2015), available at www.grantthornton.co.uk.

[62] M Nerantzidis, 'Measuring the Quality of the "Comply or Explain" Approach: Evidence from the Implementation of the Greek Corporate Governance Code' (2015) 30 *Managerial Auditing Journal* 373, 382.

[63] G Hadjikyprianou, 'The principle of "Comply or Explain" Underpinning the UK Corporate Governance Regulation: Is There a Need for Change?' (2015) 7 *Corporate Governance Law Journal* 15, available at papers.ssrn.com/sol3/Papers.cfm?abstract_id=2690687.

[64] Association of British Insurers, 'Comply or Explain' (December 2012) 17, available at www.ivis.co.uk/media/5923/ABI-Report-on-Comply-or-Explain-Investor-Expectations-Dec-2012.pdf.

[65] The Financial Reporting Council added more detail in the 2014 version of the Code on what would constitute an explanation: see 2016 version, paras 3, 4.

[66] European Commission, Green Paper, The EU Corporate Governance Framework, COM (2011) 164 final.

[67] European Commission, 'Study on Monitoring and Enforcement Practices in Corporate Governance in the Member States' (2009), ec.europa.eu/internal_market/company/docs/ecgforum/studies/comply-or-explain-090923_en.pdf.

[68] Bianchi et al, 'Comply or Explain?' 6.

not be the case in reality.[69] The thinness of the explanations has been seen as a 'recurring disappointment.'[70]

Another problem is that of legislation by the back door, or 'regulatory creep,' introducing more detailed and prescriptive provisions. This was observed after Higgs reported on the role of non-executive directors, which led to changes in the provisions on the roles of CEO and Chair, with a more prescriptive instruction for the roles to be structured by a 'clear division.'[71] So the flexibility in the Code is lost as it gets more detailed and prescriptive and in fact it could be argued that the Code in this way is more precise than some of the duties encompassed in statute such as the formulated standard of fiduciary duty,[72] so the Code then directs companies and directors more clearly towards compliant conduct.[73] This point is supported by the observations of Hooghiemstra and van Ees, who find that companies display uniformity in adopting the standards of good governance 'which is not in line with the logic of corporate governance codes and casts doubt on the effectiveness of this form of soft law.'[74] Thus, 'a one-size-fits-all approach to non-compliance seems to be emerging, which can be considered as opposed to the fundamental logic of the comply-or-explain principle.'[75] The motivations for firms to adopt this response to the Code's provisions may include reduction of costs of capital for the firm, economic motives, a desire to earn approval and respect for the firm from shareholders, stakeholders, media and competitors, as well as regulatory arrangements which may create coercive pressure to comply, eg by law or listing requirements.[76]

According to Arcot et al:

> most companies seem to think of the Code as a mandatory requirement, but at the same time they have subjective discretion on what aspect they consider to be compliant with. Shareholders appear to be encouraging such behaviour by not paying too much attention to the quality of explanations provided.[77]

They are thus, in practice, distanced from compliance decisions because they show deference to Board judgement and prefer to use financial performance as a proxy for deciding when non-compliance can be excused.[78]

[69] JB Andersson, 'Evolution of Company Law, Corporate Governance Codes and the Principle of Comply or Explain—A Critical Review' *LSN Research Paper Series No 10–19*, papers.ssrn.com/sol3/papers.cfm?abstract_id=1869916.

[70] Hilton, 'Grudging Acquiescence' 22.

[71] Incorporated in the UK Corporate Governance Code at main principle A.2.

[72] Companies Act 2006, ss 170–175.

[73] I MacNeil and X Li, '"Comply or Explain": Market Discipline and Non-compliance with the Combined Code' (2006) 14 *Corporate Governance* 486, 487.

[74] Hooghiemstra and van Ees, 'Uniformity as Response to Soft Law' 480.

[75] ibid 481.

[76] ibid 483.

[77] Arcot et al, 'Corporate Governance in the UK' 193–94.

[78] See further, MacNeil and X Li, 'Comply or Explain'.

This fact puts into further question the value of the Stewardship Code, which seeks to enhance the quality of engagement between institutional investors and companies.[79] In fact, 'the market as a whole seems to be ignoring the explanations provided.'[80] The market seems neither to factor in the value of good board governance nor to penalise poor ones.[81] What appears then to be the case is that the Code's message is being misread or not understood. This might also be caused in part by the discretion allowed in the interpretation of the Code.[82] In addition, the role of the auditors in this context is far from clear. Not only do they appear free of the obligation to provide an opinion on a company's corporate governance statement, but even if they were so obliged the lack of common structure and content among such statements and their inherent subjectivity would make the auditor's task difficult, compounded further by the complexities of the industry sectors involved, the size of a company's corporate governance statement and the quality and complexity of each separate explanation.[83]

Arcot et al also note some lack of clarity over who are the real targets of the information flows. They note that there is no formal authority established to enforce or to monitor the veracity of both the compliance statement and the explanation provided. Thus, although the Code is appended to the Listing Agreement, the Financial Services Authority (now the Financial Conduct Authority) 'makes no judgement on the quality, informativeness and accuracy of the corporate governance statements.'[84] Indeed, there is no evidence of the Financial Services Authority, or subsequently the Prudential Regulation Authority or Financial Conduct Authority, having issued any sanctions for breach of the comply or explain rule. This leads to the suggestion by O'Dwyer that the Listing Rules appear only to exist as a scare tactic to encourage companies to either comply or explain.[85]

The flexibility itself may be at the root of the problem because by allowing boards to choose their corporate structure and governance practices, it gives them more power and reduces their accountability by weakening

[79] See further, A Shaukat and G Trojanowski, 'Board Governance and Corporate Performance in the UK' (2014), ore.exeter.ac.uk/repository/bitstream/handle/10871/17354/Board%20Governance%20and%20Corporate%20Performance%20in%20the%20UK%20-%20FMA%20Europe%20submission.pdf?sequence=1. See also L Roach, 'The UK Stewardship Code' (2011) 11 *Journal of Corporate Law Studies* 463, 475 and Reisberg, 'The UK Stewardship Code' 217; Hadjikyprianou, 'The principle of "Comply or Explain" Underpinning the UK Corporate Governance Regulation'.

[80] Arcot et al, 'Corporate Governance in the UK' 193–94.

[81] Shaukat and Trojanowski, 'Board Governance and Corporate Performance in the UK' 4.

[82] Arcot et al, 'Corporate Governance in the UK' 194.

[83] Nerantzidis, 'Measuring the Quality of the "Comply or Explain" Approach' 380.

[84] Arcot et al, 'Corporate Governance in the UK' 198.

[85] A O'Dwyer, 'Corporate Governance after the Financial Crisis: The Role of Shareholders in Monitoring the Activities of the Board' (2014) 15–16, available at www.abdn.ac.uk/law/documents/Corporate_Governance_after_the_financial_crisis.pdf.

monitoring capacity either by outside independent board members or by the shareholders.[86] Observers have noted their tendency to take advantage of the flexibility they have been granted in an opportunistic manner, by adopting more boardroom-friendly arrangements when they anticipate weak performance.[87] Thus the accountability goal is lost as a result of the flexibility injection. Furthermore, evidence suggests that in fact firms are complying more with the letter than with the spirit because their explanations are not showing how their own practices represent *best* practice for that company.[88] The market has also opted for compliance as the rule, and this may be a result of the conditions of uncertainty[89] caused by lack of clarity and reflective of the fact that managers may have 'both incentives and means to hide non-compliance enabling companies to claim compliance when they are not really complying.'[90] What emerges is an isomorphic pressure to conform.[91] Mayhew points to the stigma attached to the explain part of comply or explain, which has the effect of pushing companies into compliance. In this way, comply or explain is interpreted as 'obey the law or make a plea for clemency, which is not a balanced choice.'[92]

One problem is that monitoring the accuracy of the statements is costly[93] for shareholders[94] and thus they tend to get involved only after periods of bad performance. We cannot rely on shareholders to enforce the Code, so it might be the time for adopting a formal authority to monitor the statements and to demand better disclosure.[95] Ultimately, it seems that the benefits of flexibility associated with the Code's self regulatory status are overstated.[96]

We see that in the corporate governance arena legal certainty took a back seat to flexibility, but this forgets some other key goals of a legal system

[86] Shaukat and Trojanowski, 'Board Governance and Corporate Performance in the UK' 5.

[87] ibid 10.

[88] Shrives and Brennan, 'A Typology for Exploring the Quality of Explanations for Non-compliance with UK Corporate Governance Regulations' 85.

[89] P Sanderson, D Seidl and J Roberts, 'The Limits of Flexible Regulation: Managers' Perceptions of Corporate Governance Codes and "Comply or Explain"' (2013) *Centre for Business Research, University of Cambridge, Working Paper No 439*, available at www.cbr.cam.ac.uk/fileadmin/user_upload/centre-for-business-research/downloads/working-papers/wp439.pdf.

[90] Shrives and Brennan, 'A Typology for Exploring the Quality of Explanations for Non-compliance with UK Corporate Governance Regulations' 26.

[91] Sanderson, Seidl and Roberts, 'The Limits of Flexible Regulation' 5.

[92] D Mayhew, 'Explaining Without Stigma' in Financial Reporting Council (ed), *Comply or Explain* 27.

[93] Arcot et al, 'Corporate Governance in the UK' 201.

[94] Marco Becht notes that investors are 'confronted with a multitude of codes and corporate governance statements that can be difficult to read': see Becht, 'Comply or just explain?' 13.

[95] Arcot et al, 'Corporate Governance in the UK' 201. See also Keay, 'Comply or Explain in Corporate Governance Codes'; Sergakis, 'EU corporate governance'; Nerantzidis, 'Measuring the Quality of the "Comply or Explain" Approach' 391.

[96] MacNeil and Li, 'Comply or Explain' 486.

such as predictability, transparency and participation. Ultimately as Cally Jordan suggests:

> there are several clouds looming on the horizon. Comply or explain and voluntary codes of corporate governance appear to have run their course elsewhere in the world. Even in the U.K., legislative initiatives on the corporate governance front, either domestically initiated or EU-driven, may be sapping the voluntary code of its vitality. Although the conviction remains strong in the U.K. that the flexibility and opportunity for easy, rapid adjustments are strengths of the voluntary code approach to corporate governance, the constantly evolving nature of the U.K. voluntary codes may, in fact, be an indication of a deeprooted problem: Are these voluntary codes of corporate governance, which give so much deference to industry sentiment and conventional wisdom, in a constant state of flux because they are not getting it right?[97]

NEOLIBERAL, REFLECTIVE REGULATION AND SOFT LAW LIMITATIONS

If we were to gauge the quality of the UK Code and the corporate governance system on the basis of how widely it has been adopted, we might take pride in the fact that it has been widely exported.[98] Indeed, the comply or explain principle has largely been adopted across the world: the European Corporate Governance Forum gave its support to the principle in 2006[99] and more than 80 countries adopted similar codes, most of them incorporating a comply or explain approach.[100] As Jordan points out, first the Cadbury Report was an initiative of the London Stock Exchange which was 'the most international of all exchanges at the time with hundreds of non-UK companies listed and news of the Cadbury Report would have spread quickly internationally' at a time when there was a 'great re-alignment among exchanges around the world' and there was also the old colonial network of Commonwealth countries that span the globe and which remain interconnected through judicial and legislative legacies.[101] In addition the simplicity of the Cadbury Code and the appealing personality of Sir Adrian Cadbury also helped them receive a warm welcome.[102] However, a less positive conclusion could be drawn from these regulatory increments, which is

[97] C Jordan, 'Cadbury Twenty Years on' (2013) 58 *Villanova Law Review* 1, 24.

[98] Financial Reporting Council, 'Review of the Effectiveness of the Combined Code: Progress Report and Second Consultation' (2009) 3, frc.org.uk/getattachment/3e7365ee-8826-4ac8-aedf-66093cb0fd36/Progress-Report-Review-of-the-effectiveness-of-The.aspx.

[99] Statement of the European Corporate Governance Forum on the comply-or-explain principle, 22 February 2006, ec.europa.eu/internal_market/company/docs/ecgforum/ecgf-comply-explain_en.pdf.

[100] ECGI, 'Index of Codes', www.ecgi.org/codes/all_codes.php.

[101] Jordan, 'Cadbury Twenty Years on' 5.

[102] ibid 5.

that the existing governance mechanisms and codes have actually failed to deliver, leading to the financial crisis and related corporate scandals, and then leading to invitations to 'reinforce both regulations (hard law) and governance codes (soft law) in order to increase transparency and accountability of, and to restore battered reputations and investor confidence in, financial and non-financial companies.'[103] Moreover, the proliferation of corporate governance codes may not have been stimulated by the supposed wonder of the UK's system as much as by activity of transnational institutions, issuing codes, and by the occurrence of corporate frauds.[104] The fact is that 'codes have not eliminated the problems they set out to address'[105] and 'problems of poor conduct and corporate collapse persist.'[106] As is observed by Nordberg and McNulty, 'the goal of better boards remains elusive.'[107]

What we see are codes that define and redefine the terms, seeking to learn from practice and experiences of the corporate actors. This is a form of evolution that is 'effected through language and discourse, through the use of rhetoric to persuade and ambiguity to create flexibility, in the knowledge that change will need to come again.'[108] These incremental changes are embedded in what is presented as a reflexive system. As a reflexive and soft regulatory instrument, the Code is improved and updated regularly, ostensibly as part of a continuous and ongoing process of learning and reflection.[109] Ideally, such revisions would reflect ongoing deliberative processes of 'collective learning' that encourage multilevel stakeholding.[110] This has the potential for, as Veldman and Wilmott suggest, a strong form of reflexive governance, which involves '(re)interpreting inter alia the conditions of governance, the dynamics of its practices and its (un)intended consequences.'[111]

Unfortunately, the experience in the UK has been much more restricted, so that rather than leading to 'critical scrutiny of the presence, nature and mobilisation of the taken-for-granted understandings that frame and support theories and practices of governance', we have witnessed instead a

[103] F Cuomo, C Mallin and A Zattoni, 'Corporate Governance Codes: A Review and Research Agenda' (2016) 24 *Corporate Governance: An International Review* 222, 222.

[104] ibid 228.

[105] Nordberg and McNulty, 'Creating Better Boards through Codification' 348.

[106] ibid 348.

[107] ibid 349.

[108] ibid 366.

[109] See I Ayres and J Braithwaite, *Responsive Regulation—Transcending the Deregulation Debate* (Oxford, Oxford University Press, 1992).

[110] J Veldman and H Willmott, 'The Cultural Grammar of Governance: The UK Code of Corporate Governance, Reflexivity, and the Limits of 'Soft' Regulation' (2016) 69 *Human Relations* 581, 582–83. See also C Scott, 'Reflexive Governance, Meta-regulation and Corporate Responsibility: The "Heinekin Effect"' in N Boeger, R Murray and C Villiers (eds), *Perspectives on Corporate Social Responsibility* (Cheltenham, Edward Elgar, 2008) 174; O De Schutter and S Deakin, 'Reflexive Governance and the Dilemmas of Social Regulation' (2003) 28 *European Law Review* 814.

[111] Veldman and Willmott, 'The Cultural Grammar of Governance' 584.

'learning that is restricted to making incremental adjustments and technical fixes.'[112] As a result these 'enactments of reflexivity serve simply to affirm and reproduce the dominant values of the field, with the result that the principal contribution of reflexive interventions is an endorsement and reinforcement, rather than a problematization, of the status quo.'[113] Ultimately, the corporate governance control technology ends up regularising the space in which 'repeated misbehaviour is defined, observed and ineffectually punished.'[114]

One consequence of this approach is that whilst it leads to multiple layers of regulation and constant changes, such changes often end up being repetitions of the same types of rules, being just more and more of the same, the same patterns being repeated again.[115] In the UK's corporate governance system we see this in repeated attempts to make auditors more independent, that do not work, repeated optimism in the role of non-executive directors despite continued ambiguities surrounding their role, ever more calls for more and more disclosure, particularly financial disclosure, repeated calls for more shareholder power even though they display much rational apathy, repeated attempts to curb 'excessive' executive pay through the pay for performance quest, and importantly, as Veldman and Willmott observe:

> despite the problematic empirical relation between prescriptions of 'good governance' and the instruments provided in the Code, and the evidence of failing compliance, and disregard of the spirit of the Code, the voluntaristic 'comply or explain' approach continues to be hailed as 'a non-negotiable factor in UK corporate governance.[116]

The whole approach appears as self-contradictory and rather *un*reflexive, as Bruner notes, 'essentially amounting to the claim that we must give shareholders more power because managers left to themselves have excessively focused on the shareholders' interests.'[117] In effect we are observing the old 'club' being 'able to retain the power to determine the rules and undermine tighter regulation.'[118] Ultimately the result has been a poor quality of regulation

[112] ibid.

[113] ibid 586, citing G Ailon, 'Mapping the Cultural Grammar of Reflexivity: The Case of the Enron Scandal' (2011) 40 *Economy and Society* 141, 159–60.

[114] I Erturk et al, 'Corporate Governance and Disappointment' (2004) 11 *Review of International Political Economy* 677, 704.

[115] P Sikka, 'The Corrosive Effects of Neoliberalism on the UK Financial Crises and Auditing Practices: A Dead-end for Reforms' (2015) 39 *Accounting Forum* 1, 2.

[116] Veldman and Willmott, 'The Cultural Grammar of Governance' 594, citing Keay, 'Comply or Explain in Corporate Governance Codes' 281.

[117] CM Bruner, 'Corporate Governance Reform in a Time of Crisis' (2011) 36 *Journal of Corporation Law* 309, 322.

[118] Erturk et al, 'Corporate Governance and Disappointment' 705. See also Haxhi et al, 'A Political Perspective on Business Elites and Institutional Embeddedness'.

and compliance. It is clear then the codes 'can only take a board so far along the path to effectiveness'.[119]

With these limitations, what is the attraction of this system of codification? A great pull for the flexible, hybridised regulation developed is that it is held to be helpful to markets that seek to be free from intervention as far as possible. As Apeldoorn and Horn remind us, commenting on European regulation of corporate governance: 'the purpose of regulation is increasingly assumed to be to serve the exigencies of "efficient" and well-functioning capitalist markets.'[120] They cite the words of Charlie McCreevy, past European Commissioner for the Internal Market, that highlight the tension between the need for legal certainty and meeting the needs of changing markets:

> Without legal certainty, without reliable information, without clear framework rules markets cannot work for long. So, a stable, reliable and transparent regulatory environment is essential. But it is economic freedom that lets markets best play their role ... Legislation has to help, not hinder, this process—working with the ebbs and flows of markets.[121]

The idea is that flexible regulation enables economies to grow, so soft, principles-based regulation is favoured.[122]

The traditional command and control style of regulation has numerous weaknesses in that it is costly for business to comply with, it could be viewed as too legalistic and inflexible, there are problems of access to enforcement, and it can lead to creative compliance.[123] Soft regulation is very different, usually being decentred and more horizontal[124] and therefore offering at least a perception of greater legitimacy and encouraging greater levels of buy-in, it is more flexible and responsive to changing contexts, is cheaper and has the ability to cross borders with the help of networked regulation and it is capable of establishing higher standards than formal law.[125] We see the features of 'smart mix' regulation, aiming to combine the best of both worlds. As Kinderman describes it: 'a smart mix combines the flexibility, dynamism, innovativeness, reflexivity and adaptability of voluntary market-based solutions and the authoritativeness, scope and binding force of legal regulation.'[126] Despite these possible strengths, soft law and smart

[119] Nordberg and McNulty, 'Creating Better Boards through Codification' 367.

[120] B Van Apeldoorn and L Horn, 'The Marketisation of European Corporate Control: A Critical Political Economy Perspective' (2007) 12 *New Political Economy* 211, 224.

[121] C McCreevy, 'Regulatory and Supervisory Challenges of Financial Integration' (Speech at the Lamfalussy London Summer Dinner, London, 27 June 2005), quoted by Van Apeldoorn and Horn, 'The Marketisation of European Corporate Control' 224.

[122] Sanderson, Seidl and Roberts, 'The Limits of Flexible Regulation' 1.

[123] Kingsford Smith, 'Governing the Corporation' 386.

[124] Mason and O'Mahoney, 'Post-traditional Corporate Governance' 12.

[125] Kingsford Smith, 'Governing the Corporation' 387.

[126] D Kinderman, 'Time for a Reality Check: Is Business Willing to Support a Smart Mix of Complementary Regulation in Private Governance?' (2016) 35 *Policy and Society* 29, 29–30.

mix regulation also have their weaknesses. They come with fragmented and redundant oversight, and overlapping mechanisms, and different and conflicting logics (public and private),[127] that may be in tension with each other,[128] giving rise to uncertain legality and it is difficult to work out 'who is accountable to whom, for what and how.'[129] This problem of uncertainty deepens as new events and risks and crises arise, leading to new calls for regulation. As the context changes rapidly and unpredictably, it becomes difficult to know what is acceptable compliance and so regulatees feel uncertain and at the same time they are given flexibility and discretion on how to respond to new regulations.[130]

It is also uncertain how long the regulations are able to retain their softness. There are numerous ways in which they get hardened up in practice, either by connecting them to more formal rules and institutions or by such institutions adopting them and effectively making them compulsory, or in the interpretation of the more formal laws. For example, code provisions, corporate governance guidance materials and principles may provide greater specificity to legal duties[131] and become yardsticks used by courts to determine whether directors have complied with their duties.[132] Even taken on its own terms it is clear that the system has 'not resulted in any more substantial and systematic positive correlation in shareholder value which could be identified in the empirical studies.'[133] It is a tool that has failed to deliver.[134]

One limitation found in the system perhaps follows from the political importance of large public companies. They have considerable leverage and influence over the legislator and it has been suggested that the corporate governance code could 'function as a restraint on the development of rules in company law and in particular good corporate governance rules.'[135]

[127] E Thomann, E Lieberherr and K Ingold, 'Torn between State and Market: Private Policy Implementation and Conflicting Institutional Logics' (2016) 35 *Policy and Society* 57, 59 and 68.

[128] Streeck and Schafer talk about the competing different logics of social justice and market justice. They note that people and markets are different, that for example the state's citizenry is nationally organised but financial markets are global, and that whilst citizens are usually resident in their country and cannot switch allegiance to a competing country, investors can and do easily exit: see W Streeck and A Schafer, *Politics in the Age of Austerity* (London, Polity Press, 2013).

[129] Kingsford Smith, 'Governing the Corporation' 401.

[130] Sanderson, Seidl and Roberts, 'The Limits of Flexible Regulation' 1.

[131] Mason and O'Mahoney, 'Post-traditional Corporate Governance' 3, note ambiguity in legal case history of directors' responsibilities.

[132] See eg the Australian cases of *ASIC v Rich* (2003) 174 FLR 128 per Austin J at 146–47 [70]; *Bell Group Ltd (in liq) v Westpac Banking Corporation (No 9)* (2008) 39 WAR 1, per Owen J at 528 [4362]; and *ASIC v Healey (No 2)* [2011] FCA 1003 per Middleton J at [193], discussed in Kingsford Smith, 'Governing the Corporation' 393–94.

[133] Andersson, 'Evolution of Company Law' 97.

[134] O'Dwyer, 'Corporate Governance after the Financial Crisis' 21.

[135] Andersson, 'Evolution of Company Law'.

Haxhi et al note that corporate elites have opportunity for decisive political intervention as they define the law, and they determine how it operates through comply or explain, so they can secure their political goals and their positions of power.[136] Corporate governance codes thus

> could have a negative incentive for politicians and civil servants to improve company law legislation—at least until a new scandal occurs. In the latter case the resulting legislation may be over reactive and directly harmful for the development of best corporate governance practice.[137]

Despite claims that the system leads to a race to the top in the competition for capital and the need to be seen by investors as the best, the effect of the approach in practice has been towards a short-termist and profit-oriented approach that, rather than exhibiting 'best practice', is corrosive and lies behind the successive crises experienced. We have witnessed companies operating at suboptimal levels of productivity, continued problems around executive remuneration, and levels of inequality that have led to lack of trust in the corporate or political systems. At the height of the financial crisis, for which the corporate governance has been partly blamed, Alistair Darling, then Chancellor of the Exchequor, stated that the UK was just 'two hours away from a financial meltdown' and the cashpoints running dry.[138] This is hardly suggestive of an effective legal or corporate governance system.

In a working paper for the International Monetary Fund, De Nicolò, Laeven and Ueda argue that effective implementation of corporate governance reform appears to be an important contributing factor to countries' well-being. Thus improvements to corporate governance quality should have positive effects on economic activities and influence per capital GDP growth, total factor productivity levels and growth and ratio of investment to GDP on the corporate governance quality index.[139] This suggests that if our corporate governance system were flourishing, so would our economy, but in truth the UK economy is struggling, for many reasons, including poor quality corporate governance. Thus GDP per hour is currently around 17 per cent below the G7 average and this is caused by low investment, especially in infrastructure and innovation, poor management and weak intermediate skills.[140] The poor investment levels are a result of political uncertainty and short-termism in financial markets and businesses, leading

[136] Haxhi et al, 'A Political Perspective on Business Elites and Institutional Embeddedness' 543.

[137] Andersson, 'Evolution of Company Law' 95–96.

[138] A Darling, 'We were two hours from the cashpoints running dry', *The Independent* (18 March 2011), quoted in Sikka, 'The Corrosive Effects of Neoliberalism on the UK Financial Crises and Auditing Practices' 1.

[139] G De Nicolò, L Laeven and K Ueda, 'Corporate governance quality: Trends and real effects' (2008) 17 *Journal of Financial Intermediation* 198.

[140] Valero and Roland, 'Productivity and Business Policies' 1.

to shortfalls in research and development.[141] As Sikka observes, the financial crisis has provided a justification for wage freezes, public expenditure cuts and an austerity programme. Thus the neoliberal ideologies, with their emphasis on light-touch regulation, individualisation, excessive faith in markets and pursuit of private profits, give rise to a system that has little regard for social consequences.[142]

The situation we have arrived at is that 'the worldviews of markets, profits and light touch regulation are now so normalised that they have crowded out concerns about ethics, morality, civil duty, care, altruism and loyalty'[143] and the normative approach to corporate governance in practice crowds out valid alternatives.[144] Indeed, it has been suggested that the 'metaphor of the self-governing corporation may crowd out potentially more effective interventions for the public good.'[145] The effect is that 'ordinary people have been the losers at every count. Firstly, they have been fleeced by frauds and secondly, taxpayer funded bailouts have facilitated a massive wealth transfer from ordinary taxpayers to banks and financial elites.'[146] Thus it could be concluded that the legal uncertainty that pervades our corporate governance system is intentional because its effect is in fact to reap profits on a short-term basis and for the corporate elites to benefit from those profits. Whilst the system is not working from a social justice logic, it appears to work from a competitive, individualistic market justice logic.

CONCLUSION

It might be argued that legal certainty can never be fully achieved. Indeed, it has been noted that 'the tendency toward increasing uncertainty in the law is inexorable.'[147] As Amato suggests, 'law on the books' may become increasingly uncertain due to the legislative process itself, in which new statutes get passed that create exceptions, exemptions, or privileges etc, rendering the law more complex and convoluted. In addition, rules may become more uncertain in their application, so that 'although the rules "on the books" remain unchanged, if people change their conduct so that existing rules less clearly apply to what they do, we can say that overall the law has become

[141] ibid 5.

[142] Sikka, 'The Corrosive Effects of Neoliberalism on the UK Financial Crises and Auditing Practices' 1.

[143] ibid 13.

[144] A Jansson et al, 'The Political Economy of Corporate Governance' (2016) 16 *Ephemera* 1, 11.

[145] Pargendler, 'The Corporate Governance Obsession' 42.

[146] Sikka, 'The Corrosive Effects of Neoliberalism on the UK Financial Crises and Auditing Practices' 13–14.

[147] A D'Amato, 'Legal Uncertainty' (1983) 71 *California Law Review* 1.

less certain.'[148] The ambiguous and soft nature of the UK's corporate governance system, especially its comply or explain principle, has shown that its weaknesses outweigh its strengths. The Financial Conduct Authority has sought to remove the comply or explain option for viability statements by placing a requirement in the Listing Rules for premium listed companies to compulsorily provide a long-term viability statement.[149] This is an example of the absorption of the Code's provisions into existing formal law as is suggested by Wymeersch, who highlights not only a complex interaction between the codes and the legal system, but also how gradually corporate governance rules are incorporated into statute. In the end, we find that what is supposedly a self-regulatory system is not really that at all.[150] As Hilton says:

> The perception is that light touch regulation allowed the financial system to run out of control and ultimately to blow itself and everyone else up so it is now discredited in favour of a new world of clear rules, robustly enforced and with no exceptions.[151]

Much more than a quest for legal certainty is necessary, although one improvement might be to clarify some of those key concepts that feature in the corporate governance system. Moreover, a good legal or regulatory system has many more attributes than legal certainty. The Flanders Government, for example, highlights eight features of a good quality and effective regulation. The regulation must be: necessary and effective for achieving its intended goal; appropriate and balanced—in that it improves social welfare and well-being and achieves the intended goal at the lowest possible social cost and minimises unwanted side-effects; implementable and enforceable; lawful; consistent with other rules so that there are no overlaps or contradictions with the other regulations and it forms part of a coherent whole; simple, clear and accessible; well-founded and well-discussed—evidence-based and follows wide-ranging official, social and political discussion on its objectives, options, content and effects; relevant, up-to-date, and reviewable.[152]

[148] ibid 4–5.

[149] See Financial Conduct Authority, 'Quarterly Consultation No 9' (2015), www.fca.org.uk/publications/consultation-papers/cp15-19-quarterly-consultation-paper-no-9.

[150] Wymeersch, 'Enforcement of Corporate Governance Codes' 1.

[151] Hilton, 'Grudging Acquiescence' 23.

[152] See Public Governance Flanders, Regulatory Management, 'Characteristics of Good Regulation' at www.governance-flanders.be See also LL Fuller, *The Morality of Law* revised edition (New Haven, Yale University Press 1969) arguing that valid legal rules must meet eight minimal conditions: they must be (1) sufficiently general, (2) publicly promulgated, (3) prospective, (4) minimally clear and intelligible, (5) free of contradictions, (6) relatively constant, so that they don't continuously change from day to day, (7) possible to obey, and (8) administered in a way that does not wildly diverge from their obvious or apparent meaning (Fuller, *The Morality of Law* 33–38).

A real improvement is more likely to come about by moving away from the dynamics and structures that have been shown to encourage greed and short-termism. While those same structures remain, any Code amendments are likely only to be tinkering around the edges and the same problems will keep arising. Comply or explain is also showing its age as a regulatory approach. More fundamentally, as the neoliberal order and capitalism is coming under greater scrutiny and suspicion,[153] and as globalisation introduces further challenges, it is clear that we need to think more creatively about corporate governance. As Starbuck remarks,

> More education, telework, increasing diversity, globalisation, and technological change are making traditional hierarchies less useful and making interorganisational networks more useful. This implies that alliances and interorganizational networks will replace many organizations. ... As alliances and networks replace corporations, formal corporate governance will become less relevant for actual behaviors.[154]

One such aspect which may lead to significant change and opportunities for structural change and improvement is that of the developments in artificial intelligence. This has the potential for real productivity improvements, more effective real-time compliance and risk mitigation. This technological revolution is also likely to bring with it new laws, social and political norms, and also new questions relating to ethics and regulation.[155] This may be the turning point we have been waiting for.

[153] See eg W Streeck, 'How Will Capitalism End?' (2014) *New Left Review* 87.

[154] WH Starbuck, 'Why Corporate Governance Deserves Serious and Creative Thought' (2014) 28 *The Academy of Management Perspectives* 15, 19.

[155] See eg MIT Media Lab, Artificial Intelligence and Governance Symposium (28 April 2016).

13

The Right of Withdrawal in Consumer Contracts: From the Perspective of Legal Certainty

YO TERAKAWA*

INTRODUCTION

PACTA SUNT SERVANDA is one of the fundamental principles of liberal systems of private law. However, the right of withdrawal grants consumers an option, which is conditioned on specific factual situations surrounding the contract formation or granted with respect to specific contract types. Thus, in certain situations, the consumer is entitled to withdraw from a contract within a specified period for whatever reason he or she likes, or without any reason at all.[1] In that sense, the principle of *pacta sunt servanda* is not carried through without exception. Thus, the right of withdrawal from a consumer contract has been granted in the interest of consumer protection.[2]

In this chapter, I would like to focus on the consumer's right of withdrawal especially in the context of distance selling in Japan and Germany. The reason for this is that such a comparative legal study of this right with regard to this specific type of contract will make clear the characteristic differences of the relevant legislation in each of these national laws. To put it briefly, while there are some mandatory rules about the consumer's right of withdrawal in distance selling in Germany, there are no rules about it in distance selling in Japan. However, in the commercial practice in Japan,

* The author wishes to express appreciation for the grant-in-aid for scientific research of the Japan Society for the Promotion of Science (JSPS.KAKENHI, no.15K03232). The author is also extremely grateful to Professor Antonios Karaiskos (Kyoto University) for his friendship and assistance with English translations at the time this contribution was taking shape.

[1] H Eidenmüller, 'Why Withdrawal Rights?' (2011) 7 *European Review of Contract Law* 1, 2.

[2] R Zimmermann, *The Law of Obligations: Roman Foundations of the Civilian Tradition* (Oxford, Oxford University Press, 1996) 578–79.

optional agreements with traders regarding the right to return goods play an important part. The style of legislation about the right of withdrawal in distance selling can be classified into two categories: the 'cooling-off system' and the 'goods-return system'.

The present study is undertaken in order to establish whether the right of withdrawal in distance selling could be codified also in Japan and replace the right to return goods. In doing so, I would like to examine the role of legal certainty in this context.

This chapter is constructed in three parts. The first section offers a brief introduction to the right of withdrawal in Japan, reviewing some of the short history of this right. At the same time, I will make a brief explanation of the current state in Europe, especially in Germany, to highlight some conceptual differences in approaches. In the next section, the issue of how the right of withdrawal in distance selling should be regulated will be considered. In doing so, the practical consequences of this two-tiered mechanism will be discussed, and I will try to indicate possible answers from the viewpoint of legal certainty. To facilitate this, I will further give a brief outline of legal certainty in the context of Japanese private law. The final section makes a brief summary and offers some suggestions for the way the right of withdrawal in distance selling might be re-organised.

CURRENT STATE OF THE RIGHT OF WITHDRAWAL IN DISTANCE SELLING

Japanese Law

The Cooling-off System in Japan

At present the right to withdraw from consumer contracts in Japan is generally also referred to as the right of 'cooling-off'. The operation of this right is not regulated by the Japanese Civil Code (*Mimpō*),[3] but was introduced by the enactment of the Installment Sales Act, a civil special law, in 1972.[4] At that time, this right could be exercised within four days from the date on which the consumer received the documents set forth in the Act.

[3] As to the Japanese Civil Code and recent developments regarding its reform, S Wrbka, 'Comments on Legal Certainty from the Perspective of European, Austrian and Japanese Private Law' in M Fenwick and S Wrbka (eds), *Legal Certainty in a Contemporary Context: Private and Criminal Law Perspectives* (Singapore, Springer, 2016) 21.

[4] The wording 'withdrawal of an offer' or 'cancellation of a contract' is used in the text of the law (eg SCTA, Art 58-6(1)(i)). However, the phrase 'cooling-off' has been traditionally used in general when referring to such rules. As to this discussion, see Y Yamamoto, 'Shōhisha-tekkai-ken wo meguru Hō to Seisaku' [Law and Politics about the consumer's right of withdrawal] (2012) 16 *Gendai Shōhi-sha-hō* 4, 8. See also S Kawakami, "Kūringu-ofu' ni tsuite no ichi-kōsatsu' [Study on cooling-off] (1996) 60 *Hōgaku* 1178, 1178ff.

Consequently, the consumer has the opportunity to consider, during a fixed period, even after the conclusion of the contract. The reason for the introduction of such a right was that mainly in installment sales at that time, many consumers had suffered damage by off-premises sales characterised by the element of surprise.[5]

In 1976, the provisions regarding this right were inserted in the Act on Door-to-Door Sales. The content of this Act was later expanded through several amendments. For example, in 1984, the withdrawal period prescribed in the Act was extended from four days to seven days, and in 1988, this period was further extended to eight days. In 2000, the name of the Act was changed to the Act on Specified Commercial Transactions (*Tokutei-Shō-Torihiki-Hō*; hereinafter referred to as SCTA).[6] Currently, off-premises sales are regulated by the SCTA. Subsequently, similar concepts have been adopted in the Act with respect to telemarketing sales and some contracts for the provision of services etc.[7]

However, at the moment, no cooling-off system has been introduced for distance selling.[8] In general, it is understood that distance contracts are contracts concluded over distance communication media, such as telephone, telefax, email or the internet.[9] As to the definition of distance selling, SCTA, Article 2(2) provides that it means

> the sale of goods […] for which the seller […] has received an offer for a sales contract […] by postal mail or by any other means specified by ordinance of the competent ministry […], and that does not fall under the category of Telemarketing Sales.[10]

As mentioned above, there are no provisions in the SCTA about cooling-off systems for this type of contract. The reason for this is that it has been thought that the introduction of a mandatory right of withdrawal, in distance selling as well as in off-premises sales, could impose an excessive burden on the trader who has lawfully performed his/her obligations.[11]

[5] C Mura 'Shōhisha-tekkai-ken wo meguru Nihon-Hōsei no Genjō' [Status quo about the consumer's right of withdrawal in Japan] (2012) 16 *Gendai Shōhi-sha-hō* 13, 13. See also M Dernauer, 'Verbraucherschutz' in H Baum and M Bälz (eds), *Handbuch Japanisches Handels- und Wirtschaftsrecht* (Cologne, Carl Heymanns Verlag, 2011) 575–80.

[6] Act no 57 of 4 June 1976. The English text can be found at www.japaneselawtranslation.go.jp. As to the SCTA, see also K Nakata, 'Widerrufsrechte im japanischen Zivilrecht' in K Riesenhuber and Y Nishitani (eds), *Wandlungen oder Erosion der Privatautonomie? Deutsch-japansiche Perspektiven des Vertragsrechts* (Berlin, De Gruyter Recht, 2007) 176ff.

[7] Eg Insurance Business Act, Art 309, Real Estate Brokerage Act, Art 37-2.

[8] SCTA, Arts 11–15-2 ('Mail Order Sales').

[9] G Rühl, 'Distance Contracts' in J Basedow, KJ Hopt and R Zimmermann (eds), *The Max Planck Encyclopedia of European Private Law Vol 1* (Oxford, Oxford University Press, 2012) 489, and in German 'Fernabsatzverträge' in J Basedow, KJ Hopt and R Zimmermann (eds), *Handwörterbuch des Europäischen Privatrechts Vol I* (Tübingen, Mohr Siebeck, 2009) 588.

[10] In the STCA, the term 'Mail Order Sales' is used when referring to distance selling.

[11] M Matsuoka 'Shōhisha-tekkai-ken to Mimpō-hōri' [The consumer's right of withdrawal and civil theory] (2014) 16 *Gendai Shōhi-sha-hō* 54, 62. See also Shōhi-sha Chō

In such contracts, another system is adopted in Japan instead of the above-mentioned cooling-off system. With the reform of the SCTA in 2008, if the seller has not indicated any special provisions on withdrawal or cancellation in its advertisement, the consumer can return goods during a period of up to eight days from the date on which the goods have been delivered to him/her (SCTA, Article 15-2).[12] A consumer can enforce the right to return goods in such cases.

Although these two mechanisms might look similar at first sight, the instruments with respect to off-premises sales and distance selling are not coherent. Indeed, the above text of the SCTA creates the impression that there exists a right of withdrawal in distance selling. However, a more precise reading shows that the right indicated by these provisions is not a right of withdrawal, but a right to return goods. This is the reason why in commercial practice it is understood that a different method was introduced when distance selling started to be regulated and is currently widespread. This approach is commonly known as the goods-return system.

The Goods-return System in Distance Selling

Distance selling in Japan was established during the Meiji era (which lasted from 1868 to 1912), when the post and railway networks developed nationwide, and it is said to have started from seed sales for farmers. Then, around 1980, distance selling for consumers by department stores and publishers also began, mail order catalogues became highly popular in recent years, and distance selling via the internet as well as internet auctions, etc, have been born as a new form of transaction.[13]

According to a study by the National Consumer Affairs Centre of Japan (hereinafter referred to as NCAC), distance selling queries accounted for 34.9 per cent of the total number of consultations in 2015 at government and local consumer centres located throughout Japan.[14] Nevertheless, as of today, no right of withdrawal has yet been implemented in relation to distance selling.

Torihiki-Taisaku-ka and Keizai-Sangyō-shō Shōmu-Ryutū-Hoan-Gurūpu Shōhi-Keizai-Kikaku-Shitsu (eds), *Tokutei-Shōtorihiki ni kansuru Hōritsu no Kaisetsu Heisei 24-nen-ban* [*Commentary on the Act on Specified Commercial Transactions*] (Tokyo, Shōji Houmu, 2014) 137ff.

[12] As to SCTA, Article 15-2, see also M Goto, M Saito and S Ikemoto, *Jōkai Shōhi-sha-Sanpō* [Commentary on the Cosumer Contract Act, the Act on Specified Commercial Transactions and the Installment Sales Act] (Tokyo, Koubundō, 2015) 542–61.

[13] T Mamba, 'Tsuushin-Hanbai ni okeru Henpin-Seido no Riyou-Jittai to Kadai' [Status quo and future plans of the goods-return system in distance selling] (2012) 16 *Gendai Shōhi-sha-hō* 46ff.

[14] NCAC is established as an incorporated administrative agency. It works as a core consumer advocate organisation in accordance with the Basic Consumer Act. Moreover, it handles consumer issues in collaboration with the government and local consumer centres located throughout Japan. See www.kokusen.go.jp/ncac_index_e.html.

However, goods traders engaged in distance selling have voluntarily stipulated terms and conditions that allow for a goods-return system instead of a right of withdrawal. In 1994, the Japan Direct Marketing Association (hereinafter referred to as JADMA) established, in its guidelines entitled 'Communication Sales Ethics Guidelines Implementation Standards', provisions according to which traders will accept the return of goods and indicated the conditions and the period for such return as well as its costs.[15] The number of traders that have joined JADMA amounts to around 70 per cent of domestic sales by distance selling. It is thus possible to say that the goods-return system has become generalised in Japan.[16] In many cases traders follow the above-mentioned recommendations of the guidelines. However, my impression is that the absence of a binding effect can cause uncertainty and a lack of transparency in consumer contracts.

In 2008, the Japanese legislator (*Keizai-Sangyō-shō*; Ministry of Economy, Trade and Industry at that time)[17] established provisions only about the obligation to indicate the presence or absence of a goods-return system when advertising (SCTA, Article 11(iv)). In addition, regarding distance selling, consumers have the right to return goods as set out in the law (SCTA, Article 15-2). As a result, the person who made the offer or the purchaser may withdraw his/her offer for a sales contract or cancel the sales contract during an eight-day period.

However, the Japanese legislator is not convinced that the surprise element is an integral constituent of transactions concluded via distance selling, namely, that such transactions are subject to any surprise. This attitude leads to more respect for private autonomy. Further, it is said that it would be inappropriate to accept a unilateral right to terminate a contract when consumers positively participate in the transaction, because it would impose an excessive burden on traders who lawfully fulfil their obligations.[18] In general, according to SCTA, Article 15-2, consumers have the right to return goods. However, exceptionally, if the trader indicates special provisions on the right to return goods when advertising, such rights can be excluded (SCTA, Article 15-2(1)).[19]

[15] www.jadma.org/abouts/glsummary/.

[16] S Maruyama, *Shōkai Tokutei- Shōtorihikihō no Riron to Jitsumu* 3rd edn [*Theory and Practice about the Act on Specified Commercial Transactions*] (Tokyo, Minjihō Kenkyu-kai, 2014) 311 n 16.

[17] After the establishment of *Shōhisha-chō* [the Consumer Affairs Agency] in 2009, this organisation is in charge of the plan drafting, and *Keizai-Sangyō-shō* [the Ministry of Economy, Trade and Industry] is in charge of authorisation of the traders, instructions to JADMA etc.

[18] J Ukon, 'Henpin-Seido no Arikata' [The structure of the goods-return system] (2016) 30 *Gendai Shōhi-sha-hō* 25, 26.

[19] Shōhi-sha Chō Torihiki-Taisaku-ka and Keizai-Sangyō-shō Shōmu-Ryutū-Hoan-Gurūpu Shōhi-Keizai-Kikaku-Shitsu (eds), *Tokutei-Shōtorihiki ni kansuru Hōritsu no Kaisetsu Heisei 24-nen-ban* 135–38.

To summarise, first, if there are any special provisions on the goods-return system in the trader's advertisement, the right to return goods depends on the content of those provisions; second, if there are no special provisions on the goods-return system in the trader's advertisement, the right to return goods is regulated by SCTA, Article 15-2.

Differences between the Cooling-off System and the Goods-return System

What seems to be very peculiar under the existing provisions of the STCA is the fact that 'withdrawal/cancellation' is regulated in both the cooling-off system (SCTA, Article 9) and the goods-return system (SCTA, Article 15-2). Are there in fact any differences regarding the right of withdrawal between off-premises sales (the right to withdrawal from the contract) and distance selling (right to return goods)?

In comparison with the cooling-off system in off-premises sales, the differences are as follows. First, mandatory rules versus default rule: while the provisions of off-premises sales etc are unilateral mandatory rules, the provisions of distance selling are default rules. Thus, the problem seems to lie in the fact that the Japanese legislator should select the better rule for distance selling. Second, the beginning of the withdrawal period: in case of off-premises sales etc, the period starts from the date on which the documents of the contract were handed over to the consumer. On the other hand, in case of distance selling, such period starts from the date on which the goods were handed over to him/her. Third, the issue of the costs required for taking back or returning any goods already delivered: in off-premises sales etc, the traders bear those costs, but in distance selling, it is the consumer who bears such costs. Further, in case of off-premises sales etc, there are some conditions about documents of withdrawal, whereas in distance selling there are no such conditions.[20]

Justification of the Right of Withdrawal

In Japan, there has also been much discussion about the justification of the right of withdrawal. The question that remains is whether the goods-return system is really useful to consumers. Some authors suggest that a mandatory right of withdrawal could be more useful than the goods-return system, and emphasise the necessity to introduce this right in distance selling too. For example, Kondo strongly recommends the introduction of a right of withdrawal also in distance selling because of the insufficiency of information about the goods and the lack of ability to take goods in one's hand

[20] See Ukon, 'Henpin-Seido no Arikata' 27ff.

before their delivery.[21] Further, in a more recent article, Ukon claims that there is room to examine the introduction of a cooling-off system in order to find a uniform standard for the right of return of goods, because the invalidity of agreements about the return-goods system with traders often causes difficult problems.[22] According to this opinion, the introduction of a right of withdrawal into the law is to be recommended.

Yamamoto holds a different view, derived from a viewpoint of law and economics. He positively evaluates the current state of self-regulation, namely the goods-return system by traders, and notes that it is not necessary to introduce a right of withdrawal in distance selling.[23] According to this opinion, the relationship between consumers and traders functions efficiently.

As is clear from the above, little consensus has been reached concerning the justification of the right of withdrawal. It is thus important to explain more clearly why consumers need to be granted the right to withdraw from distance selling during a certain period, without any reason at all.

German Law

Implementation of the Consumer Rights Directive

European and national legislators have implemented the right of withdrawal in distance selling. With the recent implementation of the Consumer Rights Directive 2011,[24] consumer protection is expected to be strengthened. While the right to withdrawal under off-premises sales has its parallels to the European system, the goods-return system of distance selling looks very different.

In Germany,[25] distance selling was regulated for the first time regulated in 2000, by the Act on distance selling that implemented the Distance Contracts Directive.[26] This Act was then codified into the German Civil

[21] M Kondo, Shōhisha-torihiki-ruikei to Kūringu-ofu Ken [Types of consumer transactions and the right of cooling-off] (1994) 8 *Nihon-Fukushi-Daigaku-Keizai-Ronshū* 21, 37 and 40.

[22] Ukon, 'Henpin-Seido no Arikata' 34.

[23] Y Yamamoto, 'Shōhisha-tekkai-ken no Seitouka-konkyo' [Reason justifying the consumer's right of withdrawal] (2012) 16 *Gendai Shōhi-sha-hō* 77, 93.

[24] Directive 2011/83/EU, [2011] OJ L304/64.

[25] See also Z Dönmez, *Das Widerrufsrecht bei Fernabsatzverträgen Online-Verträge im türkischen und deutschen Recht* (Frankfurt am Main, Peter Lang, 2015) 92–93. As to the developments at a European level, see P Mankowski, 'Right of Withdrawal' in J Basedow and KJ Hopt and R Zimmermann (eds), *The Max Planck Encyclopedia of European Private Law, Vol 2* (Oxford, Oxford University Press, 2012) 489; also in German, P Mankowski, 'Widerrufsrecht' in J Basedow and KJ Hopt and R Zimmermann (eds), *Handwörterbuch des Europäischen Privatrechts, Vol II* (Tübingen, Mohr Siebeck, 2012) 1791.

[26] Directive 97/7/EC, [1997] OJ L144/19.

Code (*Bürgerliches Gesetzbuch*)[27] through an amendment (*Schuldrechts-modernisierung*) on 1 January 2002. Moreover, Articles 312b to 312d of the German Civil Code were modified in order to implement the Financial Services Directive,[28] and the E-commerce Directive,[29] Articles 10 and 11 were implemented in Article 312e of the Code.

Before the implementation of the Consumer Rights Directive the German legislation had a much broader scope of application than was originally foreseen at a European level, although it also caused a complex legal technique that as a statutory right of withdrawal was limited to specific contractual situations concerning consumers or to specific types of contract. It could be particularly seen when the scope of application for individual rights of withdrawal was defined in more detail. Namely, even in situations in which the consumer could expect to be granted a right of withdrawal, there might habe been exceptions in place that exclude this right, for example, due to the nature of the goods purchased.[30] However, this situation changed a little. In particular, the implementation of the Consumer Rights Directive in the German Civil Code in 2014 integrated the provisions about off-premises sales and distance selling (as new Article 312g(1)). As to the definition of distance contracts, Article 312c(1) of the Code now provides as follows:

> Distance contracts are contracts for which the trader, or a person acting in the trader's name or on his behalf, and the consumer exclusively avail themselves of means of distance communication in negotiating and concluding the contract, except where the conclusion of the contract does not take place in the context of a sales or service-provision scheme organised for distance sales.[31]

Further, Article 312g now provides that in the case of off-premises contracts and distance contracts, the consumer has a right of withdrawal pursuant to Article 355 of the German Civil Code.

There are more precise provisions about the right of withdrawal in Article 355 of the Code. The withdrawal period is 14 days (Article 355(2)). The date when the withdrawal period begins in distance selling cases, is defined in Article 356(2)1(a) as follows: 'The withdrawal period commences in the case of a sale of consumer goods [...] has received the goods'.

[27] The English text can be found at www.gesetze-im-internet.de/englisch_bgb/index.html.

[28] Directive 2002/65/EC, [2002] OJ L271/16.

[29] Directive 2000/31/EC, [2000] OJ L178/1.

[30] R Schulze and J Morgan, 'The Right of Withdrawal' in G Dannemann and S Vogenauer (eds), *The Common European Sales Law in Context* (Oxford, Oxford University Press, 2013) 301 and 304–306.

[31] However, it is necessary to be careful about the fact that there are many exceptions regarding application (eg contracts relating to the construction of new buildings or to the substantial conversion of existing buildings, treatment contracts and contracts concluded for the use of one single connection by telephone, internet or fax established by a consumer etc) as set out in the German Civil Code, Art 312(2).

Hence, the right of withdrawal allows consumers to avoid contractual obligations simply because they have changed their mind, or, for example, because more attractive offers became available.[32] In a decision which was published before the implementation of the Consumer Rights Directive, the German Supreme Court (*Bundesgerichtshof*) held that: (1) it is a matter for the consumer's free will whether and for what reasons he or she makes use of the right of withdrawal in distance selling; and (2) the exclusion of the right of withdrawal due to the abuse of rights or the unlawful exercise of rights (German Civil Code, Article 242) can only be considered exceptionally from the viewpoint of the particular consideration for traders, for example, in the case of any malicious behaviour by consumers. Consequently, the German Supreme Court held that a consumer who bought two mattresses, trusting a 'lowest price guarantee', and then bought the same mattresses elsewhere at lower prices, could lawfully exercise his/her right of withdrawal regarding the first purchase, and that such an exercise is not an abuse of the right.[33]

Justification of the Right of Withdrawal

The reason justifying the introduction of a right of withdrawal is the missing opportunity to compare quality and price before the conclusion of the contract.[34] Recital 37 of the Consumer Rights Directive notes as follows:

> Since in the case of distance sales, the consumer is not able to see the goods before concluding the contract, he should have a right of withdrawal. For the same reason, the consumer should be allowed to test and inspect the goods he has bought to the extent necessary to establish the nature, characteristics and the functioning of the goods.

This idea is based on Recital 14 of Directive 97/7/EC.[35]

It is interesting that the discussion here is different from the one in Japanese law.[36] There is traditionally some criticism of the aims of the European legislator, as expressed for example in the Consumer Rights Directive, especially to the mandatory rules on distance selling. For example, Rühl points out that it is not certain whether the right of withdrawal improves the

[32] Eidenmüller, 'Why Withdrawal Rights?' 4.

[33] BGH, Urteil v.16.3.2016—VIII ZR 146/15. See also P Mankowski, 'Verbraucherschützendes Widerrufsrecht und Rechtsmissbrauch Zugleich Besprechung von BGH, Urteil v. 16.3.2016—VIII ZR 146/15' (2016) 71 *Juristenzeitung* 787.

[34] HW Micklitz, 'An Optional Law on Off-premises, Distance Sales and Unfair Terms for European Business and Consumers?' (2012) *EUI Working Papers in Law* 48. See also M Schwab 'Widerrufsrechte im deutschen und europäischen Verbraucherschutzrecht' in K Riesenhuber and Y Nishitani (eds), *Wandlungen oder Erosion der Privatautonomie? Deutsch-japansiche Perspektiven des Vertragsrechs* (Berlin, De Gruyter Recht, 2007) 150ff.

[35] Directive 97/7/EC, [1997] OJ L144/19.

[36] As to the justification of the right of withdrawal especially in distance selling in German law, see also Schäfer (2007) 193ff.

efficiency of distance contracts or secures the functionality of the distance contracts market. The reason for this is that the right of withdrawal creates at least two problems: (1) the contract becomes more expensive due to time delays and an increase in legal uncertainty; (2) practically worse, this right entails the risk of opportunistic consumer behaviour.[37]

Moreover, Wagner notes that the right of withdrawal should not be mandatory, but rather functions as a default solution from which the parties should be allowed to derogate if they wish to do so.[38] Similarly, Eidenmüller criticises the tendency towards a mandatory right of withdrawal in distance selling at the European level. He points out that the right of withdrawal should only be granted if, in a particular case setting, its benefits clearly outweigh its costs.[39] And then, he classifies three situations which may justify granting the right of withdrawal: information asymmetries, exogenously distorted preferences of the consumer and endogenously distorted preferences. After analysing this right, he claims the necessity for the introduction of an optional right of withdrawal. This means that, through such an optional right, consumers will be able to choose a contract either with the right of withdrawal or without it.[40]

On the contrary, Zöchling-Jud disagrees with this approach and points out that, although it is true that the introduction of the mandatory right of withdrawal leads to an increase in costs for consumers, it is doubtful whether the abolition of this right would be passed on to consumers in the form of a cost reduction. She notes that the existence of the right of withdrawal could effectively reduce some psychological barriers of consumers to the conclusion of distance contracts, which would ultimately also serve traders.[41]

Further, Höhne notes that, from the viewpoint of behavioural economics, the optional right of withdrawal could provide further incentives for showrooming, whereby a consumer examines goods in store, but then purchases the same goods online from home. As a result, he disagrees with the optional right of withdrawal.[42]

[37] Rühl, 'Distance Contracts' 491; see also Rühl 'Fernabsatzverträge' 591.

[38] G Wagner, 'Mandatory Contract Law: Functions and Principles in light of the Proposal for a Directive on Consumer Rights' (2010) 3 *Erasmus Law Review* 47, 60.

[39] Eidenmüller, 'Why Withdrawal Rights?' 2. For details, see H Eidenmüller, 'Widerrufsrechte' in H Eidenmüller et al (eds), *Revision des Verbraucher-acquis* (Tübingen, Mohr Siebeck, 2011) 126 and 163.

[40] For details, see Eidenmüller, 'Why Withdrawal Rights?' and Eidenmüller, 'Widerrufsrechte'. See also G Wagner, 'Zwingendes Vertragsrecht' in Eidenmüller et al (eds), *Revision des Verbraucher-acquis* 1, 22ff and 27ff; N Jansen, 'Revision des Verbraucher-Acquis?' (2012) *Zentrum für Europäisches Wirtschaftsrecht Vorträge und Berichte* 40–42.

[41] B Zöchling-Jud, 'Acquis-Revision, Common European Sales Law und Verbraucherrechterichtlinie' (2012) 212 *Archiv für die civilistische Praxis* 563ff.

[42] M Höhne, *Das Widerrufsrecht bei Kaufverträgen im Spannungsverhältnis von Opportunismus und Effektivität* (Tübingen, Mohr Siebeck, 2016) 81–85 and 252.

Differences between German Law and Japanese Law

As mentioned above, there are some differences between German law and Japanese law on the right of withdrawal in distance selling. More specifically, the methods of regulation for the right of withdrawal can be classified into two categories.

First, while the provisions about the right of withdrawal in German law are unilateral mandatory rules, namely, advantageous to the consumers, and a burden on the traders, in Japanese law (distance selling), such provisions are default rules. Second, there is also a difference in the understanding of the right of withdrawal. In German law, in view of the characteristics of the transaction types, the right to ensure fair trade is granted for the consumer, with the burden on the traders. In Japanese law, in order to protect consumers who might be subject to unjust influence at the time of the conclusion of the contract, consumers are given some time to calm down and rethink (ie the 'cooling off' provisions).[43]

The following section will explain that these differences occur from the perspective of legal certainty.

THE SUBSTANTIVE ROLE OF LEGAL CERTAINTY

Meaning of Legal Certainty in General

There are many meanings of legal certainty. However, an overview of the relevant studies could clarify the notion to some extent. For example, Canaris points out that legal certainty could embody any of the following concepts: legal firmness and predictability, legislative and judicial stability and continuity and practicability of the application of law.[44] According to Bydlinski, legal certainty is differentiated as follows: legal clarity, legal stability, legal accessibility, legal peace and legal enforcement.[45] Further, Hage notes that legal certainty in the context of positive law has at least three aspects: (1) certainty about the content of the law; (2) certainty that the law will be enforced; and (3) certainty that the law will be applied consistently.[46]

In a more recent article, Wrbka points out that legal certainty in the context of private law can be classified into two groups: (1) legal clarification,

[43] Ukon, 'Henpin-Seido no Arikata' 31ff.

[44] CW Canaris, *Systemdenken und Systembegriff in der Jurisprudenz* (Berlin, Duncker & Humbolt, 1969) 17. See also Wrbka, 'Comments on Legal Certainty' 11.

[45] F Bydlinski, *Fundamentale Rechtsgrundsätze* (Vienna, Springer, 1988) 293. See also Wrbka, 'Comments on Legal Certainty' 11.

[46] J Hage, 'Foundations' in J Hage and B Akkermans (eds), *Introduction to Law* (Heidelberg, Springer, 2014) 5.

which means that the focus can be put on legal clarity, stability, predictability or transparency; and (2) legal rationalisation, which means that legal certainty can be understood in a more 'value-oriented justice' way in connection with legal accessibility, legal enforcement and the practicability of the application of law.[47]

In short, it should be noted that different meanings of legal certainty can be used in each relevant field. Accordingly, it is important to observe which kind of meaning should function, in order to justify legal certainty in the context of the right of withdrawal in distance selling.

Legal Certainty and Japanese Private Law

Japanese private law is largely influenced by European civil codes, most notably by the French Civil Code and the German Civil Code, the *Bürgerliches Gesetzbuch*. With Japan's opening to the West in the second part of the nineteenth century, Japanese jurisprudence increased its efforts in modernising the domestic legal system. With the exception of the family and succession law parts, the first modern Japanese Civil Code incorporated many concepts developed in Europe.

Nevertheless, the Japanese Civil Code was comparatively short. The number of provisions it contained was roughly only half of those of the French and German models.[48] Several reasons have been identified to explain this. Uchida, for example, uses three main arguments: first, according to him, Japan felt under pressure to come up with a modern private law framework to become competitive with western nations; second, Japanese legal academics, however, widely believed that western concepts, in particular advanced family and succession law regulations, were incompatible with Japanese traditions; third, and from a legal certainty perspective (understood as enhancing the overall understandability and usability of Japanese private law) most notably, Japan wanted to retain a high degree of flexibility to respond to possible developments in various sectors, including industry, politics and society.[49] The shortage of provisions was not the only significant, structural difference. Most provisions of the Japanese Civil Code are characterised by a remarkable briefness that—with the exception of some outliers such as the complex system of sectoral claim prescriptions (Japanese Civil Code, Article 166ff)—does not distinguish between different possible scenarios that might occur in practice. In addition, the Code employed vague language that left ample room for interpretation.

[47] Wrbka, 'Comments on Legal Certainty' 13.

[48] See also Wrbka, 'Comments on Legal Certainty' 21ff.

[49] T Uchida, 'Contract Law Reform in Japan and the UNIDROIT Principles' (2011) 16 *Uniform Law Review* 705, 707.

This mixture of a low number of provisions in combination with the substantive briefness and linguistic vagueness of the Japanese Civil Code did not go uncontested. Over the years, criticism against this flexible framework has arisen. Academic research groups began to work on alternative solutions that all aimed at a modernisation process of the Code. These initiatives were launched in the latter part of the twentieth century, some decades after the—to date—only major reform of the Code, ie the revision of the patriarchal family and succession law parts after World War II. Eventually the attempt to 'complete', refresh and align the Japanese Civil Code with case law and developments by legal academia resulted in an ambitious project: the plan to critically evaluate and possibly revise Book III, the Law of Obligations. Comments on this project can be found elsewhere in the present book.[50]

The overall aim of the initiatives can be summarised as the wish to enhance legal clarity and the usability of Japanese private law. The Japanese Civil Code, case law and further developments by legal academia will be brought in line. This refers not only to domestic developments, but additionally relates to advancements in the West.

Efforts to modernise domestic private law legislation in combination with attempts to consider legal certainty in this respect did not stop at the Japanese Civil Code, but went further. The right of withdrawal in consumer contracts, ie the key topic of the present contribution, is a good example of this. Being partially regulated in a separate law, the SCTA, the Japanese right of withdrawal in consumer contracts can—as explained further above—be considered as statutorily incomplete. From a legal certainty perspective, this clearly has to be regretted. The following paragraphs add some comments in this regard.

The Right of Withdrawal in Distance Selling in Japan from the Perspective of Legal Certainty

As mentioned above, the most striking characteristic of the goods-return system is its lack of mandatoriness. Namely, while the provisions about the right of withdrawal in German law are unilateral mandatory rules, in Japanese law, provisions about distance selling are flexible default rules.

In Japan, the goods-return system is well known in the praxis. The Japanese legislator has implemented, subsidiarily, the right to return goods in the SCTA. In many cases, consumers who conclude a contract in distance selling are—due to confusing statutory law and a lack of both transparency and mandatory information supposedly provided by the traders—not aware of the existence of the goods-return system. Indeed, JADMA recommends that

[50] See ch 6.

traders clearly and legibly indicate the existence of special provisions on the right to return goods, in order that the consumers can easily understand the actual content of the agreements with traders. In that sense, self-regulation contributes to flexibility by arranging a certain balance between consumers and traders. However, this recommendation is not binding. Most traders follow it, but it is not certain whether this regulation regarding such commercial practices will ensure the protection of consumers, especially 'vulnerable' consumers such as elderly people.

Even if a consumer finds and reads the special provisions about the goods-return system in the trader's advertising, could he/she readily understand the contents of it? In this respect, it is not so easy for the consumer, who has bought the goods on impulse via the internet due to inviting terms and conditions such as a bargain price, to find out the contents of those special provisions. From the viewpoint of the transparency, the risk undertaken by the consumer when concluding a contract is much larger than that of the trader.

It is indeed not easy to define the concept of legal certainty. However, as mentioned above, several authors have attempted to define its meaning in connection with their research fields. At least, legal predictability and stability could be perceived as being core elements of any concept of legal certainty.

In whose interest is legal certainty in this case? From the consumer's point of view, he/she could conclude the contract at his/her ease. From the trader's point of view, it would be very useful to predict future costs by regulating uniformly the right of withdrawal. If there are any difficulties with consumers, traders could deal effectively and lawfully with them. That results in building a fair market. It should be noted that it is essential to increase trust in a fair market, even in distance selling. Thus, it seems natural to conclude that the right of withdrawal in distance selling should be codified, even if that means a mandatory rule. And then, the Japanese legislator codifying this right should play a law-making role from the perspective of legal certainty.

CONCLUSION

As mentioned above, the Japanese legislator is not convinced that the surprise element is an integral component of transactions concluded via distance selling. Thus, there are no provisions about the right of withdrawal in distance selling. Taking a look at findings, discussions and legislative developments in the West, in particular in the EU, this would appear to be problematic.

The main findings of this chapter are as follows: first, it is not sufficient to regulate only the right to return goods in distance selling in the SCTA; second, the consumer would suffer loss due to the lack of information about the right to return goods; finally, making a fair market requires the regulation of the right of withdrawal even in distance selling. Then, it is clear from viewpoint of legal certainty that these goals should be achieved by the legislator. A further study of *how* the legislator could effectively codify the right of withdrawal more comprehensively and, in particular from the viewpoint of enhanced legal certainty, effectively would need to be conducted separately.

14

Advertising Regulation in Japan: Legal Certainty and its Relation to Consumer Law

KUNIHIRO NAKATA

INTRODUCTION

Advertising and Legal Certainty

IN JAPAN, THE term legal certainty is often understood as requiring that the content of a provision is clear. Further, legal certainty also includes the issue of realisation and enforcement of the existing law, from the viewpoint of its relation to the general legal order.

The present chapter provides a case study of how fragmented regulation of a particular field of law can create challenges for regulators from the perspective of legal certainty. This is a practically relevant issue for topics such as advertising that cut across various fields of business. The present study will show us how this can lead to complexity and uncertainty.

In particular, I would like to examine the state of advertising law in Japan, by focusing on the following two aspects: (1) legal certainty in the clarity of the content of the provisions, namely an ex ante regulation of advertising; (2) legal certainty in the realisation of the purposes aimed at by the law, namely an ex post regulation of advertising and the remedies offered in relation to this.[1]

The Meaning of Advertising

Advertising is a means used by advertisers to appeal to prospective customers, and has an important meaning for advertisers as a marketing promotion

[1] In relation to the topic of this paper, see K Nakata, 'Gendaihogakukenkyu kara mita Kokokukisei' [Advertisement Regulation seen from the Viewpoint of Modern Law Theory] in Y Mizuno et al (eds), *Kokoku Komyunikeshon Kenkyu Handobukku* [*Advertisement Communication Research Handbook*] (Tokyo, Yuhikaku, 2015) 39 et seq.

activity. By advertising, businesses aim at selling their products or services, and provide information trying to induce prospective customers to choose their products or services.

On the other hand, advertising is also important for consumers, namely prospective customers, as an information resource when selecting and considering the purchase of products or services. It is well known that, in capitalist societies, such information is a prerequisite for achieving an appropriate distribution of resources.

In modern society, there have been many unpleasant incidents related to advertising and representation,[2] such as food fraud, including misrepresentation and representation of effects, extravagant advertisements etc. A characteristic of such incidents is that so-called typical consumer damage, namely a large number of small amounts of damage, occurs. Currently, the debate focuses on the prevention and remedy of such damage.

Advertising and Civil Law Remedies

Providing redress to consumers who have incurred damages by believing false advertising is important. The field of civil law provides a legal structure for individual remedies for consumers.[3] From a legal point of view, when purchasing a product, consumers (ie the buyers) conclude a contract, for example a sale contract, with the businesses (ie the sellers). In most cases, consumers do so because they so believe the advertising or representations made by the business, for example representations about the effects or performance of products. The law can provide remedies to consumers, by binding the business to the contract, releasing the consumer from it, or admitting a right to damages.

[2] Regarding the distinction between advertisements and representations, there is an opinion that does not distinguish between them, and another that does. From the viewpoint of legal regulation, such distinction has no meaning, since both advertisements and representations are subject to such regulation, if there is a possibility that the information communicated by them creates a mistaken belief to consumers, or hinders their autonomous and reasonable decision making. According to the wording 'advertisement or any other Representations' of Article 2 para. 4 Act against Unjustifiable Premiums and Misleading Representations, advertisements are an example of representation. Regarding the regulation of representations with a focus on the Act against Unjustifiable Premiums and Misleading Representations, see Masaharu Minami, 'Kokoku/hyoji to shohisha' [Presenting Advertisements and Consumers] in K Nakata and N Kano (eds), *Kihon Kogi Shohishaho* [*Basic Lectures of Consumer Law*] 2nd edn (Tokyo, Nihonhyoronsha, 2016) 270.

[3] Regarding the relation between civil law and consumer law, see for example Kunihiro Nakata, 'Shohishaho to wa nanika' (What Is Consumer Law?), in Nakata and Kano, *Kihon Kogi Shohishaho* 5, as well as the bibliography cited there. Further, as a recent study on this issue, see K Nakata and N Kano, *Shohishaho no Gendaika to Shudantekikenrihogo* [*Modernisation of Consumer Law and Collective Redress*] (Tokyo, Nihonhyoronsha, 2016).

However, as already mentioned, consumer damages occurring from false representations are typically of small amounts and large numbers, and each individual consumer has little incentive to file a lawsuit. From this perspective, individual redress of consumer damage has its limitations, and in some cases the unfair profit remains with the businesses who have acted illegally. Therefore, a supplementing system for collective redress of consumer damage, through monetary penalties, disgorgement etc. is required.

As can be seen from the revision of the Act against Unjustifiable Premiums and Misleading Representations, the movement for such redress is connected to the review of the regulation on advertising and representation too.[4] Furthermore, recently, a right to demand injunctive relief and administrative surcharges has been introduced, to achieve redress of collective consumer damage.

In the following, I will explain the legal framework of advertising regulation in the first two sections.[5] I discuss self-regulation in the fourth section, and conclude with a few closing words.[6]

GENERAL REGULATION OF ADVERTISING

Introduction

General Regulation and Individual Regulations

In Japan, there is no single act comprehensively regulating advertising, for example a law entitled 'the Advertising Regulation Act'. The same situation is often found abroad, as well. The reason for this seems to be that regulation regarding advertising is scattered in various acts, and it often proves difficult to unify them. However, this does not mean that it is sufficient to

[4] See K Nakata, 'Nihon ni okeru Kokokukisei no Gaiyo' [Outline of Advertisement Regulation in Japan] (2016) *Gendaishohishaho* No. 32, 4 et seq. This article has also served as material for the presentations during the annual symposium of the Japan Consumer Law Association in 2016.

[5] As to the major articles dealing with the issue of advertising regulation, see N Mukaida, 'Shohishahogo to Kokokukisei' [Consumer Protection and Advertising Regulation] (1980) 23 *Keizaihonenpo* 131; T Matsumoto, 'Hyoji no Tekiseika' [Adjustment of Representations] (2010) 200 *Jurist* 185; N Kano, 'Nihon ni okeru Kokokukisei to Shohisha no Hogo' [Advertisement Regulation and Consumer Protection in Japan] in K Nakata and N Kano (eds), *Yoroppa Shohishaho/Kokokukiseiho no Doko to Nihonho* [*Recent Tendencies of Consumer Law and Advertising Law in Europe and Japan*] (Tokyo, Nihonhyoronsha, 2011) 213 et seq, as well as M Saito, 'Hyojikokoku to Shohisha' [Advertising Representations and Consumers] in Nihonbengoshikairengokai [Japanese Federation of Bar Associations] (ed), *Shohishahokogi* [*Lectures of Consumer Law*] 4th edn (Tokyo, Nihonhyoronsha, 2013) 246.

[6] As to the literature which presents the historical development of advertising regulation, see M Suzuki, 'Kokoku no Hotekikisei no Tenkai' [Development of Legal Regulation of Advertisement] (2004) *JARO no Ayumi* [*The History of JARO*] (special issue to mark the 30-year anniversary of the establishment of JARO, www.jaro.or.jp/jaro30/index.html).

regulate advertising in piecemeal fashion, nor that a general regulation is unnecessary. The method of regulating unfair advertising within the general framework of the prohibition of misleading advertising and unfair commercial practices is used in Europe too. In the following, I will outline these two categories of advertising regulation, namely general and individual regulation.[7] In the former, there exists a general regulation applied without distinguishing between various business categories and transaction objects. In the latter, regulation applies only to specific products, services or sales methods individually.

Regulation Methods

Before going into details about the general regulation of advertising, I would like to first explain the methods of regulation found in the acts related to advertising and representation, which will be presented later in this section.[8]

Active Regulation

Under this method, businesses bear, in principle, the obligation to follow certain standards for representations they make, as well as the obligation to make certain representations. These are called representation standards and representation obligations respectively. This is an active regulation because it requires certain acts to be performed on behalf of the businesses. Such examples are the Food Labelling Act, the Food Sanitation Act, the Act on Standardisation and Proper Quality Representation of Agricultural and Forestry Products (hereinafter referred to as the JAS Act), the Health Promotion Act, the Representation of Household Articles' Quality Act, etc.[9]

Passive Regulation

This is a regulation method whereby false or extravagant representations are prohibited. The Act against Unjustifiable Premiums and Misleading Representations, which will be explained later in this chapter, is especially important in this context, since it includes a general prohibition provision.

[7] Naoko Kano, 'Shohishakeiyakuho (1) Soron: keiyaku teiketsu kateikitei' (Consumer Contract Law (1) General Theory: Rules for the Conclusion of Contracts) in Nakata and Kano, *Kihon Kogi Shohishaho* 213.

[8] It should be noted that differences may be found in the object of regulation, the content of measures taken against breaches of such regulation etc, depending on the purpose of each individual law.

[9] For example, JAS Act, Art 19-13 stipulates the labelling standards to be observed by the manufacturer, etc, regarding the matters and method of indications about the name, materials or ingredients, method of preservation, place of origin and others.

Further, the Act on Specified Commercial Transactions, the Food Sanitation Act, the Health Promotion Act etc also include such regulations.[10]

Permissive Regulation

Under this method, regulation is performed in the form of permitting only certain representations. Such is the regulation provided by the Food Labelling Act. This Act provides that representations regarding functions or effects on health of food are permitted only with regard to the following three categories: (1) functional nutritional food, namely supplements; (2) food for specified health uses, which is abbreviated as *tokuho* in Japanese; and (3) the newly-added category of foods with function claims. No permission or approval is required for category (1), but the content of representations is stipulated in the Act. On the contrary, a permission or approval by the Consumer Agency is required for category (2), and a simple notification by the business for category (3).

Basic Consumer Act

The Basic Consumer Act is an important Act for the promotion of consumer policies, and positions the adjustment of advertisements as being one of its basic measures.[11] This Act provides some conceptual rights for consumers in Article 2, and its Article 15 provides that the promotion of consumer policies is a responsibility of the state and that '[t]he State shall take necessary measures to prepare systems relating to advertisements and other representation relating to quality, etc and to regulate false or misleading advertisements and other representation, etc,' so that consumers do not make mistakes when choosing goods or services to purchase or use. This means that the state is required to regulate false and extravagant advertising to substantially guarantee the consumers' right of choice.[12]

Anti-monopoly Act

The Antimonopoly Act is a law whose primary object, according to Article 1, is 'to promote fair and free competition'. In the following, I would like to

[10] In the past, there have been many laws regulating 'food labelling' and the relation between them has been complicated, but they have been unified into the Food Labelling Act.

[11] For an overview of the content of the Basic Consumer Act, see Kunihiro Nakata (as in n 3, above).

[12] This Act is a so-called 'basic act', which does not stipulate direct legal effects regarding the rights and obligations of businesses or consumers, and does not provide for any rights which consumers can enforce through court procedures.

present the provisions of its chapter 5 related to the prohibition of 'unfair trade practices'.

Prohibition of Unfair Trade Practices and Measures to Eliminate an Act

According to Article 19, the Act prohibits unfair trade practices on behalf of businesses, and the Fair Trade Commission may order the business to take any measure necessary to eliminate an action which is in violation of the provisions of the Act.

Among the regulations of 'unfair trade practices', of special importance in relation to advertisements is that of the 'deceptive solicitation of customers', as provided in number 8 of the so-called 'general designations'. 'Deceptive solicitation of customers' means

> unfairly inducing customers of a competitor to transact with oneself, by causing to them the mistaken understanding that the content or conditions of one's own products or services or other matters related to such transactions, are particularly better or favourable compared to their actual situation or to those of a competitor.[13]

The law requires that measures are taken to eliminate such practices.

According to the Act, anyone who thinks that there has been a breach of the Act may report the relevant fact to the Fair Trade Commission, and request that the Commission take appropriate measures. This is called a 'request for relief'. However, since the procedure for such cease and desist orders provided in Article 49 of the Act lacks mobility and rapidity, the Act against Unjustifiable Premiums and Misleading Representations (see below) was established in 1962, as a special Act at that time.

Injunction Demand and Claim for Damages by the Victim

Cease and desist orders by the Fair Trade Commission bear the character of an administrative disposition. In addition to this, the Anti-monopoly Act also includes civil law remedies for the victim, namely a claim for damages and a right to demand an injunction.

Claim for Damages

The Anti-monopoly Act provides that businesses in breach of the Act bear strict liability for damages against 'victims'. Per Article 25, the scope of the term 'victims' is not limited to proprietors. However, this provision is not used

[13] The object was the so-called multi-level marketing. See for example the 'Belgian Diamonds' damages case, Tokyo High Court, decision of 29 March 1993.

so often in practice; the remedy mostly used instead is that of the claim for damages based on the Civil Code, namely a claim for damages based on tort.

Injunction

Per Article 24, a person whose interests are infringed upon or likely to be infringed upon by an unfair action which is prohibited by the Act, and who is thereby suffering or likely to suffer extreme damage, is entitled to seek the suspension or prevention of such infringements from an enterprise or a trade association that infringes upon or is likely to infringe upon such interests. The purpose of this provision is to prevent the expansion of damage based on private initiative. This injunctive relief is not limited to competitor businesses—consumers are also entitled to seek such injunctions. Damage to individual consumers is usually trivial though, and they can usually be expected not to file individual lawsuits. There has been some debate about whether to admit demands for injunctions from consumer organisations too, and such a right was in fact granted to these associations by the reform of the Act against Unjustifiable Premiums and Misleading Representations (see below).[14]

Act against Unjustifiable Premiums and Misleading Representations

Significance

The Act against Unjustifiable Premiums and Misleading Representations's purpose is to 'protect the interests of general consumers', to prevent the inducement of customers by means of unjustifiable premiums and misleading representations about transactions of goods and services (Article 1). The need for this Act was triggered by the false canned beef case in 1960,[15] and the Act was enacted in 1962, as special legislation in comparison to the Anti-monopoly Act.[16] The Act was a response to the above-mentioned case, in which canned beef boiled with soy sauce, sugar and ginger was brought to a health centre because a fly was found inside the can, and its examination revealed that the content was, in fact, whale meat. Such an unfair

[14] Regarding this issue, see T Kanai, N Kawahama and F Sensui, *Dokusenkinshiho* [*Antimonopoly Law*] 5th edn (Tokyo, Kobundo, 2015) 533.

[15] For a brief explanation of the false canned beef case, see Masaharu Minami (as in n 2 above).

[16] The Act against Unjustifiable Premiums and Misleading Representations was established to reinforce the prohibition of 'deceptive solicitation of customers', above-mentioned number 8 of the 'general designations' and of 'solicitation of consumers through unfair profit' (number 9 of the general designations). Regarding the Act against Unjustifiable Premiums and Misleading Representations, see Kanai, Kawahama and Sensui, *Dokusenkinshiho* 367.

representation is prohibited as mentioned below, as being a representation causing the mistaken belief that the product is better than it is in fact.

The Act regulates transversely all business categories, regarding unfair representation which might hinder autonomous and reasonable choices on products or services made by ordinary consumers. In this meaning, it can be regarded as a general law for representation regulation by the administration.[17] Later, an amendment of the Act in November 2014 was introduced to deal with the frequent occurrence of false representation of food products: a system for imposing surcharges on businesses who have performed such false representation. Details of this are mentioned below.

False Representation as Object of Regulation

Article 5 paragraph 1 of the Act prohibits false representation that falls under numbers 1 to 3 of the same paragraph.

Representation causing the mistaken belief that the product or service is better than it is in fact

Representations causing the mistaken belief that the quality, performance or content of a product or service is much better than it is, in fact, is prohibited. Namely, according to Article 4 paragraph 1 of the Act, any representation where the quality, standard or any other particular relating to the content of goods or services is portrayed to general consumers as being much better than that of the actual goods or services, or are portrayed as being, contrary to fact, much better than those of other businesses who supply the same kind of or similar goods or services as those supplied by the relevant business, thereby having a tendency to induce customers unjustly and to interfere with general consumers' voluntary and rational choice-making, is prohibited. The words 'much better' in this provision refer to cases where the level of exaggeration has exceeded that which is generally admitted in society. Expressions like 'nights under the midnight sun' or '24 hours during which the sun never sets' in an advertisement for a package tour in the Scandinavian countries have been judged as being different from reality and causing a mistaken belief to general consumers.[18]

[17] The competency for the Act against Unjustifiable Premiums and Misleading Representations was transferred to the Consumer Affairs Agency from the Fair Trade Commission, with the establishment of the former in September 2009. Regarding the problem of the insufficient operation of the Act after such transfer, see Noboru Kawahama, 'Shohisha to Keizaiho' (Consumers and Business Law) in Nakata and Kano, *Kihon Kogi Shohishaho* 58.

[18] Japan Travel Bureau case, Fair Trade Commission Trial Decision of 21 November 1991.

Representation causing the mistaken belief that the product or service is more favourable than it is in fact

According to Article 5, paragraph 1, number 2, any representation by which price or any other trade terms of goods or services could be misunderstood by general consumers to be much more favourable than the actual goods or services, or than those of other entrepreneurs who supply the same kind of or similar goods or services as those supplied by the relevant entrepreneur, thereby tending to induce customers unjustly and to interfere with general consumers' voluntary and rational choice-making, are similarly prohibited. A typical example is a representation where the price indicated as the reference price does not reflect the market price, and causes consumers to mistakenly believe that the price of the product or the service has been discounted, namely dual pricing.

False representations designated by the chief of the consumer agency

Article 5, paragraph 1, number 3 grants the Chief of the Consumer Agency the right to designate certain false representations, additional to the two mentioned above. Such designations serve to indicate in a specific way typical categories of false representation.[19]

Comparative Advertising

In Japan, comparative advertising is not often used. In 1987, a guideline for comparative advertising was published by the Fair Trade Commission, to make clear the criteria for admissibility of comparative advertising.

Regulation of Advertisements without Actual Proof

When it is necessary to judge whether a representation falls under the category of false representation causing the mistaken belief that the product or service is better than it actually is, the Chief of the Consumer Agency may request the business performing that representation to submit material indicating reasonable grounds that prove such representation. According to Article 5, paragraph 2, in this case, if the business does not submit such evidence, namely if the advertisement is deemed to be one without actual

[19] As representative examples of designations, there exist unfair representations regarding: (1) 'non-fruit juice refreshing drinks'; (2) 'country of origin of products'; (3) 'loan fees for consumer credit'; (4) 'bait advertising of real property'; (5) 'bait advertising'; (6) 'private residential homes' etc.

proof, such representation is deemed to be false.[20] This provision is essential to promptly deal with breaches.

Sanctions against Breaches

Per Article 7, in cases of false representation that are in breach of the prohibitions of the Act, the Chief of the Consumer Affairs Agency may order measures such as the cancellation of the advertisement or injunction against the representation. Article 33, paragraph 11 provides that the Prefectural Governor of the municipality where the breach took place can also make an injunction.

Injunctions by Consumer Organisations

When a business commits, or is likely to commit, any of the acts listed in Article 30 in relation to a number of unspecified general consumers, a qualified consumer organisation may demand that the relevant business stop or prevent said act or take other necessary measures to stop or prevent said act. However, in cases of injunction demands by consumer organisations, contrary to cases of orders for measures by the Chief of the Consumer Affairs Agency, the provision of Article 7, paragraph 2 for the mitigation of the burden of proof in cases of advertisement without actual proof does not apply, and there remains the issue of proof.

Surcharges

A system for surcharges against businesses who have performed false representation has been introduced, by which economic disadvantages are imposed upon them. This system was promulgated on 27 November 2014 by Act no 118 of 2014. The Act became effective on 1 October 2016. Under this system, surcharges are imposed against representation causing the mistaken belief that the product or service is better than it is in fact. This includes cases of advertisements without actual proof or representation causing the mistaken belief that the product or service is more favourable than it is in fact. The percentage of such surcharge is equal to 3 per cent of the sales of the product or service in question, and the maximum calculation period has been set to three years, as provided in Article 8. Further, per Article 10, to promote the recovery of damage incurred by consumers due

[20] This provision largely mitigates the difficulty in proving the inconsistency of an advertisement, and contributes to the achievement of efficiency. Further, a Guideline on Art 4, para 2 [now Art 5, para 2] Act against Unjustifiable Premiums and Misleading Representations (Guideline on Unverified Advertisements) was published on 21 November 2003.

to such false representation,[21] a system has been introduced whereby any amounts reimbursed by businesses in breach, are deducted from the amount of the surcharge.

Unfair Competition Prevention Act

Introduction

Per Article 1, the Unfair Competition Prevention Act has as its purpose to provide measures, etc for the prevention of unfair competition and for the compensation of damages caused by unfair competition, to ensure fair competition among business operators and proper implementation of international agreements related thereto, and thereby contribute to the sound development of the national economy. The Act provides for civil law measures against anti-competitive acts, such as injunctions or claims for damages. Provisions related to advertising are also included.

'Misleading actions causing mistaken belief about the quality etc'

According to Article 2, paragraph 1, number 13, the prohibition of 'misleading actions causing mistaken belief about the quality etc'[22] is especially important regarding advertising. The act of using a representation on goods or services, in an advertisement therefor, or in trade documents or electronic correspondence thereof, in a way that is likely to cause a misconception as to the place of origin, quality, contents, manufacturing process, purpose, or quantity, is prohibited. The content of this provision overlaps with the content of the above-mentioned regulation on unfair trade practices in the Anti-monopoly Act or false representation in the Act against Unjustifiable Premiums and Misleading Representations.

However, the remedies in the case of an anti-competitive act are injunction and damages, and the persons granted with the right to claim such are only competitor businesses whose business interests are infringed by such unfair competition, which means that unlike other acts, this Act does not aim at consumer protection.[23] On the other hand, under the Unfair

[21] Regarding this issue, see F Sensui et al, *Keizaiho* [*Economic Law*] (Tokyo, Yuhikaku, 2015) 310.

[22] This category is one of the 15 stipulated as 'unfair competition acts' in the Unfair Competition Prevention Act, Art 2, para 1.

[23] In Japan, the Unfair Competition Prevention Act is understood as not having the goal of consumer protection, and the remedies it provides for are different from those of the Anti-monopoly Act and the Act against Unjustifiable Premiums and Misleading Representations. In contrast, the German Unfair Competition Prevention Act that was revised in 2004 has the explicit purpose of consumer protection, and grants to consumer organisations the right to

Competition Prevention Act, penal punishment is imposed on those who intentionally, namely with an unfair purpose, perform a misleading action causing a mistaken belief about quality etc as mentioned above. In some false food cases that became an issue recently, police investigations have been performed based on this provision. This Act is important from the perspective of deterrent effects, since it provides for a system that can eliminate fraudulent false representations and advertisements.[24]

INDIVIDUAL REGULATION OF ADVERTISING

There are many acts that regulate advertising individually, based on the product or service that is traded or the type of transaction.[25]

Regulation of Representations and Advertising to Ensure Appropriate Choice by the Consumer

The Act on Specified Commercial Transactions imposes certain obligations regarding advertising and representations that have to do with mail order sales, multilevel marketing transactions and specified continuous services, with the aim of making clear the content of such transactions. Further, it includes provisions which prohibit extravagant advertisements.[26] Representations and advertising regulated in this Act are subject to injunctions by consumer organisations. There exists also regulation by other special consumer laws.

demand inunctions and disgorgement. For a recent paper regarding details of the same Act, see K Nakata, 'Doitsuni okeru Kokokukisei to Shohisha—2015nen UWG Kaisei wo Fumaete' [Advertisement Regulation and Consumers in Germany: In View of the Reform of the UWG in 2015] (2016) *Gendaishohishaho* No. 32, 48 et seq, and Nakata and Kano, *Yoroppa Shohishaho* 297; T Soda, *Dantaisosho no Shintenkai* [*New Developments of Collective Actions*] (Tokyo, Keiogijukudaigakushuppankai, 2006) also presents such developments.

[24] Apart from the above, Minor Offences Act, Art 1, no 34 and Penal Code, Art 246 (fraud) can also be applied as penal regulations.

[25] Regarding advertising regulation in individual industry laws, see H Iyori and S Yabe, *Kokokuhyojikiseiho* [*Advertising Representations Regulation Law*] (Tokyo, Seirinshoin, 2009) 140. Japan Advertising Review Organization, *Kokokuhomu Q & A* [*Advertising Legal Affairs Q & A*] (Tokyo, Sendenkaigi, 2014) also presents individual cases from a practical viewpoint, and analyses their regulation content; H Shimozu et al, 'Hyoji—Kokoku o meguru Hokisei' [Legal Regulation of Representations/Advertisements] (2010) *Gendaishohishaho* No. 6, 4, gives an overview of the regulation of representations through laws belonging to the competency of the Consumer Affairs Agency.

[26] Among the matters regarding advertising statements, representations about the existence or absence of special provisions regarding goods-return are important. The Act on Specified Commercial Transactions stipulates that if there is no statement about any special provision regarding goods-return in the catalogue or on the website, the consumer has the right to perform a cancellation of or withdrawal from the contract within eight days from the day the consumer received delivery of the goods (Art 15-2, para 1).

Regulation of Representations and Advertising Aiming at Ensuring Health and Safety

Consumer Safety Act

The Consumer Safety Act was established in 2009. Article 2, paragraph 5, number 3 of the Act provides that any circumstance 'in which a Business engages in deceitful or exaggerated advertising or any other action provided by Cabinet Order that is likely to wrongfully harm the interests of a Consumer or interfere with a Consumer's voluntary and rational choice-making' is an 'actual or potential consumer-related incident'. Advertising issues are dealt with here as well. The Consumer Agency may collect information and issue admonitions and orders against businesses.

Food

Representations and advertisements are important, not only for ensuring appropriate decision-making on behalf of consumers, but also for protecting health and safety. The Food Safety Basic Act was established in 2003 as a comprehensive law for securing food safety. This Act imposes on food-related business operators an obligation to make efforts 'to provide accurate and appropriate information concerning food', as well as the obligation of the state to take the necessary measures for ensuring food safety and for accurately transmitting information on food. Following this direction of the Basic Act, provisions on food representations have in the past been included separately in plural acts, such as the Food Sanitation Act, the JAS Act, the Health Promotion Act etc.

However, scandals related to food have frequently occurred, the words used for the same item lacked consistency, and the method of regulation was complicated. Therefore, taking into consideration the fundamental principles of the Consumer Basic Act as provided in Article 2, paragraph 1, the provisions of the Food Sanitation Act, the JAS Act, the Health Promotion Act etc related to food representation were united into one act, creating thus a comprehensive and integrated system for food representation. The scope of regulation has remained unchanged. These events gave birth to the Food Labelling Act, established in 2013 and which came into force on 1 April 2015.[27] Article 5 of this Act provides that 'persons engaged in food-related

[27] The purposes of this Act are to ensure proper food labelling by establishing standards and specifying other necessary information regarding labelling of food that is intended for sale, thereby promoting the interests of general consumers, and also to contribute to the protection and promotion of the health of the people, the smooth production and distribution of food, and the promotion of food production in response to consumer demand, in combination with the measures implemented under the Food Sanitation Act, the Health Promotion Act, and the Act on Standardisation of Agricultural and Forestry Products (JAS Act).

business, etc must not conduct any sale of food that is not labelled according to the food representation standards.'

This is how priority was given to forming a unified content of regulation, reducing costs related to the awareness of such regulation and realising the content of the regulation, to ensure its effectiveness.

Per Article 6 of the Act, the Prime Minister may give instructions to persons engaged in food-related business who are in breach of the Food Labelling Act, or order them to take certain measures. Further, per Article 11, consumer organisations may exercise a right to demand injunction if there is or it is likely that there will be a representation which is significantly contrary to the facts. These two instruments have been introduced to ensure effectiveness.

Medical Treatment—Medicine

Advertising related to medical treatment has been strictly regulated, and it is prohibited to advertise items other than those provided by the law. At the same time, a certain degree of deregulation has also been performed, to boost competition, ensure the provision of appropriate information to patients and support their decision-making. The Medical Care Act, whose purpose is to ensure the safety of medical care and to protect the health of the nation, allows advertising with regard to a medical practice only for certain items designated by laws or bulletins. Advertising related to any other items is prohibited. The content of advertisements on such items as are allowed must not be false, with penal punishments imposed for breaches of this prohibition. However, despite this prohibition, false or extravagant advertisements regarding medical products or cosmetics, which take advantage of people's consciousness for health, are increasing.

Gas Equipment/Electrical Equipment etc

Technology standards have been provided for gas and electrical equipment etc, in view of the dangers inherent in such products, and it is required that such products bear representations that they meet such standards. Further, selling products that do not bear such representations is prohibited.[28]

Regulation of Spam Advertising

Spam advertising is also regulated, as a means of advertising. It can be said that sending a large number of unnecessary spam e-mails is a nuisance

[28] Gas Business Act, Art 39-3, Electrical Appliances and Materials Safety Act, Art 27, Act Concerning the Securing of Safety and the Optimization of Transaction of Liquefied Petroleum Gas, Art 39.

against consumers,[29] and is an economic burden on them. In view of this, the Act on Regulation of Transmission of Specified Electronic Mail was established in 2002, and penal punishments were introduced by the 2005 reform. This Act was also amended in 2008, but there remain issues regarding its effectiveness.

SELF-REGULATION

Introduction

In the field of advertising, there also exists self-regulation by businesses, business organisations or third-party institutions. Such self-regulation is not a regulation directly performed by the law, but has been playing an increasingly important role.

Self-Regulation by Industry

An example of self-regulation is Article 31 of the Act against Unjustifiable Premiums and Misleading Representations. According to this article, businesses or business organisations that meet certain criteria can be certified by the Fair Trade Commission, and establish 'Fair Competition By-Laws' as self-regulation rules. Actions performed by businesses who participate in such Fair Competition By-Laws are not regarded as being problematic under the Act against Unjustifiable Premiums and Misleading Representations or other acts and are not subject to orders for action, as far as they follow the content of such by-laws.

Publication Standards of Media Companies

Media companies such as television stations, publishing companies etc, have their own publication standards. The relevant industry groups have also set similar standards.[30]

[29] As a study including comparative law analysis, see T Soda, *Meiwakumerukiseihogaisetsu* [*Outline of the Law on Unsolicited Email*] (Tokyo, LexisNexis Japan, 2006).

[30] For example, there also exist the Standards for Advertisement Insertion in Newspapers of the Japan Newspaper Publishers and Editors Association, the Code of Advertising Ethics of the Japan Advertising Agencies Association etc. However, these standards are extremely vague, and their efficiency as standards is questionable. More detailed guidelines are required to enhance legal certainty.

Japan Advertising Review Organisation

Rulings made by the Japan Advertising Review Organisation (JARO) are also a form of self-regulation.[31] The purpose of this organisation is to promote proper business activity and protect consumers, by promoting fair advertising. This organisation accepts complaints not only from member companies, but from consumers as well.[32] However, its neutrality against consumers is not guaranteed at least from an institutional point of view, since its operational costs are covered by the member companies.

FINAL REMARKS AND FUTURE ISSUES

In Japan, regulation of advertising and representations has been advancing in recent years, through a combination of public and private law regulation to achieve consumer protection. However, it could be said that the following issues still remain.[33]

First, there are many laws that relate to advertising regulation. Their mutual relationships have not been adjusted, and it is difficult to get a clear picture of such regulation. Recent incidents regarding food representations have shown that such content is unclear and difficult to understand—not only for consumers, but for businesses and legal professionals as well. This has led to an increase in compliance costs. As already mentioned, requirements and effects of the regulation are not arranged in order, even in general laws such as the Anti-monopoly Act, the Act against Unjustifiable Premiums and Misleading Representations, the Unfair Competition Prevention Act etc. It could be said that the introduction of a comprehensive act, eg an Advertising Representations Regulation Act, should be considered, to solve the existing problem of the narrowness of the scope of regulation.

[31] Regarding the analysis of self-regulation, several papers published by Professor Jisuke Nagao are important: see especially J Nagao, 'Kokokushinsei no Juyosei' [Importance of Advertising Review] in J Nagao (ed), *Kokoku no Shinsa to Kisei* [*Review and Regulation of Advertisingments*] (Tokyo, Nikkeikokokukenkyujo, 1995) 12, also for its comparative law analysis. Further, see J Nagao, 'Kiseikanwa to Kokokujishukisei no Kadai' [Deregulation and Issues of Self-Regulation in Advertising] in Nagao, *Kokoku no Shinsa to Kisei* 119; J Nagao, 'Kokokurinrikijun no Igi to Kokokushinsa' [The Significance of Standards for Advertising Ethics and Advertising Review] in J Nagao (ed), *Kokoku to Ho* [*Advertising and Law*] (Tokyo, Nihonhyoronsha, 1988) 83. As a work of another author, see K Yanase, 'Kokoku to Jishukisei to Konpuraiansu' [Self-regulation of Advertising and Compliance] (2004) *JARO no Ayumi [The History of JARO]* (special issue, www.jaro.or.jp/jaro30/pdf/1-4.pdf).

[32] The structure and activities of JARO are presented on its website, www.jaro.or.jp. Regarding the processing of consumer complaints, see I Hayashi, 'JARO ni yoserareru Kokoku no Kujo to Shori no Gaikyo' [Outline of the Process of Advertisement Complaints submitted to JARO] (2010) *Gendaishohishaho* No. 6, 12.

[33] Regarding the indications which follow, see Nakata and Kano, *Yoroppa Shohishaho* 213.

In this respect, it could be pointed out that advertising regulation in Japan lacks legal certainty, both in the stability of the legal system, as well as in the clarity of the legal provisions.

Second, no matter how many rights are included in the laws, if the system and assistance for those rights to be realised are insufficient, such rights become 'pie in the sky'. This would mean that they are not real 'rights'. For reasons of time and cost, it is not realistic to expect individual consumers to file lawsuits if they incur damage by unfair advertisements or representations. Therefore, it is necessary to ensure the effectiveness of a system for the *collective* realisation of consumer rights by consumer organisations, along with administrative sanctions.[34] A stable realisation of the content of law is also a crucial part of legal certainty. As has been shown in this chapter, there currently exists an issue of legal certainty in the sense of a lack of stable enforcement of the law. To deal with this issue, comprehensive legislation for advertising regulation is necessary.

[34] The Act on Special Measures Concerning Civil Court Proceedings for the Collective Redress for Property Damage Incurred by Consumers (Act 96 of 2013), in force since October 2016, has enhanced this direction. Further, the surcharge system in the Act against Unjustifiable Premiums and Misleading Representations is also important. Regarding this issue, see T Nakagawa, 'Kaiseikeihinhyojiho ni okeru Kachokinseido' [Surcharges System in the Amended Act against Unjustifiable Premiums and Misleading Representations] (2016) *Gendaishohishaho* No. 32, 38 et seq.

Index

www.ingramcontent.com/pod-product-compliance
Lightning Source LLC
Chambersburg PA
CBHW070908230926
51613CB00013B/111